Abebi

"WE CALLED FOR HER AND SHE CAME TO US"

Abebi

"WE CALLED FOR HER AND SHE CAME TO US"

NAILAH JUMOKÉ

**JUMOKÉ PUBLISHING
BUSHKILL, PENNSYLVANIA**

Abebi

Published by
Jumoké Publishing
Bushkill, Pennsylvania
Phone: (312)613-4404 pariswriter@att.net

Nailah Jumoke, Publisher & Editorial Director
Yvonne Rose/QualityPress.info, Book Packager

ALL RIGHTS RESERVED

No part of this book may be reproduced or transmitted in any form or by any means – electronic or mechanical, including photocopying, recording or by any information storage and retrieved system without written permission from the authors, except for the inclusion of brief quotations in a review.

Jumoke books are available at special discounts for bulk purchases, sales promotions, fundraising, or educational purposes.

Disclaimer: I have recreated events, locales, and conversations from my memories of them. In order to maintain their anonymity in some instances, I have changed the names of individuals and places. I also may have changed some identifying characteristics and details such as physical properties, occupations, and places of residence.

© Copyright 2018, 2026 by Nailah Jumoke
Paperback ISBN #:978-1-7323297-0-6
Hardcover ISBN #:978-1-7323297-1-3
Library of Congress Control #: 2018905731

Dedication

In Loving Memory of:
Victor "Uncle Vic" Yarbrough
Husband
Joseph C. Whalen and Eugenia A. Moore
Parents
Mark McElroy
Grandson
Trenese Marie Robinson
Daughter
I know you are watching over me!
You are forever in my heart.
To my children:
E'jenia, Andre, and Curtis
You are the reason that I know how to love.
To my grandchildren:
Rishona, Iniah, Johnathan, Rinesha, Kamonnie,
Amberly, Siarra, and Richael
Carry the torch that lights up the world and
let everyone see your True essence.
You are brilliant!
You are powerful!
You are magnificent!
"BE" the **change** for our world to be a better place!
You are . . . LOVE!

Acknowledgements

First, giving honor and praise to the "I AM" Presence/God for my very existence, I wish to thank the ancestral slaves of the Irwin House (former plantation) for "calling" me to come to their aid. I am truly, humbly honored and blessed to have had such an "awakening and healing" experience.

I could not have endured the five years of writing *our* story without the support, love, and encouragement from my three children and eight grandchildren. I pray that this aspect of my life will help them to understand me better and the importance of honoring those who have come before them. And to my sister, Yolanda, my brother, Mark, and my Aunt Lois, who always had a word of encouragement. I love you dearly.

To my new friend and Content Editor, Jennifer Howl, whose honesty, love, encouragement, and professionalism helped me to stay focused on what was relevant to the story. Also, a writer, she is the author of *Sit, Walk, Don't Talk (How I Survived a Silent Meditation Retreat)* and a Mindfulness Meditation Facilitator.

To **all** my friends at the NoHo Senior Artist Colony, with a special thanks to Theresa, Fran, and Queen Sylvia, who previewed my manuscript and offered great feedback. I truly appreciate you! And to my extended family, Jackie, Ramona, Lin, Cynthia, Randee, Kevyn, and Willie, whose consistent love and support gave me the motivation to keep writing. Your love and friendship are highly valued and appreciated.

Loads of thanks to Yvonne Rose with *Amber Books Publishing* and *Quality Press*. She and her creative team exemplified the highest quality of professionalism and support, which eliminated my fears of self-publishing. Their integrity and dedication to helping new writers like me become AUTHORS has been invaluable! Thank you for making the dream of being published a reality. Blessings to you, always!

A shout-out to The Java House Family! WOW! Every one of you who came through the doors of The Java House and Harriet Tubman Cultural Center is a significant reason that this story exists. Your talent, your faithfulness to us as a business, and your dedication to our purpose as a community gave me the strength to keep going when I wanted to quit. I am truly blessed to have had you all as my extended family and *teachers*. I will always love and appreciate what each of you brought to The Java House. It would not have been possible without YOU! Keep living your art!

And to my "readers," thank you so much for taking this life-altering journey with me. I hope that you will be encouraged to question your own beliefs, as well as open your hearts and minds to what you can do to help heal racism and all the other "isms" that perpetuate hatred, greed, and separation. *Our* story also hopes to offer solace and a sense of empowerment, helping to transform our self-created hells into lessons of love and forgiveness. And in all of life's challenges, remember, you are Never alone!

Contents

Dedication v

Acknowledgements vii

One: Haunted by Dreams, and Bewildered by Reality 1

Two: A Vision for Healing Manifested 32

Three: Poetry, Prophesy, Pendulum 38

Four: From Meditation to Irritation 49

Five: From Dream to Reality 55

Six: New Friends, Old Problems 74

Seven: A Night with Celebrity, Sobriety, and Sharing 80

Eight: Sharing the Dream 82

Nine: Hope for the Hopeless 86

Ten: Be Careful What You Ask For 96

Eleven: Never Take No for an Answer 104

Twelve: Giving Thanks 111

Thirteen: The Revitalization of a Plantation 114

Fourteen: The Cleansing Ritual 117

Fifteen: Unexpected Company from Both Worlds 130

Sixteen: The Gift 137

Seventeen: Revelations 139

Eighteen: Ghosts, Playing Tricks 145

Nineteen: The Findings of a Breeding Box 149

Twenty: The Sins of a Father	154
Twenty-One: Shamed	158
Twenty-Two: A Day with Daisy	160
Twenty-Three: The Proposal	165
Twenty-Four: Seeking the Good	173
Twenty-Five: Running for Governor	177
Twenty-Six: Certificate of Occupancy	180
Twenty-Seven: Tragedy Strikes	182
Twenty-Eight: Lights, Camera, Action	192
Twenty-Nine: Getting Through the Holidays	199
Thirty: Jackie	207
Thirty-One: Bitch, Moan and Laugh Until It Hurts	214
Thirty-Two: Crack	225
Thirty-Three: Chicago Bound	230
Thirty-Four: Sexual Healing	237
Thirty-Five: Plans Turned Upside Down	241
Thirty-Six: Temporary Housing	250
Thirty-Seven: Two's Company, Three's Insane	256
Thirty-Eight: What a Little Honesty Can Do	260
Thirty-Nine: Something Brewing in the Air	265
Forty: Open House	275
Forty-One: The Threat	277
Forty-Two: Restraining Order	284
Forty-Three: The Burial	296
Forty-Four: Moving On & Creating Art	299

Forty-Five: Saved by Agape 306

Forty-Six: The Message on the Wall 312

Forty-Seven: Gratitude & Family 317

Forty-Eight: A Ritual with Lady Day 319

Forty-Nine: A Reunion 328

Fifty: Theatre in the Making... 331

Fifty-One: Bitter Sweet... 340

Fifty-Two: Ghost and Homework 344

Fifty-Three: More Chilling Encounters 348

Fifty-Four: Saving My Sanity 351

Fifty-Five: Back on the Plantation... 375

Fifty-Six: Terrorized 385

Fifty-Seven: OMG, Not Again 389

Fifty-Eight: A Spiritual Quest.. 400

Fifty-Nine: Back to My World... 407

Sixty: Two Events Save the Day.. 410

Sixty-One: The Invasion of the Flies... 414

Sixty-Two: The End of a Mission.. 421

About the Author 432

ONE

Haunted by Dreams, and Bewildered by Reality

Standing bewildered in a long unfamiliar hallway lined with giant doors, my heart races like an overwound clock. Streaks of sunlight from partially wood-covered windows, showcase washed-out colors on huge, plastered walls. Although frightened, my curiosity overshadows my fears as I begin to move cautiously through the semi-darkness. My neck strains as I marvel at high ceilings, where aged, cracked paint floats to dusty hardwood floors. Silently, I question . . . *where am I? How did I get here*? Still immersed with curiosity, although with some trepidation, I continue to grope along a massive wall, while my trembling fingers disturb mounds of thick, dark dust. But, then a dark-wooden staircase leading to a second floor, gets my attention. With hesitation, I lift my foot to trail the wooden steps while resting my hands on the dusty banister for support . . . when suddenly, panic overtakes me as I feel this weird sense of a *presence* . . . like someone is watching me. I stop! Standing on the second step, too scared to go any further, I hear what sounds like . . . voices, but I can't make any sense of what's being said. It sounds like several people chattering at the same time. My whole body shakes with fear. I can barely breathe. *Come on Nailah, get it together. Take a deep breath — you can do this;* my mind coaches me. After taking a few deep breaths, I will myself to take one step at a time, while my eyes roam from left to right, making sure there's no one around. With no one in sight, and finally at the top of the stairs, I notice two more steps that lead to another landing. A giant door is off to its right. I gingerly move my feet towards the steps . . . when suddenly . . . the voices return! Only this time, louder, almost screaming! "Help! Help us!" Breaking out in a sweat, my heart starts racing again; pounding so hard, it feels like it's gonna pop out of my chest! My throat muscles tighten before I manage to swallow some saliva. Then, barely able to squeeze out the words, I nervously cry out: Who are you? Where are you, and what is this place? Just then, in the far distance, I hear what sounds like a familiar voice calling my name. I freeze! And with bated breath, I listen . . .

"Nailah, Nailah, wake up!" Somewhat dazed, my eyes slowly adjusted to the security of my bedroom and to a familiar face. "Was it the same dream? You were making sounds as if you were scared," my husband inquired.

"My God, Vic, I can't understand what it means. It's the same dream, repeatedly. I've been meditating to get some clarity, and I keep getting the feeling that someone wants me to find this . . . place."

"Yeah, I remember you sayin' it was a big house with many rooms. Was there anything different this time . . . I mean, did you see anyone or hear anything?"

"Naw, I didn't see anyone. But I keep hearing voices. It's like someone is in trouble and they need my help. For the life of me, I can't figure out what or who it is."

It had been more than a year since the dream began, and although I could often discern my night-time adventures, this one had me completely baffled.

"Want a cup of coffee?" Vic asked while looking under the bed for his flip-flops.

"Yeah, and a piece of toast would be good, too, if you don't mind."

"Of course I don't mind, baby. Jelly or plain?"

"Jelly, please. Thanks." Vic was sweet that way — accommodating and thoughtful. However, something had changed; a sense of hopelessness won out over what was once a hopeful security of a long-lasting and happy marriage.

I waited for the anticipated kiss on the forehead. The sweet taste of my beloved's mouth upon my mine, was something of the past. Married just over a year, the hot passion that once swept me off my feet, had been replaced with an occasional peck that led to nowhere. And I couldn't help but wonder what went wrong. *How did something so tantalizingly erotic, become so stale and tasteless?*

Served on a bamboo tray, Vic placed the continental breakfast on my lap while landing another "quick" kiss on the forehead. "Are you teaching today?" he asked.

"Yeah, I have to be there by 9:00. Guess I better get off my butt and get to it. It's gonna be a long day. Come by when you get off from work; I'll surely need your help. We have a small group coming for dinner around 7:00."

"I'll be there," he assured me. "James is supposed to come by tonight so I can adjust his leg. I'll let him know to come after 9:00. See you then, and don't wear yourself out. You know how you are." He was right, wearing myself out was a norm, which could have been a factor in our lack of intimacy issues.

Lying there, sipping coffee and nibbling on toast, my thoughts began to travel back to the time when we first met. Smiling, I began to reminisce about that magical night and how it all began—how everything led to this present moment of confusion and disillusionment. I was finding it so hard to believe that it all started with an unexpected trip to . . .

Paradise

Autumn colored leaves fell on my windshield as I got closer to the bright neon sign. The green palm tree with an ocean backdrop created an imagery of its name: *The Paradise Lounge*. It was "Old

School Night," featuring DJ Mack Daddy. Living in Louisville (Kentucky) most of my life, I had passed the club on many occasions, but never stopped in. Married and working two jobs, hardly left room for anything else, least of all, partying. However, working with young, troubled teens, plus working six hours at the art gallery and taking care of my sick dad, was taking its toll. God only knew a stiff drink and a little shaking my rump to the funk was just what I needed.

Although it was 1994, the visual that flashed across my mind of the DJ briefly broke my mantra for claiming a parking space, when I noticed a car pulling out of the jam-packed parking lot. Opening the car door, I was deliciously greeted with the silky voice of Marvin Gaye's, *What's Going On.* I immediately began to feel a release from the pressures of the day.

"That will be five dollars, Miss," the man at the door announced who must have served as a bouncer as well. He was big and intimidating. I reached into my purse and handed him a ten. In return, he handed me a worn five-dollar bill and told me to have a good time.

The joint was packed! And when I looked around, there was not a seat in sight. The dance floor was jammed with gyrating hips and hands in the air. While most were singing out-of-key, just about every lip in the place synced with Marvin's *"what's goin' on, tell me what's goin' on . . ."*

The smoke-filled room painted a certain ambience that added to the portrait of smooth-talkin' brothers lined against the wall, while Sistahs listened with half interest. As I looked around for a seat, an old-style bar to the left got my attention. The brothers were leaning and scheming, while some braced themselves on a rusty, chrome footed rail, checking themselves out in the wall-to-wall mirror that surrounded the dance floor. Mix-matched bar stools braced the weight of heavy and light hipped Sistahs, while tugging at high-rise skirts and blouses bursting from an overflow of pumped-up breasts.

Wearing a paisley pantsuit with a tight-fitting scull-cap, and shouldering a jacket for the night chill, I looked on, remembering my days as a fashion model, when being braless was quite fashionable. I must admit, being 5'9 and pleasingly slender, gave me an advantage when it came to wearing the latest fashions. However, now approaching middle-age, but still rather slim, my attire changed with maturity and a slight sag . . . if you know what I mean.

Still looking for a seat, round tables filled with empty and half-filled glasses and beer bottles made it almost impossible to squeeze through. Half-lit from dusty overhead red lights, the back walls were crowded with overactive levels of testosterone, while burning tips from cigarettes cast a dim glow across *hopeful* faces. I could just imagine the "line" the brothers were using. The Sistahs with rolled eyebrows and one hand on a lopsided hip, said it all—unless of course you were buying. Not only was it *old-school* music, but the rap was also just as old.

Anyway, just as I was about to give up on the idea of getting a seat and wondering if I could get my five dollars back, I looked around near the door and noticed *an* empty seat at a small, round table pushed against the guardrail. I stepped onto the raised floor and quickly sat down; took my book *The Celestine Prophecy* from my purse and began to read.

After waiting awhile and realizing that a waitress was not in the immediate forecast, I looked over at the bar and beckoned one. A tall, slender brown-skin girl danced her way over in black high-heel boots and a low-cut white blouse, revealing her bouncing busts.

"What can I get for ya, sweetie?" she shouted above the music.

"A rum & coke, please with a twist of lime," I shouted back. She pranced off waving to someone against the wall, gesturing she would be right over. I took off my jacket, lit a cigarette and resumed my reading.

"That's four dollars, please," she announced hurriedly sitting down the long-awaited drink. I handed her the worn five-dollar bill and told her to keep the change. She blushed and scurried toward the guy against the wall.

Closing my eyes, I sucked deeply from the straw. The rum was strong, and it felt good going down. I was ready to relax . . . be still for a moment and think about my next move.

"Hey baby," a strange voice spoke nearby. I heard him but didn't look up. The last thing I wanted was to be bothered by some dude.

"Hey baby, what you up to?" he encored. This time, curiosity got the best of me. Bouncing like the little white, sing-along ball, my eyes scanned this tall, chocolate, clean-cut slender man. Caught off by his smile—which could have been an advertisement for a brand-name toothpaste—left me a little unnerved, in a good way that is.

"Hi, I'm enjoying my book," I said, playing it cool and sticking my head back into the pages.

"What ya doing readin' a book in a nite club?" he asked with the authority of deserving an answer.

Not bothering to look up this time, I answered. "I always carry a book with me. I love to read."

"Wow. You're the first," he said as he managed to walk closer to my table without my noticing. An empty chair had become available behind me, and before I knew it, that smile was sitting across from me.

"I don't recall inviting you to sit down," I said looking over my glasses.

Raising his butt. . . "I'm sorry, baby. May I?"

I nodded that it was okay. He then looked me right in the eye and winked. "You know, I'm a *leg* man," he announced. I couldn't believe he used that line, although it was original.

"Is that the best you can come up with?" I responded with an attitude.

"No, seriously, I'm a leg man," he repeated smiling so hard, he looked as if he were about to burst out laughing at his own joke.

"Seriously, I make artificial limbs . . . prosthetics."

I almost screamed — covering my mouth to avoid losing my drink. I couldn't help but laugh. It felt good. I couldn't remember the last time a man had made me laugh.

"What you drinking? Can I buy you another one?" he offered. I took his offer and slipped my book into my purse and took another look at this fine man in front of me. He was vibrant, charismatic and full of jokes — just what I needed. I hadn't laughed that hard in years. And I liked the way he dressed: casual, colorful and GQish.

By the third drink, I was feeling pretty good and not giving a good shit about the fact that I was a married woman. I only remembered that I was miserable and lonely. We talked and laughed until my back hurt. So, when he asked me to dance, I was glad to have the opportunity to stretch. As I stood, I steadied myself on the back of the chair . . . checking my balance. Although I was raised by alcoholic parents, I never saw my mother stagger. She used to tell my sister and me that if we ever drank, she had better not ever see us stagger; to always remain a *lady*. However, my daddy was another story. I spent most of my childhood helping him out of ditches or off the floor.

Breaking my thought of mother's wit, Mr. Gorgeous Smile gently took hold of my arm as I stepped down. Damn, was I glad. Any resemblance of staggering would have been embarrassing. The dance floor was popping. Playing a mixture of old school and modern day, the DJ had us jamming. Then, suddenly, as if a light bulb went off.

"Hey, by the way, my name is Victor," he said, grabbing me around the waist and swinging me around. "But everybody calls me Uncle Vic."

"Nailah," I yelled back.

"What was that…?"

"Na'-ee-lah," I repeated phonetically. The swing left me a little dizzy, but I managed to keep my dignity, and the fact that he was still holding my hand didn't hurt.

"I ain't never heard any name like that before," he admitted.

"That's because you ain't met anyone like me before," I responded confidently. (Oh yeah, rum will make you cocky.)

"You got that right, baby . . . you got that right," he beamed.

"Why does everybody call you . . . 'Uncle' Vic?" I asked as an after-thought.

"My mom had a friend that started calling me that when I was really young . . . never knew why, but it stuck with me all these years. Hell, my mama even calls me Uncle Vic."

"Well, it's a pleasure to meet you, Uncle Vic."

The wee hours of the morning slowly crept into the final hour before closing. Dancing as if we had been partners for years, we had literally danced the night away. The chemistry was magnetic. And I was loving it!

While on the dance floor, a brother about Vic's height, but not nearly as fine, walked over and asked me to excuse Vic while he spoke with him. Before he turned his attention away, Vic introduced the brother to me. "Hey, baby, this is my best friend. His name is

Greg. This is . . ."

"Nailah," I interrupted. We shared niceties as he fumbled with my name before they both turned to speak in private. After a brief period, Greg returned to the dance floor to let us know his girlfriend was ready to leave and asked if I minded giving Vic a ride home.

"Just a minute, I need to check with my angel," I told them rather calmly. Before either one of them had a chance to check if I was drunk or out of my mind, I turned away to make my inquiry with Archangel Michael, whom I often prayed to for protection from harm. He was one of the many angels ("I have given you angels to have charge over you . . ." Psalms 91:11) that I had become familiar with while on my spiritual path. Everything was cool.

It was around 3:00 a.m. by the time we finally left the club. Greg had said he would meet us at the house. I felt great— tired but exhilarated. Vic was just what the doctor ordered, and I was enjoying every moment . . . almost too much.

The cool air pleasantly dried the sweat from my brow when Vic opened the door for us to leave the club. Although it was the middle of November, it was warmer than usual. Helping with my jacket and opening the car door showed that chivalry was very much alive when it came to Vic. He was a gentleman. Yet I was waiting to see if his manners would last throughout what was left of what had been a beautiful evening.

"This is it. Pull into the driveway to the right," Vic directed. He lived only a few minutes from the club. As I turned off the ignition, I got a strange feeling of déjà vu. The house looked so familiar. For a few moments, my mind drifted back to a flashback of a recent dream.

"I know this place. I know I just met you, but somehow, I know this house," I said as if reminiscing. Leaves fell from a large tree that separated Vic's house from a neighbor. I looked on in amazement as the leaves gently floated onto the windshield.

Not bothering to respond to my comment, Vic moved on as if I hadn't said a word. "Wanna come in for a minute? Greg's here with his girl. You don't have to stay long if you don't like." I reached for my purse and told him I would, for a minute. "Wait, I'll get the door for you." While Vic came to my side of the car, I couldn't shake the sensation that I had been here before.

Vic held my hand as we walked up to the door... tapping before we entered. The lights were dim as the door opened to two adjoining rooms. Except for the worn, outdated carpet, the entry room was pretty empty. On the other side, Greg and his friend, whom I was introduced to as Sharon, were slumped on a well-worn sofa. As a mother of two boys and a tomboyish daughter, the sofa showed familiar signs of playing cowboys and Indians and jumping contests.

Sharon was an attractive, fair-skinned sister. She looked to be in her early thirty's. I thought for a moment about how interesting it was that dark-skinned brothers seem to have an attraction to light-skinned women. Another one of those leftover post slave traits, maybe?

There wasn't much furniture. An overstuffed chair set by a window. A small, wooden coffee table set in front of the sofa with a broken ashtray; holding the butt of a joint, while burning incense, attempted to sabotage the familiar scent. We all spoke and made idle chit chat before Vic invited me to sit in the overstuffed chair, which had a wobbly pole lamp behind it. The plastic off-white shade was cracked, showing a glimpse of a scratched, red-light bulb, which cast a subtle glow, giving a mystique to the room. I got a little antsy sitting there and wasn't quite sure what to talk about when Vic offered to show me around. He apologized for the way the house looked and said that he had just moved back in.

"This house was a wreck; my wife..."

"Wait a minute, your wife?" I interjected as if I had the right to talk.

"Don't worry, we've been separated for a couple of years. We're going through a divorce. She and my sons moved into an apartment on the other side of town." As if to avoid the conversation, Vic quickly changed the subject. "This is the kitchen," he continued.

Although Vic hadn't noticed (or didn't care) that I was wearing an obvious wedding band, I hadn't bothered to tell him of my "similar" situation. At the time, it didn't seem that important.

"How many sons do you have?" I asked out of curiosity.

"Three, by my wife; I have an older son, too. I don't see him much, though."

The dining-room table was heavily scratched and wobbly, with mismatched chairs in which a couple of them were standing on their last leg. There was a gigantic hole in the ceiling, and I could see the room above it. The door leading to the back looked to have been the victim of a burglary. A halved two-by-four was nailed across the cracked paint to deter any further intrusions.

The walls were filthy and thirsted for a fresh coat of paint. The floors were clean but in bad shape; the tiles were broken and discolored. Next to the dining room was a small kitchen, which was in terrible shape. The cabinets had no knobs, and the corners were smudged with black fingerprints. The stove was in no better shape than the rest of the appliances. The oven door hung slightly to the right side, while the stained, chrome handle dangled by a single screw. The more I looked around, the stronger the feeling got. I had seen this house before.

"You ready to go upstairs?" Vic asked as if he were showing me a "model" home. Before agreeing to his offer to continue the ten-cent tour, I suggested that I could tell *him* what it looked like. It was coming back to me. I had a dream about this house and meeting Vic. It was all becoming clear. Even though I was accustomed to having prophetic dreams, they never failed to flabbergast me.

"The stairs are to the left of the living room," I said as a reflection.

"Yeah, but you can also get there from the kitchen. See?" Vic smugly announced, showing me the two steps that led from the kitchen, as well as the front room. "Did you see that?"

"Not really," I admitted, and continued with my dream. "At the top of the stairs, there's a bathroom to the left. There's a closet facing the stairs . . . like a linen closet. There are two bedrooms... no, three. One is across from the bathroom; two are on the right side. There are clothes everywhere–it's jacked up."

Once upstairs, we entered a small bathroom (just where I had envisioned it), and I realized it was the room that was seen from the downstairs dining room ceiling. There were several loose floorboards through which I could see the kitchen through the cracks. As we cautiously maneuvered through the other rooms, it became quite apparent that what I had previewed in my dream was amazingly on point.

"And this is my bedroom," Vic announced, flicking a light switch.

Although the furnishings were a bit shabby and the walls cried out for a fresh coat of paint, it was neat, clean, and organized. As I continued to look around in awe, Greg shouted that he and his girl were leaving and bade us both a good night.

"It was great meeting you both," I yelled. "I'm about to leave, too."

We headed downstairs just as Vic's friends were leaving. I then rushed to the door to avoid it from closing. Getting the message, Vic started walking me to my car. The deep misty-blue sky was slowly giving way to a new day's dawn. The air was crisp and clean. And just as I began to comment on how quickly the time had passed, Vic grabbed me around the waist, thrust me in the air, and kissed me so passionately that I literally lost my breath, and never even noticed that he had carried me to the car. Not until I felt him pressing me against its cool surface.

My breasts heaved up and down uncontrollably–my breathing rapid. Totally lost in ecstasy and consumed by the fairy-tale feeling that lay in the pit of my stomach, I ached with passion as his *hardness* pressed against my thigh. I was wet, lost, and falling weaker to his every roaming touch and every tongue, sucking kiss. Suddenly, right in the midst of my bliss, an invasive reality abruptly brought me back to my senses. *"Fool, you're still a married woman!"* And even though my husband, Lucas, and I were "technically" separated, there was this nagging feeling that left me feeling a little unnerved with what was happening— or what *could* happen. I desperately needed to go home.

My Husband

The sun had made its entrance by the time I got home. Getting no further than the living room, I was too deliciously drained to undress. So, I just kicked off my shoes, pulled off my jacket, grabbed some blankets from the hall closet, and slumped onto the sofa. I don't know how long it took to fall asleep, but the next thing I heard was Lucas in the kitchen.

"Good morning," I said with some unexpected energy.

"Hey, I'm getting ready to leave. I've got some business to take care of," Lucas responded from the other side of the wall, without any lead-in questions.

"What time is it?" I asked.

"Uh, it's nine-fifteen. There's some coffee left, if you want it."

"Yeah, thanks, I appreciate that."

My husband, Lucas, looked around the corner from the kitchen, just as I was grabbing a cigarette from my purse, when I realized there were no matches.

"Hey, Lucas, can I get a light before you leave?"

Lucas grabbed his jacket from the hall closet, took out some matches, and pitched them to me. He was a handsome, brown-skinned man, standing around 6'2 with large, squared shoulders. Camouflaged with wire-rimmed glasses, his eyes were dark with unusually long lashes. As I watched him put on his signature hat, I thanked him for the matches and lit my cigarette. Leaving, he said, "Bye," and that he'd see me later.

Lucas had a peculiar, nonchalant attitude these days. He was probably just glad that our decision to separate was being done in an amicable way, which allowed us both to move on without any real pressure and with a sense of dignity. Yet for some reason, I felt sad that our love affair had come to such an unpredictable and abrupt end.

You see, Lucas, like Vic and me, met in a nightclub over four years earlier. While it was not quite as fairytale-ish as my meeting with Vic, it was quite romantic. In our case, the only seat available in the club was at his table. He was smoking a cigarette when I approached and asked him if I could sit down. Smiling, he kindly said, "Sure, have a seat. How are you doing?"

We talked the entire night about everything under the sun. He was the first and only Diamond Consultant I had ever met, which I found interesting. At the time, I had just started working as an assistant to the president of a black-owned travel agency. We exchanged numbers and promised to get together soon, which turned out to be—the very next night . . . and the next . . . and the next. Before I knew it, my one-bedroom attic apartment became our love nest.

Our rendezvous lasted a year before it mysteriously ended. It appeared that somehow our careers became an issue. However, as karma would have it, two years and two relationships later, Lucas and I rekindled our relationship. This time, we made it legal.

I was a few years older than my beloved, and at the time, I had three grown children (from my first marriage with Bill) and five grandchildren with whom I made sure to keep a connection, even though they all lived out of town. Lucas, on the other hand, had only one child, a grown daughter with whom he had been estranged since she was a teenager. Although Lucas never really talked about his relationship with his daughter, I could sense that it took some heaviness from his heart when they eventually reconnected. And knowing how important it is for a girl (woman) to have a *relationship* with her father, I was happy for both of them.

We both worked and shared household expenses. And although married, we dated often, and we loved to dance. And the sex was fabulous. So, what was the problem? Hell, if I know. We weren't married two years before things changed.

Lucas... like my dad, whom I'd been taking care of for the past few years, had seizures and took medication. But for whatever reason, Lucas's condition had gotten worse and began to affect his job. One day, (they later told me after Lucas had to take a leave of absence from work), he had a seizure while on the job. Normally, he was able to foretell if one was coming on, but this day was an exception.

Now, imagine being at a jewelry counter looking at a diamond ring, when suddenly your salesperson starts shaking like he's being electrocuted. You're standing there, wondering what the hell is going on . . . and the next thing you know, he's on the floor. With your mouth open, in shock, finally, the word *"help"* falls from your lips, thus bringing the necessary attention to what appears to be a dire situation.

Eventually, forced to take a leave of absence, we knew it was time to look into getting him on disability. Which, of course, didn't sit too well with his manhood! Shortly after painstakingly jumping through major hoops and masses of red tape to help Lucas get *his* money, the seizures began to take on a life of their own. Not only had they affected his job, but they also put me in a very precarious situation. He eventually became physically violent . . . adorning my face with a black eye or busted lips . . . and then claiming he didn't remember anything. Between the unsolicited bouts, the stress of working and taking care of him and dad, I knew something had to change. That change ultimately brought us to the present situation–getting a divorce.

Taking a few minutes to reflect while drinking the coffee Lucas had made, somehow helped me to overcome the guilt, which was beginning to creep into my psyche. It almost felt like I was kicking my husband while he was already down. However, the "til death us do part" was getting too close to becoming a reality, and self-preservation simply stepped up to the occasion.

Looking around our one-bedroom apartment, the boxes that I had already packed were piling up. However, I was leaving more than half of everything with my husband: my living-room suite, half the dishes, linens, cookware . . . I did love him. Fortunately, I had to learn to love myself more. I planned only to take my bedroom suite (which my father had given me), books, and personal items.

Within a month, Vic was helping me to move, while Lucas, my soon-to-be ex-husband, looked on. I suppose one would think I was somewhat bold to have my new lover come and whisk me away from my estranged husband. However, I happen to believe that irreconcilable relationships should come to an amicable end without all the drama. Besides, we were already— over! By Christmas, I was divorced. I called it my "Lenscrafter" divorce— *done within an hour*.

Signed, sealed, and delivered.

You know, in retrospect, I should have known that our marriage was headed down a slippery slope when we went to the courthouse to get married. My soon-to-be husband–in front of me, his mother, my brother, the Judge, and God–said with uncommitted passion: "Come on now, let's hurry up and get this thing over with." Do you think that could have been a sign?

Opposites Attract

Vic and I had quite different personalities. Although we shared some common ideas about religion, marriage, children, and sex, our lives were as opposite as you can imagine. At the time, I had left my job with the travel agency and worked as a self-esteem counselor for wayward teens, a job I did early mornings a couple of days of the week before starting my job as a salesperson and a showroom designer for an African American art gallery.

Vic, a hardworking man, was considered the *black sheep* of his family, and he had recently gotten out of jail. Yes, I said jail, where he spent six months for selling drugs. Like many black brothers, Vic found the economic pressures of child-support, late mortgage payments, and a wife who felt it imperative to "keep up with the Joneses," thought it justifiable to become a 'small-time' supplier to a mainstream culture of weed-heads.

Life doesn't always paint a pretty picture, and keeping it *real* compelled me to accept people for who and what they are. Vic and I were getting to know each other—the good and the not-so-good. And while acknowledging our shortcomings, we found honor in the fact that we were both good people and still hopeful for that one thing that gave us reason to keep living… love. From the time we met, we stayed in a whirlwind of magical bliss, while I turned his house into a home. I was happy, but little did I know that I was embarking on that trail of uncertainty one more time . . . marriage.

During our rather short engagement, I introduced my husband-to-be to my world of African-rooted spirituality. When my name was changed four years prior, I was on a long-overdue path in discovering my African roots. Growing up in the South, with all its racism and post-slave mentality (which permeated the air like a dark cloud), giving up my birth name, Janella Marie Whalen, to embrace my new name, Nailah Jumoke, was only the first step to a lifelong mission. It was imperative to have some understanding of my past, as well as try to embrace some of the teachings and spiritual beliefs that sustained us as a people, giving me the strength and courage to move forward with a sense of knowing "who I am."

It took several weeks to jump through all the hoops our great American system set up to change one's identity. However, it was well worth watching my conversion take place, not only with my thinking, but also enjoying the immense thrill of seeing everything that bore my slave name, such as: debts, social security card, (unfortunately, that nine-digit number stays with you to the grave) driver's license, right down to my birth certificate being changed by due process. I had a "burning ceremony" to honor the old and a "rebirthing ritual" to embrace the new.

Soon after shedding the legal shackles of my past, I met a Yoruba priestess by the name of Shangodora, who would later become my Spiritual advisor and teacher. She would also introduce me to the principles of *"Ifa"* –a Yoruba Spiritual Tradition of divination (readings), ancestral veneration, and the worship of the Orishas. Also called deities or god/goddesses, the Orishas rule over the forces of nature and serve as emissaries to promote the well-being of mankind on behalf of Oludumare/God Almighty. You might say it is like having your own personal support system that works *with* you on behalf of God in helping with one's spiritual development and/or direction in life through the process of divination.

Once you become an initiate/student of *Ifa*, you are usually given a name that is associated with a particular Orisha, of which there are over four hundred. In my case, through divinations and several rituals that entailed personal cleansing, along with the intentions of becoming a priestess, I was given the name "Oshun" (also spelled Osun), who rules over sweet waters. Part of Oshun's duties are to aid in matters of money, healing, and diplomacy; look after the poor and motherless children, as well as govern the sanctity of women. These responsibilities, amongst others, required a spirit of "selflessness," "service," and "sacrifice" (what I call the 3 S's) as a servant of Oludumare and mankind.

Taking the initiative to embrace *Ifa* was also consistent with my reverence for the ancestors, which provided the means for me to know more about my African culture and its spirituality. And the fact that it denied any belief in a "devil" was right up my alley. Now, I'm not saying that there's not any *evil,* but what I am saying is that we need to learn to give "our" name to those actions or situations that are considered evil, or the times when we might say: "the devil made me do it." Putting our own names to our actions means we take responsibility for them (actions). After all, Free Will is also our birthright.

It's not easy to accept one's shortcomings or step out of one's comfort zone where you're expecting *someone* else to save your soul. This new path in *Ifa,* much like what I was already learning on my spiritual path, didn't allow me to shun *my* responsibility as being created in the Image and Likeness of our Creator; but rather it was teaching me to step-up to the plate and truly learn what it meant to live from the "divine" essence of myself . . . opposed to "a wretched soul." In the Yoruba Tradition, we are taught that we are gods and goddesses and that it is our "birthright" to have health, peace, joy, happiness, and prosperity.

Although being on a path less traveled (being spiritual, opposed to religious) can be lonely, I was fortunate that Vic and I were embarking on this new path of African traditions together. And during those exceptional times when he was permitted to celebrate in certain rituals, it allowed us to bond on a level that reached beyond traditional courtship. It also set the tone for a major, spiritual awakening and cranked open a door that would lead us both into an area of mystery, intrigue and long-suffering. But meanwhile, we had a wedding to plan.

Wedding Preparations

In the African culture, the bride and groom are not the only ones that wed. Both families must agree with the marriage and agree to become "one" family. And with just two days before our pre-wedding gathering, we realized that having the house completely ready by then was impossible. However, in preparation for this auspicious occasion, Vic tightened the rickety dining room table while I hung several colorful pieces of African fabric to cover the gigantic hole in the ceiling. The rundown carpet that once covered the beautiful hardwood floors lay out in the backyard along with five-gallon paint buckets, which had been set in corners just a few hours earlier. We had just finished laying the last piece of no-wax, cream-colored tile to replace the broken black & white squares that trailed from the kitchen through the dining room. You could still smell the adhesive.

The fact that the house was in shambles (at least from my point of view) and that I was barely standing from exhaustion, feelings of guilt and embarrassment as to the ill-repair of our home slowly dissipated as I watched our families come together to start the process of "joining as one." On my side of the family were my mom and stepdad, my two sons (from Indiana), my daughter (who had come from California), my brother and sister, and my mom's sister, Aunt Lillian. My father opted not to come but promised to make it to the ceremony to "give me away." On Vic's side were his mom, two brothers, and two sisters, his three sons from his previous marriage, and his oldest son from his teenage relationship. There was also his best friend, Greg.

During this time of becoming "one" family, it's tradition to ask any questions that a family member may have for the prospective bride and groom. My two sons were the only ones who asked questions from my side, basically seeking Vic's *intentions* for their mother. Vic wasn't one to talk much, as his answer was a little ambiguous. However, he assured them he would "take care of me".

When it came time for questions to be asked of me, Vic's older brother, who had apparently had a few beers already, blurted: "Now we all know that Nailah loves Uncle Vic. Hell, look at all she's done. Man, Uncle Vic's house ain't never looked this good, and they ain't even finished." After a couple of unsuccessful interruptions by his wife (sensing he was on a roll), her inebriated husband continued his ranting. "Hell, she's taken on the responsibility for my three nephews, they momma's drama, (which Vic's ex-wife was known for, particularly when it came to the boys and their visitation, especially after our marriage announcement) . . . and after paying out child support, he's broke," he continued, waving a can of Old Milwaukee. Of course, with that one, he got a unanimous—Amen! But by then, the rest of the clan stepped in and managed to change the subject by acknowledging that it was time to eat . . . and thus the feast began.

A freshly ironed Ivory antique tablecloth covered the half-sanded table as our families had filled it with their favorite prepared dishes. Huge salads, cornbread, baked macaroni and cheese, succotash, a caramel cake, two sweet potato pies, and a peach cobbler, set alongside a smoked turkey, fresh greens, and candied yams (which Vic and I spent all night cooking). It was on! And to wash it all down, Vic's brother brought two six-packs of Old Milwaukee and a jug of Zinfandel. There was also iced tea and lemonade. Yes, we had a typical down-home, southern feast. One of the *few* things I liked about the South. And in case you haven't figured it out yet, yes, we were unanimously approved to move forward as husband and wife.

Holy Matrimony

The big day was finally upon us. My aunt Lillian's yard had been turned into an African Garden. It was beautiful with all the trimmings, along with drums, dance, and food. With most dressed in African attire, about thirty of our closest friends gathered to witness our union, while two African drummers played nonstop, evoking the ancestors to this festive occasion, while the rhythmic sounds echoed throughout the small subdivision. We had two female ministers: One for the African tradition, which was facilitated by my Priestess and Spiritual teacher, Shangodora, and Virginia, a longtime friend and ordained minister, to authenticate the marriage license. We were all ready to go—but no groom.

Sitting on the floor of my auntie's bedroom, I thought I would throw up. Vic was over an hour late, and not even a phone call. I was excruciatingly afraid that my dream wedding was turning into a nightmare, while mama and auntie made awkward excuses as to why he was running late. I could tell they were afraid for me. Vic had to come. Not only for my sake but for theirs as well. They knew all too well that they would have to put my broken pieces back together . . . again.

Finally, the entire house cheered, as well as our guests, when my newly bald-headed groom came through the house as if nothing was wrong, yelling…

"Hey, baby, I'm here, baby. Where's my wife?"

Frantically relieved, my heart settled down as I wiped my tears and took a deep breath . . . as well as mom and auntie. Hugging and giving thanks to God that Vic had shown up, we redid my makeup and finished getting me dressed.

My new mother-in-law had made our wedding outfits. I sashayed in a gold, satiny two-piece with long sleeves, accented with an African print that draped over a spaghetti strap chemise. The print matched my ankle-length skirt, along with a pearl beaded veil. It was breathtaking. I felt so beautiful–Queen-like. Vic's gold two-piece traditional African garb shimmered like the sun. His chocolate complexion glistened, and that smile! I was so overjoyed that he finally showed up . . . giving my heart relief from the unthinkable possibility.

Fulfilling his promise, my father placed my hand into my future husband's as we knelt before the officiants, along with my daughter and Vic's brother. The drums were still resonating through the air while my Priestess officiator sang a Yoruba chant (a song or poem with repeated lines), which I'm sure was relevant to our wedding, before leading us into the ceremony. After the drumming ceased, we took in every word of instructions for a lasting marriage, sharing our intent and heartfelt vows. There were no rules, no promises. Only Unconditional Love would be the center of our relationship, as long as we both were committed to growth, truth, and honesty.

Right after our "I do's," the drum call proceeded its evocation to the ancestors. Prayers were made, chants were sung, and dances invoked the blessings of our ancient past. With hands locked and grins broader than life, it was time to *jump the broom,* the final tradition to a lasting union. And jump we did, landing on God's green earth, which symbolized a strong and solid foundation, where growth was imminent, and a harvest was assured. We were now *one*, and the fruit that we harvested would be based on our seedlings.

It was truly the most beautiful wedding I could have imagined. Everyone danced, drank, ate, and offered their best wishes for our future. My mom and dad, friends and family all made it a day to remember . . . as all weddings should be. And while I didn't bother to ask my wedded husband why he was late to the most important day of our new lives together, the reason would soon surface. For now, we were honeymoon-bound.

A Honeymoon to Forget

There was no doubt who he was. The wave from the far end of the baggage claim area drew in closer as father and son came face-to-face for the first time in over twenty-two years . . . since Vic's parents' divorce when he was only twelve years old. No time for nervousness, the father grabbed his son's hand and pulled him to his chest.

Vic looked like his dad. Standing shoulder-to-shoulder, Howard was a large man whose midsection showed signs of retirement and a happy lifestyle. I watched as Vic's dad gathered his manhood, fluttering his large eyes. His full head of hair sprouted strands of gray around the temples. He was a handsome man. Aging fit him well.

"Hey, pops, this is my wife, Nailah," my proud husband announced.

We hugged and shook hands as I repeated my name. My father-in-law's hands were strong and sweaty as he introduced us to his wife.

"I see you have one of those names like my wife. This is Kilana, she's Hawaiian."

Not only did our names represent our ethnicity, but recently married, she and I shared a glow that only a new bride could. Her deep, wavy black hair lay on her broad shoulders, garnered with a white flower. Her high cheekbones rose to meet her warm brown eyes with freshly arched brows. A soft pink shade of lipstick accentuated her narrow lips. She was an attractive middle-aged woman, flattered by a well-maintained body. Hugging, we all exchanged formalities for several minutes, gathered our luggage, and stepped out into a wet, dreary Seattle, Washington. We were on our honeymoon . . . my first, ever!

The night lights along the driveway led to a two-story suburban-style brick home with a two-car garage. The rain had stopped, followed by a quarter moon that hung in a starless sky, casting a shadowed glow over several homes in the quaint, middle-class neighborhood.

Kilana was delightful and maybe a little overzealous, reminding me much of myself, especially since she, too, was a Gemini. She prepared enough food for the *Brady Bunch.* Vic and I had never eaten authentic Hawaiian food before, as she delighted us with Grilled Salmon with tomatoes and capers, along with a colorful vegetable dish and rice. She also made her own rendition of Mai Tais, which took the edge off any awkwardness . . . at least for me. We floated through the rest of the evening laughing and talking, as we managed to avoid any conversation that may have prompted any past regrets.

After a couple of nights with Pops and his wife at his house (they both had their own homes), we went to Kiliana's Condo to stay for the rest of our two-week visit. Fully furnished with French Provincials and relics from Hawaii, the house was beautiful! The small kitchen was stocked with fresh fish, fruits, and vegetables. A portable bar flourished with red and white wines, while rum and mixers served as a room divider, separating the kitchen from the living room. Two large Curio cabinets lined the wall, filled with porcelain dolls and souvenirs from her various travels.

After being wooed by the downstairs with all its amenities, we gathered our luggage and went upstairs. The master bedroom was breathtaking. The oversized queen-size bed, which continued the French Provincial theme, was draped with colorful comforters and matching pillows piled high above the headboard. The covers were pulled back as an invitation to crawl into the stark white sheets. The chest of drawers and dresser were adorned with fancy perfume bottles and Hawaiian dolls, along with family pictures and postcards.

The pink and white bathroom with double sinks was a few steps away from a floor model television, which crowded a corner next to a walk-in closet. Beach size, fluffy white towels hung over a brass rod. Antique brass vanity lights draped over an oval, ornate gilded mirror. Everything was beautiful . . . perfect for the honeymoon I had always dreamed of . . . so, I thought.

An April shower wailed against the roof, while strong winds whistled through the front yard trees. It was warm and cozy inside, and I was on my honeymoon. And no matter how hard or long it rained, I was ready for the night of my life. Every fiber of my being ached for attention, and that night we would consummate our love affair—legally.

After dinner, we showered and changed into something more appropriate for a honeymoon. It had been a while since I adorned myself with lingerie. It felt good. For once, in a very long time, I felt sexy and beautiful. Vic put on a pair of silk pajamas that were a wedding gift. He looked so handsome, and I had gotten used to his shaven head; it was kind of cute. It had been a few days after our wedding when I asked Vic why he shaved his head. He said he shaved it to "signify a new beginning; to let go of the past and to start fresh." It made sense to me, so I thought no more about it.

Vic popped open a bottle of champagne while I went upstairs to get a wedding gift, one that was specifically for this night. It was the perfect game, enticing us to indulge in fresh strawberries, whipped cream, and chocolate. I set the game in the middle of our diamond-shaped legs and took out the instructions to arrange everything, according to its promise for a guaranteed night of erotic pleasure. Vic poured us a glass of bubbly.

"To us, baby," my husband said, raising his glass. And with a smile as broad as his shoulders, Vic handed me a glass.

"To us and our well-deserved honeymoon," returning his sentiments.

Our glasses rang out a high-pitched tone as we lifted our glasses before bringing them to each other's lips. The gentle, burning sensation tickled going down. It felt good. I sensuously reached for a strawberry and placed it between my teeth as an alluring gesture for my husband to bite the other end. I just knew that this would be a night of romantic conversations, lovemaking like never before, and a sense of finally being able to be together as husband and wife. However . . .

I began to sense a strong feeling of uneasiness coming from my new groom. He seemed distant and unnerved. And although my husband's kisses had recently become somewhat blasé, and his touch had lacked electricity, I was certain this would be a new beginning. I was wrong.

"Hey sweetie, is anything wrong?" I asked after eating the *entire* strawberry . . . somewhat afraid of his answer. His eyes were sad and distant as he showed me those pearly whites, while hesitantly putting his arms around me.

"No, baby, what could be wrong? It's our honeymoon."

Although there were a few laughs as we played the game and eventually ate strawberries from each other's lips and licked whipped cream from the crevices of our fingers, still, neither one of us moved to expand the sweetness. Instead of being drenched with desire, my gateway to pleasure was dry and non-responsive. Both fumbling, I wet my fingers and reached down between my legs to moisten the path of entry. Between being dry and the roughness of the carpet, it was difficult to pretend that I was having the time of my life. I prayed that it would soon be over. My prayer was answered. And what should have been the happiest night of both our lives was awkward and lacked passion... to say the least!

The next morning, for the sake of my sanity, I performed the wifely duties as if the night before was a newlywed's dream. Breakfast in bed, including a Mimosa toast to a brand-new day, was the perfect beginning. I stuffed all my insecurity and fearfulness in the hole that was in my heart. However, as usual, my husband was his bright and cheerful self and ready to move forward, as if all was well. Was it just me? Thoughts haunted me as I tried to ride the wave that Vic was gliding on. He was always so easy-going, as if he hadn't a care in the world. It had to be me.

After breakfast, we stood at the kitchen sink sharing the load of washing and putting away the dishes when my new father-in-law called to remind us that we had a date that evening for a dinner cruise.

Of course, we assured him that we would be ready promptly at 7:00 p.m. Getting back to our chores, Vic and I managed to make small talk about his dad and how much bigger he seemed. Twelve was a crucial age when his dad left, and now twenty-two years later, he was sharing one of the most important times in his life . . . with his father.

By late afternoon, the rain had stopped, and the sun broke through the clouds, giving me a ray of hope. *"Yes,"* I thought to myself . . . *"Maybe a dinner cruise along with a little dancing and a few drinks, is just what I need to chase away my blues— my feelings of unrequited love".*

The Love Boat

The four of us took pictures upon entering the boat. The soft Samba music filled the air with anticipation of a fun-filled evening. We were all dressed to the nines as we stepped aboard the lavish dinner cruiser. Inside the boat was like a Four-Star hotel, fully equipped with a bar lined with fine whiskeys and liqueurs.

The waitstaff, dressed in black & white, scurried around ready to accommodate its long list of reserved guests with hopes of it being a great monetary night. Tables draped with white linen and sterling silver, set for large and small parties, were arranged around the oak panels that separated us from the Toronto waters. A four-piece band covered a back wall, while a DJ booth sat to its right.

At the back of the ship, the savory aromas of a well-prepared meal drew us to a beautiful setting of long tables draped with purple and white linen. Floral arrangements set between several ornate food warmers. Its polished, sterling silver reflected our stylish attire. Once we were seated, Howard ordered a bottle of champagne and a gin and tonic for himself.

The band - three Brothers and one Latino - set the evening off to a smooth, saucy beat. A mixture of Afro-Cuban rhythms, mixed with modern jazz, served as the perfect complement to an array of delectable dishes. A roundtable slightly separated from the rest, lay heavy with four-layered cakes, pies, cookies, and chocolate strawberries. It was a feast to behold, and we were ready to partake.

Thanks to conversation, great music, food, and dancing, we managed to get through the evening without any regrets. I actually had a wonderful time as Vic, and I pretended that the night before was only a faded memory. We laughed and frolicked until the horn sounded our return to the dock.

The End of a Beginning

Two weeks came and went about as fast as our sex life. Howard promised that he and his wife would come to visit and try to catch up on some lost time. Howard looked as if he were going to cry, but he fought back his emotions, as I did. Vic grinned from ear-to-ear and thanked his father for allowing us to come and share our honeymoon with him. It had to have been difficult for both of them. Far too many years had passed, separating Vic from the one person he probably needed more than anyone else in his life.

The flight back to familiar surroundings was quiet. Vic slept, while I pretended to. My thoughts raced, trying to figure out what was wrong; what had happened to the hot, spicy passion I was so accustomed to, at least in the beginning. And why was Vic so different— – so distant? Was he sorry he tied the knot? Did he feel that the "paper" would change things? Nothing made any sense to me. I was dumbfounded and had no recourse as to how I was going to get through what was to be, "til death do us part." But, then again, maybe it was just an *off* week. We both had been under a tremendous amount of stress. Or maybe I was just "trippin'." You know, creating some shit that wasn't real because of my own insecurities.

Everything was as we left it. Greg had kept an eye on the house for us while we were away. He didn't make it to his best friend's wedding because of some issues with his boys... at least that's what Vic told me, later. However, Greg promised to make sure everything was cool on the home front since the house wasn't secured. It had been broken into while his ex-wife and sons were living there. She claimed that that was one of the reasons they moved. The back door was a major repair job, along with all the other work that had to be done. Yes, the honeymoon, however perplexing, was definitely over.

Still working at the gallery left little time for renovations. However, at least school was out for the summer, which gave me a couple of extra hours in the mornings and on the weekends. Wanting anxiously to make our home beautiful, being impatient was one of my shortcomings, (things had to be done "right now!"), which meant lifting and moving things on my own. However, there were times when it was necessary to wait on both Vic and Greg, like when the drywall had to be put on the ceiling in the kitchen. And once the ceiling was completed, accented with a new fan and light fixture, it was time to lay the new floor in the bathroom.

Vic's three young boys, who lived with their mother, all pitched in during their summer break, which they spent with us. During the school season, we had them on the weekends and some holidays. We got along great together during their visits, and as their stepmom, we talked openly about girls, school, and the importance of family. Every Sunday that they were with us, we ate dinner together, either at our favorite buffet restaurant or at home. It became a tradition to which we all looked forward. Vic wasn't a big talker, but on Sundays, he usually opened up more. The boys could see a huge difference in their dad, and they attributed much of it to me. It was good to know they felt that way.

A Pause to Grieve

Renovating a house is hard work, but hard work was no stranger to me. Having to learn how to fix things became necessary, especially during times as a single parent. It was enjoyable working with my hands; it was meditative, and the result was always something to look forward to. We stripped paint to reveal the natural wood on all the wood trim. The carpet was pulled up upstairs, also revealing beautiful hardwood floors. However, between renovating and taking care of the boys during their visits, I was still taking care of my father, which I had been doing for the past several years after he received a blood clot on his brain from a drunken fall, thus creating seizures, which eventually led him to give up the booze. Living only a few miles away from our home, Vic often went with me to check in on my dad or to take him shopping. They got along well, as long as dad wasn't in one of his cantankerous moods, which never bothered Vic. He thought Dad was funny.

There were times I had to argue with dad to take a bath or from going outside in only his underwear. He could definitely be a handful, and he often made my life even more insane. However, on the 22 of July, exactly three months after "giving me away," I received a telephone call around 7 a.m. from my brother, who lived with our father at the time. After hearing what my brother said, I frantically jumped from my bed and informed Vic (without any explanation) that I needed to get to my dad's house. Noticing that I was obviously concerned, he offered to go with me, but I opted to go along.

Upon my arrival, my brother, Mark, met me at the door . . . his eyes red and swollen. He didn't say anything but pointed at the floor in the dining area . . . where our father lay. . . clad only in his underwear. As I got closer, there was no doubt that he was "dead." For a moment, I just sat there on bended knees when I noticed he had what appeared to be a smirk on his face. It was as if his last vision was of something or someone . . . pleasant. Not really disturbed or sad, I knelt and kissed his cold forehead while briefly having flashbacks of all the times he was overbearing and extremely difficult to deal with, and the many times that I had wished I weren't his daughter. Strangely enough, the longer I looked at him, I found myself being relieved . . . exhaling. Not counting all the times I took care of my dad as a child (when he was around) for the past fifteen years, I had been a caregiver to a man that I barely knew as a "father." And although there were no significant, fond memories that triggered any *normal* sadness for my loss, I had *peace,* knowing that I had loved him... unconditionally.

"You know what, little brother," I said, looking up at his drawn face. "I see Dad was serious about leaving up out of this world. For the past few months, he's told me that he wanted to die... that he was tired of being here. Well, he got his wish."

After being alcohol-free for more than fifteen years, at the age of sixty-six, our father died from natural causes. However, I would *hear* from him . . . again.

I can't recall exactly how long it was after my father's funeral (at least a week or two), but on this particular day, after I had come home from my second job with the art gallery, I noticed the message light was blinking on the phone. As I was undressing to change clothes, I rewound the tape to listen. What I heard made me stop in my tracks... "Jane . . ."

It was my dad! I was in shock and unable to move as I listened to the jazz in the background (my dad loved jazz and always had it playing) as he continued.

". . . God works in mysterious ways. I'm in my world, baby. Yes, God works in mysterious ways."

After playing the tape a few more times, I finally called my mom and told her about it. Surprisingly, (since she didn't believe in 'ghosts') she believed me, especially when I played the tape for her. Vic was also quite shocked as well and had no choice but to believe it. I suppose my dad wanted to let me know he was all right... and still listening to his jazz.

TWO

A Vision for Healing Manifested

Back to the Present Day . . .

Reminiscing about the past and trying to figure out where Vic and I went wrong faded into the background once I got to school. Working through unhealthy issues with the girls was often draining, leaving me with hardly any energy to do anything else or think about anything else.

I was late opening the café that day. By the time I picked up some items from the store, it was nearly 12:00 when I got there. Still in my professional dress, I grabbed an apron, washed my hands, and started my second job for the day. I was tired, with hardly any energy to do anything else. However, creating the café was *my* idea. I was on a mission and tired or not, there was no stopping it now.

You see... it was growing up during the "civil rights" movement that had a major effect on my ideas of bringing community together, particularly amongst blacks and whites. I had watched people who looked like me be beaten down like wild animals, carted off to overcrowded prisons filled with thousands who refused to succumb to the whiplash of past generations without a fight. I had spent many years living life in a world that wasn't going to let me forget where I came from, and yet, pushed me to look beyond the illusion of skin color. I wanted to reclaim my true beginnings, and at the same time, embrace all the other ancestry that made me who I am.

So, when Vic's sister, Candy, bought a two-story building and opened a bookstore, I knew it could be the door that opened to a long-awaited vision... to create a forum for creativity (particularly for our youth) and more importantly, to help "heal" racism! Not only with another race, *but within our own.*

Candy was younger than Vic, but with a strong awareness of black businesses. She prided herself on knowing our history and the black power movement. The bookstore was her way of helping to educate us about our past and its effect on our future. We made a deal with her to rent the second floor for the café, which I thought was an ideal combination. Books for the mind and food for the soul.

Vic shared my enthusiasm about opening a coffee shop. I talked with him about what types of food we would serve, how it would look, and what we hoped to accomplish with the community. We would have open discussions about social issues and ways to create a better community. Maybe some jazz and storytelling . . . anything that would support our youth, as well as our adult community.

As a part of our plans for a café, I had made mock menus and placed them on our bedroom wall along with pictures of an espresso machine and a few other items to create a visual. "Seeing" a project was an absolute necessity if it were to manifest. Every day, I took time to visualize *The Java House Café* and often asked Vic to join in for extra energy. He was always accommodating and supportive. He used to say, "If anyone can do it, baby, you can." And since I had quit my job at the art gallery after four months into our marriage, it allowed us the time to bring our vision into manifestation.

Within six months, *The Java House Café* was a reality. And the word Cappuccino became the new buzz for those who had never heard of such. However, getting started was not an easy task. Since our kitchen was not approved for cooking yet, I ordered homemade soups and sandwiches from a local caterer, which gave us time to get our kitchen prepared for cooking. Meanwhile, we were establishing a foundation for a new type of café . . . not only as a creative forum, but *The Java House* would offer a healthier menu in a community that had been accustomed to traditional "Soul Food," which was literally killing us from high blood pressure, obesity, heart disease, and a few other life-threatening conditions. We chose NOT to serve pork, beef, fried foods, or sodas.

It took two months before we got a grill and the Health Department's required sinks and refrigeration. Admiring our homey kitchen, only a couple of suggestions were made before receiving our certificate and an "A" rating. We were finally able to bring our own creative menu to the table, thus becoming *The Java House Café* of our vision. However, with Vic still working his full-time job in prosthetics, the only problem was... that I was running the business by myself.

A Hard Decision

Business was growing, and it was hard to handle it by myself, especially after working at the school, even though it was only two to three days a week. Vic always supported me in the evenings; however, lunch was really picking up. I was cooking and serving with little or no help. And with all the thinking and worrying I had already put myself through that morning, not only about the mysterious dream about the mansion, but also the concern about my less-than-ideal marriage. So, when Vic called to see if I needed help, I was almost in tears when I asked him to come by and help me out. He assured me that he was on his way.

By the time my husband got there, a little after 1 o'clock, he looked around and was shocked at how busy it was! "Baby, how you doing this by yourself? This ain't gonna work; here, give me that, I'll finish."

I was grilling a *Last Link*, one of our specialty sandwiches, which consisted of a turkey sausage-link, smothered with grilled onions, peppers, and garlic, served on a grilled bun with Uncle Vic's secret sauce.

"Not before you wash your hands," I interjected before continuing. "It must be from that newspaper article that the Courier did a couple of days ago. The food critic gave us a good write-up. God is good." It felt good to be in the paper. Things were going better than imagined, and being grateful was an understatement. The visualization worked; we were actually in business.

Vic used the newly installed hand sink that sat alongside the two reserved for dishwashing, which still offered a homey look. The entire café had the feel of a warm, cozy home. Sofas lined the walls with tables and lamps for reading. Regular café tables filled the spaces in the middle of the three rooms. The front room had a fireplace in which we put an electric fake log that glowed at night. An old French Provincial sofa faced it, making the ambiance warm and inviting. Calling our unique look "Bohemian," the newspaper rated us three and one-half stars.

Vic called his job and told them he would be late getting back from lunch. They understood and told him to take his time since he didn't have any more clients for the day. Before long, it was three o'clock, and the brothers, Mikie and Lenny (our neighborhood boys) came to relieve Vic, which made him feel better knowing I had some help.

"Hey, baby, we gotta talk about this when I come back this evening. You can't keep doing this by yourself. I'll see you when I get off. We'll probably be busy tonight as well." We hugged, and he left to go back to work. It was a good thing that we had bought an old used van from one of Vic's friends to haul the equipment we needed for the café. It gave us a second vehicle, so Vic didn't have to take the bus, which also allowed him to come by on his lunch hour.

I was in high spirits. The whole idea of having a café was being realized, and yet I was in a fog of two emotions . . . not clear whether it would be successful, and the possibility of it becoming bigger than imagined. But for the moment, help was needed, or the latter was not an option.

We were busy that evening, well into the night, and the client that Vic was to see around nine had to be rescheduled. Mikie and Lenny took off around eleven since there was school the next morning. That night, Vic and I discussed the "what ifs". What if he left his job and we didn't have the money to pay his child support, or what if I quit my job at the school, allowing myself more time for the business? There were plenty of "what ifs," and the final solution was the fact that neither the business nor I would survive if Vic didn't come onboard.

We made the decision that Vic would leave his job while I stayed on at the school. That way, I could pay his child support and free up some of my early morning time at the café. Vic would open on the days I was at school, which would allow me to get there in time to help prepare a lunch special.

The following week, Vic gave his two-week notice, which was not taken with any enthusiasm from his employer. However, they claimed to understand. Vic was leaving to be "self-sufficient," something not too many black men are able to do, and in many cases... afraid to do.

With our alternative menu, The Java House was becoming well-known for its unique sandwiches, such as the Uncle Arnie, named after Vic's uncle from New York. The famous sandwich gave you a taste of the Big Apple, without the beef. Our rendition was grilled, fresh turkey smothered with grilled onions, garlic, green peppers, and Vic's special sauce; served on a grilled, wheat hoagie bun with fresh lettuce and tomato. Our next runner-up was the Mr. T Burger–A thick turkey burger seasoned with garlic and black pepper, grilled with more garlic and onions, topped with turkey bacon, and with either Pepper Jack, Swiss, or Cheddar cheese. This was just two of the many sandwiches that we became famous for. Some of our other specialties were Vegetable or Black Bean Lasagna (both a vegetarian delight), fresh Salmon sautéed in brown sugar and a secret seasoning, along with fresh garlic (of course) right at the end. It was served over brown rice and a lemon-wedge garnish. Fresh steamed broccoli or asparagus complemented this sought-after dish. All our unique meals were accompanied by a fresh tossed salad with green and red leaf lettuce, carrots, cucumbers, tomatoes, red onions, green peppers, and mushrooms; then garnished with raisins for a sweet finish. And to wash it all down, while savoring every morsel, we served a lemon iced tea to "live" for.

Having Vic's steady support took a load off. On the days I worked at school, there was no need to be rushed and panicky to get to the café in time for lunch. And with Vic being able to get there early, we made the decision to start serving breakfast, which went over really well. Vic had a way with sandwiches, and our breakfast sandwich of seasoned turkey bacon or turkey link sausage, along with an egg, lettuce, tomato, and grilled onions, became very popular. Fresh-squeezed orange juice, specialty espresso coffee, and fresh fruit were also an added delight.

Taking the Bitter with the Sweet

Finally, our dream for The Java House had manifested! Through vision, hard work, and perseverance, we were on our way to becoming "the" focal point of our community, and not only for great food, but rather (to my delight) a forum that would prove to go even beyond my expectations.

Although often drained from all the hard work, Vic and I were overjoyed with what we were creating and all the community support we were getting. On the other hand, our marriage had become more like we were *just* business partners, opposed to husband and wife. However, fortunately (or unfortunately), staying busy often left me no time to complain or to question our lack of intimacy. Oh, we grabbed a quick peck from time-to-time, or stole an embrace when things were slow. But, at the end of the night, Vic either hung out with Greg or stopped at Charlie's for a beer . . . or both. (Which, by the way, had become somewhat of a ritual)

On the other hand, the times when he did come straight home, and provided I wasn't too wiped out, we would manage to fumble our way through what usually ended up being a dispassionate "quickie". Yes, sex, albeit good, bad, or whatever, was becoming only a memory from a distant past.

THREE

Poetry, Prophesy, Pendulum

Six months flew by like a high-speed car traveling in the wee hours of the night. In no time, The Java House Café had become a household word. We were getting quite a reputation as a cultural venue, which aligned with my long-term vision. Young and old alike found The Java House to be the spot for great food, jazz, rap sessions about issues on male/female relationships, sex, domestic violence, the workforce, black-on-black crime, and anything else that we felt would support and strengthen the black community. But most of all, we became the threshold to the world of self-expression through the "Spoken Word."

Spearheaded by a sister who saw a vision for more community participation in the form of the Spoken Word, The Java House rocked with lyrics and beats, long into the wee midnight hours every second and fourth Saturday. One night, a couple of young brothers came to check us out. Both had their heads tied with colored scarves with a bow-like knot in the front. I could tell they were new to the scene, and they *appeared* to be gang-related (an observation, not a judgment). I knew all our customers, mostly by name, but definitely by face. This also became a signature of The Java House…a "Cheers" sort of place. Anyway, the brothers came to *spit some lyrics*.

When one of the brothers took the mic, it was obvious to me that in his spoken word, he was angry and had little or no respect for the female gender. Much like the lyrics that had taken over the radio waves, our new artist's take on his life was wrapped in a package that most of us can relate to, even though we may not admit it. Motherfucker this and motherfucker that, added with nuances of his world of bitches and hoes (whores), turned out to be the essence of both their art. Of course, The Java House family gave them respect with applause and finger-snaps. It was a rule that we would not "police" the art of the Spoken Word. As long as you acted like you had some sense, we were open to listening to what you had to say.

Now, to me, the young brothers' take on life was nothing unusual. For the past twelve years, I worked with youth who were filled with anger and resentment, and with hardly any means to express it. I was grateful that The Java House was a place of "no judgment" ... but rather, unconditional love. By not stopping an artist's creative flow, the energy and spirit of what we provided eventually led to self-governance when it came to expressing one's thoughts. And that's exactly what happened with our two new poets.

A New Twist

It's amazing how we can be impressed by our surroundings. Within two or three months, these two brothers came back with a new twist. I hardly recognized them at first. They had lost the scarves and both sported braids. I made sure I paid attention to their poetry that night. I felt something was different— which was an understatement.

Totally taken off guard, the young brothers had put together a piece that they performed together. Bitches had turned to "shorties" (girlfriends) motherfucker never showed up, and even though they expressed discontent and a strong resentment towards the ugly world they lived in, their spin, still with some profanity, took a leap that no one expected. They were "deep," as they say in the language of the Spoken Word. The crowd gave them both what seemed to be at least a five-minute standing ovation. They transformed right before our eyes. And like so many of the young people that I had the privilege to work with, these young brothers just wanted to be heard . . . not judged. The Java House was becoming a household word . . . "the" hangout for great food, music, poetry and the Spoken Word. And our extended family was steady growing.

From East Side to West Side

Before long, my vision of cultural diversity had taken a life of its own. The white kids from the East side of town found their way to the West side to gather at The Java House. One night, while getting to know my new kids, they became quite entranced with my ability to *see* some of the things that were happening in their lives, which they considered being *psychic*. However, having the ability to *see* things was just as much a *surprise* to me as it was to the person that I was shown things about. I never considered myself a psychic, per se; it was just something that happened on occasions when I least expected it. Like the few times when I've met a guy (or woman) and during our conversation, out of nowhere I would start *seeing* things that were happening in his or her life . . . like information about a partner or problems in a marriage or on a job. And the spooky thing was that the information was *always on point* . . . which prompted the obvious question: "How did you know that?" And, of course, my answer was always . . . "I don't know. It just came to me."

Then, of course, there were the times at school when my *gift* would show up while working with the students. I recall one particular incident that really stood out. It was an unusual day because we had young men join our class. The word had gotten around about the class and how down-to-earth it was. That's when some of the fellows got passes from their teachers to join us . . . after all, grades were improving as well as attendance, and some teachers felt that maybe, whatever I was doing, would rub off on some of the guys.

We role-played that day about relationships and respect. The girls really got it when the boys let them know that wearing skirts up to their ass was not what they wanted in a girlfriend. However, boys being boys, never walked up to an ass and said, *"Hey, I don't like looking at you, go put something else on."* No, that wasn't happening. But on this day, they expressed what they really admired in a lady; how they wanted to respect a girl. The problem was feeling like they (guys) were being disrespected when the girls talked down to them.

"Yeah," one young brother spoke up. "Like, check this out. Ya think you can talk to us any kinda way just cause we be hollin' at ya when you walkin' down the halls. And we be hollin' . . . Hey baby, can I take you home with me? Damn, you lookin' good. Now you're wearing some tight-ass jeans, sorry, Miss Nailah, didn't mean to curse. Then you got the nerve to ask me what the f- - - am I lookin' at. Man, y'all be trippin'."

Just as they were really getting down to the nitty-gritty, there was a young man standing in front of me. He was a big boy, but not someone most girls were trying to get with. He was talking about how he wasn't going to let anybody talk to him crazy; that he would 'f' them up.

"Yeah, if somebody disrespects me, man, I be ready to get off in they ass. Know what I'm sayin'?" The young man boldly stated.

At that point, I had to add my two cents. "Oh, so what you're saying is . . . that just because someone says something you don't like . . . you want to fight. So, are you saying you would hit a woman?" I added.

"Naw, I ain't sayin' that. But you know if some dude get up in my face talkin' crazy . . . know what I'm sayin', I'm gonna have to check him." He gets a couple of Amens from the sideline.

"So, just because someone says something you don't like, you ready to fight? Is that what I hear you saying?" I asked again.

"Yeah," he answered with no further explanation.

At that point, I stepped up close to his face—looked him straight in his eyes and asked, "What if I tell you that you're disrespecting your momma, your neighborhood, and yourself when you sell drugs to your sisters and brothers. Punk-ass nigger!" I was so close to his face that I was hoping my breath was cool. "You gonna hit *me*?" I huffed. He took a step back while the rest of the guys stepped up to him, just in case he felt he was being *dissed*.

"Ah dawg," coming from one of the brothers, "Miss Nailah all up in yo business."

The look on his face proved that I was right on point. He was so shocked that even if he wanted to hit me... just from reflex, he couldn't move. I had peeped his card.

"You psychic, Miss Nailah?" He finally stuttered.

"Aren't we all?" I replied nonchalantly. "The point I'm trying to make here, my little brother, is that *words* are just that... words. You do not have to react to someone's opinion about you. You always have the power to walk away."

"But I ain't no punk," he quickly interrupted.

"No, you're not. But it takes a man to walk away."

Feeling the need to explain further, I continued. "Now, if a person puts his hands on you, that's another story. I'm not suggesting you let someone hurt you without defending yourself. What I'm saying is, don't take it personally. Everyone is entitled to their opinion. And in most cases, it's a reflection of who *they* are–it's not even about you. Oh, and by the way, you are being watched by the po 'lice, my brother. You best be cool." With no rebuttal, the young brother looked at me and nodded. I then left the subject alone, in hopes he would get the message.

In retrospect, maybe on a deeper level, *I* was having a difficult time accepting or acknowledging that it was possible for me to have this *gift* . . . the ability to *sense or see* things in another person's life, or to receive a *message* to pass on to that person. And even though this type of thing happened more times than not, I pretty much looked at it as a . . . *coincidence* . . . *o*r it was just a *lucky* guess. For surely, this ability to *see* was for people who were far more spiritual and advanced with the metaphysical (beyond the physical) aspects of life. And although I was quite intrigued and inquisitive about this type of phenomenon, I realized that I was merely a "babe" thirsting to know more about its mysteries. Nevertheless, the *gift* had its way of presenting itself at any given time . . . and always, when I least expected it. Just as it did with my school kids, and now with my new kids.

Finally, at the end of the night, one of the girls phoned her mother to pick them up. When their ride arrived, I walked downstairs with them to meet the mother. Bending down on the passenger's side, I introduced myself. With a warm smile, the forty-something mother delightfully introduced herself and expressed her delight in the effect that we obviously had on her daughter.

"I don't know what all you're doing here," she beamed. "But keep it up. My daughter is a changed person. She and her friends love your place."

"I'm glad you approve of them coming. I love these guys. They are great kids," I graciously responded while getting a hug from each of the kids before getting in the car.

"We love you, Miss Nailah," several voices said in unison. "We'll see you next week. We're bringing some more of our friends, too. So, don't be surprised if there's a bunch of us."

"I love you, too. I look forward to seeing you all next week."

The mom thanked me again and stated that she had no problem bringing them and picking them up. It was around midnight as she pulled away from the corner.

The mic was still open. I could hear one of the poets from the raised windows; his lyrics blended with the dew of the night air. It was hot upstairs, but the inhospitable heat seemed to have no effect on the sweaty bodies that lined the stairway.

"Hey, Miss Nailah," one voice yelled above the background music to a poet's flow. "You gonna 'read' me too. Everybody say you a psychic."

"Not right now, baby, I got to get back to the kitchen before Vic gets overwhelmed. Some of you all came in here smelling like a weed factory and probably ready to eat up everything. I ain't mad at ya though."

Hittin' a joint right before coming in was definitely a plus for my business. We were guaranteed to sell out of desserts and our signature "Juice Joint," a mixture of fresh fruits blended with homemade lemonade and crushed ice, which had become a favorite. However, no one ever disrespected our place of business by smoking in the bathroom or in front of our building. They loved us too much to risk getting us in trouble or chance losing the one spot that advocated freedom to be themselves.

As I moved through the café, hot bodies were plastered along the walls, barely allowing room for me to maneuver. Thank goodness the early part of the day was not really busy. I made the *special* for the day of baked chicken with mushroom gravy, real mashed potatoes, green beans with caramelized onions, and blueberry pie for dessert. We sold out by the end of the evening.

All in the Swing

The night was finally over. Vic's client came by for his fitting and offered to help clean up for closing. It wasn't unusual for our customers or "extended family," as we liked to call them, to pitch in and help. There were many nights we could not have made it without the help of a poet or one of the teenagers who came by. But, then again, tips were always a motivation.

We believed in on-the-job training–literally. We taught the kids that came by how to take orders, which helped with their math and people skills; how to properly set a table, the importance of the dishwasher, as well as general manners and politeness when serving a customer. Of course, our customers loved seeing the youth doing something positive when they had so many other options. Plus, parents always knew they were in good hands with us, alleviating worry and concern about where they were late at night.

During slow periods, I often helped with homework or made the kids read a book, or we did role-play in how to avoid fights and conflict with their peers; the importance of being honest, how to honor and respect themselves, and the pitfalls of lying and stealing.

I recall one night when we realized that an old 22-caliber gun was missing from the top of a bookshelf. Vic and I had been looking at it a few days earlier to check out whether it had all its parts (before you start judging, it wasn't any good). Anyway, I noticed it was missing while cleaning the shelf and watering a plant. I asked Vic if he had taken it down, and his answer gave way to a little concern. The fact that all the parts weren't there took some of the fear from the equation. However, it was the fact that someone took it, that disturbed Vic and me.

I called the two boys, Mikie and his friend, Darryl, who had been working the past few nights. Knowing my babies, (what I called my neighborhood kids) I felt rather strongly about who was inquisitive enough to *borrow* it.

At the time, I occasionally did some work with a pendulum (a necklace with an elongated crystal). I'm not sure how I learned of this tool of divination, as I was always looking for ways to educate and elevate my spiritual beliefs. After ordering a book on the subject, as another means to connect with my *higher* self, the pendulum allowed me to seek answers to simple questions. So far, (after a few months of trying it out from time-to-time) it has proven to be quite accurate most of the time. Any spiritual tools that I occasionally drew upon for clarity, such as tarot cards, a pendulum, etc., I sometimes found that my strong *will* for a *certain outcome* could (or would) potentially persuade my answers to what I *wanted*, which often times meant I wasn't willing to deal with the "truth." However, in this particular case, I had no personal attachment to the outcome.

Depending on the swing of the pendulum after a question, it would serve to answer the question as a yes or no. Neither boy knew what I was doing when I asked them to stand in front of me while I asked them some questions. But this was only after I'd given them the opportunity to fess up to the crime. I also explained the dangers of handling a gun and that telling the truth was far less punishable than lying. However, both boys held their ground about not taking the gun.

As I stood next to Mikie with pendulum over his head, I asked him if he had taken the gun.

"I promise, Miss Nailah. I didn't take it," he swore, looking at me straight in the eyes. I wanted to believe him.

"Okay, this is your last chance to tell me the truth." Again, I assured them both that I would be lenient if the truth were told. However, Mikie held to his story. "Last chance," I professed one last time. Mikie's eyes rolled up into his head trying to see what I was doing with the necklace I had taken from my neck. He was small for his age. At twelve years old, he looked to be around nine or ten. A real cutie-pie, Mikie had a look that made you want to buy anything he was selling.

I moved from Mikie without using the pendulum. I wanted to see how he responded when I took the necklace and held it over Darryl's head, giving him the same options. He, too, claimed his innocence. Just then, with the pendulum hanging straight up and down in anticipation over Darryl's head, I asked, "Did Darryl take the gun?" Mikie stood back, eyes as big as an owl, watching as the necklace swung back and forth, horizontally. The answer was *no*. Darryl slumped in relief when I told him that he hadn't taken the gun.

It was now Mikie's turn to have the mysterious necklace to determine his fate. This time, as I held the pendulum over his head, I asked, "Did Mikie take the gun?" Again, Mikie's eyes rolled up into his head, only this time his eyelids fluttered up and down, fearfully. The magical pendulum swung back and forth . . . in a vertical motion. First, it swung slowly but quickly sped up to the point of almost hitting me in the face. Darryl, holding his breath while waiting for the results, stood in disbelief.

"Dang, what does it mean, Miss Nailah?" Darryl barely got out of his mouth before Mikie jumped back with tears swelling in his eyes.

"Mikie took it," I announced.

Expressing love and compassion, I asked him to go get the gun. He dropped his head and said that he gave it to the boy next door to his house.

"Go get it, Mikie, and bring the other boy back with you," I told him.

Although Mikie could not see the swing of the pendulum, he knew he had been caught. His whole demeanor showed that he was glad it was finally out.

The new kid, Mikie, and the gun wrapped in a brown paper bag, found their way back to the café. That night, the boys, as well as Vic and I, discussed the issue in depth. "How did you know where it was?" Vic asked with a fatherly severity.

"I saw you put it up on the bookshelf," Mikie admitted softly.

"Speak up, Mikie," Vic insisted before continuing. "I can barely hear you. As short as you are, how did you reach that high? Even with a chair, it wouldn't have been enough."

"I put a table by the bookshelf and climbed on it. I just wanted to show my friend. He didn't believe you had one. He bet me," he confessed.

"How much did you bet?" continued Vic.

I couldn't understand why that would be important, especially at this point in the conversation. But after looking at Mikie's face, I could see where Vic was going. While this was a serious situation, Vic got Mikie to smile—a little.

"Five dollars," Mikie shamefully admitted.

"Did you get your money?" Vic asked, trying to keep a serious face.

"No, he said he didn't have no money," the young gambler admitted, while standing next to his debtor.

"Hey son," Vic raises the boy's head, "look at me when I'm talkin' to you. You got Mikie's five dollars? It looks to me he won the bet."

"Naw, I thought he was playin'. I ain't got no money . . . see," he sheepishly announced, pulling out his pocket linings.

Of course, Vic sermonized to them about gambling and not being able to pay one's debt. It was an evening I believe will stay with those young men for a very long time, as well as an invaluable lesson for Vic and me to keep guns... working or not... out of sight and reach from young inquisitive hands.

FOUR

From Meditation to Irritation

The room across from our bedroom served as my sanctuary and where my morning usually began with my ritual of meditation and giving thanks for the day, along with a cup of coffee. I called it my quiet time, having a cup of Java with God.

To make it a place of beauty with a sense of tranquility, I painted the walls a beautiful deep lavender and draped the windows in a creamy off-white fabric, opened just enough to let the sun in. On the floor, a straw mat was placed, much like the one used during Kwanzaa. It lay on a white cloth that I made specifically for this room. Three novena candles—white, purple, and green, in which I lined the outer edges of the mat. White for purity and guidance, purple for strength and endurance, and green for a solid foundation and finances.

In the center of the mat, I placed a beautiful glass bowl, and to its right, set a crystal glass filled with fresh water to pour libation as a prelude to connecting with Spirit. As always, a prayer was said requesting guidance and protection from any negative forces that may have been looking for a window of opportunity to disrupt my intentions. I would then attempt to release any negative thoughts and seek forgiveness for any wrong that I may have done consciously or unconsciously by burning Indian Sage to remove and cleanse any unwanted energy, in which afterwards I burned Frankincense & Myrrh to sweeten the air.

On the left side of the room, there was a rocking-chair where I took the time to talk (to myself) about being open to what Spirit may have for me, and to express gratitude for all that I had while I sipped from the bitter nectar in which I considered a *natural* picker-upper from the hills of Africa; whether from Kenya, Ethiopia, Tanzania or Uganda.

After finishing my Java with God, it was customary for me to take in a deep inhalation . . . stand, stretch, and then kneel before the altar; light the candles and set my intention . . . which was to let go, breathe, and . . . listen. You see, *my* meditations were usually geared more toward connecting to my *higher self or* making a connection with an ancestor or my Orisha, Oshun, for guidance, especially if I were having concerns or challenges with a particular situation. That's when the "listening" came in. Now, that's not to say that there weren't times when I didn't just *sit* and concentrate on the breath. However, since having the recurring dreams about the *mansion,* with all its massive rooms and haunting voices, my meditations began to shift from *concentrating on the breath* to more like... moving into a deep *trance.* And my fifteen-twenty-minute sessions of *letting thoughts come and go* had turned into an hour (or longer) of black & white images that reflected the same mystified dream that came in my sleep. But no matter which *sit*, whether it was for a quick session or a timeless trance, the intrusive thoughts of: *"Did I buy enough lettuce, or do I need to order more Salmon, or will it be busy today, etc."* always made an appearance. However, what never changed, (whether in a dream or a meditative trance) were the images of this strange place, replaying over and over like a movie with no ending. And although I was still left in the dark about the dream's meaning, I hoped for some direction in the *what* and *why* of it all.

It was always a challenge for me to leave my sanctuary. Even with all the constant images and unanswered questions. As of late, that time of being still and doing some deep breathing was the most rewarding time of my day. I always left feeling rejuvenated, peaceful, and with a little more strength to handle whatever the day had in store.

Messing with My Peace

They say that time flies when you're having fun. I'm not sure how much fun we were having, or Not having. Time seemed to move at a snail's pace . . . working six days a week, twelve to fourteen hours a day. I was usually quite exhausted after working all day, and at night, it didn't take much for me to fall asleep. I'd pass out and die for the next four or five hours, often times forgetting what my dreams were about, or if I even had any.

It must have been at least two months before I realized I hadn't dreamt of the mansion. Not even in my meditative trances had the movie replayed . . . maybe because *time* had become a rare commodity, often cheating me of the quality time I had become accustomed to. With all the work and little sleep, after a while, I did good to manage ten minutes to just stop and breathe.

But even death while sleeping seems to resurrect after time. There was no rest for the weary. The meandering down long hallways and searching the massive rooms for any signs of life had returned. And with no faces or ghostly figures floating in mid-air, the voices were the only thing that my mind really focused on . . . which by the way, was no longer a guessing game as to what was being said. It was definitely a "call" for help. And it was becoming pretty apparent that *I* was the one who they expected to heed the call. However, I still didn't have a clue as to who *they* were! And so far, I hadn't gotten any messages from Spirit, either.

After what happened when I had the dream of Vic's house, it was becoming startlingly clear that the possibility of ***this*** dream coming true was not only possible, but on a gut level, I knew I was being given a "trial-run" to acquaint myself with what was to come. Meanwhile, in the real world, there was another *voice* that was quite alive and irritating!

Vic's ex-wife, Lisa, hated the fact that he quit his job. And the fact that I was paying his child support made her even angrier. I received a telephone call on our one day off from her about the child support check. Not because she didn't get it, but rather because it was *my* personal check.

"Is Victor there?" the voice on the other end asked.

I knew who it was, and from the sound of her voice, I knew it was trouble.

"Hi Lisa, no, he's not. Can I give him a message from you?" I asked, waiting for a response. Silence lingered before she rudely continued.

"Why is my child support payment coming from you? Victor always sends me a money order. This is your personal check. You tell Victor I want my money from him, not you."

"In case you may have forgotten, Lisa, I am Vic's wife. What difference does it make that it's my check, as long as you're getting your money?" I asked, bewildered.

"He was a damn fool for quitting his job, and I know it was your stupid idea. He's got sons he's responsible for . . . not you!"

"Well, right now, I'm the one who's working, so you will be getting your check from me. Plus, it helps us to keep better records." I reminded her rather calmly.

"You're a damn fool for paying it."

"Are you saying you don't want us to send you the child support, Lisa?"

"I want Victor to send it like he always has in the past. Not from you!"

"Well, sorry. If you want to keep getting your money for the boys, this is the way it's going to happen. That's all there is to it. I will let Vic know you called."

"Bitch!" was the last word I heard before a dial tone replaced the venom of Lisa's anger. My heart was racing while I tried to understand why on earth she would care where her money was coming from, as long as she got it. And the fact that she was a schoolteacher, I would think that she would have had a more *educated* response. I hated that

Vic was going to have to deal with her stupidity. For a moment, I thought about sending a money order the next time, just to keep the peace for Vic. However, it was a fleeting thought. She was not going to tell us how to take care of our business. When I told Vic about the call, he laughed.

"Baby, that ain't nothing. She's crazy. Remember when I told you that I said to my friends, 'If I ever get married again, kick me in my ass. 'She's' why. But then I met you." He smiled and kissed me on the forehead. "Don't worry about it, baby," he continued. "She's sick. And don't let her talk to you, crazy. Next time she calls talkin' crazy, hang up on her ass. Whoever heard of someone gettin' mad 'cause they get a check? Now that takes the cake." "Oh, by the way, gladly changing the subject, I've started having that dream again."

"You mean about the mansion?"

"Yeah, and the place is massive. It seems like there are even more rooms than I thought. I also get this feeling that there is a small apartment of some type in the back of the mansion, and there are trees all around the building."

"Seen anybody yet?" my husband inquired.

"Naw, but I still hear the voices crying for help."

"You got school tomorrow?" Vic asked as if to avoid any further *spookiness*.

"Yeah," I responded, being brought back to a world that was a little more realistic.

"Maybe we should go by the store and pick up some things for the café. That way, we won't have to go in the morning," Vic suggested.

"Ok, we'll need to order from Sysco, too. I'll call before going to school or give you the list, and you order it."

"Yeah, I can make the order. Let me take a shower, and then we can leave. That damn Willis broke two pieces off his leg. Hell, I told him he may as well buy a new one. I patched it up, but it ain't gonna hold too long."

As Vic showered, I realized that even our Sundays were becoming less of a day off. I lay on the sofa and mused about the dream, praying that I would be given more to go on, at least some idea as to where this mysterious building was . . . or if it even existed.

FIVE

From Dream to Reality

It was Sunday, an early, beautiful March morning. Patches of white snow glistened along the roadside, leaving traces of a passing winter. I had taken Vic's boys back home to their mom's unusually early because she wanted to take them to church. A cousin of theirs was getting baptized and, of course, she wanted them to be there.

I must have had a lot on my mind driving home because I passed the normal street exit, which meant I had to take the next one. Now, I'd lived in this city where I was born and raised most of my adult life, with the exception of the years I lived in Indiana and California, and I had taken the same expressway more times than I could count. However, that day was different.

I was driving along at least the speed limit, which was 55mph. Anyway, I'm driving along when this voice in my head says, *"Turn your head to the left."* Of course, I turned out of curiosity. Now keep in mind I'm driving around 55-60, when out of the... *dream...*

"Oh my God!" I must have screamed as I swerved and pressed on the brakes. I was so grateful that it was a Sunday, which meant there was hardly any traffic— as I'm sure there would have been an accident. However, all of a sudden, everything went into s-l-o-w motion. I couldn't believe my eyes. There it was . . . big as life! This was no dream... this was real... as real as it could get.

She was massive and surrounded by trees almost as huge–just like in the dream. Her coat of paint was worn from years of neglect; the windows were boarded, keeping out the light from the outside world. There was a sadness that permeated her strong foundation, as if ready to give up and return to the ground. An oversized sign with large, black letters with the words: "FOR LEASE," stood at attention on the front lawn while the grass traveled up its poles. I must have slowed down almost to a stop as I looked on with awe and repeated the telephone number in my mind to call for "more information." After that, I have no idea how much time passed. The next thing I remembered was running upstairs to our bedroom to the phone, repeating the telephone number until I had pressed each one.

"Hello, you have reached the Portland North Reality. Our office hours are . . ." the voice said from the recording. Of course, I didn't really expect anyone to be there; it was Sunday. While leaving my information, along with both the café and home numbers, my heart raced with each word.

"Oh my God, can this be real?" —were all the words that fumbled from my lips for at least twenty minutes as I paced the floor, with tears falling like a spring shower. I was overwhelmed with emotions that were new and unfathomable. I had *asked* to be shown— and it was given. I was happy as a hog in slop.

By the time Vic got home, I was almost like a zombie. I could not believe that the dream was playing itself out as a reality.

"Are you all right?" my husband asked with a minor concern coming through the front door. He knew I had taken the boys home and probably figured I ran into their mother. "Did you run into Lisa?"

"No, but I have the most extraordinary news," I said rather coolly. I was sitting down, amazingly calm . . . or rather comatose. "I just saw my dream . . . the mansion."

"What do you mean... You have another dream?" Vic calmly inquired.

"It's not a dream, Vic, it's real! I just saw the actual building. The one I have been dreaming about for months . . . hell, for a couple of years."

I went on to tell him all the miraculous details. Next thing I know, he's sitting next to me, just as comatose. "Look, you gotta go with me so you can see it with your own eyes." He didn't take much convincing. We got up and moved toward the front door in unbelievable shock at what we both were about to bear witness to.

Pulling into the parking lot, there was complete silence as we both stepped out of the van. With eyes widened and a dropped jaw, I would have given my right arm for a camera to capture the look on my husband's face. Less than five minutes from our home, Vic was seeing with his own eyes what had only been a dream— a figment of my imagination.

"Come on, let's walk around," I suggested, grabbing my husband's hand. "Can you believe this, Vic? This had to be a plantation. I can feel it!" We slowly moved toward the building, looking at every detail of its magnitude, its solid structure, and its call for attention. In the front to the right was a long concrete porch with huge cracks and a broken corner. From the size of the boards on the front windows, on the right and left sides, they had to be at least ten feet tall. There were four sets of windows on the first and second levels, with one in the middle over the entrance. Three concrete steps led to the front door, which was set back within a cove. An old, broken antique lamp hung from the high curved, porch ceiling.

Neither one of us said much as we meandered our way around the right side of the building, looking out at what appeared to be about an acre of land. As we both moved further from the mansion, about fifty feet to get a better look, we noticed a chain-linked fence covered with wild bushes. On the other side were railroad tracks that seemed to still be in use. Gazing up at the two-story structure, there were several windows covered with boards that continued along the length of the building.

On the second level was an ornate, octagon-shaped balcony with chipped, dark green wrought-iron fencing, held in place by an old weather-beaten, weather-beaten wooden covering.

Walking back towards the building, Vic noticed some steps that led to what appeared to be a cellar or basement of some sort. To his surprise, he discovered an unlocked door in which he cautiously entered. I quickly followed his lead.

It was damp and somewhat dark upon entering, although a nearby window provided a few streaks of sunlight as we looked around while standing in the middle of the small room. The floors and walls, made of bricks, were covered with cobwebs and soot, along with heavy traces of dirt. Dried brown vines peeked through the concrete cracks. The low ceiling supported by charcoaled beams, and the strong smell of smoke, were telltale signs of a recent fire.

While Vic took a closer look at the burned beams, curiosity led me into a back room that was even denser and darker, with only a slight shimmer of light that peeked through a small, dirt-covered window. Although the space was tight and hidden from the door, I felt an unnerving chill throughout my body. Feeling claustrophobic and a tad-bit frightened, I quickly made my way back to the front when I noticed a rusty metal hook hanging from a loose beam. Standing there in deep thought, a heavy sadness took over my initial excitement. Instinctively, I knew that it once held the weight of a slave. Maybe one who attempted to run away, or one that talked back to its Master, or maybe a field-hand that passed out from the hot, southern sun before completing his sixteen-hour day. The visions were heart-wrenching, taking my breath.

"I have to get out of here, Vic." I cried as the words were being choked by the lump in my throat.

"Yeah, I hear ya, baby, me too. It feels strange in here. I can't explain it, though," Vic stuttered as we both headed for the door.

"Did you see that hook?" I asked, looking back.

"Yeah, what you think it was for?"

"It was for us niggers that didn't wanna act right," I blurted out. "Look, I gotta get outta here, I'm getting sick."

Once out in the fresh air, I took a long, deep breath to get my bearings back, trying to get back to the reason we were there. Finding ourselves speechless, neither of us expounded on what had just happened, as we continued exploring along the length of the building. My heart raced as I gazed around in wonderment, still unable to grasp the realization of what was actually happening. That we were on a "real" plantation.

"Wow, seven windows," I exclaimed, breaking the silence. Unlike the first floor, all the windows on the second level were not boarded and were not as tall, with some panes being broken or cracked. While my gaze was lifted-up, Vic seemed to be more interested in seeing if he could find a way inside as we approached a small porch with iron railings and wooden steps, leading to a door. This time, however, Vic's attempt to enter was to no avail. And just as we stepped from the porch, I screamed, "Vic, look! It's the building in my dream that I said looked like an apartment. I know this was a plantation. I just know it! And I bet this was the slave quarters."

Vic and I were flabbergasted. It was unbelievable. But there it was. A two-room slave quarters divided by two separate entrances. Both doors were boarded. The roof was completely off, with the exception of weather-beaten two-by-fours that held rusty pieces of tin, barely hanging on one side of the building. Rusty nail-heads sprouted from the dried, cracked boards that covered the two doors— and the one window on each side.

Realizing that all we had to do was remove the rusty nails from an old latch that served as a lock, Vic found a brick and knocked it out. Not knowing what to expect, he slowly cracked open the door. Pieces of dry splinters floated to the ground as we gingerly stepped in. The light from the exposed roof cast a shadow of the beams onto an aged, red brick floor. Even with the sun's rays, the space was cold and damp; the air was thick and suffocating. It felt like death. While I tried to imagine what it looked like over a hundred years earlier, the feeling was too overwhelming . . . too heavy on my heart.

Once again, without speaking, we both left the historical sight and rejoined the warmth and beauty of the outdoors to continue our treasure hunt. It truly was a treasure in the sense that we were standing in the midst of history, bearing witness to a place where our ancestors lived and died in ways unimaginable.

At the back of the main house, what looked to have been a screened-in porch was barely hanging on to the unsound, colorless boards on the second level, extending around to the other side. There were no steps that led to it, but you could tell there had been some from the door and a small wooden platform. It too was barely hanging on.

An old, rusty fence covered with overgrown bushes separated the mansion and the small slave-quarters from a line of small houses. Backyards were filled with old tires, car parts, dog houses, and signs of small children; a tricycle that needed a fresh coat of paint; a tire swing hanging lifeless from an oak tree. The last house on the corner, next to the parking lot, was the only house that didn't scream for a paint job or a lawn makeover. Most of the entire area was stricken with desperation and a need for revitalization.

My husband and I didn't talk much on our way back home. There were really no words that could explain how I felt. It still seemed like a dream, yet I knew it was no figment of my imagination... not anymore. I began to wonder–*what was I to do now? What was the dream telling me to do with this manifestation?*

Vic must have been thinking along the same lines when he asked, "Well, what you think? It's a huge building, and it needs a whole lot of work. I wonder what it used to be?"

"You mean after it was a plantation? Because to me, it's obvious that it was definitely a plantation. This has to be what the dreams have been about. The souls here are trying to tell me something. I'm just not quite sure what it is they want. I'm gonna have to do some serious meditation. Did I tell you I called the real-estate company?" "No, what did they say?" Vic hesitantly inquired.

"Well, since today is Sunday, I left a message for them to call me back. Since there's no school tomorrow, thank goodness, I should know more once they return the call. Do you mind opening the café in the morning by yourself?"

"Naw, what time do you think you'll get there?"

"Probably around ten, I wanna meditate before leaving to get some more clarity. No telling what time they'll call, but I also want to see if it's possible to get inside tomorrow as well. I'll make sure it's after our lunch…I don't know, we'll see. Baby, I don't know what's going on, but it feels like something big is about to happen."

That night, I could barely sleep, and Vic was out late again. When he finally crawled into bed, the clock said 4:50 a.m. He had been drinking, and I had been crying. Vic's late nights had become a habit, and as most of us women do, I began to think that I was the reason. Maybe I was too preoccupied with the woes of the world. Or maybe my desire to become an entrepreneur was pushing my husband too fast. I was certainly driven, and finding time to hang out was virtually nonexistent. Vic was a hard worker, so he probably understood the importance of creating balance. All work and no play can make for an unhappy life.

With all my rationale for his late nights, fear that I no longer satisfied my husband sexually, also took up space in my thoughts. We rarely made love, and when we did, I usually had to be the aggressor, which was something rare for me. I was taught to let the man be the aggressor; don't be whorish. So instead of being *forward* and showing my husband how much, I missed his touch, I threw my legs across his still body and finally drifted off to sleep–only to see visions that made me never want to dream again. And, believe me, it wasn't about no mansion.

As usual, no matter how late my husband stayed out, he was always the first to rise. "I hate the mornings," I managed to slur with one arm hanging off the side of the bed, lifeless.

"No, you don't. You love the mornings. You love them so much, you hate for them to be over," my husband so eloquently reminded me. He may have been the quiet type, but he sure had a way of making sense when he did speak. He was absolutely right! I loved the mornings. And although we may have been estranged in bed, we had an uncanny way of being able to know what the other was about to say or want. The times when Vic couldn't get his thoughts lined up, I was able to complete his sentence, and he could sense when I needed something before I asked.

"Have a nice time last night?" I inquired while trying not to be too nosy.

"Yeah, me and Greg hung out at Charles' joint and had a few beers. We got to talkin' after he closed. . .you know how Charles is. Hell, I thought we would never get out of there. He was complaining that his bar was turnin' into a gay club."

"Yeah, I noticed that the last time we were there. This one girl was checking me out, kinda tough. I think she got the message when she saw me all up under you. Oh well, as long as they respect my preference, that's their business. Besides, their money is green, too.

Hey, I'm supposed to hear from the real estate office today."

"You think you will get to see it today?"

"I don't know, but I'm sure gonna try. Since you have to be at the café, maybe I can get my friend, Carolyn, to go with me. You know, my redhead girlfriend. The one I met while working at the art gallery, and she thought I was crazy for marrying you. She said she heard that you beat women."

We laughed while he undressed to take a shower. I knew Vic wasn't the type to hit a woman. Not only was he quiet, but he was usually rather passive as well.

"You know, she was probably talkin' about Greg," he yelled from the shower. "People get us mixed up at times. Now, he's good at hittin' on women. I told him bout that shit, but he claims they start it. As much as I've wanted to knock the shit out of Lisa, I couldn't do it. Now, I've pushed her to get her off me, but I ain't into hittin' on women."

"Yeah, you right. When I met his last girlfriend, she mentioned that they fought. Why women stay with men who beat on them, I will never understand. Well, Carolyn admitted that she was wrong once she saw how happy I was. I'll give her a call. You mind if she goes instead of you? You know, we could close for a while if you really want to go."

"Naw, baby, one of us has to be at the café. We need to make all the money we can. Hell, we got a mortgage and rent, plus everything else. I don't know how you keep everything paid. That's why I just gave you my check when I was working. You are damn good with keepin' things straight. Hell, baby, for a long time, you ran the café by yourself. I can handle it till you get back. Only a few guys come for their regular sandwiches in the morning. It'll be cool. You take your friend."

I loved my husband. He was the kinda guy you could depend on, and he was always understanding and supportive. Although usually quiet, there were times he'd be really talkative, particularly when he had a buzz. Damn, he was funny! He would get on the mic during Spoken Word and have everyone cracking up. And the times he couldn't finish a sentence–everyone else filled in the blanks, which made it even funnier. His smile lit up the entire room when he came through. Everybody was, "Hey, baby. What's happening, baby"?

Being married to me brought out the radical side of Vic. He often followed my lead when it came to expressing our African culture. Growing my hair and wearing dread-twist inspired Vic to grow his hair, also. He would braid his hair in several plaits and twist them all together, and when he unbraided them, whichever way they stuck out, that's how he rolled. He looked good, no matter how he wore his hair; even when wearing a mandatory scarf, Vic had a special flair. He loved wearing bright colors, even before it became fashionable for men. I loved that about him; we were both alike in that manner. We had our own unique styles, and we didn't care what people thought.

The Call

"Hello. Yes, this is she speaking." The real estate call came around ten. "Well, I would like an appointment to take a look at it today, if possible. Late afternoon would be best... say around five thirty? Yes, I understand. I'll call if anything changes. See you then."

My heart was racing like the time I got baptized; thankful for my young soul being saved and not going to hell but scared to death that if I ever made a mistake, God might forget that I was just a kid and send me straight to hell. *What was I getting myself into?* Thoughts ran rapidly with possibilities and impossibilities. But first things first, I needed to call Carolyn.

I called Vic before leaving to see if we needed anything, and then stopped by the store to pick up a few items. I must have gone to the grocery every day at least once . . . sometimes three times. Running a café was no joke. A twenty-four-seven job, even on our off days. I suppose that's the price you pay to be self-sufficient.

I got to the café right before lunch. There was no time for a lunch special, and I decided to prepare one for dinner during our downtime. It was a relatively quiet Monday, and we had been taking note that Mondays were generally slow and thought about closing on that day. This would give us a little more time for ourselves and maybe have a little fun . . . at least me. Vic always made sure he took his fun-time, and as of late, he didn't ask me to hang out with him as much as he used to.

After further discussion, we agreed to start making announcements that we were closing on Mondays and put it on the answering machine. Little did we know at the time that days off would practically be null and void.

"I have an appointment at five-thirty this evening," I told Vic while putting up groceries. "I also spoke with Carolyn, and she said she could meet me here, so we can go together."

"Have you given any thought about why you want to look at it?" my husband asked with reservation, as if not to incite any wild ideas he knew I was famous for.

"Not yet, I didn't get much in my mediation. But I feel like once I'm inside, it will come to me what to do next."

Carolyn arrived at five o'clock. My husband, despite my friend's past feelings about him not being good enough for me, towered over her with a welcoming hug. She tiptoed to reciprocate his kind gesture while her ruby-red lips spread into a warm and sincere smile.

Before leaving, Vic and I gave Carolyn another quick tour to show off our recent accomplishments. Although she had visited when we first opened, some things had changed once we got our own equipment and Certificate of Operation. She was super excited and wished us well.

Carolyn and I had met several years earlier at an art show where I worked as a gallery designer. She had recently moved to Kentucky from San Francisco, California, which we found as a commonality. We hit it off immediately and became friends, thereafter realizing we shared many personal experiences.

One day, Carolyn and I were talking about spiritual stuff. Jewish and a confessed Atheist, my friend held onto a lot of anger and believed that there was no way there could be a God. We both had horror stories about life and its unfathomable reason for existence. And, like me, in trying to find answers to life and make some sense of it, she had dabbled in some metaphysical stuff like Tarot cards, tea leaves...that sort of thing, which somehow led to the subject of ghosts. Again, being a skeptic, Carolyn didn't believe in such things as *ghosts*, which turned out to be the perfect segue into telling her about my first encounter with the *unbelievable* . . .

It was a late, southern summer night, and my little sister and I were all alone in my grandmother's house. I had just turned eight that June, which made my sister around six. Our house, a huge two-story with dark green, tar-like shingles set on a half-acre facing one of the two major roads that led into our quaint community. The front was framed with a long concrete porch, supported by three huge white columns. Under the living-room window set an old, rusty, white, iron sofa-swing. As you entered the front door, there was a creaky staircase that led to the second floor, which we hardly ever used. Living with daddy's momma, we grew up with minimal facilities; we had no electricity and no running water. We used oil lamps and had coal stoves; one in the kitchen, which was used for cooking, and the one in the dining room was used for heat during the winter.

On this particular night, lying on blankets on the living room floor, my sister and I, wearing only T-shirts and panties, were trying to sleep, but it was too hot. The only light came from the full-moon, casting a soft glow throughout the large space. We hardly ever stayed in this particular room, except in the summer, because it seemed to stay a little cooler. There was a long striped green and white, silky-smooth sofa –a hand-me-down from one of my grandmother's white employers. Next to the sofa was an old piano with music rollers in the middle that played various musical tunes just by pressing a paddle. There were many times I had sat on the piano stool, stretching my feet to the big paddle while spreading my long skinny fingers across the Ivory keys, and pretending to be playing for a live audience. I would even turn to take a bow!

Right next to our makeshift bed was a big rocking chair where Grandma used to rock us and read storybooks. To help us fall asleep, I began telling my sister the story of *The Three Little Pigs.* As I was "huffing and puffing" to blow the pig's house down, a sound came from the piano. I looked up and saw one of the keys pressed down as if someone had played it. I looked at my sister, who was now sitting up, and told her that it was probably a mouse. I continued with the story ... huffing and puffing.

Just then, the rocking chair, which was only inches from us, began to rock— and there was no one in it. I thought it was my imagination and continued to tell the story. But it rocked again. This time longer. I knew that for a mouse to be rocking it, it had to be as big as a cat, and

I wasn't willing to stick around to see it. And since my sister was facing me, she didn't know what was happening.

"Come on, Lonnie, we got to get out of here," I whispered while grabbing her arm to raise her up.

"Why, what's wrong? I want to hear the rest of the story."

I tried to explain that it was too hot to stay and that we needed to go up to Aunt Lucille's.

As we stood up to leave, the piano played again. This time, more of a melody.

"Is the mouse playing the piano again?" my little sister asked nervously.

"Probably so, Lonnie, let's go," I insisted. Lonnie stuck her thumb in her mouth as we headed for the front door. Just as I grabbed for the doorknob, for some reason, I looked toward the staircase. The stairwell was dark, but I could still see a tall, man-like figure descending the stairs. Large, dark, hollow-looking eyes were the only thing that resembled a face, and it appeared to be wearing a long black cape with a hood. I was so scared! I couldn't move for what seemed like forever. I couldn't even scream.

Finally, I was able to open the door. We ran out so fast that the door slammed shut behind Lonnie. As we ran toward the end of the porch, I noticed a strange man sitting on the sofa-swing—gently swinging back and forth. He was wearing a white shirt and dark trousers; he never said a word, and he never stirred.

My hair must have been standing straight up when we fell into Auntie Lucille's back door, huffing and puffing.

"What on earth is wrong with you, girl. What are you two doing so out of breath?"

"I-I-I-I saw a ghost," I stammered with beads of sweat popping out on my forehead, and it wasn't from the heat, as I continued out of breath. "It was comin' down the stairs, and a man was sittin' on the porch swing, and he didn't say nothin', and the rockin' chair was rockin', and the piano was playin'. We scared Auntie." Lonnie stood there looking bewildered, sucking her thumb; apparently, she didn't see what I saw.

"Now, you know there ain't no ghost," Auntie tried assuring me. "Come on in and go in the other room where the fan is. You girls can watch television."

Aunt Lucille was Daddy's older sister who lived further up the backyard on the other side of the "outhouse." She had long, black, shiny, wavy hair, and little red freckles all over her face. I loved going to my auntie's house; she had electricity and a gas stove.

It didn't take long for Lonnie to fall asleep. Auntie had given us some Sassafras tea and a slice of pound cake. Still a little frazzled, it was during the "Jack Parr Show" when I eventually felt safe enough to drift off into dreamland.

Needless to say, sharing my beliefs and dreams was something I felt safe in doing with Carolyn. Even though my ghost story was a little hard for her to swallow, she at least chalked it up as a *childhood experience* that was at least a *possibility.* However, the one thing that she did understand was what we were trying to accomplish in our community and our plight. With her own cultural challenges and as a recent newlywed to an African American, Carolyn had been delightfully supportive. So, asking her to be a part of our next quest was a given. However, it proved to be . . .

A Hard Sell

We arrived about ten minutes early to meet the real estate agent. And just as we pulled into the parking lot, Carolyn suddenly gasped for breath.

"Is this it?" she questioned.

I assumed the first impression was not necessarily a good one.

"Yep, this is it," I responded. "Isn't it beautiful?"

There was silence. But, of course, I ranted on about how beautiful it was going to be.

"Are you looking to lease this?" my friend stammered.

"No, I want to 'buy' it," I said with authority. "Vic doesn't know it yet, but I believe I'm supposed to buy this building."

Before we could further debate it, a car pulled up next to us. An average height man removed himself from the car that advertised his real estate company. He was slightly bald with a little grey around his temples. He wore a wool, grey jacket with black pants. His horn-rimmed glasses provided sight to his light green eyes. And from the look of his midsection, one could see he stayed at a desk most of the time. Carrying a leather briefcase and a large industrial-sized flashlight, we both walked towards him and introduced ourselves.

"There isn't much electricity in the building," he announced, not knowing which of us was the interested party. "The owner has a temporary, electrical pole that will only allow me to show a small portion of the building. But I have this flashlight as well."

As the agent spoke, he scrambled around in his pockets and briefcase, only to realize he didn't have the key to let us in. "I'm sorry, I don't seem to have the key," he shamefully admitted. "But I can run around the corner and get the owner's key if you don't mind waiting." Embarrassed, he waited for our response.

"No, I don't mind at all," I quickly spoke up. Carolyn smiled in agreement. The man left, promising to be back in fifteen minutes.

Carolyn and I walked around the building while I did most of the talking, which was mostly about the dreams. Even with that, my dear friend could not comprehend *why* I would entertain the thought of *buying* this building. And as hard as it was to believe in the possibility, I knew that it was possible and that it would, in fact, happen.

We heard a car door and returned to the front of the building. As the real estate agent promised, he was back in fifteen minutes with keys dangling in his hand. By now, we were standing on the porch waiting for the boarded door to be opened. He fooled around with a few keys until one fit. I was anxious. My heartbeat moved up into my throat, but I remained cool on the surface as the agent opened the door.

"You know, there was a small fire here," he began explaining. "And even though the owner had offered to open the door, the firefighters chose to use an axe instead. I never have been able to understand why they do that." The three of us managed a chuckle as he pushed open the door leading into a dark foyer.

Right as we entered, there were two giant doors which had to be at least twelve feet tall–one on the right and one on the left. The cold, stiff air gave me a chill. For a moment, I was speechless. The bright light from the agent's large flashlight inched away the darkness, exposing an ebony staircase leading to a second floor. Looking behind the door, he retrieved the temporary electrical pole. Once turned on, a huge wire-encased bulb quickly shed a wide stream of light on the stairs, which were cluttered with old newspapers and boxes speckled with paint shavings. The surrounding walls were laced with years of cracked paint, while individual pieces and clumps protruded, waiting to be brushed against, freeing them from their cold surface.

We all moved toward the right of the staircase, entering a giant door that led into a large room where we were met with burnt pieces of hardwood flooring scattered across the room, exposing areas of the cellar beneath. Black soot plastered the four enormous walls. In the background, as I gleamed with the possibilities, Carolyn was whispering, "Oh my God, no Nailah, you can't do this." Her slightly round face twisted in disbelief and horror.

"Remember to watch your step," the agent alerted us. "A fire was started in the cellar below. It's believed to have been started by some homeless people trying to stay warm." While listening to him and watching my step, all I could envision was a finished product.

"Carolyn, this is going to be a formal dining room," I finally said.

"Oh my God!" Carolyn chanted.

For the next hour, we ventured through the twenty-two rooms. Some of the huge rooms were filled with old, dusty antique office desks and file cabinets. At least three of the rooms had handcrafted, marble fireplaces. All the windows on the first floor looked to be about ten feet high with fourteen-foot ceilings. Trash was everywhere, connected to years of cobwebs. Stacks of old newspapers and faded blueprints lined the gigantic walls and halls. Large holes exposed 2x4's and dangling out-of-date wiring. Broken commodes and sinks were the only traces from the once commercial and private bathrooms. Still, I could only see the possibilities as we moved from room to room; our footprints leaving their mark on the mounds of dirt and dust that covered the creaky, wooden floors.

So many times, I had walked the long hallways and visited the many rooms while in a deep sleep. However, now I was wide awake, seeing with my own eyes what the visions and dreams had given me a glimpse of. And regardless of the horrific sights and the massiveness of the work that would have been involved, which was intimidating enough, my heart danced as I gave every room a purpose, and in many instances, a name. All I could see was its beauty, its elegance, its grace.

While I couldn't quite understand my purpose, or the reason I was shown this plantation in my dreams, (let alone try to explain this to Carolyn) instinctively I knew that a great work was to be done, and it had everything to do with the former slaves that once walked these halls: those that cooked, cleaned, cried and died in ways that I hated to imagine. However, I could feel it.

As the agent moved along with us, and as I described each approaching room, while Carolyn continued to call on the very name she claimed to have no belief in, the agent asked if I had been in the building before.

"If you can understand," I began explaining. "I have been all through this house but not like you may think. I have had many dreams about this house and have walked through every room. Do you know what it was, just recently?" I enquired.

"It was the Southern Railroad Headquarters. They shut down about fifteen years ago. It's been empty since."

"Did you know that it was once a plantation?" I asked, figuring he could have cared less what it was.

"Uh, I don't know anything about that, ma'am," he stammered. "Mr. Murphy, the owner, may have some information."

Once back into the light of day, the exhilaration I felt was taking my breath. I managed to take a few deep breaths before asking the agent when I could meet the owner.

"You know, the owner is a contractor, and it's going to take him about a quarter of a million dollars to fix this place up," he began to explain.

We met eye-to-eye. By now, based on the side comments from Carolyn, it was probably obvious who was the interested party.

"And your point?" I stared with intensity while waiting for an answer.

"Uh, I didn't mean any harm. I was just stating that it was going to take quite a bit of money, even for a contractor . . ."

"Yes," I interjected. "I think it's quite obvious that it's going to take quite a bit of work and money. Again, when can I meet . . . did you say Murphy is his name?"

"Yes, Mr. Murphy, can I have him reach you at the same numbers?"

"Please do. I look forward to hearing from one of you soon.

Thanks again for showing us the place. Have a great day!"

Carolyn and I stood on the porch as we watched the agent drive off. He smiled and waved.

"Nailah, you can't be serious about this place. He's right, it's going to take a whole lot of money. Plus, it's going to be hell trying to fix this place."

I could see the tears as they began to form in Carolyn's hazel eyes, which she managed to hold back, while her perfectly arched brows creased with fear.

"I know it looks impossible, but I know it can be done. I have to do this."

"If you just have to have the property because of what it represents to you, why not just bulldoze this... this building and build from scratch?"

Her thin red lips, slightly trembling, I knew she meant well as she pleaded for me to look at other options.

"It's the building itself that has the importance," I attempted to explain. "If the dreams mean what I think, the ancestors will make a way for it to happen. Oh, Carolyn, it's going to be beautiful. I know you can't see it now . . . but just wait . . . you'll see."

The short drive back was quiet and awkward. My dear friend already thought I was crazy for starting a business with credit cards and marrying a man that had spent some time in jail. I could only imagine what was going through her head when I tried selling her on my "dream." It was virtually impossible to get her to understand the importance of purchasing the former plantation. Hell, I could barely understand it myself.

SIX

New Friends, Old Problems

Uncle Vic was serving a newcomer when I got back after saying good-bye to my distraught friend.

"Hey, baby, come and meet Martha. She heard about us through a friend."

Martha was a very pleasant, middle-aged woman with dark blonde hair cut in a short, curly style. Her hand was small and warm as we shook, and she appeared to be short in stature as I leaned down to give her The Java House greeting.

"Welcome. My name is Nailah. How do you like our little place?"

"Oh, I love it. It reminds me of New York. They have places like this in Manhattan. Hey, the food is excellent. Uncle Vic made me an Uncle Arnie, and it was the best sandwich I've had since I've been in Kentucky. Your husband's a damn good cook. I've been trying to find out what is in the special sauce."

"Well, good luck with that one. Everybody tries to get it. Can I get you some more lemon iced tea?"

"Oh yeah, this is awesome," taking a large swig. "I understand, it's homemade."

"Yeah, we try to do as much homemade as possible. You know, give it a homey quality. I'll be right back with your tea."

One of the unique qualities of The Java House, besides the food, was how it was attracting people from all ethnic and cultural backgrounds. We served a broader community, creating unity and camaraderie, establishing a foundation for trust and forgiveness.

The three of us sat and talked for a while, getting to know each other. Also Jewish, Martha was particularly proud of our establishment and what we were accomplishing in our community. Having some understanding of our plight as descendants of slaves and how we still found ourselves constantly battling the disparities that were placed upon us as a people, she would eventually become a confidant and a supporter in our mission.

Sharing with My Daughter

After our new customer left, I remembered that I needed to call my daughter, Jenia, to share my good news. Unfortunately, I hadn't seen my oldest child since our wedding. However, like with my sons, we tried to talk at least once or twice a month. Needless to say, I had been so busy working that it had been at least a month since we last talked. She, too, had been busy as well, working and raising five kids. Grateful she had an older son, Mark, who was a teenager, was able to be a big help with his younger siblings, especially since school was still out for the summer.

"Jenia, you are not going to believe this." I started off the conversation.

"What mom? Believe what... is it good news, because I don't know if I can take any bad news right now."

I could hear the youngest crying in the background at the top of her lungs.

"Yes, it's good news! Remember the dream I was telling you about . . . you know, the mansion?"

She agreed that she recalled the dream while yelling to Mark to get the baby.

"Well, I just saw the actual building . . . the dream was showing me this building that I just saw in real life."

I continued, excitedly giving her the full story while she occasionally asked me to hold on while she attended to one of the kids. Needless to say, not only was she fascinated with the whole thing about the building, but extremely ecstatic with the fact that my dream had become a reality.

Before we got off the phone, she shared that things were looking a little better because her husband had gotten a job, and that he was helping more with the kids. I encouraged her to keep praying and to take care of herself. She assured me that she was attending church with the kids and doing her best to keep her faith.

"Hey, before we get off the phone, let me say hi to the kids."

After speaking with each of my grandchildren, including the youngest, who stopped crying long enough to say, "Hi gamma," we ended our conversation agreeing to talk again soon and to keep her posted on everything with the mansion.

Just after I got off the phone with my daughter, a stream of customers came through until around ten o'clock that night, keeping us busy. My little friend and poet, Daisy, came through. She offered to stay and help us clean, which she often did when she came by. Daisy was about sixteen or seventeen and was still in high school. She was an excellent rap artist, which is what she often did during a poetry night. She was cute and petite and wore her hair wrapped as a part of her Muslim religion. Her dark skin showed the menacing signs of being a teenager... pimples. She loved to talk and often talked with my husband for advice on boys. I thought it was cute that Vic served as a father figure to a girl, since he had all boys.

On one occasion, when she and I were having a girly conversation, she alluded to the *possibility of liking* a *married man.* Of course, I went into the... *girl, don't even think about it... It's a dangerous road to travel, and believe me, it's not worth it, mode.*

Being on both sides of *adultery,* I sheepishly admitted, I explained to her about an experience I had once shortly after my first divorce.

Young and dumb, I believed the man when he said he wasn't married. Plus, there were no signs, such as a wedding ring. After a couple of months of promises and intimate encounters, I got a phone call from his "wife." Shocked, I stammered, trying to explain to her that I didn't know . . . that he said he wasn't married. She admitted that I wasn't the first. Surprised and curious, I asked why she stayed with such a man. She explained that she had three kids and no means of supporting them on her own, and that having a father for her children was important. And even though he was a cheater, she admitted that she loved him. Naturally, I assured her that she didn't have to worry about me seeing her husband again.

From my own personal experience, I knew all too well her situation and how painful it could be. The difference between her and me was –I took my three kids (and was pregnant with my fourth) and left. After sharing with Daisy, she shyly hung her head and agreed it was a bad idea. We never had the conversation again.

We finished cleaning around 11:30 p.m., and Vic gave Daisy a ride home. I went home, took a bath, and reminisced about the day. I visualized and spiritualized the possibility of the dreams about the mansion coming into fruition as I soaked. The scented bubbles gave me a feeling of being away at a resort, while my exhausted body gave way to the ambiance. A glass of Chardonnay had me relaxed while Olive oil made my skin feel soft and silky like a woman— something that was rare. Most of the time, I felt like an old, beat-down hag. I could only hope that my husband didn't share the same sentiment.

I must have been in the tub for about an hour, and Vic still hadn't come home. I figured he went by Charles'. I was so tired that it really didn't matter. By the time I slipped between the cool sheets, the clock said 1:30 a.m.

Same Old, Same Old

That night, I never got the chance to tell Vic about seeing the mansion; I was in a deep sleep by the time he got to bed. In my dreams, my soul traveled to unknown places, showing me things that were so unsettling that I wouldn't allow myself to accept them as a possibility, let alone prophetic. So, to avoid the stress of giving it any reality, I once again chose to chalk the dream up as merely a nightmare . . . brought on by exhaustion.

The alarm went off at 6:30. As always, Vic got up before me. I rolled over as he started to get out of bed.

"Hi baby. What time did you get home last night?" I asked casually to avoid any possible need for defense.

"Oh, I don't know, probably around two or three. I stopped by Charles'."

"What's old Charles up to?"

"Same old, same old— Hell, you know how he likes to talk. Hey, you don't have to get up right now. I can open. You know how you love the mornings."

I gave a soft moan and thanked him. My back was killing me, as usual.

I tried to go back to sleep, but flashes of the disturbing dream flooded my mind. There was just no way I was seeing the truth. Maybe it was my own insecurities. My past relationships with men never failed to leave me drained of any hope of longevity, but I was sure my relationship with Vic was different. After all, I had sought spiritual guidance from Shangodora (Yoruba teacher) through divination regarding our relationship. We were meant to be together. We had a great work to do, even though one particular reading said that Vic was carrying a secret. But hell, we all have secrets, so I never really gave it much thought. We were happy (for the most part) with each other, and we were doing more things in the two years of our marriage than most couples did in twenty.

However, between being a student of *Ifa* and the priestess-hood, the dreams of seeing the future and seeing Spirits, plus the rigorous work of working two jobs, there were times I thought I was losing my mind— or already crazy. And there was never an option of Not overcoming the challenges that surfaced from day to day. However, driven by something much deeper than any need to rest or give up, I had no choice but to keep pushing forward.

SEVEN

A Night with Celebrity, Sobriety, and Sharing

April showers never stopped the pouring in of Spoken Word and Hip-Hop artists. It was the fourth Saturday, and as usual, the place was packed. I had picked up some more fresh fruit for the Juice-Joints. Gee, they sold like blunts to a weed-head. You would think they gave you a buzz. They were good, if I say so myself. And at $3.75 a drink... that was my *high*.

Earlier that evening, Vic and I attended a performance at an Arts Center for a poetry slam, featuring well-known writer and poet, Ms. Jessica Care Moore. During the show, I hollered and screamed so much that the MC and a friend of The Java House Café acknowledged Vic and me as being in the audience and had us stand. He then asked over the mic if we would be interested in a late-night jam at The Java House. Well, you already know what I screamed back.

As we were leaving, a young man approached us and vivaciously explained how great it was to meet us, and that he had heard a lot about us and the Spoken Word. He was hyped as he introduced himself as Jack B. and expressed his intent to come by.

That night, we were packed, and to my surprise, Ms. Moore showed up with her significant other around midnight. A hundred long individual braids fell on her shoulders. She was more beautiful up close than on stage. We introduced ourselves formally before half the room recognized her and stood in line for an autograph.

Ms. Moore spoke of a black revolution while interweaving the importance of black love. I was amazed at her wisdom and devotion to who we were as a people, while offering homage to those who came long before us. She was hot! And we were honored beyond expression for her presence and her gift. Our new friend, Jack B., took to the stage as well. It would be the beginning of a five-year love affair of flowing lyrics . . . his "poetic justice" to maintain his sobriety and a need to belong.

Late nights were common for The Java House, especially on poetry night, but that night, we didn't close until the next morning. The Java House was on fire! We were jamming, and Jessica and her guest didn't leave until around four. Vic and I made breakfast (our treat) for those who had passed out on sofas and chairs, including my stepsons, who had found spots on the carpeted areas for refuge. There were also those who managed to keep us awake with stimulating conversation and a few cups of coffee. Thank God it was Sunday.

Finally, around ten that morning, we were able to persuade the last few over-niters to leave. Tired, couldn't begin to describe what I felt. I was drained... and my back felt like it was breaking in half. But what else was new? The agony of pain had become an everyday part of life and was getting worse as the days went by. I couldn't wait to hit the sack. I believe I made record speed in driving home for fear of passing out at the wheel. Vic and the boys weren't far behind me. I must have run to the bedroom because before they got in the front door, I had flopped on the bed— too tired to pull back the covers. Vic came in, and as if I were a child, he undressed me and put me under the covers. I couldn't tell you whether he came to bed or not. I passed out not a moment too soon.

EIGHT

Sharing the Dream

The scent of marijuana brought me to a sit-up position. I stirred around to see if anyone was upstairs. The scene behind the curtains exposed a full moon. I threw on a robe and went downstairs. Voices came from the kitchen, where the scent got stronger as I turned the corner. Vic and Greg were smoking a joint and drinking beer.

"Hey sis, what's going on? Vic said you all were up all night last night," Greg uttered with smoke oozing from his lips.

"Hi Greg, yeah, it was crazy. We didn't get home till this morning. How you doing?"

"Ah, it's all good. You know how it is. There ain't no point in complainin'."

"Hey, baby, you must have been real tired. It's eight o'clock," Vic jumped in, surprised I had slept so late.

"Yeah, I was. Where are the boys; are they gone already?"

"Yeah, I took them home bout an hour ago. You know I wouldn't be doing no smokin' if they were here."

"I know. I wish I could have said goodbye. Did they eat dinner?"

"Yeah, we all went out. Greg went with us. We just got back a little while ago. You hungry? I can go get you something or make you a sandwich," my husband offered, while I reached for the joint that was between his fingers.

"Naw, baby, you don't want any of this," he announced while taking it from my hand. "I'll roll you one. Back still bothering you?"

"Yeah, I need to get in the tub and soak with some Epsom Salt. That's what you can go to the store and get me, if you don't mind. And bring me back a fish sandwich from Burger King, please."

"You want fries?"

"Yep, and make sure they are good and hot."

Vic handed me a fresh, ultra-thin joint with a pack of matches. I didn't bother to ask what was in the one he and Greg were smoking. Whatever it was, he knew better than to give it to me. I only *assumed* that it was probably hash or cocaine.

"Hey Greg, did Vic tell you I went to see this mansion a few blocks from here?"

"Yeah, he told me bout it, said it looked like a castle." We all laughed.

"Ah, you know how Vic exaggerates. It's big, but it ain't no castle."

We all talked for a few more minutes. I took a couple of hits and a swig of Vic's beer before I went to the living room to crash on the sofa. They both left. I lit some Frankincense and did some stretches, which smoking always propelled me to do. I felt a little more relaxed as I waited for Vic to return.

The fries were hot and fresh. I finished eating while we sat around talking about the mansion. Boy, I tell you, my husband was hilarious. He started talking about how big and awful the mansion looked. He had me and Greg rolling. I laughed so hard my back ached even more, but this was a good ache.

". . .and man, you could tell the white man had us hangin' from those big-ass trees. Those damn trees have to be a hundred years old. Hell, I could still smell the blood. Then we went down in this dungeon, right... the walls and shit was all burnt. And . . . and then my wife showed me this hook hangin' from the ceilin', know what

I'm sayin? . . . and man, we knew they had our asses hooked on it, beatin' the hell out of us. The place was spooky as hell, man. I told Nailah I had to get the hell up out of there before I started seein' ghosts and shit. Man, it was somethin' else."

In between the screams of laughter, I tried to tell Greg about the dreams and the fact that I felt the ancestors wanted me to help them to leave, that their souls were stuck. Greg nodded and grunted an "Umum" from time to time. I could see that he was trying to make some sense of what I was saying.

"You mean to tell me that you believe there are some ghosts in the building?" he asked, taking a toke from the joint.

"Well, I call them Spirits, and yeah, I believe there are Spirits there. What... you don't believe in Spirits or ghosts?"

"Naw. I believe once your ass is dead, it's over," Greg proclaimed, passing me the joint.

"Now you be cool, you know your ass can't smoke," Vic chimed in.

Greg laughed in agreement.

No Rest for the Weary

We must have laughed and talked for a couple more hours. I was getting sleepy again and ready to crawl back under the covers.

"Hey baby, me and Greg gonna go drink a couple of beers round Charles'. I won't be gone too long. Oh, and I put the Epsom Salt on the kitchen table."

"Thanks. My body certainly needs it."

"You need anything else before I leave?"

"No babe, I'm okay. Tell Charles, hey."

I looked on, somewhat disappointed that he wasn't staying. But I didn't want him to think I was trippin'. Besides, I was ready to go back to sleep. He gave me a peck on the cheek, and Greg gave me a hug and wished me a good night. I listened as the van left the gravel driveway.

I threw out the beer bottles and emptied the ashtray before going upstairs. The bedroom felt cold and empty. Suddenly, I felt strangely alone. I missed being held, kissed, and made love to. I crawled between the cold sheets and cried.

The sun had made its way to the surface, shedding light on the fading night while birds sang their welcoming song. Vic hadn't noticed that I was awake when he crept into bed. The clock said 6:45 a.m. I decided not to speak. I sank deeper into my tear-stained pillow and pulled my knees to my chest, trying to comfort the pain I felt in the pit of my stomach. I had had another terrifying dream. One that I tucked away . . . again. I was relieved that we had made the decision to close on Mondays. Otherwise, I don't think I could have gotten through the day with any grace or enthusiasm. I felt lifeless.

NINE

Hope for the Hopeless

It was 9:45 when the phone rang. I rolled over to get out of bed when Vic called me to the phone. He was already downstairs. I could smell the coffee. Trying to sound like I didn't just wake up; I answered the extension on the dresser with a high-pitched voice. "Good morning, this is Nailah speaking."

It was Mr. Murphy, the owner of the mansion. He apologized for the lateness in getting back to me. We made an appointment to meet on the following Wednesday evening at five-thirty. After a long and tearful night, I managed to smile.

"Hey, Vic, that was Mr. Murphy, the owner of the mansion," I yelled from the top of the stairs. "We have an appointment for Wednesday. Is that coffee I smell?"

"Yeah, want me to bring you a cup? You know I don't really drink the stuff that much, but I knew you would want some. Hey, you don't have to get up if you don't want to. Remember, we decided to close on Mondays."

"That's right, thank God it's Monday. I am beat, even though I slept most of yesterday. I can come down and get the coffee; there's no sense in me being that lazy, unless of course you wanna spoil me." I yelled while heading to the stairs.

I laughed as Vic stood at the bottom of the stairs holding my favorite mug with a slice of raisin toast.

"Oh, you didn't have to bring it to me," I said, blushing.

Vic looked like he had gotten an eight-hour, good night's rest. I couldn't understand how he did it. How he could stay out all night, drink beer, smoke, and no telling what else, and then manage to go all day on a few hours' sleep.

"So, you're meeting the guy at five-thirty, Wednesday, right?" he asked, meeting me at the top of the stairs.

"Yep, he said he was working on a job uptown and couldn't make it till later in the day on this side. I told him it wasn't a problem and that it worked for me." After handing me my continental breakfast, Vic and I sat on the bed.

"You and Greg have a good time last night?"

"Same old thing . . . after we left Charles, hell, I ended up staying at Greg's house till damn near four or five o'clock. Those boys of his are driving him crazy. The oldest one decided not to go to school for the past week. Hell, Greg didn't even know it."

Vic shared his night with me while getting dressed to go to the café. He wanted to mop the floors and clean the grill. I decided not to question the time I knew he came in or what he was doing the rest of the time before he came home. The thought of being lied to made me sick.

Catching Vic in a lie had become common, and there was never a way that I could really prove that he was lying. Remembering the time, I found condoms in the van and asked if he was seeing another woman. He looked at me and stated that he wasn't seeing another woman. But he couldn't tell me *why* there were condoms in the van. "Maybe they Greg's or one of my other friends that borrowed the van," he had said.

I tried so hard NOT to be "that woman" who was always accusing her man of wrongdoing. However, Vic's lack of intimacy, including kissing, made me question myself and made me afraid to ask any questions for fear of the answer. There was this one time when I extended my beloved a kiss just because I wanted to—only to get a quick *peck* on the cheek and the ridiculous question, "You really love me, don't you?" he asked, looking at me and then walking away. The rejection hurt so deeply that I couldn't even say anything. From that point, I forced myself to be less affectionate by keeping my distance.

After Vic left to go to the café, instead of being super excited about the upcoming date to see Mr. Murphy, I lay around most of the day contemplating the dreams that had been haunting me. And these dreams were not about the mansion. They were much bigger and more fearful than any ghost or Spirit. They didn't intrigue me or have me seeking to find out more. No, these dreams made me never want to close my eyes again–not if it meant facing something that would tear me apart; destroy everything we had built as husband and wife, and as a family.

I managed to drudge through the day and finally started cleaning, just to get my mind off the dream. Cleaning has always been meditative for me. I loved thinking about the finished product, especially with our home. There was always something new that needed to be done: Painting, stripping walls, washing the tons of clothes that piled up quicker than I could keep up. However, the time passed quickly.

I decided to make some chili before Vic got home, figuring he would be hungry. After cooking, I showered and poured a glass of wine; got a cigarette and flopped on the bed when I heard Vic come through the back door. It was the first time we had seen each other since that morning.

"Hey, what happened to you?" I asked. Grease was all over him. "Was the grill that dirty?" We both laughed.

"Naw, the damn van stopped on me, again. I think I need a new battery. What you cooking? I ain't ate nothin' all day." He went straight to the basement as he pulled off his shirt.

"I made some chili," I yelled.

It became strange not to offer my husband a kiss for no particular reason, or for the fact that I hadn't seen him all day. Confusion settled in and made itself comfortable. And needless to say, our sex life had become virtually nonexistent.

The Appointment

Wednesday shot around as if Tuesday decided to take the day off. I was excited! It was almost time to meet Mr. Murphy about the mansion. A smile surfaced as I thought about the possibilities.

"Hey, Vic, I'm gonna run home and take a quick shower before I meet with Murphy. You think you can handle things while I'm gone?" I asked, even though there were only two customers. However, there was always the chance for a sudden rush.

"Of course. I got it. Anyway, if it gets busy, Mikie and Lenny should be comin' through anytime now. You do what you gotta do and don't worry about comin' back after your meeting. You'll probably need the rest. We got it."

I left feeling good about the situation. It had taken a while for me to leave things in other capable hands. For some reason, guilt often surfaced when I took time off or left others to do what I had been accustomed to doing by myself. I was definitely growing.

Vic called to make sure we were still having the meeting. He reassured me that everything was cool and that the boys had made it over. "Look, if it stays slow, I'll probably close early. I told Candy I would do some hauling for her."

Candy was remodeling the bookstore and changing out some furniture in her apartment. I was glad to see that they were on good terms; things had been getting strange with her, almost as if she were jealous of the success we were having.

When I arrived at the mansion, a man was walking the grounds. "Mr. Murphy?" I assumed while extending my hand. He was a little taller than me and was wearing a plaid shirt and dark trousers. His pale skin marked the resemblance of a fading tan. An inviting smile spread across his full face, and his eyes were soft and revealing. The art of delegating and rich cuisine showed around his midsection. "Yes, Mike Murphy, and you must be Mrs. Yarbrough," he acknowledged with a firm handshake. "Pleased to finally meet you."

We talked briefly while walking the grounds. The grass had become long, and weeds were moving up along the sides of the porch and steps. He later got a large flashlight from his truck, and we both went inside. Everything was the same as before, except Mr. Murphy had a lot more information to share with me about the building and his purchasing it.

"Well, as you can see, it needs a lot of work. I had planned to fix it up to lease, but I've been so busy working on other jobs that I haven't had time to work on this building. I bought it over two years ago for the taxes owed on it. The railroad company had it as its corporate headquarters but abandoned it almost fifteen years ago. All this time, it has been empty."

I looked around and asked some general questions about its history, particularly before the railroad company bought it.

"Did you know this used to be a former plantation, Mr. Murphy? That it was built by my ancestors . . . former slaves?"

The shock of my abrupt questions sort of took him off guard. We both walked out the front door and stood in front of the mansion as he looked at me with that not quite how to answer look.

"Well, I'm not sure whose ancestors, but I did find some information that proves that it was built by slaves. I understand that there's some information in the archives at a private club that keeps those types of records. You seem to know something about the history."

"Yes, I do. However, I was given the information through dreams. And when I say, *my* ancestors, it simply means that I recognize a connection with all of those whose DNA flows through my veins, particularly those of Africa," I explained proudly. I then shared a little about my dream as he listened in astonishment.

"You probably think I'm crazy, but it's the truth."

"No, I don't think you're crazy. I'm Irish and wouldn't be surprised if what you're saying is true," he shared as if there was some commonality. I interjected that I had great-grandfathers and grandmothers who were Irish as well. "What do you intend to do with this building if I lease it to you?" It was now my turn to look at him strangely.

"My intention is to buy it, Mr. Murphy— not lease it," I proclaimed as we both stood face-to-face.

"Well, Miss Yarbrough, I have no intentions of selling but I will consider leasing it to you. Do you plan to have your café here?"

I stepped closer to my new Irish friend and looked him straight in his hazel eyes . . . placed my hand over his heart and said...

"Mr. Murphy, former slaves built this place, and as descendants of those slaves, it's time for 'us' to take it back. I don't want to lease it. I want to own it!"

Invading his private space, I stood very close to him and tapped him on his plaid shirt right in his heart center. "Now you go and talk to your God about it," I continued. "And I'm sure He will tell you what to do. I look forward to hearing from you soon."

Somewhat stunned, Mr. Murphy agreed to think over my "intention" and to call by the first part of the following week. He smiled as we departed, going our separate ways. I had never been that direct or so sure of anything— but somehow, I knew we were to buy this building. Although I didn't have a clue how it was going to be accomplished, there was no doubt . . . it would happen.

My entire body shook when I got in the car. I eventually took a few deep breaths and just sat there. Thoughts raced out of control about how I was going to pull off this untamed idea of taking possession of this enormous piece of property. A few more deep breaths and a quick prayer finally provided the energy to turn the key and leave the parking lot. It appeared that the enthusiasm to see my dream come true was now turning to panic, and I wasn't even sure if Murphy would sell . . . Yes, I did. I knew he would sell. That was my real fear!

By the time I got back to the café, it was around 6:45. Thank God the day was about over. It felt like I had been on a nonstop rollercoaster, and I was in no shape to cook or serve anyone. As I dragged myself up the stairs, I noticed there were only a couple of people. Vic assured me he had it under control and ordered me to go home, which was music to my ears. I promised my husband that I would tell him about the meeting when he got home.

As soon as I hit the door, I made a mad dash to the kitchen and poured myself a glass of wine, then headed upstairs to our bedroom and immediately lit a long-awaited cigarette. I spent the rest of the evening *trying* not to think about what had happened— what the ancestors had gotten me into. Just thinking about it made me nervous.

I'm not sure how long I had been sitting, but the next thing I heard was Vic's voice. "So, what happened with the guy about the mansion?" walking in with a six-pack of beer.

"Hey there, I didn't hear you come in. You scared me."

Vic pulled a can from the plastic covering and popped the lid and took a long swallow.

"It was cool. I told Mr. Murphy that I wanted to buy the mansion."

"You want to what? — you kidding, right?" taking another swallow and belching.

"No, I was serious. He said that he would have to think about it because he had no plans in selling . . . only leasing. I explained to him how I felt about the fact that our ancestors built it and that it was time for us to take it back."

Vic calmly leaned against the bedroom door. For a minute, I thought he was going to leave. The half-stripped doorway framed his sleek physique. His smile glistened as he looked at me with those laughing eyes.

"You're serious, aren't you. You really want to buy that place?"

"Of course, I do," I stated, putting my hand on his shoulder.

"Don't you agree that black folks should have that building?"

"Yeah, but it ain't gotta be us," he countered. "Where we gonna get the money, and who's gonna fix it?"

"I don't know babe. I just know that it will work out. And believe me, I understand how you feel, but this is something I know has to be done. I hope you're with me on this. But even if you're not, it's something that I know I have to do."

Vic grabbed what was left of the six-pack as we both headed downstairs to the kitchen and pulled off another can before placing the rest in the fridge. We both sat at the table to continue our unpredictable conversation. Before long, I, too, had a cold one up to my lips, hoping that the alcohol content would calm my jitters. Two hours later, we had finished the six-pack and a joint, while I attempted to give my husband the courage and confidence that was needed for us to move forward in what was a rather dubious situation.

"You know, baby, you have more faith than anyone I've ever known." Vic finally said, laughing . . . (probably more so to keep from crying).

"I'm with you, baby," he continued with obvious reservation and shaking his head. "Think he'll sell it to you?"

"He doesn't know it, but he doesn't have any choice but to sell it to me. This is beyond him or me. The ancestors are all over this one."

Along with Vic, hearing myself make that statement, I started laughing and shaking my head as well. Yes, it was unbelievable . . . but it was happening.

Later that evening, I called my daughter and gave her the update. She, too, was overwhelmed with the news.

"You can do this mom. I've got a good feeling about this. Have you told your sons yet? You know how my brothers are about you taking on too much work. With them both working and living out of town, they may not be around to help out."

My daughter spoke as if she knew things were gonna work out about purchasing the building. She was already seeing it as a done deal.

"Yes, they know. And you're right, they're already worried that it will be too much for me. I reminded them of me doing Vic's house, but they both said that it was one thing doing six rooms, but doing twenty-two rooms was a whole different ballgame."

"Well, they have a point, especially with your bad back. But if you think you can do it, mom . . . I know God will make sure you have the support you need. Tell Uncle Vic hello and hang in there with you. I know he's probably a little apprehensive".

"Yeah, he's a little scared, but he seems to be onboard. We'll see."

"I love you, Mom, and don't forget to keep me posted."

"I will. Give the kids my love."

"Oh, Mom, I forgot to tell you, I registered for school. I figured I could take some classes while the kids are in school. And my girlfriend, Jean, said she would keep the two youngest ones."

"Wow, baby, that's great. Will you still be working?"

"Yes, but only part-time, and since I'll be studying social work, it will help with my job."

"Are you sure you can handle it? That's a lot of pressure."

"I've figured it out. Mark is willing to help as much as he can. He's a great son. Plus, since Ronnie (her husband) is working, I can afford to work part-time. It'll be okay."

"All right, if you think you can handle it . . . I'm sure it will work out. Looks like we both have some major changes happening. Well, take care, and I'll be talking with you soon; hopefully, with some real good news. Love you!"

Just as agreed, Murphy called that Monday. My heart raced once I realized it was him. When he asked if he could give me an answer the following week, I was surprisingly relieved. Since he and his wife had planned to go to the Derby, which was the following weekend, Mr. Murphy assured me that he would have an answer shortly thereafter. My knees were shaking as I hung up the phone and sat down. *Just one more week,* I thought to myself, but for now, work needed to be done. The Java House was having its first Derby.

Living in the West End, where 90% of the residents are African Americans OR poor Whites, we had been "cut off" from the major traffic coming off the expressways. The distinguished guests and high-profile celebrities attending the Derby were "led away" from the possibility of going through Louisville's less "appealing" neighborhood, which meant that black businesses were not privy to making the kind of money as our more affluent neighborhoods.

Nevertheless, due to the fact that The Java House Café had become the center of attraction, so much so that during the Derby weekend, we were graced with the presence of the well-known activist, scholar, and nutrition expert for the Bahamian Diet, Mr. Dick Gregory. After eating our famous veggie burger, he honored us by saying: "It's the best— not one of the best but <u>the best</u> veggie burger I've ever eaten. And I mean that!" He ordered three more to go... without the bread.

Our first Derby was also blessed with a couple of other artists, including "Just June," a comedian we had met on one of our visits to Cincinnati. She was famous for her impersonation of Jackie "Moms" Mabley, a renowned standup comedian and veteran of the Chitlin' circuit of African American vaudeville. Yes, The Java House and its first Derby proved to be quite lucrative . . . in spite of.

TEN

Be Careful What You Ask For

The phone rang at nine o'clock that Monday morning. Vic was already gone. I was still wiped out from the night before and had no plans in getting out of bed before noon. But as usual, my plans went out the window.

"Good morning." My voice was deep and drawn.

"Good morning, may I speak with Mrs. Yarbrough. This is Mike Murphy."

"Oh, hi, Mr. Murphy, thanks for calling."

I didn't wait for a response, as I nervously kept talking.

"How was your weekend, and did your horse come in?" I enthusiastically asked. He chuckled and announced that his friend's horse came in and "placed" in the main race.

"I guess you can say I won a little," he said shyly. "By the time I counted my losses, I came out a little ahead."

"I'm glad that you won, even if it was a little. Have you got some good news for me?"

I must have held my breath while waiting for his answer. He didn't just come out with a yes or no. He had to go into speaking about it to his wife, how he hadn't had time to work on it. But finally!

"Well, Mrs. Yarbrough, I have decided that I will sell it to you." My heart must have dropped to my lower stomach.

"Hello. Are you there?"

"Oh, yes! I'm here," I finally responded. It took everything I had to keep from screaming and running across the room. "I'm so happy to hear that," nervously continuing. "You made the right decision, and you have made the ancestors happy. So, what do we do next?" I asked with my most professional voice. You know, the one that's sure of itself—confident? The one that says, no problem, no matter what is about to be asked of you, particularly money.

"Well, I'll contact my real estate agent and have him fax over the paperwork to get started. I haven't decided on a price yet, but I'm sure we can negotiate a price that works for the both of us. By the way, there will be a $500.00 deposit required as a "good faith" gesture. It will later be subtracted from the negotiated price. Do you have a fax number I can give to my agent?"

"Yes, . . . yes, I do." I managed to say without explanation. "Got a pencil?"

I gave him Candy's fax number at the bookstore. I really didn't want her to know my business, but I didn't have a fax.

"I suppose you'll have a real estate agent working with you," he asked, as if strongly suggesting that I did.

"Yes, my mother has a referral. She and my stepfather just recently bought a home, and I'm sure she'll explain the procedure. Mr. Murphy, I can't tell you how excited I am. Thank you so very much!"

"Well, I think you're the right person to have it and I hope everything works out for you. Take your time. There's no hurry. Just get back to the agent when you are ready to proceed. If you have any questions beforehand, call me. I look forward to working with you. By the way, I understand you and your husband are doing great things over there. It delights me to be able to sell you the mansion. Good luck, and I'll be talking with you in the near future. Oh, you do understand that it will be sold 'as is.'"

"Yes, Mr. Murphy. Not a problem!"

I was happier than a hog in slop! After putting the phone down on the cradle, I ran around in circles for about five minutes. I couldn't even get the words *"Thank you, God,"* out loud. But the silent gratitude screamed out, vibrating in every part of my body where God, Herself, heard every syllable loud and clear. Then it hit me! Standing in the middle of the floor, dizzy and crying, I thought out loud . . . *"Nailah, where in the hell. . .excuse me God. . .are you going to get five-hundred dollars?"*

Vic wasn't surprised when I gave him the terrifying news. We were about to own a former plantation along with the entire drudge that came with it. At least, that's what I felt for the next few days. I had no way of knowing how any of it was going to work. How we were going to get the down payment and then find a bank that would loan us the money (once negotiated), plus finding the people to help with all the horrendous renovations. I was stunned and petrified of all the possible things that could go wrong. *What the hell was I getting us into?*

A Little Motivation

Since I had been acting as if we already had the mansion, I had spoken with my mother about a real estate agent long before Mr. Murphy agreed to sell, so she had a referral, like I told Mr. Murphy. I had also tacked up a blown-up picture of the mansion on the café wall with a sign-up sheet for those who would support us when the time came for creating it into the look that my dreams had shown me.

Everyone was excited. Well, just about everyone. I wasn't quite sure how my sister-in-law felt. Our relationship wasn't considered congenial, and the conclusion had been drawn that she was a little jealous of our success and the unexpected attention we were getting. Vic had certainly noticed a change in her attitude, which was mostly directed towards me since The Java House Café was *my* idea. Even with that, I suppose Candy didn't think anything *big* would come from our *little* coffee house. Once we started having Spoken Word and jazz, it led to a surprise call, in which she expressed her dislike and concerns.

"I didn't think you would be doing music and stuff like that," she rudely expressed. "That's not what I rented it to you for, and there ain't no place for my customers to park," she continued. "I thought you was gonna just sell coffee and sandwiches."

What I felt as an attempt to be diplomatic didn't go over too well. My sister-in-law was fuming with bitterness. I could feel it! So, I simply listened until she finished with no rebuttal, other than to say, "Sorry you feel that way, Candy. I'm looking into other possibilities. I'll keep you posted. Have a good day." I hung up the phone before she could say bye.

Even before her rude announcement, her *distant* attitude served as a motivation to start seeking another location for our business, even before the possibility of the mansion. My life was challenging enough, and putting up with some unnecessary bullshit was not in the cards. Initially, I thought she would be thrilled that we were doing well and reaching out to the neighborhood. She was extremely Afrocentric and believed in educating us as a people. And whatever little success we had, it certainly played a major role in her being able to pay her rent and utilities.

On a lighter note, she did like our food. Candy often ordered our vegetable lasagna and the veggie burger, which is more than I can say about my family. The mere fact that I wasn't selling fried chicken, pork, and anything else that spoke "soul food," most of my family wasn't interested in anything that resembled "healthy."

Doing business with my sister-in-law wasn't the best situation; however, because of her initial support, it allowed our business to exist. And for that, we were grateful. Things in life change, and you do what you got to do until you can do better. Meanwhile, I continued to pay our rent on time and stayed out of her way as much as possible, while looking forward to our new venture and how to make it all possible.

Granny to the Rescue

Not only were my family members rarely customers, but I was also going to have to rely on one of them to spot us five-hundred big ones. Unfortunately, most of my family was as broke as we were. But, as the good news got around, I received an unexpected phone call from my grandmother.

"Hello Jane. (Grandmother never did accept my new name) Well, well. I hear you're going to buy a big old mansion. Your mama told me that you and Vic found a great new place for your restaurant."

"Yes, ma'am, we did," I told her, along with the short version of the dream and our intentions to buy the mansion. Surprisingly, she asked me how much I needed to put down.

"I have to put up five-hundred dollars as a down payment for what they call 'earnest' money or 'good faith' money, grandmother. That will reserve the property, so that no one else can bid on it."

"Well, honey, I can give that to you. When do you need it?" As usual, her voice was soft, but without the stern quality that she was known for. "And look, don't worry about giving it back," she continued.

"Grandmother, you sure? I know that's a lot of money for you." It was hard for me to accept gifts without an *I'll pay it back, tag.*

"Look, child, if I didn't have it to give, I wouldn't have offered. Now, when do you need it? Can you come by tomorrow to pick it up? If you need cash, you can take me by the bank, and we can get cash, or I'll write you a check," she asked with her words strung together without pauses.

I was stunned and relieved at the same time. My grandmother was allowing us the opportunity to move forward. This was a first. My grandmother had never lent me money before, but then again, I had never asked for any. As prayed for, everything was unfolding in a surreal sort of way.

Grandmother was waiting downstairs when I pulled up in front of the apartment building. I blew my horn as she had instructed and waited until she came out of the glass doors. I rushed to meet her to assist her in coming down the steps. Dressed in her Sunday best, her worn, black heels cradled her swollen ankles, while gout had become a constant reminder that she could stand to change her diet. Her large frame hiked up her dress in the back, exposing the nude colored, rolled stockings that knotted right below the knee. Grandmother's soft white curls peeked from a worn, red Beret while a light pink lipstick covered her thin lips and high cheeks. Large, costume pearl earrings practically covered her small ears, while a tarnished, gilded necklace draped over her polyester black dress. Grandmother always did believe in looking appropriate when she left the house. She would often say, "You never know who you might meet."

Eighty-two years was no match for her beauty. Proud of her Irish and Native American heritage, grandmother's creamy light complexion was still radiant, and her mind insisted on being full of life, along with the enthusiasm of certain longevity.

Less than a couple of minutes from the bank, and using the drive-through window, it took no time to cash the check. After receiving the brown envelope, it was obvious that my grandmother was as pleased to give it to me as I was to accept it. Expressing my gratitude more than once, my grandmother reassured me that there would be no need to pay it back. It was her gift to help fulfill a dream.

Before heading back to grandmother's apartment, we went across the street to the grocery store to pick up a few things for her dinner. She never did like buying too many things at once, since it was only her. The fresher the better, she would say. As we strolled down the aisles toward the meat department, I listened as she explained that her doctor had told her to stop eating red meat, but that eating lean pork (the "other" white meat) would be okay. But, knowing first-hand how pork had been a "killer" in our community by causing high blood pressure, obesity, gout, and a few other maladies, I just looked at her and shook my head, knowing that I dare not contradict her doctor. I learned a long time ago not to mess with old folks and their doctors. That's God in a white coat.

Hitting the Jackpot

The check was in the mail, and price negotiations were just about underway. It was understood that Murphy would start high, but I also knew not to accept any offer until I saw the price I was "shown" by Spirit during one of my meditations.

My realtor called me after we made the first counteroffer, which was declined. Well, I wasn't concerned. For an entire week, I had meditated every day to get a clear understanding of the right price to accept.

It was the third offer that got my fullest attention. I countered back five thousand dollars less than what was asked for. Amazingly, three hours later, the next price that came over the fax machine was the "jackpot." I screamed when I saw those numbers—$90,000.00. I knew then it was a done deal.

I called my realtor and told her to accept the offer. She said it was late and that I probably wouldn't hear anything that day. The next morning, my realtor called and said the magic words . . . "Nailah, they accepted your offer. When can you come and sign the papers?"

It still amazes me, even now, as I reflect back on how important our ancestors are and how they're here to guide and support us. I know it may sound spooky, but believe me, *life is everlasting.* They (Spirits) may not be visible on this side (in most cases); however, they are with us. And by now, even though my family was far from believing in certain metaphysical antics (ghosts or Spirits), I had learned that they do exist and to listen and obey. And in this case, $90,000.00 was the *exact* figure that the ancestors had shown me to accept.

Wow! It was time to jump for joy, right? But the cold fact was that there was another crucial element–getting a bank to lend us what I knew would be several hundred thousand dollars to purchase and renovate this twenty-two-room mansion.

My young business was less than a year old. I had no collateral, except for my eight-year-old car, and of course, my excellent credit, which was the only thing that gave me any leverage. Meanwhile, doing a business proposal to present to prospective lenders was taking weeks of serious thinking and writing, in which, oftentimes, the language was ambiguous, meaning I had to be extremely cautious with regard to interpretation and my choice of wording.

Once my business proposal was completed, I had a couple of my friends, including our new friend and customer, Martha, to go over it to make sure I wasn't too unorthodox, which I tend to be. For example, the section that required information regarding my "competition," I stated: "I have no outside competition; I am my only real competition. If I'm giving 100% to everything I do, how someone else chooses to operate their business is of no concern of mine. There is room enough for everyone who seeks to fulfill their dreams."

While my friends thought that a traditional answer would have been more appropriate, I stood on my premise, as with a few other unorthodox answers. However, after a final review from a couple of friends who critiqued my proposal, I was given the thumbs-up to proceed. Now, it was time for the real test—the bank. And I had only ninety days to find one.

ELEVEN

Never Take No for an Answer

Have you ever had a situation where you know something is going to happen, but you just don't know how? I was sure that I would get a loan. The dreams and meditations were for a reason, and everything that I had been led to do up to this point was on target.

Of course, the first bank I approached with our vision was my own bank, which I had been banking with for a few years. I never wrote a bad check, and I paid my credit card bills on time. However, it wasn't enough to impress the manager to jump onboard.

"Well, Mrs. Yarbrough," the loan officer started, leaning back in his chair... "You've been a great customer, and you have great credit. But I'm afraid you don't have the necessary collateral for the substantial size loan that is needed to pull off this type of project. Restaurants are a very risky business. Sorry, maybe once you've been in business a few more years... at least five, we can take a look at it again. Good luck."

I reached over and shook his hand, thanking him for his time. He stood up and wished me luck, again. I told him that I was sure I would find the right bank. However, the next bank gave me the same answer, except quicker. I wasn't in the office five minutes, during which the loan officer barely looked at my proposal.

"Sorry, Mrs. Yarbrough, we don't finance restaurants. You may have a problem with this one. Most banks want you to be in business at least five years. It's too much of a risk, but good luck."

We said our goodbyes, and I left feeling like I was defeated, although I didn't let him see my frustration. It was time to seek some more guidance. I knew the vision wasn't brought this far, only to be let down. There had to be a bank. There were no other alternatives as an option to finance this project. There was a bank somewhere—I had to believe that!

One day, during my regular meditation, it came to me about a town meeting I attended over a year earlier. Although I was considered an advocate and quite vocal on community issues, I didn't attend meetings that I felt were politically driven or those that espoused the negative issues that were obvious to anyone with eyes or ears.

Crimes were widespread, our youths were out of control with gang-related violence, and unemployment for those of color was at an all-time high. Shit was bad, period. The sad thing was, there were never any real solutions to these everyday challenges. None! However, this meeting got my attention. It served to inform the community of a new type of bank that would cater to the needs of minorities (I hate that term) and women-owned businesses. I had forgotten about this bank until now, during my meditation.

It took me a couple of days to get all the pertinent information as to its location and its proposed intent to the community. Fortunately, The UnCommon Bank was up and running and lending money— and loads of it. Surely, this was the bank I had been seeking. I gathered all my paperwork, placed it in a new folder, and called my friend, Martha, later that evening. I explained to her about the bank and my intentions to go and apply for a loan. She agreed to go with me for support. Not only did she support me by agreeing to go with me, but she offered me 25,000 dollars of her own money—just in case. You see, after Martha and I became good friends (remember she was my other Jewish friend besides Carolyn), we often shared personal information, in which I learned that she had inherited quite a large sum of money after her husband's death. Now, how much, I had no idea. That information, she didn't divulge. However, the $25,000 was a drop in the bucket compared to what I needed. Nevertheless, the gesture was appreciated.

I called the bank the next morning and asked the receptionist to speak with Mr. Roland. During my investigation, I had read that he was the senior loan officer. Surprisingly, I was put right through without any screening. After introducing myself and explaining the purpose of wanting to meet with him, he made an appointment for the following week but suggested that I drop off my proposal the next morning so that he could review it before our meeting. I agreed and expressed my looking forward to our meeting on Tuesday at 9 a.m. Although our conversation left me feeling comfortable and hopeful, my hands shook as I put down the receiver. It was actually happening!

Martha was almost as excited as me when I gave her the good news. She also reminded me that she would attend the meeting with me. I let her know that I was dropping off the proposal the day before, so it could be reviewed prior to our appointment. We also agreed that we would meet at the bank. Later that evening, I took one last look at the proposal, making sure I hadn't missed anything. With a new light blue clear folder, along with a beautiful color photo of the mansion on the front cover, it looked professional and ready to be dropped off on Monday morning.

The Interview

As planned, Martha met me in the bank's parking lot; both of us were dressed to impress. Before entering the double glass doors, we held hands as she wished me luck. Upon entering, huge floral arrangements decorated both sides of the wide hallway entrance into the bank. The scent of fresh paint and new carpet still lingered in the air. Several rich, cherry desks and high-back leather chairs lined the walls on each side of the enormous room. Two private offices set to the right with glass walls. There was another private office in the rear. The door sign read: Kevin Roland, Senior Loan Officer.

Its mission for "equal employment" was evident as we looked across the room. Smiles greeted us as we moved through the room, when a voice offered to assist us.

"Good morning, and welcome to The UnCommon Bank. How may I help you?" a well-dressed young lady asked with a pleasant and professional voice. Her dark skin blushed with rouge and matching red lips. Long, silky black hair lay softly on her shoulders. I felt welcomed.

"My name is Nailah Yarbrough. I have an appointment with Mr. Roland. I'm a little early."

"Yes, I see," she acknowledged, browsing a large appointment book. "And you are a little early. He's still in another meeting this morning, but I'll let him know you're here. Are you two together?"

"Yes, we are," I responded.

"Well, you both can have a seat over in our waiting area. Can I get you some coffee or anything to drink?"

We both agreed to coffee with cream and sugar. I looked around, noticing all the African art and artifacts. More fresh flowers adorned the corner tables and the receptionists' desk. There were no Tellers or counters, no lines of people waiting to cash checks or make deposits. This bank did nothing but loans, and its sole purpose was for business owners and wanna be's. I was in the right place, and I prayed to God it was the right time. I have to admit, I was nervous.

Martha and I talked a little, but I was too busy thinking about the meeting to really get into a deep conversation. She understood.

"Excuse me, the ladies' room?" I asked the receptionist. I figured I had better take one last look to make sure I didn't have lipstick on my teeth or lint on my navy-blue suit. It was a good thing I did. There was lipstick on my chin from drinking the coffee. Returning to my seat, I started imagining what I would have looked like if I hadn't looked.

"Good morning, Mrs. Yarbrough?" The voice was strong and courteous.

I raised my head from the Fortune 500 Magazine and was met with a smile. He was tall, well-built and wore a pair of designer glasses. His handshake was firm and deliberate. We looked eye–to-eye as we continued our greeting. He, too, wore a dark blue suit with a pink shirt and a blue & pink pin-striped tie. He was a very nice-looking brother and had all the signs of being married—besides the band on his left hand . . . not that I was looking at him like that. I just happened to notice. He turned and acknowledged Martha with the same pleasantries and requested that we follow him.

It was a typical boardroom with a long cherry table that sat twelve. A large glass vase, filled with Lilies and Birds of Paradise served as an eloquent centerpiece. Bookshelves lined the walls filled with an array of leather and paperback books. Antique, floral prints mixed alongside of old Kentucky black & white photos gave the room a reflective quality.

The three of us sat at the head of the table with Mr. Roland in the middle. I sat to his right, while Martha was on his left. We went over my proposal page by page, gradually moving toward the *bottom-line* decision–was I worth the risk?

I won't bore you with all the back-and-forth details of the meeting; however, I will share with you a pivotal moment. The discussion was becoming very passionate as Mr. Roland and I were on another level. This wasn't just your run-of-the-mill qualification ritual but more of a *meeting of the minds*. However, during our conversation, I noticed that Mr. Roland's body language was beginning to communicate an 'I don't know type attitude, which prompted me to take a *different approach*. I had to get him to understand that this wasn't just about going into business. This was far more than that.

So, I looked into Mr. Roland's eyes real intense-like. I raised up, then bent down on one knee and looked up into his eyes. Then in one long breath, I said . . .

"You know Mr. Roland this is not about you or me… this is much bigger… this is about the community… an opportunity to divert gang violence and racism… this is a mission… we have an opportunity to bring something really positive to the community… you've heard what The Java House Café is doing and it's a good thing… so you *have* to loan me the money… we have to work together… this is why this bank exists and I'm a perfect candidate… You will not be sorry."

Finally, after I took a breath, Mr. Roland looked at me as if I had lost my ever-loving mind, and his face really said it. *Now, I know she didn't just get on one knee and tell me that I **had** to lend her this money.* I could see it all over him as he helped me up. But I had done just that–with no shame.

Two weeks later, I got the letter: "Congratulations-Approved." I fell to my knees, kissed the floor, raised my eyes to the Universe, and gave thanks. I believed it, and at the same time, I couldn't believe it. However, again, the ancestors were right! But don't think this was a simple task—Oh no!

Getting a *signature* loan for almost a quarter of a million dollars is no simple feat. I was put through the wringer. They checked EVERYTHING, and I mean everything. No rocks unturned. And signing one's name to that amount of money is not like taking an order for a Mr. T Burger. I prayed with every piece of paper I signed . . . about twenty-five. I tell you, it pays to do your best in everything you do because someone is watching. Overwhelmed with joy as my husband cosigned, and mixed with just a little anxiety, small beads of sweat formed around Vic's brow. This was doing big business— and it was just the beginning.

Now, since we were approved, I was able to move forward with the contract to buy the property. There wasn't any point in getting the building and then not being able to pay for it. I had a few more weeks before my time expired to purchase, and as the ancestors would have it–it was right on time.

Signing the dotted line for the property wasn't as shocking as the bank situation. However, the hardcore reality of renovating twenty-two rooms was enough to send me into a brief panic mode. However, it was far too late to change the course of action now. We were now— like it or not—the owners of a former plantation, along with an arduous mission of renovating. Yes, I was scared, and so was my husband. He had agreed to support my vision and to come along for the extreme, uphill ride. We were in it together.

That evening, we went back to the café and worked as usual, and we didn't talk much about the fact that our lives were about to drastically change. Business was good that night, which didn't leave us much time to take in the reality of what had just happened. We did, however, share with some of our best customers the good news. A faithful few promised to be there to support us if we needed any help, and we gladly accepted.

And as promised, when we got home, I called Jenia and told her the good news. Not at all surprised, my daughter screamed with delight.

"I told you mama . . . I knew you guys were going to get the building! I am so happy for you. And mama, don't worry . . . everything is gonna be fine. Tell Uncle Vic congrats. And I'll tell the kids their grandma just bought a mansion."

TWELVE

Giving Thanks

Wow! I couldn't speak for my husband, but I needed a break. But most importantly, I needed to thank my ancestors and the Orisha, Goddess Oshun, for showing me the way, and for the guidance and instructions in making all that had happened–thus far. There was so much more to be done, and being in a position of gratitude and listening was imperative.

Along with the usual altar setup and cleansing myself with Sage, it was necessary to go to the water in order to make an offering to Oshun since she governed prosperity. She loves sweets, and I usually took her oranges and honey to make my appeal. Before heading out to the river, I took a few moments to breathe deeply so as to reconnect with my Higher Self and to request permission from Elegua (Gatekeeper between the living and the dead) to evoke Oshun, which is a prerequisite before any ritual or communication with an Orisha can be done in order to be in the proper mindset; to understand what you are being told regarding your request or intention.

I lit a candle and placed white flowers in the center of my mat and prayed, giving thanks to all the other ancestors who had been my support system. I wanted to be certain that we were on the right track and that I hadn't forgotten anything that may hinder the success of our mission, even though I was still a little uncertain as to what that was, exactly. Although I felt it had something to do with helping to release the trapped souls of slaves, I still hadn't received any confirmation regarding that theory, and it was my hope that meditating would offer some answers. So, I began to breathe slowly and deeply. With each deep breath, I began to feel a closer connection to my guides, and before long, my body began to move in a circular motion . . . a sign that I had made a connection, after which, I silently began to ask questions seeking to know if we were on target.

The answers were usually shown to me according to the directions by body moved. When it circled to the right, it was a *yes* answer. When circled to the left, it was a *no,* or if I was to move back & forth, it usually meant *not yet*. Basically, my body served as a pendulum, and however weird that may sound, it worked.

The presence of the ancestors always made me feel warm and secure, and I loved being able to communicate with them through meditation. There was no fear or any reason to doubt their directions or their realness. I can't really explain it, but it's like having all the answers to any questions right *inside* me, but from something Higher than my ego mind or thoughts. Anyway, during this particular meditation, the ancestors (whom I also recognized as Guardian Angels and Spirit Guides) *showed* me that I was on the right track and doing well, and that they were always with me whenever guidance was needed.

After I gathered my oranges and honey, to head to the river, I wrapped my head and smudged again with Sage, making sure I was still clear of any negative energy before approaching Oshun. I shared with Vic my intentions and asked if he wanted to go, but as usual, he opted to stay behind, feeling that it was meant for me to go alone. And, as always, he assured me that I had his full support.

I prayed all the way to the Ohio River, and even after parking the car, I sat in the parking lot to pray some more before making my appeal to Oshun. Emotionally charged, tears began to flow as I humbly expressed my gratitude for her presence in my life and how honored I was to be her daughter. By the time I headed towards the water, I was at peace and confident that my appeal would be heard.

There was a soothing, cool breeze blowing over the river, a comforting relief from the hot, mid-July sun. As I searched for the perfect spot, I noticed that there weren't many people in the area, which was more remote, opposed to the riverfront. There were two older couples sitting on benches under a shaded tree. One had a small dog; it yelped as I got closer. I spoke and moved further down where it was a little more private. Giving an offering isn't something you broadcast to everyone, especially when you're throwing stuff in the water and yelling out names of ancient deities.

I took off my shoes as I approached the edge of the water. The sand was warm and damp from the gentle waves. As I sat down, the fragrance of Honeysucker and various other flowers filled the air. It was sweet and pleasant, an added ambience. The waves were calm and awaiting my voice to stir up the life of Oshun. With each deep inhalation, I grew calmer and more serene. Finally relaxed and ready to make an appeal, I took out my offering.

The orange was sweet, even before the honey. Its nectar ran down my chin as I took the first taste, which is customary before giving it to a deity, making sure that it's safe and pleasing to the palate. It was good. As I spoke her name— "Oshun, Oshun," the mild winds carried my voice across the vast waters, and her waves rose to great peaks splashing my naked feet, letting me know she heard me.

As I released the sweet oranges to the waves, I made my appeal for guidance and a request for love, prosperity and a life of peace. I could hear her gentle, motherly voice speak to me . . . calling me her precious daughter while the waves carried my offering out into the distance. I was comforted with her love and felt a sense of peace, and feeling strengthened by our union—once again.

THIRTEEN

The Revitalization of a Plantation

Vic and I had agreed to do most of the general work and hire subcontractors to do the serious stuff such as electrical, plumbing, heating & air and the installation of the hood for the kitchen, which required licenses and professionalism. On top of major repairs and renovations, equipment had to be purchased as well. Refrigeration, a stove, grill, tables & chairs, etc.; would all be necessary to run an efficient kitchen. The problem was the fact it all had to be done on a mere "shoestring" budget. Yes, things were beginning to feel a little overwhelming, to say the least. So, making the decision to be my own contractor seem to make sense, a means of saving money. Now, mind you, I had no idea as to what it would take to be a contractor, but I was about to find out, and so was my willing husband.

The next couple of weeks were like walking through a fog. Sometimes I didn't know what direction to take as I kept telling myself that everything would work out—that we would find the right people to bring it all together. Yet every time we went to the mansion to take note as to what had to be done, it seemed as if every room got bigger; the trash seemed to triple, and the "help" that was so willingly offered, was nowhere to be found. And to top it off, the "unexpected" presence of "trapped souls" started showing themselves in ways that took me completely off guard.

All Women Who Cry the Blues Ain't Black

It was early August, and the heat was stifling. I entered through the front door which was still half boarded. When I stepped in, it felt like a refrigerator, which was a welcoming relief. It was dark except for the sunlight that came from a three-paneled, dusty window over the door and through the cracks of boarded windows. I stood there for a moment before being prompted to go upstairs.

As I cautiously ascended the creaky stairs, the glow from my flashlight gave just enough light to avoid the stacks of old newspapers and magazines that ladened the path to the top, where I continued down a long narrow hall. Suddenly, an intense, unsettling emotion abruptly stopped me as I approached a door with a sign that read: Ladies. I hadn't noticed the sign the other times I had wandered the hall, but this time was different. I slowly opened the door to a small closet-like area. To the right was an opening that led to what obviously was once a large restroom. Two broken toilets and basins laid on an old, tiled floor. Rays from a bright sun, streaked across the room through cracked and broken windows.

While standing in the area looking around, I thought I heard a cry. Not sure what I actually heard, it prompted me to stop and listen. It was definitely a cry, only this time it was more like . . . cries. Spooked, I was ready to get the hell out! But just as I finally stepped back to leave– that's when I saw the faces of three white women huddled together and whimpering as if they were afraid someone would hear them. Each was costumed in long dark-colored dresses with white aprons, which appeared to be from the late 1800s. White bonnets were set back on their heads, exposing the fronts of their pulled-back hairstyles. Although the vision was in black and white, their pale skin flushed with fear, while their lifeless, tear-filled eyes focused upon mine.

Unable to react by running like hell, I was immobilized by their stark presence, and too scared to say anything . . . out loud. Of course, in my mind, I was asking questions like: *"Who are you? Where did you come from?"* You know, the usual questions when enquiring minds wanna know. Not really expecting any response from my *thoughts*, I was ready to make a mad dash when one tried to speak. I could only watch as her trembling lips formed words that fell upon deaf ears but, but I could hear and *feel* her words telepathically as they all began to tell their plight as women in a world of tyrannical men.

Although they were not women of African descent, they, too, had horror stories of being verbally, physically, and sexually abused. They swept with their heads hung low, as if embarrassed to speak their truth. Sad, despondent, and pissed, I found myself sweeping too, realizing that there was nothing I could do. They were stuck in a time that had long passed to the rest of the world, but unlike most who had long departed, they found themselves unable to move from this virtual hell.

Suddenly, their images faded–but not without leaving behind an aura that clung to my heart and soul and activated a few thought-provoking questions regarding my own plight in the scheme of things. Everything had been moving so quickly that I still wasn't able to fully understand *why* the dreams and everything else that had preceded them. One thing for sure, it was a lot more than *expanding* The Java House. It was more than helping to eliminate violence and providing a creative outlet, while somehow teaching us to accept each other and our differences. Whatever the *real* reason for our presence on a former plantation, I sensed that those three women were crying out to me for help, just like those voices that haunted me in my dreams. But what *kind* of help was the question, and how? Little did I know that the *answer* would soon become undoubtedly clear.

FOURTEEN

The Cleansing Ritual

It was an unusually warm September afternoon, and before we could move forward with any major cleaning or renovations, it was customary, as in African culture, to first seek permission from the ancestors and to get their blessings. Vic and I had done some initial cleaning, which was necessary before the ritual. The last thing you want to do is invite ancestral Spirits into a place that's unfit and undeserving of their presence.

Nasheed, my friend, and *Ifa* Priest (also called a Babalawo) came early to help set up. I loved this man. He looked so— priestly. Dressed in a traditional white African attire, he stately stood about six feet tall, and his weight was well-maintained. And his peaceful-looking face, with eyes of passion, was very pleasing to the senses.

We had been talking over the last few months about my dreams and the mission that I felt I was being called to do... although uncertain as to what exactly that meant. Rather than go by his thoughts on the situation entirely, he sought answers through divination for assurance and guidance, which showed that I had definitely been called to aid in the ancestor's cry for help. We briefly talked a little more about the situation and agreed that I would be *shown*, without a doubt, just what I had been *called* to do.

Vic was already dressed for the occasion in casual attire when he came from upstairs to help with the preparations. However, as a priestess initiate, like Nasheed, I had to wear white, along with a headdress. So, I went upstairs to get ready while Vic and Nasheed put everything in place.

By the time I returned, our customer and friend, Sasha, had shown up to participate in the ceremonial ritual. As a Yoruba priestess for a few years, she was eloquently dressed in white. Her thick, well-groomed locks fell from under her white headdress . . . draping her radiant, cocoa-colored skin. She truly mirrored an African Queen, in all her glory. We knew Sasha's attendance was a blessing and that she served a significant role in seeking the ancestor's permission to move forward with the cleaning and renovation of this historical and sacred site. She was honored to have been asked to offer her gifts and talents in what she felt was a historical event.

You see, in the Ifa culture, rituals and ceremonial events should not be initiated or implemented without first seeking guidance from our Ancestors. *Ifa* teaches that we MUST honor, acknowledge, and seek guidance from those who came before us . . . those we came *from*. Much like Guardian angels and Spirit guides, our ancestors also support us on our unique paths by helping to build our characters and by helping us to understand our divine purpose. Much of this guidance is through meditation and divination.

You know, even before I embraced *Ifa*, I somehow knew the importance of honoring and loving our ancestors–like grandmothers and grandfathers, and their parents and those before them. I'm not sure when this awareness actually started, but I knew for sure after my paternal grandmother made her transition and then appeared to me in a dream. I loved my grandma! She bought my first book, as well as all my childhood stories that rescued me from a world of fights and drunkenness. Besides being a major influence in my love for storytelling and the reason that I love to read, she was also my anchor as a little girl, showing me glimpses of happiness and laughter. So, when she came into my subconscious, via a dream, carrying a coconut cake with blazing candles, I sensed that I was never alone, and that maybe life was "everlasting."

Her silvery grey hair was neatly pulled back into a bun. She was wearing a patterned dress, which was unusual. I hardly saw her wear anything other than the uniform she wore as a maid. I watched as she looked at me with those twinkly eyes, telling me to "Make a wish."

In the dream, it felt like I was a little girl, although in reality, I was in my thirty's. I closed my eyes and silently wished "*For more love in the world,*" and blew out the candles. She then looked at me and said, "Jane, you can call on me anytime. I am always here for you." From that day forward, I not only Believe that my grandma Ella Whalen is with me, I Know she is! I will always honor and pay homage to her and all the other ancestral souls that share my DNA. I am grateful and blessed to have all the countless Souls that continue to support me on this rather precarious journey.

After I got dressed and cleansed with Indian Sage, Nasheed, Sasha, and Vic took their turn to be cleansed before our guests arrived. The room had been set up much like a Kwanzaa celebration. We had a Mkeka (place mat) to symbolize the earth; Mazao (fresh fruit); a Kikombe cha Umoja (a communal cup for unity and giving thanks), filled with fresh water and a Kinara (candle holder), in which we placed one black candle (opposed to the traditional seven) to symbolize the African peoples. We also placed two additional white, glass candles to provide extra light. All of the items were important to the ritual because it encouraged us to always honor those who came before us; maintain unity in the family, community, race and nation, and to keep our focus on the right to freedom—the very principles The Java House Café stood for.

All dressed in African attire; the drummers were the first to show up strutting their Congas painted in colors of the Mother Land and covered with various animal skins. Their excitement and honor were obvious. There were at least nine of them that came to represent; to be a part of invoking the ancestors and the Orisha, Shango (Lord of thunder and lightning) which the Congas emulated for this honorable occasion. And once they uniformly began to play, the intensity of the rhythmic vibrations began to transform the entire area.

Each moment, as I watched our participants file in like proud soldiers, dressed honoring the Homeland, it was apparent that they were eager to participate in this momentous occasion. This was not your average building. We were embarking on Sacred and Holy ground, and we all knew we were all about to be amongst the ancestors of a former plantation, whose history had affected all of us – – black and white.

Without any prompting, the drummers started beating their drums to summon the ancestral deities as each gallantly lined up to stroll through the smoky, Indian aromatic plant before entering, so as to forego any possible negative energy. Once the drummers entered the room, their rhythmic beats bounced off the walls, echoing throughout the building. They were so in sync with each other, one would think they had practiced together for hours. However, most of them had just met for the first time.

As the rest of our guests walked through the dense smoke, along with the drummers, each one took a seat in the circle of arranged chairs. After everyone was seated, I stood back and gazed around the room. It looked like Africa! My insides shook, and my heart pounded as rapidly as the drum beat. Here I was, in the most important ritual I'd participated in as a priestess initiate—I was hyped! However, it was mandatory that I kept my composure and stay alert and aware during the ritual.

In Full Swing

It was still light outside, but the windows were still covered with the weather-beaten boards, making the room dark . . . except for the candles that burned brightly on the table. Everyone was seated quietly and attentively as Nasheed stood before us, requesting that the "Elder" in the room raise their hand. It was Mama Yay, a well-known and respected spiritual leader and teacher of the African culture. Expressing great honor, she gave her permission to proceed with the ceremony.

Immediately after Nasheed prayed and sought the guidance of Elegua to move forward, and Sasha had poured libation, the drummers once again began their call to invoke the Ancestral Spirits. Caught up in the intense energy of the drums, I watched in amazement how each hand moved up and down effortlessly as if led by some unknown force. Before long, the room was electrified with the added sounds of cowbells, tambourines, and vocal techniques that the ancestors were sure to recognize. The ceremony had begun and was moving into full swing.

As a priestess initiate, I sat on the opposite side of the room basically watching over everyone, as it is customary to be available to assist if a Spirit chooses to communicate through anyone. Not sure what to expect, I watched intensely while allowing my eyes to roam the room.

We had been in session for only a short time, but already the syncopated, rhythmic sounds were penetrating the thick walls, calling out to the heavens to be joined by our forebears. Our guests had fallen under the spell of the call as weightless heads bobbed up and down. Bodies gyrated, pulsating to the beat, while many moaned and groaned . . . crying out to the ancestors. Some began to speak in unknown tongues, while others softly sang songs. Although there were only about twelve people, plus the drummers, the room felt packed. It was hot. Small beads of sweat sprouted around my wrapped temples; my bare feet started sticking to the century-old, wooden floors.

As I observed, I noticed that Thomas, one of our regular customers, stood up and began to sway forward . . . then backward, ever so gently. I took note to look closer and to make sure he was all right. His eyes were closed, and his sway began to deepen . . . almost tipping over. Then, suddenly he stopped and started turning around in circles. That's when I decided that I needed to get up and "cover" him—to serve as a protective shield. But just as I stood up, his 6 feet, 200 plus pounds– hit the floor—BAM!

I jumped from my seat and watched as the hardwood floor gave in like a sponge to his weight; his body bouncing as if jolted from an electric shock only to land again . . . like a feather. Although one might think that the situation warranted me to move with a quickness, I calmly walked over to Thomas' stiff body, once again awestruck by the works of the Spirit. There was no concern about his being hurt in any way. I had witnessed on many occasions Spirit's way of "showing up," and never witnessed any harm to anyone.

He laid there on the floor like a baby as I knelt beside him, waiting for him to come back to himself. It was no more than a few seconds before he opened his eyes and looked up at me, as if wondering why I was practically on top of him. Not wanting to seem unsympathetic, I asked him if he was okay.

"What happened?" he asked, trying to raise himself up. I smiled and lifted his head from the floor while trying to assist him to his feet.

"You're okay. You were just moved by the Spirit," I assured him.

Not saying a word, Nasheed came over and helped to get Thomas off the floor. Heavy and still not able to fully gain control of himself, we finally managed to get him up. Still dazed, he gingerly followed my lead to a nearby chair while Nasheed went back to his perspective place at the head of the circle. Seeing an empty chair further down, I gently shook the person next to us and asked them to move down a seat, and in-turn they asked the next person—playing musical chairs until Thomas had the seat next to me. Whatever or "whoever" was on Thomas, left him practically comatose and sitting like a zombie, waiting to be led . . . anywhere.

Feeling that all was well, I knew Thomas would be all right and more than likely not even remember what happened. Everyone else was still caught up in the Spirit while the drummers appeared to be spellbound, with dreadlocks flopping to the timely beat. Sweat glistened on their ebony and bronze skin, while each drop was caught by the colors of Kente cloth or some other semblance of Africa's vivid colors. Completely in a trance, Sasha danced vigorously . . . her back arched as the rest of her body jerked uncontrollably, while her feet moved in syncopation with the fast tempo of the drummers, who were now in a zone. The Spirits of our ancestors were in the house.

I could tell Thomas was still dazed. He sat beside me with eyes closed, gently swaying from side to side. Everyone else in the room was overcome by the heavy presence of unseen Souls. I, too, was being drawn into the mystic sounds that seem to cast a spell upon those of us that were willing to be taken beyond the walls that surrounded us—beyond the present—beyond death. It was like everyone had been possessed.

Understanding My Purpose

I have no idea as to how long I sat there before beginning to feel a strange sense of being separated from all that surrounded me. Everything seemed to become elongated, stretched far into the background. The loud and pulsating sounds of the drums were now like a faint echo in the far distance. It felt like my body was leaving its familiar surroundings. As this feeling consumed me, I became unaware of everything around me. There were no sounds of drums–no voices–nothing. Then, like a crystal-clear hologram, they appeared.

Black as Africa and stoutly built, she sat on the floor before me, wearing a two-toned scarf wrapped around her head. With her broad shoulders and back half facing me, I could see that she was wearing a patterned, short-sleeve dress. The skirt of an apron lay pulled to one side, ruffled by a restless young girl who was cradled in her deep-seated lap. Appearing to be four or five years old, the girl's dark skin backgrounded her tattered light-colored dress. Her unkempt woolly hair crinkled from her loosened braids. Obviously frightened, she clinched her frail arms around the woman's neck . . . with her head laid against her large bosom . . . crying.

"Please, please don'ts let dem takes me. Please don'ts lets dem sells me." Spellbound, I watched with humility. The woman rocked the distressed child back and forth like a newborn, trying to assure her that she would keep her safe. That's when she turned around and looked straight at me. Drained of life, her large eyes were cold and distant. Her body language shrank to defeat as she tilted her head back just enough for me to get a good look at the pain in her face. Fixed upon her gaze,

I watched as her thick, dried lips parted to speak. Taking a noticeable breath, her nurturing breast rose to meet her chin before she exhaled to make her declaration in a language that was foreign and forced. Her voice was strong but wavering. However, clearly and with conviction, she stared at me and declared: **"Yous done been chosen, my child. Yous been chosen to heal da hate, so's dat my soul cans be free and my chil'ren's souls cans be free."**

Although accustomed to hearing from the other side, I had never been given such a direct order. At that pivotal moment, there was no doubt as to my purpose, and no doubt as to what the dreams had been preparing me for. I had been given charge over helping to "free" the tormented souls that continued to live in a constant, living hell!

Slowly dissipating into the darkness, the woman and young girl mysteriously vanished as mysteriously as they appeared—leaving a dusty, shadow-like film lingering in the open space. I didn't know whether my eyes were open or closed until the vague image of the drummers unfolded—their sound becoming louder and louder, until I realized I was—back.

There was no concept of time when I came back to reality... if in fact, it was a reality. I looked around and saw that everyone was still absorbed. I was still in shock, so I just sat there. Then, I heard a woman's voice . . . in my head. It whispered as to not disrupt the ceremony, but loud enough to make sure I got her instructions.

"Move. Move into the other room . . ." the voice quietly demanded.

Not sure what room, I asked in my mind.

"What room? Which room are you speaking about?"

"There was once a fire," the voice continued. "The room where there was a fire—over the cellar."

From experience, I had learned that when in a state other than what appears to be reality, there's a tendency to do what is asked without asking questions. So, I looked around to get Nasheed's attention who had stopped praying and was surveying the room, looking to see if any ancestors were coming through. I stood to walk toward him, and immediately he knew I had been visited.

"What is it Oshun, what happened?"

Hearing the sound of my Yoruba given name, I had a brief moment of being Proud and Grateful for all that was happening, and my part in it.

"I was told that we need to go to the other room... the Henrietta Marie room." I whispered loudly as he knelt to hear me.

"Let's go. Lead the way."

In an orderly fashion, Nasheed and Sasha let our participants know that we were moving to another room. Everyone fell into sync as if the move had been a part of a formatted agenda. Not a beat was missed . . . literally. Walking and drumming in sync, each drummer moved to our new spot, while everyone else quietly picked up their chair and followed us into the appointed room.

The circle was quietly duplicated, and I could feel the energy becoming even more intense as our guests took their seats. The drummers tapped quietly while keeping a steady beat, while I asked if everyone was okay or if anyone had any comments about what was happening. Some spoke of feeling a presence, while others heard voices. Then there were those who said they were in prayer and meditation to assure that the space was free of negative energy and that we continued to stay open for any Spirits to make their presence.

After sharing for a brief period, I noticed that Vic was standing by a boarded window. His gaze was so fixed on the covered window that it looked as if he could see right "through" it. "They're comin', they're comin' in droves," he started ranting. "It's so many of them. O my god, they are everywhere!"

Not sure what he was talking about, Nasheed moved closer and asked, "Who, Uncle Vic. Who's coming?"

"Slaves. They're comin' . . . out a huge field . . . so many, running!" His voice raised with excitement and awe, while the look on his face looked like he had seen a ghost. Well, in this case, several ghosts. Vic was so believable that we all rushed over to the boarded window and started looking as if there was a clear view of a slave stampede, coming in our direction. Of course, no one else was able to witness what Vic was seeing, but nevertheless, many acknowledged that they "felt" the ancestors' presence. Instinctively, the drummers began to raise the volume and heighten the rhythm—moving us into phase two.

Vic took a seat along a wall where Sasha and Nasheed had placed the glass candles. Silhouettes of the group danced across the plastered wall, creating a mural-like image. As I turned to go and take a seat, I suddenly felt an uncontrollable impulse to dance. As my feet began to move, the rest of my body joined-in, moving frantically . . . keeping in time with the spastic beat of the drum call. Everything else around me was oblivious. I was in a world *other* than my own. Sweat poured from my tightly wrapped head. Beads of salty water trailed down my eyes, curving around my nose to find its way to my slightly parted lips before falling to the dusty floor.

I must have danced for at least an hour, if not longer. My headwrap had loosened itself, falling upon my shoulders before hitting the floor. I felt the energy of someone picking it up as my body began to release to its promptings to end the dance. Slowly, I became aware of my rapid breathing and racing heartbeat. Finally, coming to an abrupt stop, my body slumped onto a nearby chair. I sank in gratitude, wondering how on earth I could have danced the way I did. Now, don't get me wrong. I love to dance! It's like therapy. However, something or someone had taken over my body, and all I could do was . . . allow.

The Ripped Dress

Somewhat still drunk from the intoxicated takeover, and with no intentions of my own, my delirious attention was taken to one of the three boarded windows that sat inside a concave wall in the middle of the room, which were about twelve to fourteen feet away. Somehow, I was able to notice that the middle window's dry, knotty pine had a tiny hole, about the size of a pea. I know, you're probably wondering how in the hell I could see a pea-sized hole, especially so far away. Well, trust me, I was wondering the same thing. The only way I can explain it—is it was like I was Wonder Woman, with biotic vision. Anyway, I wish I could better explain these strange occurrences, but it's hard to put into words. A trance is the closest thing I can think of.

Once again, the surrounding sounds began to fade as I miraculously looked out the pea-hole . . . out into a cinematic view. I saw her as if I was at the movies. She appeared to be young, around twelve to thirteen years old. She was wearing a plaid dress, (although I couldn't determine the color since it, too, was in black and white) with the right sleeve torn off her shoulder. Not only did I "see" the girl, but our thoughts connected—A telepathic conversation ensued.

"What happened to your dress?" I asked. Her kinky hair stood at attention with four plaits pointed in different directions. As I watched, I mentally noted that her tall, slender frame was running across the *yard* when I then heard a voice correcting me: *"She's running across the 'field.'"*

"Why are you running . . . what happened to your sleeve?" My questions traveled telepathically!

Unlike the woman with the child, the girl never looked at me, but rather straight ahead while she began to *show* me how her dress was torn! Suddenly, her slow forward movements—stopped! Next, everything started moving fast and—backwards, as if the scene was being rewound. The next thing I saw, she was in the cellar crouched on the dirt floor with her back pressed against a brick wall; her arms wrapped around her trembling legs, crying and begging the man in front of her to stop. Wearing a white shirt and dark trousers, he crouched in front of the frightened girl. His dark, thick hair fell limp over his right eye, which was furious . . . red and wild looking. It was like watching a movie of flashbacks from my own life as he tried to pry open her young legs. With her face contorted and her mouth opened wide, she made no sound . . . "Scream!" My mind cried out.

"They's will hear me. I's will gets in mo trouble if'n they's finds out I's was in da cellar."

Her transferred thoughts troubled my mind. I was furious and helpless. Strong and determined, she spat and kicked to keep this monster from stealing her innocence. Unable to move, I held my breath as she freed her right leg from his tight grip—raising her bare, dusty foot. Then, with all the strength she could muster, she kicked him right between his partially, spread legs. He let out an embarrassing and excruciatingly deep groan and lost his grip in trying to pry open her legs. Infuriated and holding on to his throbbing testicles with his right hand, he grabbed her right shoulder with his left. Then, with venom and rage, he spat out the words, "You nigger bitch!" Ripping her dress and falling back, the horrified girl quickly charged pass him . . . running for her life!

Like before, the silence was broken with the distant sound of drums. My heavy breathing slowed, and the drums got louder as I came back to reality. Still sitting and trying to get a handle on what had happened, I felt a hand on my shoulder. It was Nasheed, asking if I was okay. I could only nod. I had no energy or the words to describe what was just seen. Gazing around the room, I noticed that Vic was still sitting on the floor against the wall, while others were gathering their composure—coming out of their trances. The ritual had reached its climax.

One More Surprise

It was late afternoon when we had gathered for the ritual; however, when we opened the door to bring it to its end, we were greeted by the soft, reddish tones of a rising sun along with a brisk, fall chill. Everyone began to casually file out one at a time, as most were still trying to gain their composure from the unforeseen events that had taken place over the past twelve hours.

Exhausted, there was little to say as we hugged our guests and bade each other farewell. The night had been long but welcoming, and now we could move forward in both the restoration of the building and the freeing of trapped souls that sought refuge from a literal . . . hell. However, the mystical events were not quite over.

Completely worn out, Vic and I took the time to make sure all the lights were turned off before leaving, even though there were only a few. Although we were still running our electricity from the temporary pole that Mr. Murphy had set up, keeping the cost at a minimum was essential. Convinced that all was well, we made our way to the parking lot to leave, and as we were pulling out of the drive, for whatever reason, I turned to look back at the building. Maybe I was still mesmerized at the fact that we were owners of a former plantation. Or still overwhelmed with what had happened just a few hours earlier. I don't know. Whatever the reason, that's when I noticed a light in an upstairs window.

"Hey, Vic, I thought we turned out all the lights."

At that point, he, too, turned around.

"Hell, I know I turned off everything," he assured me.

That's when I saw him!

"Vic, you see what I see?" I whispered, pointing up at a second-floor window.

"I be damned. Is that a child?" he nervously asked.

We both sat there for a moment unable to talk as we gazed up at a little white boy who stared back at us before disappearing into thin air. I don't know what happened, but after seeing and communicating with disembodied souls for the past twelve hours, you would think that seeing one more was no big deal—*You would think!* But, instead, I damn near burned rubber pulling out of that parking lot. Why? I haven't a clue. Vic and I never even mentioned it again as we rode home in complete silence.

FIFTEEN

Unexpected Company from Both Worlds

Day after day, Vic and I worked for hours on end, taking one room at a time, which was hard for me. I wanted to work on several rooms at once, thinking we could get more done. However, Vic convinced me that it was better to clean one room at a time . . . that way we could stand back and say . . . good, now that room is DONE! Admittedly, at the end of a long day, seeing a room completely finished gave me hope and the boost needed to keep going. There were many times I wondered what would have happened if Vic hadn't quit his job. Just the thought of having to do most of the work by myself without his help was terrifying. And no matter what other issues we had, every day I thanked God for my husband and his tireless support. We were definitely in it together.

September had come and gone. The brisk October air was a reminder that a forecasted, brutal winter was right around the corner. However, this particular day, a warm sun peeped through the side windows of the front entrance when I heard a knock. Once again, I was alone. When I opened the door, I was greeted by a strange woman. After a friendly hello, she began to explain that she had heard about us and decided to stop by. It was always good to meet prospective customers, so I graciously invited her in.

She was average height, full-busted, and thick around the hips, wearing a heavy sweater to ward off the chill. Her dark, smooth complexion needed no makeup; a natural glow highlighted her high cheeks. Horn-rimmed black glasses set off her dark eyes and oval face. After entering, she stopped and stood for a few moments, gazing up at the staircase. Then something happened that I was not expecting, at least not from a complete stranger.

"Have you met her yet?" she asked softly.

Clueless! "Met whom. Who are you talking about?"

"The girl with the plaid dress."

Shocked, excited, and a tad reserved, I asked her what the girl looked like. She then began to describe the girl I saw in the cellar and went on to tell me more about her.

"She keeps the banister polished," she continued. "I can see her doing the ritual with a sense of being carefree and bouncy."

Amazed, I anxiously began to tell her about the vision I had during the night of the ritual. Not surprised, she continued to my astonishment.

"Her name is Bessie. She was named after one of the white women of the plantation whose name was *Betty*—which she didn't like, so she called herself Bessie. She feeds the children and hides them under the porch."

"What do you mean, she hides children?" I quickly interjected.

"That's probably why she was afraid of anyone knowing about her being in the cellar." She went on, not bothering to answer my question. After another pause, she continued.

"There's an opening in the cellar that leads to a tunnel from the Ohio River, where slaves are brought in from boats and barges. Umm, shaking her head slightly. That was probably a part of that guy's job who attacked her."

Her words rolled off her lips as if she were afraid she would lose them, with an occasional quick pause in between, and then start up again.

"When children were brought through, Bessie would sneak down and take them food."

Hanging on her every word, I restlessly sat on the edge of the bottom step. Her story sounded authentic, for I had heard about the tunnel from some of the locals, and I was now certain about the girl.

"The dress she's wearing is her favorite. She loves the different colors."

Her full lips widened into a smile. "I see her tapping on the steps, signaling the children that she's coming with food."

A quick chuckle interrupts her stream of words . . . "She steals the food off the kitchen table."

Again, she pauses…."There's a long room here that has two doors."

"Yeah, that sounds like the room over here," I announced, jumping from my position on the step, eager to have her follow me to the initial room where we started the ritual.

"Is this the room?" I enthusiastically asked.

"Yes, I believe so," she stated with little hesitation. "You see," she chuckled. "She comes through this door," pointing at the door nearest the back. "She then grabs food off a long table that sits in the middle of the room and then runs out the opposite door. The woman who prepares the food is a big woman. She acts as if she's trying to catch her . . . but not really."

"Was this the original kitchen?" I inquired.

She looked around the room as if she were checking with her unseen resources. "Yeah, I believe it is."

"You know, I think you're right."

I didn't bother to go into the story about the woman I saw during the ritual. Hearing more about Bessie was intriguing, as well as a validation. The stranger had my full attention as she slowly walked around the room; her eyes fluttering like a bird's wings. I could tell that she was still being "shown" something as she verbalized what her mind's eye was witnessing.

"The children were taken from their families and were to be sold to other plantation owners, but in many cases, the girl, Bessie, was able to help them escape to nearby fields, giving them a chance to possibly connect with the Underground Railroad. She was a brave girl to be so young."

To confirm my curiosity about her age, I asked her how old she thought Bessie was. Pausing... she then continued.

"It looks like she's twelve or thirteen years old. She's tall for her age and skinny." At that point, without a doubt in my mind, the young girl she saw and the one in my vision were the same. She was no longer a figment of my imagination. And now, she had a name. After several more minutes of sharing and a deep expression of my gratitude, the stranger left as unassumingly as she had come. I never saw her again.

Chef Spirit

You know that old saying, "Time flies when you're having fun?" Well, I'm here to attest to the fact that it flies when you're "not" having fun. I don't know what happened to the time, but November had come in like a thief in the night along with its brutal chill. There was no heat in the mansion, so Vic got a couple of kerosene heaters.

As usual, Greg spent quite a lot of time with us. Every night that we were there, he was there, also. Every day (well, maybe not *every* day, but it sure seemed like it), Greg was as much a part of our marriage as if all three of us had vowed to love each other till death do us part. If he wasn't in our home, my husband was at his house or at Charles's or wherever. However, there was one particular incident that kept Greg away from the home front... at least for a couple of days.

One night, we were all sitting around the kerosene heater, robed in heavy-duty coveralls, thermal underwear and T-shirts, and at least two pairs of socks. It was in the wee hours of the night, and we were drinking wine and passing a joint while telling Greg some scary tales about the things and people (or Spirits) we had seen during the ritual.

In the midst of our last laughter, we heard a loud noise from the rear of the building.

"Did you hear that?" Vic whispered as if not to be heard by anyone other than the present company.

"What?" I asked, whispering back.

Greg sat there holding the joint, frozen. That's when we all heard it again–clanking pots and pans as if someone was in the back cooking. With ears perked, we continued to listen just in case we were trippin'–– when suddenly— there it was again. We knew that someone was in the kitchen. However, the only people who could have been in the kitchen were sitting huddled around a heater, trying to stay warm and minding the business at hand. Without saying another word—the three of us quietly, but with a quickness, turned off the heater and took off towards the front door—And not looking back! By the time we made it to the car, we could hear each other as we gasped, finally taking a deep breath— but still not saying a word.

We were at least two blocks from Greg's house before he fired up the roach that was still attached to his fingers. And after taking a long toke, he finally spoke.

"Hey, you guys, I'm gonna be tied up the next couple of days, but I'll get back at ya next week."

"Yeah, man, not a problem. I'll catch up with ya later." Vic assured him.

We pulled into Greg's driveway, let him out, and said our casual goodbyes. As usual, Vic and I didn't mention what had happened.

Ever since I started having paranormal experiences, even before the ritual, in which Vic had one as well, one would think that nothing else could rattle us... especially me. After all, I never felt any fear or sensed any danger or any need to be afraid. And yet, seeing the little boy in the window and hearing the commotion in the kitchen made me wanna run for cover.

While I was musing over the situation, I thought about another similar *scare* I had a few days earlier, which really made me think about why *hearing* (what we knew as ghosts or Spirits) frightened me. During this other time, when I heard what I call "chef Spirits," I was painting in the foyer. Standing on a twelve-foot ladder and painting the ceiling, I was listening to some music when I heard a loud clanging of pots and pans (pretty much like with Greg and Vic), only that time I was alone. And I wasn't smoking or drinking.

Thinking maybe it was the music, I turned down the radio that was sitting on top of the ladder. I heard it again. Louder!

"What the hell is that?" I thought out loud.

But before I could answer the obvious, (since no one was in the house but me) I damn near slid down the ladder trying to get the hell out!

Now, maybe with Vic and Greg, I could blame our taking *flight* on the fact that we were *high*. But as for my burning rubber out of the driveway when I saw the little boy in the window, and the incident when I was painting, the only thing I can *assume* (because I really don't have a clue) is that I was in my *normal* state of consciousness. I wasn't under the influence of a *trance, meditation, or dream state*. But, then again, when I saw the three women that I mentioned earlier (All Women Who Cry the Blues, Ain't black), I wasn't in a ritual or meditating . . . they just showed up. And yet, although initially a little shaken... you might say, I found myself unable to move as I became a part of their world, almost magically.

With the three women, as well as the woman with the child, and with Bessie (so great to have a name), it was like I went into another dimension in space and time while having no control over anything, as well as being oblivious to everything around me. With no concept of time, I never knew how long I was "out of *my* mind" (but rather in the minds of others) before coming back to *reality*. Believe me, to this day, I cannot explain *how or why* I responded to these different scenarios from the perspective of what appeared to be entirely two different energy fields. I'm still baffled.

Once we arrived at the house, my steadfast husband and I grabbed a bite to eat and took a shower before going to bed, virtually in silence. We managed a quick peck on the cheeks before falling into a deep slumber. And like I said, we never again spoke on the ghostly activities that day. And why . . . who knows.

SIXTEEN

The Gift

The Christmas holidays were on our heels, and with both our efforts, Vic and I were having a rough time trying to make sure there was money for the boy's Christmas. And to top that off, I had decided NOT to go back to school after the Christmas break. I hated to do it, but the time had come to let my children go, which was one of the hardest things I had ever done. However, between the classes, being a stepmom, the business of the café, and the renovation task, it had become an added wear and tear on my physical body, as well as a drain on my mind. But I made myself look at the bright side. I had given ten years to one school in helping to promote self-esteem, pride, and self-love, all with the hope of stimulating my students' young minds to the importance of an education. Along with the intentions to help create an awareness of their power "within," which would eventually become a foundation for their success and happiness, it was time to trust that our sessions had not been in vain. For now, with all that was facing me, it was the next chapter in my life that needed my undivided attention. And even though we were virtually broke and needed all the money we could get, my health and well-being took precedent.

It had been snowing most of the day as Vic, Shorty and I were bringing our fourteen-hour day to an end. Damn, what a blessing Shorty was. Between him and Larry, our other carpenter angel, God only knows how we would have made it through. Shorty was the younger of the two. Larry was in his fifties and more experienced in some areas and was the first to come onboard. And as I have probably mentioned many times, we didn't have much money to work with, and both of these guys worked for practically peanuts. Anyway...

This particular night, we had been talking about being broke. Between the three of us, we couldn't rub two dimes together. And neither our friend, Shorty, nor I had gas and were trying to figure out how we were gonna get some money to buy some. Looking like we had just left the cotton fields, we were walking out to the parking lot when Shorty noticed a white envelope on his windshield. It was still pretty light out, so it was quite noticeable. Vic and I started teasing Shorty about having a secret admirer and that it was probably a love note. Rushing up on him like it was something tantalizingly juicy, Vic and I waited in anticipation as Shorty carefully opened the envelope.

Like two kids with bulging eyes and held breath, we watched as Shorty looked inside. Dumbfounded, he surprisingly pulled out THREE—CRISP—TWENTY DOLLAR BILLS, along with a note.

Still holding on to the three bills, Shorty began to read out loud.

"I know times are hard. Thank you for what you're doing. God bless the three of you."

I'm not sure how much time went by before one of us broke the silence and decided to breathe. But after catching our breath, Shorty handed me and Vic a brand new twenty-dollar bill. Still looking at each other, we were shocked and in disbelief. Of course, we tried to rationalize how it got there; however, there was no rationale. So, we surmised with great certainty that it was a gift from God . . . sent by an Angel. Is God good or what?

After Shorty got in his truck and started backing out of the driveway, Vic and I waved like two children waving to their grandparents who had just dropped off gifts before going back into the mansion to get my car keys. Needless to say, we were still amazed about the miracle that had just taken place, realizing that once again we had been blessed. Only this time . . . in a monetary way!

SEVENTEEN

Revelations

By the time I stopped to get gas, it was nearly 1:00 a.m. before we got to the house. The work was taking a toll on me, but it didn't seem to bother Vic. I thought that it was because he was a man and had more stamina than me, only to find out much later that his stamina had nothing to do with gender. Exhausted, I went to bed. Vic, on the other hand, always seemed to find energy to go out, and that night he had money as well.

Before leaving, Vic planted a quick kiss on my cheek and assured me he wouldn't be gone long.

"Where you going?" I asked as if I didn't know his response.

"Charles', I won't be gone long. I need to get some air; have a couple of beers."

I don't know why I felt so uneasy about him leaving. Maybe it was the disturbing, recurring dream that gave me that sick feeling in my stomach. in which I also used as an excuse to do what I did next – I followed him! I know. That's pitiful! Whenever I heard a Sistah talk about following her man, I swore I would never do some dumb shit like that. Never—say—never!

Not only was I nervous creeping along the snowy, narrow quiet roads that led to Charles' place, but I felt like shit! *What the hell was I doing?* Even though the question burned away at my consciousness, it didn't stop me from continuing my little escapade as I sheepishly drove around.

It took only a few minutes to notice that Vic's van was nowhere in sight as I got closer to the club. *"Maybe he was parked around the corner."* I thought to myself. So, I slowly drove around the corner—and the next corner—and a few more corners for at least a half mile, no van.

When I pulled back around close to the side entrance of the club, I noticed there was no music and Charles' car wasn't anywhere in sight, which I hadn't noticed earlier, too busy looking for my husband's van . . . I suppose? It was 2:00 a.m. No van, no music, and no husband.

By now, I felt like I was going to vomit. Tears blurred my vision as I drove away from the club. *Where was he?* I made the familiar path one more time, to no avail. And the sick feeling grew into a full-fledged panic. Although I asked myself over and over about the whereabouts of my husband, I was more afraid than not to know the answer.

After sitting parked for a few minutes to collect my composure, I finally pulled off to head back home. I felt lost, defeated and STUPID for doing what I had vowed NEVER to do. As I got closer to the house, I prayed that Vic hadn't come home to find that his wife was gone. I knew there was no way to explain my disappearing act, at least nothing that wouldn't be a lie. Just when I was ready to turn onto our street, a sickening, gnawing feeling replaced the nervousness that I was feeling in the pit of my stomach. A voice in my mind demanded that I take the route that would pass Greg's house. It was 2:30 in the morning.

The darkness barely hid the familiar van that sat in the driveway. I knew I shouldn't stop, but my car seemed to have a mind of its own as it pulled along the deserted street. Like a thief in the night, I eased out of the car as if someone would surely hear me. As I crept along the graveled driveway, trying not to disturb the tiny pebbles, a dim light showed in the basement window. *I dare not go any further . . .* I thought as I continued to tiptoe toward the basement window. Like catching a robber trying to break into your house, I was taken completely off guard when an automatic detection spotlight caught me dead in my tracks.

Oh shit! What was I going to do if someone came out? For a brief moment, I froze . . . unable to move an inch. No one came. I started backing up quietly and slowly— at first. As I got closer to my getaway car, I ran like a rabbit, jumped in the car, and sped off. Rushing into our driveway (while making sure I matched my tire tracks in the snow from when I left), my heart pounded like I had run a marathon and came in last, but relieved to be at the finish line. Huge beads of sweat poured down my face like it was a hot summer night, while the December's bite evaporated them as quickly as they appeared. Finally, I was at the front door, which was cracked open. I had forgotten to close it—which in this case, I was glad.

Had Vic and Greg heard me? Was Vic right behind me ready to ask me questions I wasn't ready to answer? As I reached the top of the stairs, my heart raced as I angrily pulled off my clothes and put them on the chair where they were when Vic left. Then, like a snake, I slivered into the cold sheets trying to hold back the built-up, tearful waterfall. But the stream of tears could not be held back, as they released themselves into the deep crevices of my pillow. Ashamed, mad and afraid of my worst nightmare, my thoughts haunted me until sleep prevailed. However, not before the moon took cover to make room for a rising sun, and still . . . no Vic.

"Hey, sleepyhead!" Vic's voice roused me as he towered over me. "You really do love the mornings." He reminded me.

My eyes felt glued. I was afraid to move too quickly. My head was letting me know that it was ready, willing, and able to wreak havoc.

"Do we have any aspirin?" I whispered, trying not to make any sudden moves. "I have a sinus headache."

His rationale about me and the mornings was right. I loved the mornings because I hated to get up before ten, especially if I had worked like a Hebrew slave the day before— or in this case, riding around being . . . stupid! (AND using up the gas that I was just blessed to get)

"I can tell, and your eyes are swollen, too," Vic announced. "Where did you have the aspirin last? You know I don't take that stuff, since I've never had a headache."

"Never?" I asked, not really caring if his head ever hurt or not. Obviously, he had never cried all night, or worried about his wife being involved in an affair—or worse.

"No, never!" He bragged as he continued.

"I often wondered why. Like the only time I've really known pain was when I had a toothache— I pulled it myself with wire-pliers."

"Damn, I wonder what drug he was on," I asked . . . in my mind.

"So, you've never been sick?" I mischievously asked, thinking it was the next obvious question.

"Nope, never! Except for a cold . . ."

"Oh, and don't forget that time you had a sore throat." I had to interject.

"Yeah, that's right . . . the sore throat."

And while he recalled that situation *only* after I reminded him, my memory of that time was quite vivid. You see . . .

After months of sparse, lukewarm sex and non-arousing foreplay, there was this particular time when I was feeling all hot and bothered and decided to corner my husband in the doorway to the kitchen. My hands roamed his tight thighs. My tongue licked along his salty neck. I was so hot for my husband's touch . . . his wet kisses and long, lost passion. I wanted to feel that feeling—you know—sexy, like a woman, and turn my husband on. I could tell he had been smoking; he was easy and willing to be led as I lured him into the living room. Our favorite chair welcomed our weight. My hands prowled his body, Revelations caressing the all too unfamiliar. I tugged at my own clothes, sensuously disrobing myself while breathing heavily with anticipation. Damn! I was gettin' me some. And this time, it was like OLD times.

Feeling like a limp rag and deliciously drained of all my woes, my weight sank into his sweaty chest. His heart was pounding rapidly as we both gave into the release. I had my husband back. So, I thought.

The very next day I attempted to get a "replay," pushing up on my man with my sensuous charm. I moved close to his face with slightly, opened pooched lips when suddenly . . .

"No, don't kiss me! I have a sore throat," my husband proclaimed while pushing me away.

I wanted to think that he acted so anxiously because he didn't want me to catch anything, concerned for my well-being. But the *push* seemed to have a different energy. Rough–like guarded anger. "A sore throat? When did you get a sore throat?" I asked, puzzled and thrown off balance.

Backing still further . . . "I don't know . . . the last time you kissed me . . . I guess."

"You guess? Vic, I ain't got no sore throat. You didn't get it from me!"

Shocked and pissed that he would fix his mouth to even say something so ridiculous, I felt humiliated and completely baffled. It hadn't been twenty-four hours since we had made passionate love; and now, my husband doesn't wanna kiss me? What the hell? I couldn't even talk about it anymore. From that day forward, I never felt my husband's tongue again.

Back to Reality

"I found the aspirin! They were in the medicine cabinet. One or two?" Vic asked, jolting me back to my present, unrequited fairytale.

Although the kissing drama had happened more than six months earlier, I couldn't help but think that finding Vic over to Greg's had a connection. I felt it. And I was too horrified to allow myself to believe what my gut was screaming at me through my dreams. The "one" dream that's too hard to talk about . . . let alone, believe.

"Two." Vic handed me the aspirin and a glass of water.

"Thanks." I threw back the aspirin and silently prayed that they would ease the pain. "Well, it's a damn good thing that you don't have headaches. They are NO fun. Sometimes I get them so bad, I have to vomit to get some relief."

"Yeah, I've heard other people talk about havin' them. I guess I'm pretty lucky."

"By the way, what day is it... Please say it's Sunday."

"It is. So, you can go back to bed and sleep as long as you want. I'm gonna do some work downstairs and then go to the café. I'll check on you before I leave."

No sooner than he said the words, *go back to bed,* I fell back onto the bed . . . said, "Thank you God," and pulled the covers over my head.

EIGHTEEN

Ghosts, Playing Tricks

"*P*rince's" big hit, "*Party Like it's 1999*," blasted on the radio, temporarily taking my mind off my neck pain. Standing on a twelve-foot ladder with brush in hand and head tilted back, I was painstakingly painting a hand-carved, floral design. Like most of the crown molding that continued along the ceiling on both sides of the focal point, the plastered, floral motif that served as a center for a chandelier, was the first thing you saw when you came in the front door. So, I decided to paint the oversized petals with several vibrant colors, making it alive with brilliance. Perfect for the gigantic, brass chandelier I found at a salvage yard. And thank goodness, Vic had experience with plaster as a prosthesis. His creative genius came in quite handy when it came to recreating several pieces of broken or missing molding.

I was alone that cold February day since Vic had to see Charles for some used equipment, which is something he did as a side business. I was grateful that we had finally gotten some real heat from the installation of the new furnace, even though we still had to use kerosene heaters upstairs. Things were finally moving forward with the major part of the renovations, such as plumbing and heating... at least for downstairs.

The electricity was getting its final approval from the City Building Inspector this particular day, and I was expecting our electrician, Marvin, to meet with the Inspector at any time. So, when I heard a knock on the door, I was happy to take a well-needed opportunity for a reprieve from being Van Gogh. My neck was killing me. And, as you know, I usually don't have sense enough to quit when I'm in pain.

"Hey Marvin, how's it going?"

Bundled up like an Eskimo, Marvin was tall, dark, and slightly rounded in the midsection, as well as handsome and strong, looking like one of those Mandingo brothers.

"Ready for this inspection, Miss Yarbrough. Looks like you doing some more painting. Things are looking good."

"Yeah, thanks. I'll sure be glad when it's all over. Can I get you something warm to drink... take your coat?"

"Naw, I'm cool. The Inspector should be here any minute now. I'll go ahead and make one last check before he gets here."

Marvin had been through the entire house before he called the Inspector a couple of days earlier to get his work approved. Everything was working just fine. However, with forms on a clipboard, Marvin proceeded towards the back. I guess one more run-through couldn't hurt.

When the Inspector got there about ten minutes later, unlike Marvin, he wore only a jacket and a hat. Short and stocky, upon entering he nodded and took off his hat and tucked it under his arms. As Marvin proudly walked the Inspector through the entire house, checking out certain areas, I tagged along behind them, just to see for myself that everything was cool. About fifteen minutes into the inspection, Marvin led the gentleman into the room over the cellar— the one where we completed our cleansing ritual. So far, all was looking good.

Casually walking to a light switch on a back wall, Marvin flipped the white lever while the three of us looked at the fluorescent ceiling fixture. Nothing happened! No light! Looking bewildered and confused, he flipped it again . . . and again . . . to no avail. He then went to the main box in the next room and checked to see if anything had tripped. All looked to be working fine. He tried the light switch again. Still, nothing.

"Look here, Marvin, . . ." (scratching his balding head while obviously perturbed for what he felt was a waste of his time) ". . . you obviously missed something. Look, why don't you recheck everything and call me back?"

The rosy cheek man walked toward the door, while Marvin looked on in anguish.

Lost for words, Marvin fumbled with an excuse while trying to convince the Inspector that everything *was* fine.

"Look, I don't know what's happening, man . . . but everything was working fine. I just checked out everything a couple of days ago, and before you came . . . I don't understand it."

Reiterating to call him when he had everything working, the Inspector put his hat on and headed out to his car. After the official car pulled from the driveway, Marvin meandered across the room to the switch he knew should have worked. He took out a screwdriver from his bag and started to take off the covering.

"Marvin, before you take off the plate, try turning it on again." I'm not sure why, but I felt a strong urge to tell him that.

With head half-cocked, Marvin looked at me, squinting his eyes while putting his screwdriver in his back pocket. And as if he were talking to himself, I could hear him muttering.

"This damn light better not come on."

I had never heard him curse before. He was always professional. But for that moment, all of his professionalism and the whispering went right out the window when he flipped the switch, and there was … light.

"I be damned! This is some crazy shit! I'm getting out of here. I knew there was something not right about this place, and this ain't the first time something like this has happened. I've seen lights go off and on without my hitting the switch; I've seen strange movements and nobody there."

I stood there looking with a half-smirk on my face as I waited for him to take a breath. He looked so serious. And I did everything I could to keep from cracking up. I knew he wouldn't think the shit was funny.

"Look, I'm gonna just have the Inspector come back tomorrow morning." He continued while avoiding eye contact.

Then, with a quickness, he grabbed his tool bag and headed for the door . . . still ranting.

"You're a good one. No way I could stay here . . . no way."

The next morning, he and the Inspector returned. This time, we were warranted a Certificate of Compliance. However, Marvin had no desire to stick around for his final payment. Hurriedly walking out the door, he yelled back at me.

"Mail me my final payment. And good luck. You're gonna need it."

NINETEEN

The Findings of a Breeding Box

The Heating Ventilation/Air Conditioning (HVAC), and plumbing contractor, along with his small crew, pretty much had everything installed downstairs. At least to the point of having some heat. On this particular day, the owner of the company was working upstairs while a couple of his guys were working outside. I was upstairs as well, laying some floor tiles in the bathroom.

"Hey, Mrs. Yarbrough, I found something up here in the attic. Wanna come here and see what you think of it?"

When I heard his voice, he sounded a little bewildered. So, I took off my gloves and went into the room where he was working. His mocha-colored face seemed a little flushed as he attempted to keep his cool. Showing a little dust and dirt, his white, thick turtleneck sweater pronounced his medium-built physique, accentuating ripped muscles in his biceps and shoulders–surely capable of fighting off any apparition–if need be.

"What is it? You see a ghost or something?" I asked, trying to be funny. I could tell that he was slightly apprehensive as he climbed down from the ladder and invited me to take his place.

"Naw, I ain't scared. It's just strange looking . . . some sorta box or something. You know some weird things have been going on here. I just ain't said nothing. But this is . . . I don't know. I ain't never seen nothing like it before. You'll see."

I bravely climbed the ladder until I reached the opening. It was about five feet away from where I stood, with my body partly in. The ceiling was tall enough for me to stand up halfway as I moved closer to this— thing. At first, I thought it was some type of coffin, but it was too long and wide. Kneeling to get a closer look, I noticed what appeared to be fossilized feces . . . now as to whether they were human or not, is another story. The outside of the mysterious box was made from wood, mixed with some type of metal, making it strong and solid. The inside was layered with a shiny surface, like a thin tin. Being curious, I climbed in and lay down on the cold surface when an intense, strange feeling came over me. It made me shudder! I quickly jumped out . . . almost falling.

"Hey, you all right?" The contractor yelled with obvious concern.

"Yeah, I'm okay."

"What is it? Do you know what it could be . . . have you ever seen anything like it?" He stammered as his questions came one after another, giving me no time in between to answer.

"I'm not sure." I yelled back after a brief moment. "I *feel* like it was some kinda place for breeding … you know, slaves put together to make babies."

"Are you kiddin' me? No way!"

"I'm not sure. It's just a feeling. I'm gonna ask a friend of mine who knows about these types of things. He'll know for sure. He can do a *reading*."

"A what?"

"Never mind. It's hard to explain. Anyway, I'm coming down. I'm feeling sad and mad at the same time."

I lowered my body back toward the ladder and slowly climbed down, still pondering on what I had just witnessed. The plumber sorta shook his head and mumbled something about my place being spooky, which is probably why later in the job we *found out* that most of the plumbing and heating & air-conditioning units were installed incorrectly—thus leaving the entire building with inadequate heat, poor plumbing and hardly any cool air. Maybe they were . . . "spooked?"

Regrets

You know, I thought I was doing the *right* thing by hiring folks who *looked like me*. You know, keep the money in the *community.* Well, let me put it this way. The plumber's work was so messed up, I had to take him before the *State Licensing Board* to get some results, which was only after I tried to get him to "do the right thing" and fix the problems. However, since he was dealing with a "woman," primarily (Vic left all the business and contractors to me) he probably figured that I wouldn't know a duct from a PVC pipe, which would have been a major mistake on his part. And what I didn't know, there were friends in my life that did!

The day that we went before the Board, was a horrible experience. It was the last thing I wanted to do; however, the plumber gave me no other choice. The weather had gotten pretty cold, and not having sufficient heat was a major problem. We had already suffered through smothering heat and poor plumbing—something had to be done.

The room was small with just enough room for a long table and a file cabinet. Present, were the contractor and his wife, three board members consisting of two males and a female, and of course, my husband. After we were all seated and introductions were made, along with our former complaint, I immediately raised slightly from my seat and leaned half-way across the table. I then purposely and defiantly made direct eye contact with the plumber, and the next thing I knew, I was pouring out my frustrations.

"You know, my 'bro-thur,' it breaks my heart that we have to bring you before the 'white man' to get you to do what's right. I took great pride in getting black folks from the community, so as to support each other in our business endeavors . . . and you failed us!

How could you take a talent . . . a gift that God has given you and completely abuse it?"

Although I was extremely hurt and disappointed, I somehow managed to stay relatively calm . . . meaning that I didn't raise my voice to the point of screaming! I continued to look at him while he tapped his pen gently on a manila folder while occasionally looking away from me. His wife, whom I had never met, sunk her small frame back into her chair; her eyes lowered in shame, while I continued.

"We had a written contract, in which you were paid-in-full to do a professional job, and not one thing is working right!"

Sheepishly, he raised his eyes to meet mine and tried to blame his "workers".

"Look!" I quickly interjected.

"You are the one that's responsible for your employees! You should have made sure that the work was done correctly. Your name was on our contract, not your employees!"

Adding to his defense, he announced that his work was inspected by the City and "approved."

"Yes, you're right." I agreed as I directed my attention to the board members. "Tell me, how can an Inspector stamp an 'approval' on this man's work? As far as I can see, they need to be investigated as well."

Of course, my comment was not answered directly; however, after a few more comments and questions directed to each of us, the three of the board members looked at my husband and me and apologized for all our inconveniences and suffering. We were assured that the situation would be investigated and that another Inspector, from another district, would come by The Java House and facilitate another inspection.

After gathering all of our substantial documents, such as, contracts, canceled checks and a copy of the "approval" sticker, the board members stood, shook each of our hands and promised that we would have a decision within 15 working days, and that Vic and I could also expect a call to set up an appointment for the inspection. Now livid,

I could feel myself shaking on the inside as we walked past the contractor and his wife. Neither of us said another word.

As promised, there was another inspection in less than a week, and within two-weeks, we received a Certified letter from the Licensing Board that our claim had been approved and was awarded a check in the amount of $10,500.00. Although this was a shoutin' moment, we ended up having to hire another plumber do redo *some* of the work. Unfortunately, there was more fixing needed than we had money.

Anyway, back to the find in the attic . . .

A few days later after our find in the attic. I received a phone call from Nasheed who had inquired about the mysterious box through divination. He confirmed that my *feelings* were correct—it was a "Breeding Box." Once again, I was astonished! Not only about the Box, but the fact that I was correct in my intuition.

TWENTY

The Sins of a Father

All alone and working like a Hebrew slave, my daily grind was interrupted by what sounded like a knock at the front door. I turned down the classical music to listen. It *was* a knock. I was somewhat surprised since it was late evening and I wasn't expecting anyone. My immediate thought was that someone was coming to help. I got excited. The glass pane that surrounded the front door was still covered with newspaper, so I couldn't see who was on the other side. I opened the door and was met with a chilling wind, along with a white man who was obviously drunk, swaying back and forth with beer in hand. I have to admit, surprised was not the word. I was taken completely off guard.

"Good evening, can I help you?" I asked quite curiously.

He stood there adjusting himself; pulling at his tattered, dark pea coat with missing buttons and shuffling his feet as if his well-worn shoes would spark up some warmth. Average height and frail, my strange guest looked harmless. His dark hair, sprinkled with gray around the edges, limped over his ears and down his neck; his eyes were distant.

"Hey ma'am—Do you know where you are?" His speech slurred as he struggled to stand upright. "You know we don't have yo kind round here and we don't want it to be no trouble. Do you know where you are?" He asked again as if I didn't hear him the first time.

"Do you know where you are?" I redirected. I couldn't be angry. The fact was, I knew exactly where I was and what came with the territory. "Come on in. Looks like you can use a cup of coffee." His eyes widened as his cheeks rose up to meet them. He raised his unsteady hand and tilted his head back for one last, hopeful swallow from an empty can.

"By the way, my name is Nailah."

He stepped inside the door in front of me.

"Russell, but everybody round here call me Smiley." His thin lips parted into an uncontrolled grin, exposing teeth that knew tobacco all too well.

Keeping late hours, I usually kept a pot of coffee on, as so I did that night. I invited him to have a seat and poured us both a cup of coffee . . . and then, it was on.

We must have talked for over an hour, while he cried off and on as he confessed his dislike for colored people.

"You know, I've been livin' round here most my life. My daddy, God rest his soul, used to tell me to stay way from niggers. He say they troublemakers and up to no good. When they started mixin' colored and whites in schools, my daddy made me quit. Said he wasn't gonna have his son in the same room with no nigger. He say the only thing those coloreds are good for is makin' the white man rich."

It took every ounce of strength I had not to get mad. My right leg shook as if there was a crying baby on it. Something I did when I got nervous or while trying to control an emotion. Getting all worked up wasn't gonna do anything but make me sicker, and I was tired of being sick. Sick about slavery, the injustices, the cruelty, the 400 plus years of suffering and its "after math" of a slave mentality, which was still prevalent—hanging over our heads like a heavy, dark cloud just waiting to rain down more hell.

But three cups of coffee later, and sharing my own story as to "where" we were, Smiley was sober by the time he got ready to leave. His eyes had softened, and his cheeks blushed as the alcohol drained from his face. He wasn't a bad-looking man; he was rather nice-looking. As he stood up to leave, he gave a warm smile, thanked me, and asked if he could give me a hug. I extended my arms. We embraced.

"I'm so sorry, ma'am, and thank you for bein' here and good luck to you."

As we headed for the front door, Smiley stopped suddenly. "Oh, by the way, I thought you might want these here." Reaching into the inside of his ragged jacket, I couldn't believe what he pulled out. "Here, ma'am . . . me and some of my friends took this off yo property some time back."

My hands trembled as I held it in my hands. Tears swelled without warning, and my knees weakened. I stood there, unable to move, as I meticulously inched my fingers along its surface, surveying every inch of the small, cold **shackles**.

"There was also some bigger ones," he continued. "I think they was used round the neck. The boys that have em said they likes lookin' at em and makin' jokes about em and gettin' a good laugh. I tried to get em to give em to me, so I could give em to ya, but they said they's was gonna keep em."

Still shocked, I tried to slip one of my hands inside one of the locked holes.

"Are there keys?" I asked still trying to force my hand into the past, and yet afraid that the pain would be too unbearable if I felt the weight and confinement of the heavy iron.

"Naw. That's all I have. I ain't seen no kinda key," he solemnly admitted as he watched my tears make their escape. He put his hand on my shoulder and apologized, again. I deeply expressed my gratitude and applauded him for having the balls to come by and express his concerns about "where I was," but more importantly, to return a piece of history that only a descendant of a slave could appreciate.

Being angry with Smiley or his kind, I realized, was a waste of energy. He, like so many others, was a product of his environment–Hatred, based on ignorance. At least now he could form his own opinions about "colored" people. Besides, he must have felt something good about "us," for he could have chosen to be like his friends and kept the symbol that represented four hundred years of "bondage and enslavement"— for a "good laugh." That night was not only proof of my visions for healing, but it was another confirmation as to my *calling*, and another hard reality check as to how much work needed to be done.

I invited Smiley to come back once we opened. However, like the strange sister, I never saw him again. Meanwhile, I continued to trudge through the task at hand.

TWENTY-ONE

Shamed

Trying to keep an unbiased mind about the plight of my people when it came to having to deal with the *powers that be,* often left me checking my own racist meter to make sure it stayed in the area of . . . I *can't hate you because I'm being tested on "love your enemy."* On too many occasions, the spindle swung heavily in the red zones of hatred, anger, frustration. However, it took a *wake-up* call to remind me that the racism and disparity I experienced couldn't hold a candle to what my ancestors went through.

I recall one day when I was having a pity party from being so tired from all the hard work, and the feeling that it was never going to end. I was lying on the floor with weary arms stretched out as if I were being crucified, looking up at the high, monumental ceiling with tears coasting along my cheeks, eventually resting at the corners of my lips, screaming to God . . .

"Why God! Why? I can't do this. Couldn't the ancestors have found someone else?"

Well, somebody heard me whining, and it wasn't God.

"GET UP!"

The voice of a female jolted me. Shocked, I moved slightly — rolling my eyes from side-to-side — checking to see who was there.

"GET UP, I SAY!"

The voice repeated its demand with a sense of urgency and even louder than before. Frozen, I couldn't do anything but listen as she continued.

"You's ain't doin' nothin' child. We's built this place wid our bare hands . . . even made da bricks. You's just doin' sum decoratin'.

Now you's gets up and stop yo whinin."

Her every word vibrated through my entire body. I shuddered with fear and shame, wanting to disappear into the floor like a vapor as the tears continued to flow—only this time out of remorse. I immediately began to cry out loud.

"I am so sorry. Please forgive me."

My words resonated through the empty space as I hoped that the unseen presence heard my plea. I laid lifeless on the floor for a while, breathing in dust particles mixed with tears of humiliation, while ruminating over the horrors of what my ancestors faced on a daily basis for over four-hundred years. Talk about being shamed!

Needless to say, I got my black butt up and diligently went back to my "decoratin."

TWENTY-TWO

A Day with Daisy

I couldn't help but notice Daisy's excitement when she came by the mansion, unexpectedly. Her stomach, at least seven months and counting, she glowed like any seventeen-year-old having her first child. Petite and average height, and wearing an oversized blouse with a wrapped skirt, her pregnancy was becoming. Her skin glowed; she wore no make-up, and her Muslim head-wrap accentuated her slender face. Her once smaller breasts rose to the occasion, doing their part in her metamorphosis.

After greeting her with a hug, I nervously offered to show her around. I hadn't seen her since we left the other location; however, I had heard the news of her pregnancy. After touring the first floor with a little history of each room, I offered to show Daisy the upstairs. She was completely surprised and thrilled with our accomplishments.

"Oh, Miss Nailah, I can't believe it," she exclaimed as we headed upstairs.

"And this is the *Isaac Murphy* Theater, he was the *first* African American Jockey to win three Kentucky Derbies," I proudly announced.

Extending almost the length of the building, the room was one of the largest. In the theme of the Derby, we accented the mustard-colored walls with a deep, brown and gold wallpaper border of horses intermittently breaking their stride with six, ten-feet windows. Continuing the floral design from downstairs, the carpet was throughout, except for the stage, which took up about one-third of the space, but leaving plenty of room for a cabaret-style setting. A beautiful fireplace added a unique ambiance, even though it wasn't usable. We moved awkwardly across the hall as I continued to showcase all our hard work.

"The office, as you can probably tell," I announced.

The dark-stained wooden floors had a different feel from the plush carpet. Though not as comfortable, the solidness and vintage appeal gave a sense of nostalgia. The cracks and crevices held years of sweat and blood from bent-over backs, swollen knees, and rough, red knuckles.

"Here, have a seat," I offered, gesturing her toward a large winged-back, green-patterned chair, accented with a small wooden table and lamp. "How your back feel?"

"Oh, not too bad; it hurts a little. I'm just a little tired. I can't believe what all ya done. It really looks good, Miss Nailah. You and Uncle Vic did real good. Do ya live here, too?" she asked shyly.

"Yeah, we finally got some things over here, so we don't have to keep going to the other house. You feel up to seeing the rest . . . where we live?"

"Yes, ma'am; I probably need to walk more anyway."

She pushed herself up with the aid of the back and the large, round arms. I tried with everything not to give in to the nervousness I felt in the pit of my stomach. I demanded the racing thoughts to go away –to no avail.

"This is a huge kitchen, Miss Nailah. It's got a lot of windows. Are you gonna have a stove or just use the one downstairs?" asking in a way that sounded as if she didn't know what to talk about. Nervous, I suppose. We both were.

"I want one up here, so I won't have to go downstairs when we're not open and when the boys are over. I'll cook up here on my day off; I don't even wanna think about having to go downstairs every day!"

Daisy continued to look around the large space, admiring our work. Looking over to the right, there were two steps that led into a bedroom.

"Is that where you and Uncle Vic sleep?" she asked timidly.

Surprised that she would ask such a question, I walked behind her as she entered "our" bedroom. Standing next to our bed, she rubbed her protruding stomach before sitting on the edge of the bed, running her hand across the two-toned, striped bedspread. I wanted to run–to vomit!

What was wrong with me? How on earth could I talk with her, give her a grand tour as if nothing was wrong, as if her carrying my husband's child was perfectly natural? Yeah, you read right— carrying my husband's child. It took everything I had to keep from grabbing her . . . no, that's not true. I never wanted to grab her or to hurt her in any way. I just wanted one of them... her or Vic to just tell me the truth. Stop the lies!

There were so many times I could tell she wanted me to know. And at the same time, I knew she didn't want to hurt me. I had been like a mom to her. I loved her. I counseled her. I trusted her. What angered me the most was the fact that the times I counseled her about the pitfalls of messing with a married man, I didn't have a clue that the married man she was talking about was my husband.

I began to think about all the times Vic gave her a ride home. Daisy often stayed late to help clean the café after closing. I was usually so tired that I welcomed her help. I thanked God for her love for the café and what it meant to her. She lived her art there. Her rhyme and reason. Some nights I would leave before them, knowing that Vic would make sure she got home, especially if I had the boys. I'd give her and my husband a kiss goodnight, a "thank you," and I'll see you later. Damn! And now, I'm giving her a tour . . . now go figure!

"Look, Daisy, I have to get back to work," I explained, forcing myself to be civil. I couldn't blame her. She was a child. Vic was a grown man.

"Yes, ma'am; I need to be gettin' home anyway. When will Uncle Vic be home?" She couldn't help herself. She had to ask about him.

"He's out buying equipment," I managed to tell her as we walked to the door. "I'll tell him you asked about him. Take care of yourself."

I could only imagine how unbearable it had to be. To pretend that your unborn child belonged to some teenage boy who got lucky one night. We both knew. The look in each other's eyes spoke volumes as I hugged her goodbye. To *hear* it, however, was another feeling altogether, and one I wasn't ready for, but one I needed to be ready for. There needed to be a confession . . . a telling it all . . . But I guess Vic and Daisy never bothered because they knew . . . I knew. However, later that night, I tried one last time to get my husband to admit the agonizing truth, and this time I had some unexpected help.

Flying Saucers

It was late, and Vic and I had finally decided to call it a night. Before we went upstairs, I had mustered up the nerve to ask him to tell me the truth about Daisy's pregnancy. He was standing in the kitchen, while I stood in the doorway of the dishwashing room. An entire room separated us, as my eyes began to swell with tears. I could not hold back the pain any longer; I had to know. I had to hear it from his own mouth.

"Why don't you tell me the truth?" I cried literally. My insides quivered, and my heart was pounding so hard, I could feel it in my ears, in my throat.

"What are you talking about?" He asked, knowing exactly what I meant.

"You know. The baby, it's your baby," my voice wavered from pent-up emotions. "Why do you keep lying to me? You know I can see. You know I have dreams. When I looked at her, I could tell she wanted me to know. Please Vic, just tell me the truth. Daisy is carrying your child."

Standing in front of the pantry looking at me as if I were crazy; as usual, Vic started stuttering as he tried to convince me that I was wrong. Sick and tired of his lies, I walked towards him; wanting to just shake the hell out of him, and to make him tell me the truth. Then suddenly, right before my eyes — before I could take a step, a plate from the pantry bolted past Vic's head—crashing against the wall. Vic stood there, unable to move. His disbelief left him in shock momentarily before realizing what had happened. Looking down at the broken glass, his body trembled. There was no need to *look* to see who may have thrown the plate. He knew no one was there, and so did I.

"See, I told you!" I screamed! "The ancestors know you are lying, and they don't like it!"

Something raised up in my spirit—letting me know that the ancestors knew my pain and that they were on my side. I almost laughed seeing how shaken he was. His eyes were bulging, and obviously nervous, he tried to move past me without showing his urgency. I grabbed his arm and explained again how the ancestors were looking out for me, and that they, too, knew he was lying. Pulling himself from my grip, Vic rushed out through the side door, leaving me with my tears and anguish; however, I was grateful to know that I wasn't alone.

I didn't bother to bring it up again. I was more than convinced of the truth and only hoped that one day he would confess . . . not so much for me, but for himself. Meanwhile, I carried on as if everything was peachy cream, storing my pain in the back of my mind. I had no choice if I were to survive. I had two businesses to get up and running, followed by a trail of debt. And if that wasn't enough . . .

TWENTY-THREE

The Proposal

Trial and error became an everyday occurrence as we serendipitously moved toward the completion of our arduous task. Nevertheless, things were finally looking up. All the labor pains of hopes and foresight for our new home and business were birthing into a reality. Carpet laid, walls painted, and workable plumbing led to our door being opened—at least for Spoken Word–served with a cup of Java or a cold brew.

It must have been around the middle of July, the day my dear friend, Virginia, came by, accompanied by three unfamiliar women. It had been at least six months since we had seen each other. I had officiated her wedding in the Henrietta Marie room a few months earlier. At that time, it was the only room that was finished.

"WOW! I can't believe what you all have done," Virginia exclaimed before turning to her entourage, stopping briefly to introduce us. "Nailah, this is Dr. Schaffer, Mrs. Timber and Miss Riley."

We all did our hello's as I scoped them out. It's not like Virginia was any more racially unbiased than me, but I was curious as to why her associates were all white. They looked harmless. No two-piece suits or briefcases; no vacuum cleaners or insurance pamphlets. However, being that they were all women with large purses, it crossed my mind that maybe they were there to inform me that the "Pink Cadillac Ladies" had branched out to include a new product line for "women of color."

Moving through the various rooms, giving the twenty-five-cent tour, the doctor asserted that she had read some great things about us and the positive effect we were having on the community. Of course, between the ooh's and ahh's, I shared with them a little history of the building and the fact that it was on the ten most endangered list, with the threat of being torn down. Niceties were espoused while heads turned in different directions with necks tilting back to admire the tall ceilings and carved cornices. They were quite impressed and intrigued by its history.

After the tour of the downstairs, Virginia apologized that there was no time to go upstairs . . . that they were on a schedule. I invited them into the Fredrick Douglas Library where we had about an hour of an unforeseeable and unbelievable conversation. I was shocked, to say the least.

"I am honored that you would consider me as the perfect candidate to run for such a prestigious office, but I am completely taken aback. I knew when Virginia brought you here that it had to be of some importance—maybe become a Board member or something on that level. I would have never expected *this* conversation in a million years. I have to bring my husband in on this one."

Excusing myself, I went to the bottom of the stairs to call for Vic, who was upstairs laying our kitchen floor.

"Hey, Vic," I yelled. "Can you come down for a minute? I have something to ask you."

We could see my husband as he descended the stairs. Dressed in some overalls covered with glue and a red bandana, he immediately noticed Virginia and shared his contagious smile. And just as he got to the end of the stairs, I announced. . .

"Hey, baby, Virginia and these ladies here want me run for **Governor**. What do you think?"

"Oh, I think my wife would make a great governor," he announced with a huge grin. Hell, maybe he thought it was a joke. Entering what was previously a debating chamber, Vic spoke to our friend. "Hi, Virginia, long time no see," he announced while giving her a warm hug.

"Hey, Uncle Vic, I know. I've been busy teaching some little knuckleheads. This is Dr. Schaffer, Mrs. Timber, and Miss Riley. They're all with the *Natural Law Party*."

"Pleased to meet you," shaking their hands. "So, you want my wife to run for governor?" Vic asked as if I had been asked to have a bake sale. "That would be great. What's the Natural . . . what did you say the party was?"

Simultaneously, the women proclaimed, "The Natural Law Party." (NLP)

"I tried to tell them Vic, that I'm not political. I hate politics." I stated as if the idea was absurd.

"That's one of the reasons we think you would be great," interjected Miss Riley. "We want someone with principles. What you have accomplished with the youth and your community is a great part of what the Party stands for."

As if I could read Vic's thoughts, I quickly moved the conversation to answer his inquiring mind—why me?

"I have to admit, based on what I've been told today, I do agree with the platform this Party stands for: Self-governance, sustainability, prevention . . . really, they're commonsense laws, and they promote meditation."

"That's right up your alley, baby. You're always meditating," he blurted.

"And we will even train your wife in Transcendental Meditation (TM) if she agrees to run," Dr. Schaffer began to explain. "You see, we want someone who's well known and respected, active in the community, and preferably a business owner. And even more important . . . a woman. Virginia gave us your wife's name, which, by the way, is well known around this city! As I mentioned to your wife, I've been following you both in the papers. I congratulate you on the great things you're doing for the community. And after our conversation with Nailah this afternoon, we believe she's the perfect candidate."

Of course, I jumped in and reminded everyone that we were trying to open our business and finish renovating.

"We understand your concerns as far as having the time," the doctor eagerly interjected as she continued. "I can see you guys have a massive project."

"Yeah, like twenty-two rooms." I quickly reminded the doc.

"But the good thing is, we will do most of the work," continuing her sales pitch. "You will have an entire crew supporting you. We'll raise the money, make the phone calls, and all you'll have to do are a few interviews and a little door-to-door campaigning."

"I don't know. Look, let me pray and meditate on it . . . How much time do I have to decide?"

"Two days," the doctor said, as if to encourage a quick decision.

"You're kidding, right?"

"Well, maybe three days," she offered. "You see, we have to hire an out-of-state crew to collect signatures to get your name on the ballot as an Independent. And, we have only five weeks to get five thousand signatures . . ."

"Five thousand?" I exclaimed. I knew that was almost impossible.

"Yes, then they have to go to Frankfort. Look, I know this is not a lot of time, and I apologize. But we have not been able to find the right candidate... until now."

Adding another two-cents worth, Vic jumped on the sales team.

"Hey, baby, we're almost done with the downstairs. I think you can do it if they're willing to do most of the work."

"So, are you saying that if you don't get the five thousand signatures, I can't run?"

"That's right—we won't be able to go on the ballot."

Um-um, maybe that will be my way out, I thought to myself.

"Okay, call me Monday. I really need to sleep on this."

The doctor then reached in her purse and got a pen and a small notebook. "Mrs. Yarbrough, you will be doing The Natural Law Party and this state a great service if you do this . . . your number?"

"Well, we'll see." I gave her the number to the café and the best time to reach me. I had two meetings on Monday and an application to complete and mail for our 501-C 3 status, for the Harriet Tubman Cultural Center. Already time was becoming a major issue. Nevertheless, we all hugged while agreeing to talk on Monday evening after seven.

Caught Off Guard

I didn't think much about the offer over the weekend. Neither had I taken the time to meditate. Besides the obvious work that kept us busy, I felt the whole thing was a bit far-fetched. Not that I *couldn't* be governor, but having the time to do it and getting over five thousand signatures was the concern.

The phone rang. It was precisely seven-thirty; Dr. Schaffer was right on schedule. Bypassing any long, drawn-out conversation, the doc got straight to the point: "So if you don't mind, I can come by in about an hour and give you more details on the process and get your signature to move forward."

"Okay, Dr. Schaffer, I'll see you soon," I begrudgingly agreed.

Hanging up the phone, I sensed a surge of urgency... almost a panic. Realizing that I had not sought any guidance, I sat down, took a few deep breaths, and began to pray and call on the help of my ancestors. I stood there for a moment or two, comprehending the fact that I was about to make a decision that would not only be historical, but MORE WORK.

The knock at the door brought me back to the present. It was Dr. Schaffer. Forty-five minutes had passed, and it actually felt as if it were ten.

"I asked for a sign," I announced to the doc. "I told the ancestors that I needed a sign so as to know what to do."

Dr. Schaffer looked on with an intensity, raising her brows, forming tiny wrinkles on her forehead. She was an attractive, plain-looking, petite woman with a low-maintenance short hairstyle. Her persona, strong and assertive, was guided by a humbleness as we sat and spoke for two hours. Our conversation covered more than either one of us could have anticipated. I learned that she wanted to leave her practice as a dermatologist and plastic surgeon and move to the country. Getting away from a hectic lifestyle would give her more time with her two small daughters. And since I hadn't shared with her about "the dream" during our first meeting, I figured I would give a quick synopsis of my mission.

"Look, I know you may be wondering what the heck I'm talking about when I say that I need to 'get a sign' from the ancestors. It's rather hard to explain, but I started having dreams about this building a couple of years ago, which eventually led to a mission... not only to purchase and renovate this building, but to help free a few trapped souls who have been unable to move from this dimension."

While my doctor friend continued to look perplexed, she nodded from time-to-time as if to understand what I was talking about. However, I knew it was a hard pill to swallow, but I continued.

"And because of this mission, I meditate and communicate with those who have 'crossed-over' to get clarity from time-to-time on what to do in any particular situation . . . such as this one."

"So, have you gotten a sign?"

She eagerly asked, trying to get back to what was important to *her* mission . . . getting me to run for governor.

"Well, to be quite honest, I haven't taken the time to really inquire as to what I should do."

Looking rather pensive and not quite sure what to say, I knew that an answer to her question (had I gotten a sign) was all she wanted to hear. "Look," I continued with some assurance. "If you raise the five thousand, plus signatures to get me on the ballot, I'll run for governor. That will be my sign."

"Well, Nailah," finally smiling. "I know that we'll get those 5,500 signatures. Get ready, you're about to become the first African American, male or female, in Kentucky's history, as a Gubernatorial candidate."

The Petitioner

It was shortly before the canvassing was to begin when Dr. Schaffer came by the mansion to introduce the four out-of-state young white men who had been assigned as my petitioners. They all beamed with enthusiasm while shaking my hand, and each vowing to do all they could to assure enough signatures to get me on the ballot. Completely overwhelmed with what was happening, and admittedly filled with a little anxiety, I thanked them in advance for working to get me on the ballot. From that day forward, each one drove, walked, or biked across the state of Kentucky soliciting on my behalf. And although I didn't really see much of them once the canvassing started, one day I received a surprise visit.

Summer was making its debut while the June sun danced upon the dark green blades of fresh, cut grass. Rich, pink, blossomed Dogwoods lined the back corners of the yard. It had been three weeks since the canvassing had begun, and I was planting some Tulips when I heard a somewhat familiar voice behind me.

"Miss Nailah," the voice spoke my name with excitement.

I turned suddenly, trying not to be startled.

"Do you have any idea how many people know you?"

"Who's that? I can't see you," I asked, shielding my eyes with my gloved hand. And with the sun blinding me, I couldn't recognize the young man.

"Oh, sorry, Miss Nailah, it's Jake. We talked a few weeks ago. I came by with a few other petitioners to introduce myself."

Jake grabbed my left hand, helping me to my feet. With one eye half closed, I could finally see his familiar face.

"Oh yeah, I remember. How's it going?"

He was a lanky, average height young man, kinda cute, too. His thick, blonde wavy hair fell over his left ear, while the other side was cut close to the scalp. His perfectly straight white teeth (probably from wearing braces most of his life) glistened from the sun as he spoke. His eyes were soft and friendly.

"My God, everybody knows you," he continued. "I've been all over this state, and everybody I talked to knew about you and The Java House." He beamed with perplexity.

"Oh yeah, think we might get the numbers we need?" I inquired somewhat nervous. Of course, I was still thinking or maybe hoping, deep down that the numbers would fall short.

"The way it's going, it looks good. You must be pretty cool. In all my time doing this type of work, I've never seen this much excitement and enthusiasm before. Some folks wanted to know if they could sign twice," he announced rather vivaciously.

I smiled with bewilderment and took a deep breath as the haunting thought flashed across my mind—My God, what if. Jake and I chatted for a few more minutes after offering him a lemonade. It was hot and humid, but Jake didn't seem to mind as he scurried off. His excitement was contagious, although not really warranted. Just the thought of adding more to my plate was cause for panic. Hell, we weren't even open yet.

TWENTY-FOUR

Seeking the Good

Spoken Word was up and running. It didn't matter that the kitchen wasn't serving up some old favorites, as long as there was a mic and some lemon iced tea, the Harriet Tubman room was filled to its capacity for a Saturday night of spittin' lyrics, crooning a tune, or camouflaging your voice to spit out the latest beats. It was on.

The word had also gotten out to The Java House family that I might be running for governor. There was excitement as well as the unspoken tune of . . . who do you think you are playing in the background of forced smirks and half felt hugs. Not only had I facilitated a business that had become a household word, but now I had the *audacity* to consider running for the highest, political office in the state. How dare I!

Being the subject of sidebar criticism was not new to me. "How dare I" was becoming a norm in many of the conversations that took place at local beauty salons, small and mega churches, as well as some family members who thought that NOT selling fried chicken or pork swimming in greens was an unadulterated sin and a disgrace to the African American community. Oh well, back to what's really important.

Just when I thought things were falling into place, with the inside at least, we learned that one of the double-door refrigerators didn't work, as well as one of the double ovens we bought from a guy who sold used restaurant equipment. Not willing to replace or exchange the equipment, (let alone give some of our money back) it became evident that virtue was not one of this man's qualities. But we had to keep it moving.

Damn! It's hard when you're running your own shit. If it wasn't one thing, it was ten. Making things happen on a "shoestring budget" can be a bitch. And if I wasn't praying to somebody—be they ancestors, angels or deities, I could not have moved forward in what was becoming more and more challenging.

While renovations on the inside were pretty much under control, the roof over the upstairs kitchen had started *raining on my parade,* which was causing damage not only to the ceiling but to the floor as well. With the help of a friend, we went onto the roof and patched several areas with hot tar. Plus, I was trying to get the outside of the building painted before we opened. Vic was afraid of heights, so that part of the renovation (painting the outside building) was on me, as well. I personally did over 90% of the painting inside as well, so as to free up the guys to do the heavier work, like building stages and putting in new ceilings and moving extremely heavy equipment. Even though many times I felt like I could do *anything* a man was capable of doing, Super Woman, I was not!

As I stood in the center of the café, admiring its purple walls and white trim, I smiled at the makeshift stage that framed a large wall along with huge speakers and a stand-up microphone. I couldn't help but reflect on the past year as I continued my walk through the downstairs area. At least looking at our accomplishments, I'd hope it would deter the frustration that was slowly building into another moment of asking, "Why me?"

There was the *library,* which we named after *Fredrick Douglass,* a free man and the first African American to speak at a Presidential Inauguration (Lincoln's) that sat to the left when you entered the front door. The mint green walls with white trimming, adorned with reflections of African culture, outlined a replica of an antique sofa that faced an original marbled fireplace, and where a hand-drawn picture of Douglass looked over the room.

In the next room, leading from the library, was the brightly orange-colored *Amistad* room, named after the ship of the slave uprising in 1839. Appealing to those who just wanted to chill with a cup of Java or something stronger, this room was warm and cozy with a small, overstuffed love seat and an old-style coffee table. The walls were decorated with a small, hand-carved wooden slave ship and wooden plaques of the famous statement by *Malcolm X, "By Any Means Necessary."* Malcolm X was an African American Leader and a prominent member of the Nation of Islam.

Off from the *Amistad* room was an actual vault. The door leading to the mid-size space was made of cast iron. Once inside, the fourteen-inch-thick concrete walls were lined with metal shelves. An original *Wells Fargo* safe with faded letters and an ornate design barely showed through the rusty black finish. The door, which stayed open so as not to lock (we didn't have the key) must have been at least eight inches thick. One could imagine stacks of Confederate money, along with gold and silver coins that once filled the cold slots of various sizes. After putting in more bookshelves, loaded with books donated by a school, the *Vault,* as we called it, served as a children's library and storage room.

After leaving the *Vault,* and as I continued to roam from one room to the next, a sadness invaded my thoughts, along with a deep longing to cry out to the walls that were forcing me to remember the cold, bare and neglected state they were in before the fresh coverup. I then walked out to the newly carpeted hallway and walked toward the front entrance. The room on the left, *The Henrietta Marie* (a slave ship) was the only room downstairs besides the hallway and stairs, that had carpet. Its dark green background with a deep, colorful floral print looked period. It fit right in with the antiques and old furnishings. The *Henrietta Marie's* walls were painted an unusual color, which came with a unique story.

One day while meditating, I was given instructions on what colors to paint in what would become the Henrietta Marie, formal dining room. I was shown that there were two fireplaces once, which were replaced with walls, leaving a deep space surrounding the concave windows where we built a stage. I was told that because of all the rapes and killings that took place in the cellar below, I was to commemorate those who died and shed their blood. I was instructed to paint the two fireplace walls a deep, reddish brown to give the appearance of old blood, while the rest of the walls were to be painted a pale purple to signify a life that was once royal and free.

Although the rooms were enlivened with bright, vibrant colors, I could still smell the blood . . . hear their stories, while their souls pleaded for a long overdue freedom. I could feel their presence watching me . . . us, as we brought back a semblance of how it used to be.

TWENTY-FIVE

Running for Governor

The phone call was unexpected — or when I least expected it. Time was moving so quickly, I had forgotten that several people were out canvassing the state of Kentucky to get me on the ballot as a candidate for governor.

"Nailah, we did it!" the voice of Dr. Schaffer was almost screaming, which was far from her usual composure. "We got the signatures to get you on the ballot!" she continued ecstatically.

I must have stopped breathing. Finally, her voice paused long enough to realize that I had not responded.

"Did you hear me? You are running for governor."

Forcing a chuckle and taking a deep breath, I finally responded. "Wow! You're kidding, right? How short were we? There's no way we got close to six thousand signatures. What's it been, three, four weeks?"

"Nailah, we got 7, 755 signatures! More than enough! I knew we could do it! There are a lot of people out there that know of you, and what you're doing," she joyously declared.

"Wow!" was the only word I managed to say while fumbling around my immediate area for a place to flop. My legs jellied. My stomach sunk as the harsh reality of doing everything that needed to be done with the renovations AND run for governor caused huge beads of sweat to sprout around my forehead. I was approaching panic.

"Uh, so what happens now?" I managed to ask with a sense of composure.

"Well, we have to start preparing to campaign," Dr. Schaffer eagerly continued. "There's a lot to be done..."

"But..." I interjected. However, before I could finish expressing my fears, talking a mile a minute, Dr. Schaffer ranted on.

"And don't you worry, like I told you before, you will have plenty support. Our team will do most of the legwork. You will primarily have to be available for interviews and do some canvassing. Oh, I'm so excited, Nailah. I know you're going to make the Natural Law Party very proud of you. Look, I have to run now and start getting things together. I'll call you tomorrow."

Before I could even say good-bye, the dial tone ended our conversation.

The next couple of months were a combination of upstairs renovations, cooking, canvassing, preparing for a wedding (which I was to officiate), and trying to keep up with the current events by reading the newspaper and listening to the news like never before. Never in a million years did I think that I ever would be in politics. I had little or no respect for those in political office, and to find myself being scrutinized and analyzed by reporters was something I was to get used to, like it or not. Meanwhile, the harsh reality of managing a business was taking precedence.

It felt good being able to hire a staff. Although paying wages was scary, it had to be done. I had been making the mortgage payments along with the renovation expenses from the construction loan. I missed the money from school, but my life was more important than a few extra dollars–that is, if I was going to run two businesses and now run for governor . . . I had to keep living.

Damn, how did politicians do it? I was used to having photographers around because of the café. And when I could, I made sure Vic was the one posing for the pictures. However, this go-round, I was the face plastering the newspapers and television, along with numerous radio interviews. One radio announcer blasted over the airwaves: "She wears a nose ring! She's against growing tobacco and espouses that growing Hemp would be a better replacement. What will the farmers think about that one?"

Of course, these questions and comments were a drop in the bucket compared to what was to come. Nonetheless, I had answers!

I never read the newspaper that much in my life. There was never any "good" news as far as I was concerned; however, it was imperative that I was knowledgeable about the various political stances that were being argued. . . which candidate was saying what. In order to "stand" for what the NLP supported, I needed to be well prepared for the big, televised debate at the end of the year.

My newly found political journey was arduous, to say the least. I felt pulled in several different directions for the next few months. The campaigning took me through various parts of Kentucky—at least half of its 120 counties. I was amazed by the support, especially from the younger generation. I had the honor of walking and talking with many of them as they shared their concerns of hopelessness. No matter what the race, our youths were crying out for a chance at the *pursuit of happiness.*

Although I was supported by most of the African American community, there were many that were appalled that I would have the audacity to run for such a high office, while many from *other* communities thought I was a *breath of fresh air* to the arena of politics. Honesty, integrity and commonsense had been a long time coming, and the Natural Law Party espoused just that — A platform that called us to self-governance, proven educational programs, holistic health care, renewable energy, sustainable agriculture, and other forward-looking, prevention-oriented programs. The Java House Café/Harriet Tubman Cultural Center and the Natural Law Party shared many commonalities.

Although the first of my race to run for such an esteemed political position, I somehow didn't really see it as a *big* deal. My question was *why* was I the *first?* I had a strong suspicion that the ancestors had their hands in this aspect of my career, as well.

TWENTY-SIX

Certificate of Occupancy

It had been a long, hard and arduous road getting as far as we had with the mansion. Many of those who promised their support fell by the wayside. However, thank God for a few true friends and supporters, as well as those family members who thought I was out of my mind, but were there pushing me on in support of the vision. Then there were those that dropped out of the picture after a few months of lending a major helping hand, like Shorty and Larry, who taught me a lot about being a contractor, as well as working like Hebrew slaves, themselves. There were also the other folks who dropped in on occasions, taking out trash, sweeping, or just there to keep me company. And I can't forget an ex-boyfriend of mine, Albert. He came through so many times, offering his handyman skills for the price of materials (or free), that there was no way we could have made it through without him.

Without a doubt, if it were not for the few men and women who supported us in bringing the dream to a reality, it would have been virtually impossible for us to have made the progress we did during the past year. And although we had our problems, my husband worked harder than anyone else — in the snow, heat, and the rain.

I recall one night in particular. It was cold and raining. Vic and I were in our rain gear. With shovel in hand and boots up to his knees, Vic continued shoveling the hole he had started earlier that day. I held the flashlight and a broken umbrella while he dug another three feet into the muddy terrain. We both tried to stay positive as we occasionally muttered our disdain for the lousy work that had been done by the previous plumber. And in order to save money after hiring the new plumber, we had to do most of the work to facilitate the new water pipes that had to be installed. It's amazing how we both managed to stay focused on the work, despite the fact that our marriage was falling apart. Vic was a hard worker. That I couldn't take from him. Working together, we had come a long way. Thank you, God!

The kitchen had slowly manifested into a working, commercial kitchen with a touch of home. Handmade curtains with tiebacks hung over pull-up windows and a partially glass door that led to a long, back porch with a cast-iron grill for smoking turkeys. Working refrigerators, a grill, and an eight-burner stove (with one working oven) set evenly under an overhead industrial hood with fans and fire extinguishers. Pots and pans, working tables, a slightly rusted-edged steam table camouflaged with floral, patterned contact paper, and a heavy-duty microwave made it ready for the return of the famous "Mr. T" and the seductive "Java House Café lemon iced tea."

Although the floral contact paper cost us one point, which we were encouraged to keep, we were proud of our 99% rating from the Board of Health. With just a couple of weeks past our target date to open, we were now ready to do some cooking! Grateful for everyone's time, love, and hard work in getting us to the point of a "Certificate of Occupancy," Vic and I were finally able to move into our new home... legally, that is. It had been rough! But we had made it.

Things were a little slow for the first couple of weeks, and we made no effort to advertise. For me, *slow*...was good. I was completely exhausted. However, Vic seemed to always stay *up* and be ready to go. Eventually, through word of mouth, business picked up, and that was good... and very good... until...

TWENTY-SEVEN

Tragedy Strikes

It was our first Spoken Word since we had opened "officially." It had taken a year and two months of blood, sweat, and tears, literally. And now the melody of lyrics from songs to poetry was sweeping through the freshly painted rooms and hallways on that mid-September eve. Drumbeats and jazz CDs vibrated with each poem and song, with finger snapping and foot stomping. The energy was high and intoxicating. The Tubman room was so packed that customers spilled into two other rooms, which meant spreading out the speakers so that everyone could hear.

Although my day had already been long and tiring, the exhilaration from the crowd was contagious. I worked that night, dancing through crowded tables and slipping through bodies that crammed any free space. For the first time in a year, The Java House Café sandwiches and lemon iced tea were again ravaged with the familiar sounds of finger-licking, lip-smacking delight. While the "Grand-Opening" was still a few weeks away, the power of the *word* had us back in business, and I must admit, it felt great to witness the excitement of the Spoken Word again.

By the time 2:00 a.m. rolled around, I damn near had to make people go home. Even Vic was starting to feel the wear and tear of an outrageously wonderful night. He, too, had to strongly encourage folks to leave. Even when everyone was out the door, it took at least another hour for some to leave the parking lot. I was beat and ready to crawl into bed, and of course, my dear friend, pain showed its ugly head—big time.

Wired, I grabbed my book on *Angels and Life After Death* with the hope of falling asleep faster. As of late, I had found myself reading books on the subject more than usual. It was the second book on the subject I had gotten from the library in the past couple of weeks. It was soothing to find that there was life after death . . . not that I didn't already believe that, after all, I was listening and obeying Spirits that had crossed over for some time now. However, the books I was reading had a more mystical and alluring perspective; death wasn't so... morbid.

As I was about to doze off, the telephone rang. "Who the hell can that be this time of night ... or morning?" I slurred out loud.

Vic was still downstairs cleaning, so I had no choice but to get up and get it myself.

"Maybe someone left their purse or keys or something," I thought, staggering to the kitchen.

"Hello. Yes, this is she."

"Hi, Miss Nailah, this is Jean, Jenia's friend," she said rather softly.

It was only around 11:30 p.m. California time, so I didn't think too much about it. However, I was a little surprised that my daughter had Jean to call me.

"Is Jenia all right?"

There was silence for a moment.

"It's Mark! Miss Nailah."

"Mark? What's wrong . . . what happened?"

For a moment, I thought he did one of his running away tactics. He was seventeen and swore to be in love.

"Is he in trouble? Did he run away, again?"

"Miss Nailah, there was an accident."

There was a disturbing pause before she managed to continue.

"Mark is dead!"

To repeat the word dead, and to make sure I heard her right, wouldn't or couldn't come from my trembling lips. I have no idea how much time passed before I could speak. I kept hearing her say my name, but nothing came from my mouth until finally... "Where's my daughter... where's Jenia? Is she all right?"

Of course, I couldn't fathom how dumb that question was, but I asked anyway.

"She's not so good, Miss Nailah. There's a few of her church members here; we're praying with her. She keeps asking for you. She wants you to come and to let her brothers know. Can you get here, soon? She's in bad shape!"

"Tell my baby, I'm on my way. I don't know how long . . . just tell her, I'm on my way."

After I hung up the phone, I felt as if my entire stomach came up in my throat. My heart raced; my legs gave way to the cold floor that took the weight of my body as I cried out... beating the floor . . . "NO! NO! NO! Oh, my God! My baby, my baby. Oh, Jenia! Mark, no, this can't be true . . . you can't be gone!"

Suddenly, I heard his voice.

"Grandma, I'm all right. I'm all right. Stop crying. Please stop crying . . . I'm all right."

I lifted my head and looked around, hoping that somehow, I had imagined all this, and that Mark was truly all right. However, everything in my body and soul told me otherwise. I knew, my first grandchild was—gone! And the pain was—indescribable!

Vic must have heard me screaming. He came into the kitchen to find me on the floor. Confused and concerned, he asked me what was wrong as he bent down to help me up. I couldn't move. My legs wouldn't work, and my breath escaped me. He grabbed me under the arms and assisted me to a nearby chair. I slumped into his chest as he bent down to hold me; his chest rising and falling as if breathing life back into my body. Finally, somehow the words fell from my mouth. Mark . . . Mark is dead. Vic slowly raised himself up, dropping his head as he allowed himself to let go of the agony. His cry echoed my pain as he fell down to his knees to embrace my stiff body. There were no more words for either of us. We sat. We cried. We sat. We cried.

Time moved like a snail. I'm not sure how or when, but I managed to call both my sons. I thanked God that they both only lived less than a couple hours away in Indiana. I can't remember what happened during the time before they got there, or even once they got there. I just remember more crying and more pain, and trying to figure out a way to get to my daughter. My youngest son at the time worked for a major corporation, and we used his corporate credit card to book an emergency flight.

When we got to the airport, the lady at the counter checked our reservations. Looking rather stunned, she looked at us and announced that the doors had been shut and that we could not get on the flight. We knew we were not late, so she apologized, admitting that the plane had taken off a little early. As dazed as I was, I must have panicked! All I can remember is screaming: "YOU HAVE GOT TO GET ME TO MY CHILD!" The next thing I knew, they had made arrangements for another flight and got someone to drive us to the next gate since it was already boarding.

The non-stop flight was vague, but I recall that an attendant offered complimentary wine to help calm me down. I was a wreck! The only semblance of any comfort was being in both my sons' arms, as they both tried to keep their own emotions together enough to be my strength. Within nine hours from the time I received the phone call, my two sons and I had landed in Fresno, California.

Other than a somber greeting, the ride from the airport was quiet. Ronnie, my son-in-law, was just as grief-stricken, and none of us were able to really have a conversation. Riding along, the early morning had given way to scattered streetlights that lined the quaint neighborhood, while my mind drifted in and out of the whys and hows of the tragic news. My grandson, dead at seventeen! What was I going to say? How was I to help ease my daughter's pain . . . a pain that I, too, understood all too well? Although my "other" daughter, who died over thirty years earlier at the age of two from an acute pancreatitis, the unforgettable pain took residence in the deepest part of my heart and soul. Never to be forgotten!

"How's my baby, Ronnie?" I finally asked.

Jenia was the oldest of the three, but she was still my baby, as were all my children.

"She's doing as well as expected."

I don't recall any more of the conversation that may have taken place before we drove into a driveway, in which a front porch light was still on from the night before. Curtains covered a bay window where manicured shrubbery and patches of familiar flowers laid underneath. We followed my son-in-law as he led the way into a small, dim lit hallway, where we were immediately greeted with the muffled sounds of deep-seated moans and supplication. I felt numb and lifeless as my sons held my hands, while following Ronnie to a darkened, back bedroom. The bed, encircled with several women bowed down in prayer, was the first thing my eyes adjusted to from a dim-glowing lamp, taking in a panoramic view of hips in various sizes. Most were wide and thick, while a few fell within the slim category. That's when I saw her.

Although it had been a couple of years since I had seen my child, I recognized her body at once. I knelt down beside her as my sons stood behind me.

"Jenia..." I whispered.

I called my daughter's name a second time before she heard me. My sons then knelt down behind me while laying their hands on our shoulders. She stood without speaking, slumping into my arms.

The supplication had heightened while some *spoke in tongues* and others sang one-liner hymnals, which only intensified the horrific pain that had no place to hide. My screams of *why* only rang loud in my spirit. I had to be strong. I couldn't give in to the desire to fall apart, to curse God and denounce all I ever believed. No, this was not the time. My daughter desperately needed me to be strong; she was on the edge. Shattered, dismayed, and filled with unadulterated anger, I knew deep within that God was the ONLY ONE that could give me the strength to get us through–the Only One!

Through the grace of God, we were finally able to get Jenia to go to bed. I suppose that's when I fell asleep as well, for the next thing I heard was . . .

"Grandma, grandma."

The tiny voices spoke in unison as they rushed into the bedroom. Lined alongside the twin bed like stair-steps, were Iniah, Johnathan, Kamonnie and Siarra; their ages ranging from eight to one and a half (Jenia's friend, Jean had taken them to her house the night before, where they spent the night with her two children). Smothered with hugs and kisses, I temporarily forgot the pain that laid heavy upon my heart. I only felt the presence of—love! What a joy!

Bill, my first husband and my children's father, whom I hadn't seen for quite a while, flew in the next day. Like my sons, Bill lived out of town and had also remarried a few years earlier. He went with our sons to identify Mark's body. There was no way that either Jenia or I could take that final look; no way we could acknowledge the fact that he would never be around again. Even the thought—was unbearable.

The next few days were difficult, although we all managed to grab what joy we could, when we could. The children made it a lot easier to keep going as they ran around the house; not fully understanding that their big brother would no longer be around to play hide-and-seek with them; to tickle them until they begged for mercy or to discipline them the only way a big brother could. They couldn't quite understand the constant tears that flowed from their mother's eyes, or why she screamed out Mark's name in the middle of the night, or why she never wanted to leave the bed.

Soon the questions would come — ones that would lead to the storytelling of Mark going to heaven and becoming an Angel. Questions that would lead to answers that only brought uninvited tears along with hope that one day Mark would come back and play with them, again. No one knew that in the coming years, the memories that were stored in their hearts and minds would one day be released, bringing confusion and anger. But for now, the story of being an Angel and being with God was their protection from a devastating reality. And even greater than that . . . to them, Mark was still around.

It was at the breakfast table when Kamonnie saw Mark. Jenia was standing up, eating from a plate of food brought over by a church member, when Kamonnie exclaimed, "Momma. Der's Mark, momma; he's eatin' off yo plate." She had just turned four years old a month earlier, as she rose from her seat, pointing toward her mom. That's when Siarra, the baby, bounced up and down in her booster chair, echoing her sister, and calling out Mark's name. I could tell it was hard for Jenia.

Mark's father and grandmother got there a day before the funeral. It was good to see them. Big Mark, as we called him, looked different. He had gained weight, quite different from the slender young man I had known seventeen years earlier. While my grandson wasn't a junior, he had his father's name, first and last. Mrs. McElroy hadn't changed much, and I could tell that losing her first grandchild was no less unbearable. We cried together, sharing memories of our grandson as a toddler while living in San Francisco and Oakland, which is where she and her son still lived. *Big* Mark managed to be strong and supportive for his son's mother, while his distant eyes carried a pain that we all shared.

There's no such thing as a *good* funeral. However, Jenia's minister, a young man who had moved into the high rank as Bishop, delivered a message so powerful and beautiful, that to show a glimmer of joy was no challenge. Somehow—somewhere deep within, we were able to find comfort in accepting that Mark had gone home.

On the way back from the funeral, Curtis, my youngest and a minister, sat next to me in the limo. Holding my hands, he quietly asked, "Mom, how do you do it? How do you find the words to give my sister comfort? I'm a minister, and I have not been able to console her; the words have not come; and yet, you seem to have the perfect words at the right time. How can you be so strong and in control?"

I looked at him and smiled, giving him the ONE and ONLY answer there was—GOD!

The following day after the funeral, my sons and Bill left early, while Big Mark and his mother stayed until late evening, since they only had to drive to Oakland. It was hard to see everyone leave; however, there were jobs and responsibilities to get back to. I knew I couldn't leave, not yet. I knew I had to be with my child at least a few more weeks before she would be able to find some strength to keep going. So, I called Vic and told him to tell the couple whose wedding I was to officiate the following week that they would have to get someone else, and to offer my apology. It would take some time to get Jenia to try to get back to a life; to go back to her college classes; to comb hair and give baths without falling apart every few minutes. And I was grateful to God for giving me the strength to be there for her.

As with their two children, Ronnie had spiritual gifts, too. He was not a seer like Kamonnie and Siarra, but he could *hear* Mark, who began to speak to his mother through him. Ronnie had served as his father for the past five years, as well as to his sister and brother from a previous marriage. He became a conduit for Mark to speak to his mom; and one day, I was there to witness a message first-hand.

Jenia's grief left her immobilized at times, and this particular day as Ronnie lay next to her in bed, trying to calm her uncontrollable wailing, I noticed a strange look come over his face. He moved closer to my daughter and began to speak, real softly. *"Tell momma that if she believes in God the way she says she does, then she should know that God does not make mistakes. Tell her I am free, and that I can go around the world quicker than I can say the words. And tell her I love her and will always be around her."*

Being able to *hear* Mark's message, a calm came over my daughter as she stared at her husband. It was a look that I cannot explain, particularly since she had just been crying uncontrollably.

"Okay, okay." My child whispered. "Tell Mark, okay." A few moments later, she was sound asleep.

The Final Night

During the time with my child, we talked about my grandson's final hours. It all started when Jenia and Ronnie took in a young, beautiful lady who had been in Foster Care with another family. However, since she had just turned eighteen and pregnant, she was asked to leave. Since Jenia worked in social services, and the young lady had no place to go, she and her husband decided to take her in until they were able to help her find her own apartment. During this time of living in my daughter's home, Mark, became completely infatuated with this young woman.

On this particular night, the young woman had borrowed a friend's rented car, who was visiting some friends in town. She asked if Mark could go out with her for a drive. Ronnie told Mark that he couldn't go — that he had to stay home with the kids while he went out for a short period. However, once the kids were asleep—and with the expectation of Jenia coming home soon from her night classes at school, he decided to *sneak out.* Unfortunately, that one night of being disobedient put Ronnie in a position that he probably could have never imagined –forwarding messages from Mark's *spirit,* in hopes to bring a little comfort to his grieving mother.

I'm sure, at some point, Ronnie must have asked himself, *what if he hadn't left . . . maybe Mark would still be alive?* We all asked, *what if.* What if Jenia hadn't taken in the young woman who had no place to go. What if Mark hadn't fallen in love with her, even though pregnant with another man's child. And on the last night of his life, w*hat if* the young woman had STOPPED at the stop sign — avoiding the oncoming *Exposition SUV* — killing Mark, instantly!

However, with all the "what if's," only God knew why my grandson departed this earthly realm on September 19, 1999. And despite the horrendous grief we were all feeling, we were truly grateful that the young woman and her unborn son (who had to be delivered through a cesarean birth) were spared, virtually unharmed.

TWENTY-EIGHT

Lights, Camera, Action

After two more emotional weeks with my daughter and grandchildren, getting back home was no relief. The race to the governor's seat was quickly moving towards the finish line. The televised debate was getting closer, and I was beginning to feel like a turtle trying to win a race with three rabbits. I had been through a lot over the past year, and some family members thought I should bail out, which I understood. But when one of my opponents tried to *buy* me out to acquire my votes, I was bent on finishing, no matter what happened or how busy I was. I had to stay in the running; there were people depending on me, which reminded me of a newspaper article that was written by an African American, female reporter. She had made a negative comment about my running for governor . . . "*as to why or how did I think I had a chance of winning.*" However, she changed her tune once she interviewed a young black female, a high school graduate who was voting for the first time.

"The fact that Miss Nailah Jumoke-Yarbrough is running for governor as the first African American in Kentucky's history has shown me that I can do whatever I desire in life. She is my inspiration." As a first-time voter, she also stated that she looked forward to casting her first vote for me. It was then that the reporter realized that whether I had a chance of winning or not was not as important as my fulfilling my "right" to run. She then wrote a public apology stating that she made a mistake in her judgment.

Newspapers, quotes, magazine articles and every argument that had been made during the past few months, covered my California King bed. Highlighted views and opinions were transcribed to a large, yellow writing pad to focus on the areas that I thought would be asked during the debate. And yet, I reminded myself that the most important thing was to *speak my truth*. However, I also knew that our government had not always relied on *truth, common sense* or what was best for the *whole*.

Uncle Vic and our scant employees worked extra hours during my absence. Being back was almost like I was still gone. I barely had time to keep the books, shop, or create programming for the Harriet Tubman Cultural Center. I was now public property with last-minute impromptu interviews; my time was not my own. But then again, what else was new?

My husband was being – different. He was supportive in ways he hadn't been in months. Since my return, he stayed home more; no more late night rendezvouses. For the time being, our problems were put on hold. No more talk about the baby; no need for lies about his whereabouts when he came in with the sun. We went to bed together, and just being able to put my arm across his body, my estranged desire for intimacy resurfaced . . . only to be tucked back into its dwelling place.

With everything I needed to do, meditation and my spiritual practices were still a major factor in keeping some sense of control or balance in my frantic life. Taking a quick trip to the river to make an offering was occasionally squeezed in on my way to the market. Candles were picked up from a local botanical shop, and prayer requests were made from a few stolen moments on the telephone. I needed spiritual support — more than ever.

Prep for the Camera

It had been a long time since I had been in a television studio. Vic and I had become local celebrities and had been invited to do a few cooking demonstrations and interviews on two local stations, which were fun and great for business. The Java House was the newest and hottest spot in the city, with some of the best sandwiches in town. However, the Public Broadcast Station was no cooking show, unless you consider having me on the hot seat as an entree.

As I entered the makeup room, I was wearing a T-shirt and jeans. The young, vibrant artist enthusiastically spoke and grabbed a cape to put around my shoulders as I sat before a large mirror.

"Now let me try and match the colors you're wearing," she announced.

"Did you think that I was wearing this?" pulling at my T-shirt. "Are you kidding? Look, I'm already wearing a nose ring, and you may have noticed that my hairstyle isn't your standard look for politicians."

She smiled as I immediately got up and went to the other room where I had my suit. "This is what I'm wearing," raising up the plastic covering, displaying a two-piece, button-down mauve-tone ensemble (which my mother bought for me), along with a deep brown velvety, pull-over hat.

"Oh, that's beautiful, and are you wearing the hat as well?"

"Yep," I answered. "I'm going to pull my hair back so as to not bring unnecessary attention to my African twist. Believe me, wearing a nose ring is creating enough buzz."

"Well, let's get started," she insisted. "We don't have much time before the cameras will be rolling."

Once the foundation was applied and the cheeks were blushed with color, the young artist scanned a palette of eye colors.

"Do you mind if I use eyeshadow"?

"No, not at all," I responded. "Make me look beautiful for the camera."

"This color will look nice and bring out your eyes," she stated with confidence. She continued my makeover by lining my lips and adding a soft, neutral color. She then asked to see my hat so that she could style my hair accordingly. Within five minutes, hairpins and a little hairspray transformed my African, carefree hairstyle into a tamed French bun. It didn't take much time to get dressed, and after a few minutes of adjusting my skirt and cocking my hat to the side . . . just right, I was looking candidate-appropriate. However, I had one more important thing to do –- I had to find a quiet place to pray.

The bathroom was empty; the perfect place to sit and be quiet, and there was no one but me. I first admired my conservative style, which I had not seen in quite a while. No jeans, T-shirt, tennis shoes, or scarves tied around my head. I felt attractive and professional. I looked pretty darn good—hat and all.

My conversation with God was straight and to the point. "Look, God," I started. "You got me into to this running for governor, and while I understand the message that needs to be heard throughout this state, I still don't know why I was chosen as the messenger. But here I am—here WE are about to go on public television for all of Kentucky to see, and WE cannot make a fool of ourselves. I need YOU to take over and speak **through** me. My ego will remain in the bathroom stall while YOU go out and do Your thing. I completely let go—and let You take over. My voice is now Your voice. Thank you, God, for this opportunity, and again, let Your Will be done. So be it—and so, it is!"

As I stood at the podium with bright lights, TV cameras, microphones, and surrounded by three other candidates, I was completely at peace. No shaking legs. No nervous stomach. I felt beautiful, confident, and completely assured that God was in control. Standing between the Incumbent Governor and the Republican candidate, it was now "action" time.

The questions were coming fast and furious; however, I always paused for a moment before answering, and my answers were usually straightforward and succinct. I was well-prepared . . . for the most part. I had read the papers, studied the various opinions and topics of the day; however, I was not up to speed for one particular question which the moderator asked the other candidates. With composure, I stood there praying to myself.

"Okay, God. I don't have a clue what he's talking about. Please, don't let him ask me to respond to that question. Remember, we're on TV and everybody is really paying attention to me. I'm the first Black and they're just waiting for me to mess-up. So please, let him pass me on this one." Thank God, I was saved from embarrassment.

It proved to be an evening of debatable promises and at times, downright bullshit. There were times when my dubious opponents resembled a third-grade classroom with a substitute teacher. It got crazy. And while everyone else was throwing darts, I stood there in my most regal stance, giving thanks to the Creator for having *some* common sense.

After the debate, I immediately gave a mental shout-out to God: *"Good Job. We did it!"* And before I could step away from the podium, I was swarmed with cameras, enthusiastic campaigners, reporters, and guests, expressing accolades. At one point, a group of young, Caucasian females offered to campaign for me. The problem was that they were already working with one of the Republican candidates. Not only did the wife of the governor, on two occasions, hug and thank me for a wonderful job, she went on to say that she hoped her husband (as if she knew he would serve a second term) would use some of the Natural Law's Platform. And although the least experienced in politics, the consensus was that I had "won" the debate and made a major impression on all those that doubted my ability to run, including the Incumbent.

And the Winner Is

By the time election day came at the end of November, I didn't know what to expect as I watched the numbers come in. I was given an election party with all the trimmings of a "Win," even though the possibility of that happening was practically nonexistent. Not so surprisingly, as I looked around the room, most of the people cheering me on did not represent the African American community, but rather a community that The Java House was known for — diversity. One woman who happened to be Caucasian, and whom I shall never forget, came up to me and said something that I was totally not expecting.

"You know, I hope you take what I'm about to say in the love and in the sincerity that I mean it."

I looked at her, ready to embrace whatever she had to say. After all, nothing would surprise me at this point, and whatever it was, she was saying it to my face.

"*I hope you don't win . . .*" she stated rather emphatically.

I tried to make sure my expression didn't change and to suppress the urge to interject the question, 'why.' Without my interruption, she continued.

". . . What you are doing here in this community as a whole is far more important than being governor. No governor has accomplished as much as you have with our youth and gang violence. Furthermore, what you have created as a forum for this community, concerning the arts, has never been done on the level that The Java House has provided. And everybody knows that no matter where you live."

My enthusiastic supporter followed up her warm, kind and genuine words with a loving embrace. And I totally got what she was saying. I returned the hug and thanked her for her honesty and her support of what The Java House was doing. We were being "self-governing," taking responsibility for ourselves, our business and our community.

I learned a lot about myself during those arduous months of working and running for governor. Before then, I enthusiastically denounced being political. However, after giving some serious thought about the NLP's platform on "**self-governance,**": being the 'head' or 'controlling' factor of your life, creating and setting policies for **self** and family; becoming the **first** to live by principles that assure a sense of well-being, responsibility, self-sufficiency and respect for others, I came to the realization that — "I am" policy/politics; thus, the statement *"We The People..."* (which is espoused somewhat loosely without any real understanding) provokes us to accept the responsibility as the *true* government, which in term means that if any changes are to be made for the **good of the whole**, it starts with the individual, thus subsequently becoming . . . We the people!

Okay, let me get off my *soapbox* and get back to the *real* life — one of sex, drugs, lies, and ghosts–that is, right after I tell you the outcome of the race. Kentucky ushered in the Incumbent's second term as governor for the new millennium, along with a promise to implement at least part of the Natural Law's policies on education and prevention. Yes, the new year was going to bring in some new changes and challenges, both politically and personally. However, it was the *personal* changes and challenges that I would find to be even more daunting then some of the things I had already been through. Yes, it was about to be on and cracking. However, first, we had to get through the illusions of the bearded man on a sled.

TWENTY-NINE

Getting Through the Holidays

It was our first official Christmas in the Mansion and the last one before we ushered in the 21st Century. Although I didn't believe in or celebrate this month of consumer rip-offs and lying to our children about a big white man coming down a chimney and leaving gifts, I did have my stepsons to think about and my small grandchildren whose eyes would light up from Christmas tree lights and wrapped surprises. So, I succumbed for my grandchildren, stepsons, and to those of the Café family who thought Christmas was the best thing since *white* bread.

In the Henrietta Marie dining room, an eight-foot fresh-cut pine sprawled across the concave stage, adorned with miniature white lights that blinked to a rhythm only they could hear. Huge, red satin bows hung strategically on thick, foliaged branches; large, silvery, shaped balls reflected smiling faces and peppermint sticks. Boxes of various sizes, laid in wait for the taking; some wrapped in African print, while others glittered with silver and gold tones held by carefully scalloped ribbons. Wide bands of red and green ribbon intertwined throughout the room made the holiday season bright, despite the hype.

We were successful in creating an ambience of a traditional holiday, underlined with a nontraditional Truth. We didn't fall prey to a white man with a long white beard and red suit or the lie of a particular birth but instead praised the gods of creativity and sharing.

We used this season to Lionize the Seven Principles of Kwanzaa; to live each Principle in celebration and in honoring ourselves, our families and our ancestors.

It was my family's first Christmas without Mark, and not having Jenia and the rest of my grandchildren made the occasion difficult. We all tried not to be sad—telling ourselves that Mark wouldn't want us to be unhappy. So, we told stories—the good and the not so good, about our times with my grandson, their cousin, their nephew. In spite of our loss, the memories jolted us into bursts of laughter as we reminisced about his protective nature; his genius and his stubbornness as we sat lined on both sides of a long antique wooden dinner table.

My three grandchildren (from my sons), mischievously led by my three stepsons, ran throughout the twenty-two rooms as if they were on a fantasy island, looking for treasures. The gaiety that filled the large open spaces flowed like Jamaican beer–robust, full-bodied, and free. It was our first big family celebration in the Mansion, and it proved to be the highlight of the season.

Spoken Word continued to take center stage during the countdown to the new millennium. No matter how precarious the weather, the café vibrated with joy and thunderous celebration for the "word." Lyrics of revelation and revolution fell upon the ears of desperation for a reprieve from hate, ignorance and lack of consciousness. The falsehood of Christmas was being deconstructed and exposed to its high ideal of capitalism and falsehood, with its intentions to bamboozle humanity from its truth; to rob from the poor, creating more debt, more anxiety, and ultimately more division in the black family. However, that was not the only thing that was being deconstructed and divided.

The actual weather of sub-below temperatures bore a chilling semblance to the stoic matters of the heart. My relationship with my husband had managed to continue its slippery slope of deceit, drugs, and infidelity; sliding into a new year of more broken promises, heartache, and the need for ancestral intervention.

Let the Truth be Told

Vic woke up early to shovel the walkway leading to the parking lot. It was the first Wednesday of the New Year and our first day open after the holiday. Vic had already put salt down to melt the ice that had formed during a freezing, heavy rainstorm. I stood there looking out the window from the *Fredrick Douglas* library, looking out as far as I could see. The wintry morning looked like an oil painting on canvas. Tree branches gave way to several inches of ice, drooping like rabbit ears, while the ground, frozen solid, took its hiatus from birthing green grass and wildflowers, waiting for spring to come forth with new life.

As I positioned myself to see more of the house, I took note of several sharp-pointed icicles hanging uniformly along the gutters like ice soldiers. It made me smile. Vic was at the edge of the sidewalk before he turned around and noticed that I was in the window. He waved. I waved back, struggling to raise a half-frozen window, just enough to be heard.

"Hey, you wanna come in for a minute and warm up?"

The cold air gushed in, causing me to shiver as I yelled from the narrow opening.

"Naw, I'm okay; I'm gonna do the rest of the walkway around the building, and then I'll be in after that. Think we'll have any customers today?"

While Vic seemed to be one with the weather, I was freezing.

"Who knows, it's pretty cold, and it is after a holiday."

Just that quickly, my fingers felt like ice. I breathed into my hands, trying to warm them up, but to no avail.

"I'll make a *special* just in case. Hey, look, we can talk when you come in."

Vic chuckled and nodded as he went around the corner. I hurriedly pushed down the window and locked it. Damn, it was cold!

Although Vic and I were on the outs, we both made the effort to be civil towards each other. I was too tired to argue. I heard the news that Daisy gave birth to a son and that she had moved back to Washington with her new husband. I was relieved that I didn't have to deal with the embarrassment of having the baby put in my face; to have everyone whispering behind my back about what they thought I didn't know. My husband had fathered another son, making it the magic number . . . five. I wondered if he saw his son, if he arranged to be responsible for his welfare. Even more interesting — I wondered why I even cared.

I missed being a wife, a lover, a friend. I was lonely and tired. Vic accused me of staying tired, which was probably true. I needed to be rejuvenated; to feel appreciated, adored, understood and listened to. There were no hugs or intimate kissing, not even the occasional, quick and deliberate peck. I prayed for sleep to come quickly. At least, I could dream . . .

I lay there naked. His eyes roamed the curves in my arched back, which he trailed with his tongue. I breathed deeply and slowly, ravishing in the glory of bliss. I knew him not by name, but I felt we were longtime friends getting reacquainted after a season of separation. My body shook with gratitude and freedom as he devoted himself to my pleasure...

My back was straight against the padded headboard as I sat up with my arms folded, . . . perplexed.

"Vic, we need to talk. I'm dreaming about another man and that's a problem." Although I had no idea who had creeped into my dreams, the affair was deliciously refreshing and welcomed by all of me. I had no idea how Vic would take my abrupt honesty — and I didn't care. My husband barely moved from his upright position with his head hanging down, struggling to give me eye contact.

"Oh yeah? Uh, who was it? I mean, what happened?" Vic stumbled with his seeming concern.

"I was made love to, and I have no idea who the guy was. It's kinda embarrassing, but I feel it's important that we talk about it."

My stomach began to knot as I started telling my husband about my unsolicited, late-night rendezvous.

"I don't know when the last time was, we made love—or had a quick fuck for that matter," I reminded him.

The word . . . fuck sounded so nasty to me; foreign to my vocabulary, but I had hoped that by using such language, Vic would realize that even if he didn't *make love* to me, I would have settled for merely *gettin' off*. . . which would surely warrant a touch, maybe even a real kiss. And ultimately . . . a release from all the pressures I felt were smothering me.

"I feel so . . . useless, unwanted . . . as if you don't desire me or love me . . . or if you ever did love me."

I continued my unforeseen bearing of my soul. The trail of thoughts fell from my lips without any room for comment. Not that Vic would have had anything to say, especially in a case such as this. Although he was the greatest listener I knew, he was never much for communicating. However, now I needed him to tell me something—anything!

"I really don't know what's happening anymore, Vic."

Vic moved around nervously on the bed, as if trying to find a comfortable position while keeping his eyes far from mine.

"I know. I know that you deserve to be loved . . . that I haven't been there for you . . . and I can't say why." I wanted to jump in and ask, "why not," but Vic was on a roll, so I decided to just listen.

"I love you in my own way . . . I mean . . . I do love you, but not the way you need to be loved. I have never met a woman like you before in my life," he continued, still unable to look at me. I moved closer to my husband and put my hand on his shoulder. He didn't move.

"Vic, will you look at me... please?" My husband slowly turned his bowed head and hesitantly looked at me. His bloodshot eyes swelled with tears that did not fall. I wanted to just stop the conversation and move on with our lives, just for the sake of not hearing the horrifying thought of our marriage being based on an unrequited love; that Vic could not love me as a wife... as a woman. I waited with bated breath for his next words.

"Nailah, I know I've hurt you, and I know that you love me. Sometimes . . . sometimes, I don't believe I deserve your kind of love. You love so hard. I mean, you expect so much in return."

"You mean I shouldn't expect your love in return, Vic? Are you saying that for me to want your love... is something that I *shouldn't* expect?" I couldn't help the interruption. I couldn't understand what he was saying. "Am I that terrible? Why, what's wrong with me?"

This time, *my* eyes swelled with tears; only mine fell... and fell with a vengeance. "What should I expect, Vic? What is so unusual about wanting, expecting my husband to love me back?"

"Don't get me wrong." Vic continued, almost whispering. "You know how I am about tryin' to explain myself. I get mixed up with my words. I do love you . . . just not the same way you love me."

Not only was I bewildered, but I was also numbed by his truth, and I had no idea what I was supposed to do with it. Now *I* was at a loss for words.

"Look, it's not that I don't love you . . ."

"Yeah, I know, Vic. You said that twice already. I get it!"

My confusion turned to anger, and just the thought of my finding fault with myself or thinking I had done something wrong went right out the window. I was determined that I was not going to make "me" the problem. It was time to accept Vic's truth, whatever that meant, and make some changes so that I could move forward. I wiped my eyes — grabbed a cloth napkin from a nearby tray of leftovers and blew my nose. Then, I rose up on my knees.

"Okay, Vic. This is what's going to happen."

I took my husband's hands in mine, tilted his head-up and began to lay down the new rules for my life.

"I am going to find me a lover." Vic sat there, speechless.

"I'm serious, Vic. I can't keep going like this."

"You got someone?" He asked as if worried that I had found someone to take his place.

"Not yet," I somberly replied. "You know, at one point I thought that if we talked, we could work something out— even with the baby situation."

Before the lie fell from his lips again, that it wasn't true, I soldiered on.

"The truth is, I need someone who is going to love me, and you just told me that you're not capable of doing that — not in the way that I need as a woman. And you know what? I understand. I'm not even upset. I can't cry anymore or try to figure out what went wrong.

It is what it is."

Hearing my words made me chuckle with pain. I got it. I finally got it. After five years, it was time to give up the ghost... the illusion of thinking that marital bliss was something attainable. That the man I married would understand my emotional needs for support and intimacy, a shoulder to cry on. Hell, living the life of a Hebrew slave, as well as having to be an Amazon of a woman, exuding strength and courage, *all the time,* was taking me over the edge of sanity. And according to my husband, my occasional bouts of weakness were not permissible. As far as he was concerned, I probably had no right to cry, feel weak or get tired. After all, I asked for all this work... and got it.

Not so surprisingly, Vic agreed that I deserved more than he was able to give and accepted the fact that I was going on a "love hunt," which meant adding one more thing to my *to-do* list. However, the weeks of freezing rain and unusually low temperatures postponed any possibility of seeking out a willing and able partner. However, my sexual desires were not taking a back seat to time, yet there was never any real desire for self-pleasuring, which was void of the passion of a sensuous kiss and the hardness of a man. So, I waited patiently for the night when dreams mirrored my fantasies of true love filled with the sweet pleasure of release, without drama or guilt.

During the next couple of months, Vic and I said very little about my plans after our dubious but truthful realization about our marriage. It was more important that we kept a good business front for our customers and the community-at-large, rather than highlight our lusterless relationship. We were the ideal couple in the public's eye, and for the sake of business, keeping up the illusion was crucial to our success.

THIRTY

Jackie

It was late in the afternoon on this particular rainy day, and it was pouring down pretty heavy when my friend, Jackie, walked in as if she were half-dead—loaded down with books and an oversize, dripping umbrella. It wasn't funny, but the look on her face made me laugh.

"Hey sweetie," I chuckled. "Looks like you waited too late to open your umbrella. You are drenched."

"The damn thing wouldn't open right cause the damn wind was blowing so hard. Hell, by the time I got it opened, I was at the door. What the hell you laughing at? I'm wet as hell, and my braids are soaked," she lashed-out as her distorted face gently softened into a warm smile—her mocha skin glistening from the rain.

"Poor baby, come on in and take off that drenched coat," I sympathized. "Want some coffee?"

"You know I do, and I need to get something to eat, too. Hell, I ain't ate all day. And you know a bitch ain't got no money; I'll have to pay you later."

Jackie cursed like a sailor, which was as much a part of her beautiful personality as all her other attributes. And if she referred to you as, "Bitch," that meant you were *truly* a close friend.

Short in stature and built like a brickhouse (well-endowed in all the right places), as well as being beautiful, Jackie was a strong and confident woman. And unless you really pissed her off, she was one of the most loving and spiritual people you could meet.

"What you doing here on a Friday afternoon, not that I'm complaining, I'm happy to see you... It has been a while. But I thought you were working today."

"Shit, I took off early, since I didn't have any more clients after my court session with one of my teenagers, and you know my ass gotta be in class tonight at seven. Hell, I needed a break."

Working a full-time job with the state as a social worker and attending night classes on the weekends (including Sundays) to get her Master's, needless to say, I didn't get to see her much. And she hated the fact that she couldn't make it to poetry nights; she had heard about how awesome they were.

After taking off her drenched coat, I suggested she sit in the library while I got us both a cup of coffee. I already knew what to order from the kitchen; she was a die-hard Uncle Arnie fan, and it was extremely difficult to get her to try anything else. However, I was able to get her to try the Mr. T *once*. She admitted it was good... but she stuck to her favorite.

Jackie and I met while the Java House was still over the bookstore. She had come by with a co-worker who was already a customer. From that day forward, we became the best of friends . . . somehow, we knew we were kindred spirits. Eventually becoming more like a daughter, Jackie and I shared a lot about everything. She was only in her mid-twenties but was wise beyond her years. Gifted as well in the spiritual realm, Jackie "sensed" energies opposed to "seeing," which meant she *felt* the energies around a situation, while picking up intuitive information. Needless to say, there were times when she was able to shed some light on a few of my issues.

"Hey, baby, how you doin'?" Uncle Vic strutted in the library with his signature smile and placed Jackie's food on the coffee table before giving her a hug. Standing on her toes, she managed to reach her arms around his shoulders.

"Besides working like a damn slave, school is kicking my ass. That's about it. How's it going with you?"

"Just keepin' busy, baby. It's been pretty slow all day, so we let the staff leave after lunch. I'm back there roastin' a turkey for some more Uncle Arnies," Vic said, still smiling. "Look, don't be no stranger and enjoy your food. I put a little extra *special* sauce on your sandwich when Nailah said it was for you."

"Ah, thanks, Uncle Vic. I appreciate that. I know it's the bomb, as always."

After a final hug and kiss, Vic scurried back to the kitchen, while Jackie dived into her food.

"Catch me up, bitch . . . I ain't talked to yo ass in a month or so,"

Jackie asked in between bites. "Damn, this sandwich is good."

"Well, other than being happy that we are finally doing some good business, although today, it's been a little slow... It's pretty much the same. As with the renovation, we still have a few things to do downstairs. It's the upstairs that still needs a lot more work."

"Bitch, I don't know what else you can do downstairs; this place is fuckin' amazing. But with yo perfectionist ass, you would find something else to do. What about you and Uncle Vic? That's what I wanna hear about."

"Like I was saying, things are pretty much the same. After my grandson was killed . . . "

"Yeah, I still can't believe that shit," Jackie interrupted. "How's your daughter?"

"As well as can be expected . . . she's still in school, but she and her husband are having problems, too. As one can expect, it has been really hard on both of us. At the time, running for governor sorta helped to keep my mind off of it."

"Girl, I was so proud of you. Hell, I hurried up and registered to vote, just so I could vote for yo ass . . . anyway, back to you and Uncle Vic."

"Like I was saying, after Mark's death, Vic stopped going out as much. He actually paid me a little more attention . . . not sexually, unfortunately, but he at least let me cry on his shoulder; and he didn't make me feel bad if I complained about being depressed or tired. But that didn't last long. He's back to hanging out with his friend, Greg, and hanging out over at Charles' . . . you know, the bar I was telling you about."

"Yeah, I remember. Well, as we have talked about before, there will probably come a time when you will have to make a decision as to whether or not you want to stay in the relationship. I know you love Uncle Vic and all, but my main concern is . . . you. I mean you gotta do what's best for yo ass. And whatever you decide . . . just know that I am always here for you."

"Well, one thing I haven't told you is . . . it's kinda embarrassing."

"Come on, bitch. You know you can tell me anything"

"Well, I had this dream; it was about me making love to someone else and I told Vic about it."

"What the fuck! Who was it? What did Uncle Vic say?" Jackie asked, damn near all-in-one breath.

"I have no idea who it was. I just know that it was beautiful and so real."

Jackie, while taking a break from eating, looked at me with her mouth open as I continued.

"I told Vic that I couldn't deal with our lack of intimacy any longer and that I was going to find a lover."

"What the fuck did he say to that?"

"After a full explanation about our love life, or lack thereof, he   actually, agreed that I deserved to have someone to love me in the way that he couldn't."

"Naw, girl . . . you kidding, right?" Jackie exclaimed.

"I couldn't believe it either . . . but he admitted that he couldn't love me as a wife should be loved."

"Damn, this is some crazy shit. I can't believe that he actually said that to you. So, you gonna actually look for someone else?"

"Yep, I sure am. I don't know when or how . . . but something has to change. I can't keep going like this."

"I ain't mad at ya, girlfriend. You have every right to be happy. I don't know what's happening with Uncle Vic, but you gotta look after yo needs. Hell, I'm happy that he's at least being honest."

"Yeah, you're right . . . even though his being honest hurt like hell. Anyway, what about you? I know you're working and going to school . . . any man in your life?" I asked, needing to take the conversation off me. I could feel the tears beginning to swell.

"Are you fuckin' kidding . . . between work AND school, when would I find the time? That's why I keep a vibrator right under my pillow, so when a bitch needs some, at least I can take the edge off. Hell, every bitch should have one . . . and plenty of batteries."

I just about fell off the sofa from laughing, while agreeing with her sentiments . . . even though "self-pleasuring" had become boring, as of late.

"But, on another note," she continued. "I've decided that once I finish school in a few more months . . . thank you Jesus . . . I'm thinking about getting the fuck out of Kentucky . . . maybe Buffalo, New York."

"What! You serious? You know somebody there?"

"Serious as a heart attack! I have a girlfriend who moved there last year. She said it shouldn't be a problem getting a job in my field. I'm putting my resume together now to start sending it out. But you know me, bitch, I ain't worry about that. I can get a job."

"That would be great, Jackie. I would hate to see you leave, but I know that would be good for you. You deserve to spread your wings."

"I know one damn thing, wherever I go, yo ass will have someplace to come if you need to get away . . . that's for damn sure."

"Thanks, sweetie, sometimes I feel like I need to get the hell up out of here . . . and don't you leave without letting me know, first."

"Don't worry, yo ass will be the first one to know. Hell, you'll probably know before my own mama," she said, eating the last raisin from her salad.

After another cup of coffee and both of us indulging in a slice of sweet potato pie (which was Jackie's other favorite), it was well into the early evening when we were interrupted by a customer coming in. It was one of my regulars and my signal to get back to work. Besides, Jackie had to get ready for her class.

"I'll be right with you," I yelled. "You can put your umbrella in the corner behind the door. Thanks for coming out in all this rain."

"Take your time," he responded. "I'm in no hurry."

Both realizing our girl-time had come to an end, Jackie hesitantly pulled herself together to brave the weather and head to class. This time, "I" made sure her umbrella was fully open—right after opening the door.

"Now let's hope this bitch stays open until I get to the car," Jackie expressed with some concern of being drenched... again.

And once again, I laughed as I watched her fumble with her books (which by the way, she never cracked open) while trying to keep the windblown umbrella steady.

"Bye, Mama Java," she yelled, trying to get into her car. "I'll get your money to you next week when I get paid."

"Hey, don't worry about it. This one is on me."

"Are you sure?"

"Yeah, I'm sure. Now get in the car, I've got to get to work."

"Thanks, I love you . . . keep me posted."

Trying to avoid getting wet, I hurriedly waved back, echoing her sentiments as I rushed to the dining room where my customer was reading a damp newspaper.

The rest of the night was pretty slow, so we decided to close a little early. However, by the time we cleaned up and mopped floors, it was still after ten o'clock. Although it hadn't been busy, my back was bothering me a little more than usual, probably because of the rain. As I started heading upstairs, I called out to Vic, who was still in the back.

"Hey, Vic, will you check all the doors before coming up and turn the thermostat down? My back is acting up a little, so I'm gonna soak in the tub. I need to be ready for poetry tomorrow night."

"You think it's still gonna be busy if this rain keeps up?" he yelled back.

"It could be raining cats and dogs, and it wouldn't stop them from coming," I reminded him.

"You got that right," he agreed as he got closer to the stairs. "Hey, look," he continued while looking up at me. "I'm gonna head over to Greg's. He wants to go over to Charles's and hang out for a couple of hours. I'll be sure and check everything before I leave . . . I won't be out too late."

Not surprised, I smiled at my husband and said to tell the fellows hello. Agreeing to do so, he headed towards the kitchen, and I headed to our bedroom . . . once again, alone.

THIRTY-ONE

Bitch, Moan and Laugh Until It Hurts

It was one of those days when I really felt alone and afraid. Vic was gone to get some more kerosene. The fierce winds whistled through every crack in the house, exposing the incompetence of the heating contractor who was also the plumbing contractor — and you know how that went. The poor installation of the furnace, particularly in our living quarters upstairs, was like having no heat at all. We had to use kerosene heaters in our bedroom, bathroom, kitchen, and office while closing off the rest of the rooms. The smell was often overwhelming, but better than freezing.

The crisp, cold air crept through cracks and crevices of the heavy plastic that we used to cover up the large openings of what used to be a covered porch at the back of the house. Closing the porch off did little good to keep the brisk cold air from moving under the doors like a misty fog, hovering over the bare wooden floors. I was angry as hell. All that money spent on having adequate heat was a total waste. And believe me— money was the last thing we could afford to waste.

"Damn it! What the hell do you want me to do?" I cried out to the ancestors. *"Is this what I get for trusting 'my' people to do a good job?"*

Kneeling at the altar, I felt the cold breeze encircling my feet and moving up my pant legs. Wearing a sweater and long-johns with a wool tam pulled over my ears made little difference to the harsh reality of what the problem was. And the fact that we had four beautiful fireplaces, offered no solace from the Midwest's cold temperatures—one more thing the City Inspectors felt prone to stamp a "no" onto. Too old, too unsafe. I was beginning to wonder who really owned this plantation. Who was I to the "powers that be" on this historical site? Was *I's* still a slave... just a nigress trying to have more power than she deserved? After all, I had been asked more than twice . . . "Who do you think you are? And who told you that you could be self-sufficient?"

I prostrated myself in front of my ancestral altar, begging, screaming for answers, which was something I had promised never to do again, since the time when an ancestor reminded me that . . . "I wasn't doin' nothin' but some decoratin." But here I was whining like a spoiled brat.

"Can't a Sistah want anything in life without having to fight for everything... all the time? You brought me here! You gave me this mission! Why does it all have to be so hard?"

A mist escaped from my mouth after every word. The glass of water on the altar was nearly frozen; the apple was cold and hard. The candle gave off just enough heat to keep my glove-covered fingers warm. Even the tears rolled down my raw cheeks in slow motion before landing on the wool scarf around my neck. I was freezing, tired, alone, and having a meltdown.

I must have cried, begged, and bitched for a couple of hours before I heard Vic coming up the stairs. He sounded so full of life as he called out my name.

"Nailah, I got some kerosene. Where are you?"

I hurriedly wiped my eyes and rose from my sore knees. God knows I didn't need him complaining about me crying and asking awkward questions that he really didn't want answers to.

"I'm in here . . . in the office," I yelled, watching the vapors from my mouth fade into the air. With as much strength and acting ability I could muster up, I sat in a nearby chair next to a heater pretending to warm my hands. There was barely any heat coming from it. It bordered on empty.

Vic pranced into the room carrying a large, gray can. He was wearing his thick, navy-blue coveralls, boots, and brown gardening gloves.

"Hey, I got five gallons of kerosene. It should last us a couple of days. Damn, it's cold in here. Did you turn on the oven? You're shivering."

Vic grabbed the heater and filled it up, looking everywhere but directly at me, which was nothing unusual since our talk. He never noticed my bloodshot, swollen eyes.

"No, I didn't turn on the oven since I was working here in the office. We need to watch the bill. Last month, it was close to a thousand dollars, and that's without the furnace working right. I can't understand how someone can claim to be professional and not give a damn about the kind of work he does."

"Hell, now you know half the damn people working on any kinda job don't care. Shit, when I was working in prosthetics, people were coming back a month later cause it wasn't done right, and then I would have to end up trying to fix someone else's shit. I never liked that guy anyway. Too bad we didn't know about the furnace when we took his ass to court last year. Hell, we should have gotten all the money back."

It was rare for Vic to express his disdain for certain people, especially if they were present. He always left it to me to speak on injustices or poor work ethics when dealing directly with the individual. And I usually had no problem with speaking my truth, not even with him.

After Vic filled all the heaters, we went downstairs to finish building the small stage for the Harriet Tubman room. Until now, the poets had marked a spot for their readings in front of the purple wall. Our friend, Henry, came over just as we were finishing. His face, framed in a sheep's wool hat covered with black leather and rabbit ears, looked nearly frozen, but his smile warmed the still air as he entered the door, while removing his fogged glasses and wiping them. I hadn't seen him since he built the stage in the Henriette Marie dining room.

After a few agreed sentiments about the weather, Henry got up the nerve to tell me that I didn't look too well; that I looked tired. I looked at him and said . . .

"No shit. Hell yeah, I'm tired."

We laughed at the truth of it all. Vic even put in his two-cents worth . . .

"Yeah, man, she's always tired. But we both have been working like dogs, man. You know, I thought my wife was crazy when she said she was buyin' this scary place. I don't know what she was thinkin' about." Vic laughed, and Henry joined in. I laughed, just to keep from crying.

"Baby, this shit ain't no joke. Look here, man . . . the other night, man, me and Nailah almost left up outta here. We were upstairs in that room next to the last in the back . . . you know which one I'm talkin' bout?"

"Yeah, man, next to the porch; it has a fireplace." Henry agreed, hanging on to Vic's every word. He knew he was about to hear some creepy shit.

"Yeah, that's it," Vic acknowledged. "Anyway, we were cleaning, and it was kinda quiet. We wasn't doing no talkin'. Hell, it was going on two o'clock in the mornin'. Anyway, I heard somebody whisperin'. So, I stopped what I was doing and listened. Now I knew wasn't nobody in the house but me and my wife, right? So, I looked over at my wife, and she wasn't sayin' nothin'."

Vic shrugged his shoulders as if he knew you either thought he was full of shit, or he knew that you knew from personal experience that he wasn't making the shit up. Henry didn't budge and stood there with one arm across his chest, supporting the other arm with his hand under his chin. Vic then started whispering.

"So, I asked her. . . Did you hear that? She looked at me and said, "Hear what"? (Typical, right?) So, she got quiet, and I got quiet, right? Did you hear . . . like a bunch of people talkin' . . . whisperin'?"

Now, of course, he had my attention. Not that I was shocked. I knew exactly what he was talking about. Hell, I was glad to hear that somebody else heard it besides me.

"Listen. Man, I tell ya, me and my wife both heard them . . ."

Henry takes off his headgear and places it under his arm. His tightly curled, mixed grey hair lay sweaty against his scalp. He continues listening to Vic's story, intensely.

". . . But then she said that she had heard them before. Baby! It sounded like they were in the same room with us. Shit, neither one of us could figure out what they was sayin'. But I could imagine in my mind them all standin' round together lookin' at us and wonderin' what the hell we were doin' there." Henry and I both laughed.

"Man! I done seen some shit I ain't even told my wife about. You know there's Spirits in this house, don't you?"

"Yeah, man," Henry eagerly acknowledged. "I know." "Hey, baby, did you ever tell Henry about that time you showed us some stuff in a candle?"

"Naw, I didn't." I admitted. "Now that was some really weird stuff that night."

"What stuff? What candle?" Henry asked as if he was really getting a kick out of the stories we were telling.

"Henry, it was amazing. You see . . ."

I began telling Henry about a particular night when me, Vic, Shorty and Bill were working late, and I discovered something quite unexpected. And this time, I had a few witnesses.

Story in a Candle

In the main dining room, along the long wall which separated the two doors, I had placed a long table to serve as an ancestral altar. Fresh white flowers, a plate with a slice of sweet potato pie, a glass of blessed water, a white candle, and a fresh banana, along with sweet-smelling incense, kept me motivated during those times I wanted to quit and chalk it up as an "experience," which I found myself often wanting to do. The candle was a five-day candle, like most of the candles I burned.

On this particular night, the candle, which had just burned out, seemed to have an impression in the wax residue. As I went to take a closer look at it, I noticed that the banana was still firm and had maintained its bright, yellow hue. The pie looked as though it was freshly baked; the flowers stood tall and full of life. This was nothing unusual; I was familiar with the fact that an altar would often show no signs of losing its savor. This usually meant that the ancestors were pleased. On the other hand, if the setting lost its zeal only after one or two days, it could very well mean that the ancestors were not pleased or that the energy around it was negative. In this case, I was pleased that the ancestors were in harmony with what we were doing.

The room was barely lit by an overhead, single light bulb, but I wanted to see what the impressions were in the candle. So, I raised the candle to the light, turning it slowly. I was amazed and shocked at what I saw. On one side, there was an impression of a mountain and a woman with her head wrapped in mounds of cloth, as well as around her body, standing at the top and looking down from her high place. The wax impression was so detailed that I could see the profile of her keen, facial features. It was obvious to me that she was of great stature and authority. Her slender hands came together in a prayer position. Still, slowly turning the candle, it became apparent what she was looking at.

Right before my bewildered eyes, I vividly saw the gruesome, detailed image of a man walking through a swamp. His hands, raised from the murky waters, were shackled; his head turned as an alligator or crocodile moved towards him. (I know you're probably wondering how in the hell I could see all that in some candle wax) I understand; it was hard for me to grasp as well. But that's not all— as I continued to turn the candle. Behind what I would imagine to be a terrified, shackled slave was what appeared to be a field of tall wheat, overgrown weeds, or grass. (More than likely, it was probably cotton.) There were several head images grouped closely together, and as I continued to view the images, I intuitively knew that the heads were those of slaves trying to escape through the fields and swamps . . . in an attempt to reach freedom. I inched the candle for one last turn to see the final image of . . . praying hands.

Taking one last look before calling the guys to come and witness what I thought I had just seen, my breath shortened, and my balance became unstable.

"Vic, Shorty, Bill, come here," I yelled. While I waited with bated breath, I took another look just to make sure that everything wasn't just in my head. Nothing had changed. I felt the guys hurry in from the other room, almost fearful that something was wrong.

"Hey, baby, everything okay?" Vic asked, moving closer to me.

"Hey, you guys, you ain't gonna believe this," handing Vic the empty glass candle.

"What's this?"

"Hold it up to the light," I urged him. "What do you see?"

Vic turned the candle several times, not sure what he was looking for.

"What does that look like to you?" I asked again, pointing at the shackled image. "Don't you see it?"

"Yeah, kinda look like a man with handcuffs."

"You mean shackles," I interjected. "Now what else do you see?"

"Damn, baby; I don't know. What do you see?" he asked, not sure exactly what I wanted him to see.

Before answering him, I handed the candle to Shorty, who was standing close by, looking up at the raised candle.

"Shorty, look at this candle." I insisted with excitement and curiosity. "The wax left some residue. Now slowly turn it around and tell me what you see," I instructed.

In an attempt to get the candle closer to the light, Shorty stretched his short arm. For a few moments, he stood silent . . . slowly turning the candle.

"Yeah, I see something," he exclaimed. "Looks like a woman on a ridge."

Excited, I shouted! "Keep turning it . . . not too fast, slowly. Do you see anything else? Do you see the man with the shackles?"

"Wait a minute. I think I do. Wow! This is crazy. I see it! There's some kinda . . . Is that an alligator?"

I was so excited that I just started showing him everything I saw, while Vic leaned in to see what we were seeing. Meanwhile, without our knowledge, Bill was interested in something else.

"Bill, come here," I asked, not noticing what he was doing.

"Damn, this pie sure is good. Did you make this?" he asked, chewing and moving in our direction.

I lowered the candle to see what he was talking about. Shocked, my voice raised another notch.

"Where did you get that pie?"

"Off the table here," he admitted, pointing at an empty plate on the altar.

Vic and Shorty stood quietly to see how Bill would react after finding out what he had just eaten. Taking a deep breath, I softly said,

"Bill, you just ate the ancestor's pie. It's a week old."

Looking like a cat who just ate the canary, he swallowed the last piece.

"Really? Damn, it sure was good. Taste like it was just baked," he sheepishly admitted, while his expression changed to confusion and concern. He then scanned our faces and asked, "Will the ancestors be mad?"

"Naw, but if you get sick, dude, we ain't got no insurance," I alerted him.

We laughed, and I was relieved that someone else was able to see the story that was told in the wax images, and that I had not lost my ever-loving mind. But what wasn't funny was the fact that it ended up being another one of those times when the ancestors were reminding me of what they had been through... what they had to deal with, and once again, reminding me that I had NO right to bitch or moan about anything, let alone hard work.

The phone ringing and a knock at the door simultaneously broke up the storytelling hour, although I was able to complete my story for Henry. I answered the phone, and Vic went to answer the door. Henry gestured to me as he headed for the front door, where he said his goodbyes to Vic. It was my mom on the phone, checking to make sure I was okay. I was coming down with a cold the last time we talked. I had been sick for a few days, but couldn't afford to stay in bed. I drank herbal tea, sucked on cough drops, and took a dose of Castor Oil, per mom's adamant instructions.

As always, Mom asked about Jenia and the kids. My daughter and I spoke at least a couple times a week. Mark's death was still hard to believe. The kids were still saying that they could see him, something that Jenia was not able to deal with. She admitted that the thought of actually seeing him, knowing that his handsome face would simply fade away, that his 6'2, lean body would disappear right before her eyes, was far too much to bear. I totally understood; her feelings were quite mutual. Seeing the Spirits of those you don't know is one thing – – seeing your child or grandchild is entirely another story.

The guy at the door was one of Vic's patients, who had come to get his new leg adjusted. He was bundled in thermos coveralls with a Davie Crockett-looking hat, framing his rosy cheeks and hazel eyes. He spoke in passing, apologizing for interrupting our work. I assured him, it was no problem, as he followed Vic to the back of the house. I ended my conversation with mom and finished putting the mic and speakers on the new stage. Stepping back a couple of feet, I stood there admiring our handy work. We did good.

By the time I got back upstairs, the heaters had taken the bite out of the freezing temps. I took off my hat and scarf and removed my gloves. It felt quite comfortable considering the fact that a couple of hours earlier, I was walking around blowing in my gloved hands, cursing out the heating contractor and screaming at the ancestors! Anyway, at least I could get some work done.

Just for a moment, I reflected back to what Henry said about me looking tired. He was right. I did look tired and worn out. My face looked sullen and dry . . . no life. My long, beautiful hands were feeling more like cardboard these days, dry and calloused. I hadn't had a professional manicure since our wedding, and trying to keep my toes polished was almost impossible. I was not only looking tired, but truth be told, I was tired!

Vic's client hollered his goodbyes and wished me luck with everything. I walked to the top of the stairs to bid farewell and expressed gratitude for his well-wishes. Vic also said his goodbyes, saying he was going over to Greg's and then going by Charles' place for a while.

"Tell them both I said hello, and tell Charles if he gets any more restaurant-size pots and pans, I could use some."

"I won't be gone too long, just for a couple of beers."

Vic stood in the doorway, and the cold air moved straight up the staircase.

"Hey, it's raining again. I'll see if I can get some more kerosene while I'm out. What we have will probably only last during the night."

"Yeah, okay, and close the door. It's freezing and rain is blowing in on the carpet. I'll catch you later."

Vic closed the door and I headed back to our kitchen where I was washing dishes, cleaning floors and putting up curtains. Enjoying our private kitchen, it felt good the times when I could cook in my robe and flip-flops; not bother to comb my hair or cover it with a scarf. It made me feel like I had a separate life from the café and cultural center, at least for a few hours out of the week.

Rays of sunshine began to peep through the streaked windowpanes, adding warmth to my mood. Things looked brighter when the sun was shining. And even though the rain had stopped, the strong wind whistled through the cracks. Suddenly, I felt a ray of hope and a sense of pride in all that we had accomplished over the past fourteen months. Although not sure what had changed my mood from the despair and gloom I had felt just hours earlier, something had shifted. Something had changed.

THIRTY-TWO

Crack

It was a bright and cheerful, Monday morning. I got up early to tidy up from the weekend and to wash a few dishes. Cleaning had become meditative for the most part. I did so much of it, I decided to make it work for me. Washing dishes was calming; the hot water was soothing and comforting to my tired hands. Cleaning the restrooms usually prompted freedom songs as I polished porcelain and chrome. Vacuuming brought back memories of the times before the carpet was laid, and the thought that was put into making sure it complemented its 1800s architecture.

Normally, I would clean after closing, just so I didn't have to face it the next morning. However, we had spoken word Saturday night until about three in the morning; I was completely exhausted, so I slept just about the whole day, Sunday. I got up only to eat and pee . . . period. While I rested, Vic and the boys worked on the back porch and cleaned up around the grounds. The rest surely did some good; however, I was still restless and feeling down about the way I looked and felt. I needed a break — badly!

As I was musing about how I could fit in a much-needed break, the humming of the vacuum served as a type of background mantra to calm my mind. That's when I saw it! The crystal-like rock stood out like a black eye against the colorful pattern. Not sure what it was, I bent down to pick it up to get a closer look. I was petrified and livid! I immediately knew what it was. I had seen it before, years ago, while living in Los Angeles, watching it destroy the life of someone I cared for very much – overnight.

Standing there, shaking and barely able to move. I wanted to scream but was afraid the boys would hear me and come running in the house, only to find that I had found **Crack Cocaine** lying in plain sight.

"*My God!*" I thought to myself. "*What if someone else found this?*"

Of course, I immediately tried to believe that it could have come from any of the hundred-plus people who had walked the halls over the weekend. But deep inside, I knew who it belonged to. Just a month or two earlier, while cleaning the dishwashing area, I found a glass pipe under the unused dishwasher. When I asked my husband about it, nervously, he disclaimed any knowledge of it and accused his half-brother of possibly being the culprit.

I barely knew Vic's half-brother. I had met him a few times after we acquired the mansion. He even came over and helped out a few times, and he seemed to be a decent man who was a couple of years older than Vic. They hadn't been close, but since seeing his dad again, Vic decided to try and have a relationship with his estranged brother, the only other male his dad had fathered. Raymond was brown-skinned like Vic, and his slender build was also a Yarbrough characteristic. There was also a resemblance in the face, but Vic was better looking.

When I approached Raymond about the mysterious pipe, he, too, denied any knowledge. However, unlike Vic, looking me straight in my eyes was not a problem. I also sensed that he knew the truth. I could tell in his eyes that he felt pity for me—suggesting that my concern that my dear husband was on *Crack*, was in fact, a valid concern. He gave me a hug and told me to stay strong.

After ruminating about the pipe, along with what I had just found, I put it all together in my mind, realizing I had reasons to be extremely concerned about my business. Things were beginning to add up–like why Vic always had so much energy, or the times when he would repeat an order four or five times before getting it right. At the time, I thought it was he was probably still trying to get back into the swing of things. Oh, yes!

I had big reasons to be concerned. This was messing with MY life and everything we had worked for. And there was no way I was gonna let Crack or anything else destroy it!

Later that day, after Vic had taken the boys home, I confronted him with what I had found. At first, I thought I would be calm and handle the situation with some diplomacy. However, I lost it after I took a good, hard look at my husband when I showed him the crystal. I didn't have to ask – it was written all over his face.

"I know it's yours, Vic. How in the hell could you be so careless?" I screamed. Tears swelled in my bloodshot eyes as I continued to confront him. "Do you realize we could be shut down if this was found by someone else and they decided to report us? Do you even give a shit?"

Vic stood there unable to say a word, while I stood there crying profusely. This was it! This was the straw that broke the camel's back.

"Damn-it Vic, for the past few months I have been through the wringer. I have worked my ass off with this damn renovation. I ran for governor, lost my grandson, and I still haven't had the time to grieve his death. And I'm trying to keep my daughter from losing her mind while trying not to lose my own — And now drugs?"

Unable to comfort me or assure me of his innocence, Vic paced back and forth, pleading for me to stop crying.

"Hey, stop crying, you'll get sick. Please, stop. It's gonna be all right. I promise you!"

I walked over to the man that I still loved, and lay my head on his shoulder, hoping for a hug or something. Nothing! I eventually stepped away to dry my eyes and catch the snot that was running down to my mouth with the bottom of my T-shirt. Vic was right. I did get sick –sick to my stomach about the whole damn thing. It was time for a major change! So, I took a deep inhalation, sat down on a nearby stool and calmly spoke.

"Vic, first let me tell you that I will call the Fucking police myself if I **ever** find any more Crack or pipes or anything else that could jeopardize everything I've worked for!

And I don't care who it belongs to. This is it! I'm not hearing any more lies or excuses." Vic leaned against the refrigerator and hung his head.

"Also," I continued. "I'm gonna take some time off."

Vic finally spoke, raising his head to make eye contact.

"What you mean... how long? You know we're gettin' real busy."

I looked at Vic like he had lost his mind before I answered, and this time I didn't give a shit about being calm or losing my temper.

"You know what, Vic . . . HANDLE IT!" My voice continued to escalate as I came off the stool, moving towards Vic, my hands flying in different directions while spitting out months of pent-up anger and pain.

"At this point, I don't give a damn about it being busy. That's why I hired employees. I need a break before I do something I might regret — like tear all this shit up and say fuck it! Vic, I am tired of you and this business. You obviously don't give a fuck about this business . . . or me! Look at me, Vic! I haven't looked like a woman in what seems like . . . forever . . . not that it would matter to you."

I looked ragged that day, more than usual. I even tried to avoid seeing myself in the mirror. It made me want to cry. The life had drained from my eyes, and I looked old and worn out. Vic remained plastered against the refrigerator.

"Why are you cussin' so much? It don't sound right comin' from you."

I stopped momentarily to catch my breath and gain some control before I started hyperventilating.

"Are you kidding me, Vic? My whole fucking world is falling apart, and you're asking me why I'm cursing? Nigguh, please!" There was silence for a brief moment.

"Like I said," taking a deep breath, "I need a break. I don't know when or where I'm going, but I've got to get the hell away . . . soon!"

THIRTY-THREE

Chicago Bound

It had been a week since my blow-up with Vic, and although I had calmed down considerably, I desperately tried to find the time to get away. However, Black History blazed through like an inferno, and the spoken word celebrating our blackness, spit lyrics like never before. "Is What?!" —a rap, beep-bop, jazz group from Cincinnati came through that night after a local engagement. Napoleon, leader of Is What?!, introduced a newcomer he had been working with from Chicago.

    He was a poet and a rapper, and he was bad! His handsome, dark presence at the mic was magnetic, as he gingerly rocked from side to side while holding what appeared to be a bottle hidden inside a brown paper bag, in which he occasionally turned up to take a swig. I watched like everyone else, wondering what was inside his crinkled bag. A beer? Wine? I felt like I was judging him as I watched him turn it up. Then, after about ten minutes at the mic, with his last words falling like thunder, he stepped back, slid the paper bag from its mysterious hold only to reveal a—32-ounce bottle of *water.* He mischievously raised the clear liquid to a raving audience and made a toast to a standing ovation. Although the newcomer was a *virgin* to our mic, his erotic and tantalizing lyrics left everyone screaming for more. Talk about poetic justice, he was damn near illegal.

    It was one o'clock in the morning before I was able to sit down.

Although I was beat, the high energy of poetic sentiments gave me the needed strength to make my congratulatory rounds to our family poets and to our Chicago guest. I wanted to thank him personally for gracing us with his captivating performance, and to assure him that he was welcomed anytime as part of The Java House family. However, I had no idea he had something for me, as well.

"Mama Java? Is that what they call you?" He stood, as I sat down.

"Yes," I declared, looking around the room.

"I never thought I would ever have these many children. And believe me, most of them act like I'm their mama, for real. However, my real name is Nailah."

After a firm handshake, he sat down and drank from his *bottle*.

"My stage name is Baruti," he announced.

Just saying his name, his posture shifted to a more upright position. "It means, *teacher*. My slave name is Tomas—Thomas, without the h. Tomas Willis, but please call me Baruti".

We talked about twenty minutes before he reached into his leather folder and took out a flyer.

"There's a play showing in Chicago some friends of mine are doing. I think it's around 300 miles from here, but I think it's worth the trip," he continued handing me the flyer. Little did I know that that flyer would land me the opportunity to take that break I so desperately needed.

On the Road

The sun glistened on the wet interstate along I-65. The sun's warmth penetrated the windshield, warming my face and making the chilled February afternoon feel sunny and warm. It felt good as I bounced to the loud music from the radio. For once, I felt free as I headed to Illinois. It had been almost two weeks since I received my invitation to Chicago, and not to my surprise, Vic was down for my getting away.

Baruti's directions were perfect, leading me right to the college campus. As I drove into a large, nearly empty parking lot, a well-lit marquee hanging over double doors advertised: "Final Weekend." *I Remember When the Blues Was Hot.* I had a two-hour wait before the eight o'clock performance, and my stomach reminded me that I hadn't eaten since I left Kentucky, a little more than five hours earlier. Being on a college campus meant plenty of fast-food choices, so I stopped by a burger joint, bought a fish sandwich, fries, and a cup of coffee.

I took my time eating while enjoying my book, *"Friendship With God,"* by Neale Donald Walsh, also author of *"Conversations With God."* His books were another outlet from the mad world I found myself merely surviving in. I heard my own voice in every page screaming, hallelujah—Truth at last! And with every truth, Ego screamed to keep its position, insisting I had no right to *talk with God*. But it was too late. Talk about a revelation!

By the time I got back to the theater, the parking lot was full. I was still about a half-hour early, so I bought my ticket and sought out the ladies' room to freshen up. It was the second time I had worn the suit my mother bought me for the governor's debate. I looked professional and business-like, as I smoothed back my long, micro twists. And with a little makeup, I looked good; I even had a little glow.

The theater was small, seating about 70 people. It filled up quickly. Chatter filled the room as I sat there and watched the young sisters and brothers find their seats, while the gutsy sounds of yesterday's blues filled the room. I tapped my feet to the familiar sounds as I gazed around, thinking that maybe I was a little overdressed, but then again, I was there on business.

Our unique custom of being on CP (colored peoples) time had not taken a backseat as the MC enthusiastically graced us with his presence 15 minutes after the hour. He was welcomed with a thunderous applause—probably because they were finally starting the show. However, he proved to be quite comical and rather pleasing to the eyes, which for me, made it worth the wait. By intermission, I had stomped my feet, laughed out loud and worn out two tissues wiping my eyes. It was definitely time for another trip to the ladies' room.

The cash bar was small, basically only serving beer and wine. I ordered a white Zinfandel and casually walked around listening to comments about the show. Family members and fans who had seen the show more than once or twice, gave kudos to the fact that the show had gotten better. First-timers, like myself, seemed to be equally impressed.

I had managed to take the last sip of wine when the lights flashed off and on. I was feeling just a little tipsy as I made my way back to my seat for the final act. I was truly enjoying myself. For a few moments, I gave way to the thoughts of why I was really there, or at least what I told myself, for I had already surmised by the end of the first half that the show was much too large for our budget. Paying for their round-trip transportation from Chicago to Kentucky, plus time and talent, there was no doubt that hiring them for the cultural center was merely wishful thinking. However, on the other hand.

As he walked up to me to get my opinion on the show, his cute boyish look aroused my curiosity— in more ways than one.

Standing just a little taller than he, I offered my honest opinion about the performance, letting him know that I did enjoy the show very much, with particular interest in his performance... of course. Before we knew it, we realized that the theater was just about empty. That's when we decided that I follow him to a local bar, have a drink, and continue getting to know each other. That's when it also became evident that we hadn't even introduced ourselves.

"Oh, you think we should at least know each other's names before I venture off with you for a drink?"

Of course, I went through the pronunciation routine of my name and got the usual compliment of it being unusual and unique.

He smiled and moved in closer, "Trey Donald, and it's a pleasure to meet you. You smell wonderful."

"Lead the way. I'll be right behind you," I said, blushing . . . just a little.

It only took about fifteen minutes to get to the club, as I followed him to an empty space for street parking.

As we walked into the music-filled room, I had a flash of déjà vu. As I looked around at crowded tables along with hot, sweaty bodies on the dance floor, my heart raced for a quick moment as a flash of that momentous moment when I met my soon-to-be estranged husband brought water to my eyes. I made a quick adjustment to my emotions as my new friend and I meandered along narrow aisles searching for seats that could not be found. We opted for the dance floor.

While dancing, he backed away just a little bit to take a look at me. I admitted that I wasn't very good at following, as I took a deep breath to relax. I was so accustomed to being the leader in everything, that I found it difficult to follow a man — even dancing.

"You're doing fine," he assured me. "Besides, I'm not all that good at dancing, period."

We both managed to chuckle and stayed on the dance floor for at least a couple more songs before we ventured off to find a seat. This time we were a little more fortunate; however, it was next to the thunderous speakers, so trying to have a conversation was almost impossible, as well as getting a drink. Trey got up to go to the bar, but not before making a confession first.

"Uh, I hate to admit this, but I don't have much money," he quietly stated. "I can buy you a glass of wine, if that's okay."

"Not a problem, a glass of wine is fine... Chardonnay."

Somehow, I knew that was the case. That seemed to be my MO. They were either broke, near broke, or paying out the ass for child support. Anyway, I was glad to know that he didn't have an issue with pride. His situation wasn't anything new; like most talented people, many of us fell into the category of "starving artist."

By the time he returned with the drinks, a couple had left giving us the opportunity to get away from the speakers. We talked and laughed as he sipped his beer and I savored my wine. He had a gentle look—a quiet demeanor. It was almost as if he didn't know what to say to me. Maybe because I was older, or should I say he was a lot younger. Like the age of my daughter, younger. Well, he didn't seem to mind, and neither did I.

During our conversation, it was obvious that Trey loved being an actor, with intentions to pursue it as a career. And based on his performance, I could see he had the potential to be quite good. Well, it didn't take long before the real conversation took over our idle chitchat. The more personal side of who we were finally made its way to the heart of why we were making goo-goo eyes at each other. By happenstance, we were both married and both on the verge of a separation. (Now wasn't that convenient!) Neither one of us were eager to elaborate or make that somber conversation a highlight of our evening. So, we managed to make a quick jump forward to the topic of when and where we were going to see each other... again. We decided that two weeks from that night would be a good time for our next meeting.

After walking me to my car, and a quick impromptu kiss, I took one last, long drool at my prospective love *dream;* one last look at his clean-cut, boyish handsome face before departing to make my way to a nearby hotel. I had planned to be back on the road by ten the next morning so that I could take my time, and maybe even stop to have lunch along the way before getting back to the uncertainty of my life.

What is it about . . . affairs? What makes them so deliciously tantalizing and forbidden? Not that I'm accustomed . . . I'm just asking. Besides, it wasn't gonna be a "real" affair, my dear husband and I had an "understanding." Now, Trey, on the other hand, was biding his time while his estranged wife allowed him to stay until he could afford to move.

The anticipation of seeing Mr. Dream Man again made the next two weeks feel less like hell and more like having a winning lottery ticket. Colorful memories flashed through my mind of our innocent flirting, prompting me to smile when least expected — raising questions from inquiring minds. Of course, I dared not tell, but instead

I'd offer some half-baked tale about . . . anything. However, Vic knew something was up, but also knew not to question my actions. Technically, I was no longer his wife. What could he say?

Although it was still February, the weather was changing. It was getting much warmer, particularly for that time of year. Or maybe it was because *I* was warming up. Maybe after the long draught, I was beginning to feel like a woman again. When I thought about Trey, I couldn't help but think about the time when I met Vic. After all, it was almost the exact scenario. I was married when I met Vic, albeit on the rocks. I had met him in a nightclub just when I felt like I could not live on . . . as with Trey. And although my meeting with Trey was not nearly as intense, he stimulated a ray of hope; a deep, burning desire to be loved–to be held–to feel alive.

THIRTY-FOUR

Sexual Healing

The Sunday morning drive to Chicago was smooth and easy. Our decision to meet the following month for a few hours was worth every minute. Not quite 50°, it felt like a spring day–a day anxiously ready to bring in the debut of March flowers with fresh, green grass and budding trees, a day of new beginnings.

"Reservations?" The hotel clerk was warm and friendly, as she searched for my name in the computer and made an attempt to pronounce it correctly. Once checked in, I went across the street to the drugstore and bought cigarettes when I noticed the display of condoms. I had never bought condoms before, but I had made sure to take a few from our basket in the restrooms, where we offered them to our customers for free. I had picked up Regular and Magnum... just in case.

Situated on a busy street corner near downtown Chicago, the hotel was in the midst of heavy traffic. And the fact that it was Sunday made little difference with the sound of beeping horns and blasting stereo music. My room was warm and cozy with a king-size bed, which awaited my tired and restless body as I slumped down, kicking off my shoes. Propping myself on pillows, I took a deep sigh and lit a cigarette. The cool, menthol flavor lay in the back of my throat before I slowly exhaled a long stream of smoke into the open space. It felt good.

I had tried quitting this terrible habit on a couple of occasions, but life just wasn't allowing that to happen. Besides, I never really considered myself a *real* smoker. I only smoked when I was extremely nervous or if I was drinking alcohol, and I usually had to put them in the refrigerator to keep them fresh. However, as of late, I was smoking more than usual. It was almost a ritual. I found myself having a glass of wine accompanied by nicotine before I passed out at night after a sixteen-hour shift. And since I had made a commitment to not smoke in my car, it had been at least 5 hours since I'd had a cigarette. Talk about waiting to exhale.

The radio clock by the bed said one-fifteen. I had time to rest and freshen up before Trey would arrive at three-thirty. I snuffed out the hot cinders from my cigarette and set the alarm to wake me at two-thirty. Before lying down, I took out my hardly ever used black lingerie and spread it across the bed. I stood there a few moments thinking about the times I used to get cute and sexy with my husband and shake my money maker for a hot, steamy night. However, those nights had long been over... until now!

Ready or Not

The music from the hotel's radio jolted me as I jumped up and looked around, briefly forgetting where I was. Remembering, I smiled as I deliciously soaked up the ambiance of the tranquil jazz and the elegant space. I took a long shower; oiled my body with Shea Butter and dabbed on some Egyptian Musk. I felt rested, SEXY, rejuvenated, ready, willing and *hopefully* able to have an evening of divine pleasure.

As the mind would have it, just when I was all hyped up, my musing for a pleasurable evening was interrupted with two disturbing thoughts: Other than the fact that my legs had not been in the "spread" position in like . . . forever, my hip had been kicking my ass. Was I *able?* And did this *young* man know *how* to do the do? Damn, I would be pissed off and mad as hell if he didn't. And doubly pissed off if I couldn't move to the groove.

Trey arrived a little after four o'clock. Like me, it was obvious he was nervous. We laughed and talked for a couple of hours. I didn't want it to seem like I was ready to jump his bones as soon as he got there. We ordered room service and opened the bottle of Cognac he brought.

Only after a few sips, I was feeling its effect. Giggling and feeling loose and carefree, I finally gave in to his touches… his kisses …his everything.

For the next three hours, I didn't even know I had hips. There were no fireworks –no thunderous eruptions, but rather a peaceful, steady flow of tranquil waters gently beating against mounds of stagnation and forgotten territory. The dam had broken. My parched thirst for intimacy had been quenched. We lay frozen in the moment. I was completely drenched. Every muscle melted– my limbs lightly trembled with surges of energy. Maybe it was the Cognac. Or maybe it was the prayer that I prayed to the Universe that I would let go and relax. That I would be so happy to "get some" that my mind wouldn't think about my aches and pains, and most importantly, maybe my plea to be guilt-free was heard and honored. Whatever it was, I was submerged in gratitude. As we lay in silence, Trey gently held my head next to his hairless, dewy chest. I cried.

Making More Time

Trey and I met at a halfway point every other Sunday morning at a hotel in Indianapolis, to eat from the *forbidden* fruit… so to speak. Our long talks on spirituality, poetry, acting, and the mysterious world of ancestors in the form of Spirits that roamed the familiar twenty-two rooms took up many hours. He was intrigued by my knowledge of the ancestors, my spiritual wisdom, and my running for governor. He was even more flabbergasted when I took his wife's side when sharing with me their challenges. I wouldn't allow him to find fault or minimize her to condone what we had. He was forced to look at his own shortcomings, as well as I. It was always easy to judge another or make someone else the "reason" for seeking more than what life was offering . . . or not offering. With his youngness and inexperience, and my experience and acceptance of reality, we both learned to take ownership of our actions and where we had ended up on the spectrum of what we called… life!

Strange and wonderful things happen to a woman when she is being loved—or an equivalent thereof. Trey swore that he was "in love" while I wasn't even sure what love was. I had tricked myself into believing that I was wrapped in the thrones of this mysterious bliss so many times that it was becoming a myth. I doubted its authenticity. However, for the next three months, my tired, worn body took on a life of its own.

I slowed dance without a partner in dimly lit rooms and hallways to a tune that came from no radio. My face glowingly transformed as if with child. I wrote and read seductive poetry to the tune of wild drums and smooth jazz. I was emerging from the darkness of a cocoon into the bright hues of a butterfly. Whatever this feeling was, I was ready to soar to whatever heights it would take me.

Vic had come to a resolution about my decision to move on with my life. And although I was quite adamant when I told him of my intentions, he shared with my auntie that he didn't think I would actually *do* it. That I would seek out someone to care for me . . . to listen, hold me, let me cry . . . let me feel alive! But like she told him, "If my niece says she's going to do something, you better believe she's going to do it. I would think by now, you would know that."

My husband's decision to move to the back of the house gave our estranged arrangement more validity. He often shared his private space with a former girlfriend, who shared his recreational drug use. Not that he was doing anything new; however, now it wasn't hidden from my "awakened sight," and I wasn't going into bouts of hysterics and sleepless nights. Yes, the life we once knew had changed drastically, one that would prove to push us even further apart in a way that I would have never imagined, EVER!

THIRTY-FIVE

Plans Turned Upside Down

My altar brightened the dark corners of my lonely room. And the fresh, white Daisies gave the energy around me a spark of life. My prayer requests to the ancestors had moved from the usual "getting directions type" regarding my mission with the mansion, although I was still seeking their guidance. However, now I needed support in understanding what I needed to do with the separation I was feeling toward everything and everyone around me. My motives were changing, and I could feel the resistance in the pit of my stomach. I didn't want my relationships to change, at least not with my staff or my extended family. Anyway, after meditation, it became clear that it would be best to just let my staff know what was up.

It was after our lunch shift when I called my two waitresses together for a quick meeting. I decided to go ahead and tell them about me and Vic's decision, and about Trey.

"Look, you guys, as you probably already know, Vic and I are having problems, and I want to make sure that you understand that we have an agreement."

Looking rather pensive and a little surprised, both girls gave me their full attention as I continued my confession.

"Technically, we are separated . . . so if you see either one of us with someone else . . . it's cool. Vic and I both will be seeing other people, and as a matter of fact, my new friend will be moving here sometime next month, and Vic is supposed to be moving back to our old house."

I assured them that we would continue to move forward as if all was well. That Vic and I would continue to work together, even after he moved out. Suddenly, I found myself getting teary-eyed, as if I was hearing about our separation for the first time. Both my waitresses rose from the sofa and gave me a warm and sincere hug while expressing their sorrow for our separation. They both admitted that they already felt something was wrong but didn't want to interfere. We hugged again before getting back to the duty of preparing for the next shift. I felt relieved.

Spring Had Sprung

It was the end of May 2000. Various forms of scented flowers sprang up around the mansion, taking away the gloom that had fallen upon its massiveness. The Dogwoods budded to greet the warm sun that was sure to stick around for a few months. The dead grass sprouted with new life, and the birds once again perched on rooftops and tree branches.

While the season for new growth, beauty, and warm weather rose to the occasion of welcoming the summer, the perfect couple was vanishing like the occasional ghost that appeared and then disappeared, and I had become the bitch that was destroying the very fabric that held our artistic community together. The news had gotten out about my illicit love affair, and the talk about Vic leaving his hard-earned haven, which he had vowed to do by June 17th. However, it was understood that he would continue to work in the business. We did work well together, and this way our customers would still have us as "the couple" —only not so perfect.

Meanwhile, Trey talked with his family and told them of his decision to move to Kentucky. We had talked about him telling his wife about us, and to be completely honest… lying was not an option. Neither one of us was sure what we were doing. It was like walking on a tight rope, realizing that each step we took could lead to a great fall.

I could only hope that there would be a net to catch us. Especially since Trey felt being with me would be a *spiritual journey* that he couldn't pass up. Funny (or not so funny) ,I seemed to always pick the guys that didn't quite have it together. I had this delusional sense of *seeing* their innate capabilities . . . their good qualities, as opposed to the **reality** that was staring me in the face.

I decided to keep the news about Trey moving in on the downlow, at least until it was close to the time for Vic to leave. Trey wasn't coming until around the 20th, which was enough time for him to finish his last acting class and make a few dollars from his gig. The transition would be smooth and easy... so, I thought.

I hadn't shared our plans with anyone except with my dear friend, Saria. She knew all about the issues that eventually made the split between Vic and me. She had read the Tarot Cards for me on several occasions and often tried to skirt around some of the horrible truths that showed up. But the truth was something I had to face –like it or not. At least that way, I was able to be prepared for the turmoil. Like the old saying: Forewarned . . . Forearmed.

My conversations with the ancestors weren't always clear, but getting some confirmation, even if vague, helped to ease my concern as to whether or not I was doing the right thing. If I were doing things according to God's plan. Here of late, I had gotten pretty good at being selfish, thinking about my own happiness for a change. However, I realized that I couldn't keep that attitude and expect peace and order. So, I was back to asking that God's Will be done, while crossing my fingers that there would be a little joy and happiness in the process.

My altar's white candle was burning dark, which meant there was negative energy around my plans. Was it that I shouldn't let Trey come? Could it be that Vic and I should resolve our differences and get back to "the way we were"? Hell No! That couldn't be it. But what was it? I checked with Trey and he confirmed that his intentions had not changed. That's when I decided to talk with Vic again about his plans to move.

Our hired chef had left for the day, and Vic and I were left to manage an unexpected rush of evening diners. Everything went smoothly, like old times. Working as a team was never a problem, even when we weren't speaking. By the time we had finished, it had gotten close to midnight, and I really wasn't in the mood to have *that* conversation, but I knew it had to be done. We quietly cleaned and set everything up for lunch for the next day. I was filling the salt and pepper shakers when Vic announced he was going out for a couple of hours. I no longer inquired as to where or why he was leaving, but I wanted to have *the* talk before he left.

"You still planning to move on the 17th?" I asked with my back to him. His hesitance in responding made me turn to see if he was still there. With his scarf removed and a fresh shirt, he leaned against the door entrance.

"Uh, I'm not sure," he muttered. His tone was dry and disconnected as he continued. "We can talk about it tomorrow. I'll see ya later."

I watched as he casually walked toward the back. Neither one of us said anything else. A few minutes later, I heard the back door slam. Suddenly getting a queasy feeling in the pit of my stomach, I knew something had changed. Something was wrong.

I solemnly finished what I was doing . . . got a glass of Chardonnay and sat in the library. I was tired –mentally and physically. With my feet propped on the coffee table, I took a big swallow of wine and began to think about the candle on the altar, and the fact that it was burning black. With only the walls to hear my audible thoughts, I cried out. "Damn! What's getting ready to happen now?" Whatever it was, the ancestors were trying to give me a heads up.

Conversation Still on Hold

The sun broke through the crack of my bedroom drapes. The hands on my bedside clock were straight up and down. It was six o'clock. I sat on the side of the bed before I decided to look outside to see if Vic had made it in. He had not. I went back and sat on the bed just to reflect for a minute on what to do if he didn't show up. I began to think out loud. *"My cook will be here, and I can help if he needs it. Plus, I have two waitresses scheduled. If Vic doesn't show up . . . it should be just fine."* I relaxed.

Still tired, I tried going back to sleep, but racing thoughts about Trey coming, Vic leaving, and all the *what ifs* . . . I finally got up. As I moved about to get my day started, I heard the downstairs door. I looked out again and noticed Vic's van; he had returned. Everything was so different. No more questions, answered with lies. Vic was free to do as he pleased. And, whatever he did, I no longer gave a good shit . . . Or did I?

On his way to the bathroom, Vic and I passed each other in the hallway. We still shared the bathroom upstairs, since the one in his living quarters needed some work. Cheerfully, and with a nonchalant attitude, I spoke first, "Good morning." Damn, I was so cheerful, I almost sang it. He looked rested and well awake.

"You up early," he said, looking at me quite surprised. "Is this a good time to use the bathroom? I'm gonna have someone over to check my shower head in a couple of days."

His slender frame brushed against me, and for one brief second, a sadness settled in my heart.

"Yeah, wasn't sure whether or not you would make it, so I got up to get things started. Go ahead, I can take a shower later."

"Now, you should know I wouldn't leave you stranded. Hell, I still live here. I'm gonna always do what I need to do," he stated. His eyes were wild and strange-looking. I missed his huge smile and the way his eyes used to twinkle. "It's a nice day today and it's Friday. We should be busy," he continued as if wanting to have a conversation.

"Yeah, it probably will be. I'm gonna make baked chicken and dressing with mashed potatoes for the Special. What you think?" "Sounds good. I'll peel the potatoes. How many you think you'll need?"

We were being civil and actually kind . . . not a "put-on."

"I don't think there's that many; may as well do all of them. I can make rice if we run out."

Vic went to his part of the house and got fresh clothes and a razor before getting back to take his shower. I left to make my bed and to put on some coffee before going downstairs. In the corner of my bedroom, I glanced over to see what was happening with the candle; to see if it was still burning black. And, sure enough, it was. More than half had burned, leaving a thick, black layer of soot. The queasy feeling returned.

By nine o'clock, the chicken and vegetable lasagna were in the oven. Vic had the potatoes cut up and ready to boil. I made a large, fresh salad and five gallons of our signature lemon iced tea. By ten, I had my shower, dressed, and was ready for the day. Our scheduled employees were all in and ready to go, and I was grateful.

As predicted, we had a gloriously busy lunch. The Special sold out by twelve-thirty, and for those who had short lunch breaks, the Special was ideal; and from the numerous comments, it was also delicious. By two-thirty, things had slowed down, and all of us were ready for a break. The girls had made some good tips, and one offered to work that evening as well. Vic and I usually worked it ourselves, but she also offered to work for tips only . . . now you know I jumped on that. And by eight that night, it was beginning to look like a poetry night. I was so happy I had help. The three of us were humping up until closing.

The Shit Hits the Fan

The month of June eased its way in without any warning. Before I knew it, I was being reminded that I had passed the golden age of 50 and was now 51 years old. It was my birthday, June 4th. I received calls and well-wishes from family and a few friends, including my estranged husband, to wish me a happy birthday with hopes of many more. Trey sent a card which happened to arrive on the day of. I have to admit, being another year older led to more self-reflection and questions of my sanity. There was no celebration like the year before, when I had been taken totally off guard with a surprise party. I truly had no clue. That day, when I walked in the house after returning from the store, I looked so bad I had to go shower and change before I could join in the celebration. However, this year showed no resemblance. My life had completely changed. And as optimistic as I was for happier times, I was in for a rude awakening.

For whatever reason, Vic and I had never gotten back to our conversation about his *leave* date. Before my celebratory day came to an end, I decided that it was a good time to talk. We both were in good moods and on good terms. No arguments as of late, and I was feeling pretty mellow after drinking a couple of glasses of wine and a one-time hit off a joint, which was a present from Vic. Needless to say, I would have no problem speaking my mind.

The night was moving into the beginning stages of a new day. It was around midnight, and Vic and I were sitting in the library. He was nursing the last of an Old Milwaukee while I savored the last sip of wine. We both had been unusually silent –it was Sunday, and we had spent the entire day cleaning. We were pooped. The night before was poetry night, and by the time it was over, it was nearly 3 a.m. before I hit the sack.

"Have you decided if you're gonna go back to the other house? "I inquired softly. It took a few minutes before he responded. So, I waited, making sure there was no indication that he was being rushed in any way, although anxiety was present.

"Uh, I'm not sure," he finally spoke. "I don't think it would work for me if I had to stay somewhere other than here. I mean . . . our old house is empty . . . I would have to buy furniture, have stuff turned on . . . and I don't have the money for that." Vic slouched in the chair and raised the beer can to his mouth before crushing it. The noise from the can was the only sound for the next few moments. I was busy trying to unknot my stomach and get the lump out of my throat before attempting to respond in a calm and rational manner. I raised the wine glass to my mouth in hopes that there was at least one more drop to wet my dry tongue. But, like my tongue, the glass was dry.

"So, what are you saying?" I asked, taking a couple of slow, deep breaths, trying not to let Vic see that I was pissed.

"You not moving like you said you were? You said you would move out on the 17th and now you're telling me something different?"

My heart raced a little faster, and my volume had begun to escalate.

Vic sprang from his chair like a cat ready to pounce . . . "I can't afford to leave . . . so, I'm staying here," he stammered as if his pronouncement was as big a shock to him as it was to me.

"I can just stay in the back like I am now, and we can continue to run the business together. You want some more wine?"

I nodded and handed him my glass; took a cigarette from my pocket, lit it, and took a long, deep drag, hoping it would help calm my nerves and stop my knees from shaking. Now, it all made sense why the candle was burning black.

I hadn't told Vic about Trey's moving in with me. I figured it was none of his business, especially since he was supposed to be moving. And now that it looked as though all my plans were being detoured, I frighteningly realized that things could get really shitty. So, I kept repeating to myself that everything would be okay and took a sip from the chilled wine before setting the glass on the table. I then looked up at Vic and quite calmly said, "Vic, you will not stop me from living my life. You will not stop me from being happy. You have always done *exactly* what you wanted to do, and you never cared how it affected me. What goes around, comes around, Vic. I just hope you can handle it. I'm going to bed. Have a good night!"

Before I hit the cold sheets, I found myself hitting the wall with my hands before falling to my knees at my altar; my sobs wrenched at the deepest part of my stomach while trying to suffocate the intense pain of hurt and confusion. Followed by a stream of salty tears, I cried out to my ancestors.

"Why, why do I have to keep going through this? Don't I deserve to be happy? I've done everything you've guided me to do. I can't keep giving and not get anything back. You have got to work this out. You've got to help me!"

I was too tired to wait for an answer, and I wasn't sure if I would like their response, anyway. After all, estranged or not, I was about to bring another man into our home.

THIRTY-SIX

Temporary Housing

It was after 2 o'clock by the time I came out of dreamland. The late afternoon sun made the upstairs feel like a sauna. Our costly air-conditioning fell short of providing any relief. Just the thought of the half-ass work made me even hotter. So, I tried to put it in the back of my mind, opened the windows, and found a fan. After a quick cup of coffee, I grabbed a cigarette and took a couple of quick puffs before dashing off to my car. It was time to freshen my altar with fresh flowers and a new candle. There was some major beseeching to do with the ancestors, and I knew I had to come to them, right. So, I made a quick run to the store.

A dozen white Daisies alongside a white candle were a starting point in resurrecting the life back into the space where I normally found energy and strength. Wilted flowers and black residue from the candle were a sure sign that it was time for a change, in more ways than one. I retrieved an apple and a banana from the grocery bag, double-checking for any imperfections before meticulously placing them on the mat. After burning some sage to clear and cleanse the space, as usual, I burned Frankincense and Myrrh to top it off with a sweet scent.

After a shower, I took the sage and moved it up and down and around my body and over my head, praying for the releasing of all negative energy as the smothering stream of airy, gray smoke dissipated into the dampness of my skin. Smudging was an important part of the preparation for making my appeal to the ancestors, and I really needed to clear my energy. As of late, it had been pretty funky.

Before kneeling, I poured libation with fresh, anointed water. My nakedness was draped with a white towel, as was my hair. My chest rose as I took in the warm air around me, consciously allowing it to escape for the next inhale. And with each breath, my shoulders slowly released the anxiety that had me bound. Everything around me had been moving like a whirlwind of uncertainties, mixed feelings, fears and doubts. I could no longer bear the burdens. Something had to be done, and I could only pray that the ancestors had answers, or at least some guidance.

It was over an hour that I sat before the altar — before the peace of sweet serenity gave way to my restless spirit. And although tranquil, I felt energized and ready for whatever was in the cards. At least, that's what I thought.

Deciding to meet Trey at Saria's house, wasn't the original plan. However, since Vic had reneged on his promise, Saria thought it would be best if Trey came to her house to stay until we figured something out. Husband and boyfriend living under the same roof. (Yeah, I can hear you gasping now, and I can't say that I blame you–that was a hard one for me, too).

Just to give you an idea of the love that was around me and supporting me, Saria was a Real Sistah. Her rich, dark complexion glowed with pride from her Jamaican roots. She sported dreadlocks, wore conservative long skirts and dresses, and wraps that covered her arms and upper body . . . as to honor her religion as a Muslim. And she smoked plenty of Herbalicious, if you get my drift, in which she called 'a spliff.' She was truly a Rasta! She was a Queen, a spiritual healer – one who communicated with her guides and ancestors through divination and rituals. She was an amazing singer, and on many occasions, graced our business with her rhythmic Reggae tunes, many of which she penned herself. She was a mother who raised her three children to obey the Laws of Allah, and worked a full-time job in social services, aiding others to get through tough times. I was inconceivably blessed by her presence and spiritual guidance.

Saria made a great space for Trey and me. The upstairs room, just large enough for a full-size mattress, a small bookcase, and a portable radio, was perfect. Just outside our private space was an open area much like a sitting room, which led to another small room with a window. Fresh flowers sat on a table next to a large, overstuffed chair, and Saria had candles burning on a dresser, along with some incense. We were much alike in many ways.

The excitement of seeing Trey was dampened by the sudden turn of events. However, for the next few weeks, we managed to move through the turbulence that was slowly but surely bringing forth thoughts that I felt I was too spiritual to have. On top of wishing I could just disappear into the abyss of La-La land, I found myself doubting my purpose, my assignment, which was not good. Doubt, by all accounts, can make you believe in Satan.

Of course, by now, Vic knew the whole story about Trey, but it didn't seem to make him wanna forego his new decision to stay. It was rough! I was feeling torn between dropping everything and finding a new life, or to go deep within my soul and *grow* through this manifestation of trials and tribulations, in which I could blame no one but myself. I had really created some shit this time.

Unbelievable

It was on a Saturday, a little after midnight, and I was putting together an overnight bag for my nightly getaway. It was an off night for poetry, and I couldn't have been happier. The thought of getting out at two or three in the morning was exhausting just to think about it. Vic and I continued to stay civil with each other, which helped. We managed to talk and have decent conversations without getting into our personal struggles. However, it was hard for both of us. The pain was real, and it was deep.

Wearing his signature smile, Vic approached me as I was about to leave.

"Hey, busy night tonight . . . almost like a poetry night."

He was so close, I could smell his fading cologne. I have to admit that I was also a little unsettled. We hadn't been that close in months.

"Yeah," I mumbled. I was tired and not in the mood for any drama. "Glad it was over at a decent hour and that we're off tomorrow. I can use the rest."

"Look," he continued. "Why don't you have your friend . . . What's his name?"

"Trey, his name is Trey," I answered.

I had no idea what he was going to say, but I damn sure didn't expect what came out of his mouth next.

"Yeah, that's right; you know how I am with names. Why don't you have him stay here? It don't make no sense for you to keep havin' to leave your own home every night. It's got to be wearing you out," he suggested with no hesitation while sitting on the step at the bottom of the stairs. I damn near dropped my bag. But I was cool.

"What are you talking about?" I stammered. "You mean you want me to have Trey come here and stay while you're here?" I can only imagine the look I had on my face. "You kidding, right? What have you been smoking?"

"No, seriously, it has to be hard on you. And things are hard enough as it is. I understand that you need somebody." Vic adjusted himself and stretched his legs to lean back before continuing. "I did say that I was gonna leave. Hell, everybody knows what's going on anyway."

I motioned for him to make room for me to sit down, took a deep breath, and sat on the next step. I needed to make sure I heard what I thought I heard. This was deep. Trying to stay positive as I listened to my husband invite my boyfriend to our home and business, my ego led me to think some real weird stuff as to whether or not it was some type of plan to get us together to... well, I won't say what I was really thinking. Let's just say that skepticism quickly became a priority. However, after discussing it for nearly an hour, Vic eased my suspicion. It appeared that his concern for my welfare seemed to be legitimate. Now the question became, was I ready to find out just how serious? But first, I needed to run it past my lover.

"What! You mean your husband wants me to come while he's still there?"

Beads of sweat surfaced along Trey's hairline as he listened to me trying to explain what my husband and I had talked about. I could read it on his face that he, too, must have been thinking along the same lines as I did, as to my initial response to Vic's suggestion. Needless to say, neither one of us was able to make any sense of it. So, I did what I normally do, or at least sometimes. I called Saria to do a query with the Angels to see if our concerns were, in fact, warranted. All three of us were pleasantly surprised by the answer.

I remembered when my dad, who, on occasion, would say something that actually made sense. Especially, when he found it difficult to believe that his daughter, the one that he beat, pulled knives on and treated like shit most of her life, would be the very one that took care of his cantankerous ass, which led him to say, "God sure works in mysterious ways." This was one of those times when those exact words were my sentiments exactly. However, the answer also showed that there were going to be some *challenges.*

It was Sunday, and Trey and I stayed in bed most of the day, managing to get a little TLC in the mix. A little hugging and kissing, along with a nice, long massage, put me in the mood, although initially, I swore that I was too tired *to bust a grape.* Needless to say, all I needed was a little convincing that not only did I *want* to make love... I *needed* to. It had been a rough week physically and emotionally, but more importantly, mentally. And Good sex is a Must if your sanity is at stake. And believe me, I knew what it felt like to be on the brink of insanity. Ooh, ooh, ooh, what a little "intimacy" can do.

After releasing in a most pleasurable way, Trey served brunch in bed, which was the perfect ending to a great afternoon. Being a little more relaxed, we continued our discussion and decided to wait until Monday (since we were closed) to officially move him into our home. Nonetheless, no matter how much we talked about it, or what the Angels said, or the fact that we had *released* some stress, the entire situation was still strange as hell.

While Trey was finally able to fall asleep (which normally happens after some *good loving)*, I was nervous, unsure, and a little confused about how I was gonna pull this whole thing off. *What would I say? "Hello, Vic, this is my boyfriend. Trey, my husband, Vic."* This was getting more weird than I thought . . . now that I was actually thinking about it. I played the scenario several different ways in my head, and they all sounded crazy. Bottom line, whatever was going to be said . . . would be said.

THIRTY-SEVEN

Two's Company, Three's Insane

It was late evening before we finally made our way to Trey's new living quarters. We didn't see Vic that night. I could never tell when he came home, unless I looked to see if his truck was in the yard, which on this occasion, I did... and it wasn't, which allowed both of us to calm down and to see our perceived dilemma positively. After all, we had sought the advice of the ancestors and Spirit Guides, and besides, it was Vic's idea. He appeared serious when we talked and showed legitimate concern for my well-being. So, what could be the problem?

Trey was in awe with the massiveness of the place he now called home. His eyes widened as he took in each room, while his responses were mostly preceded with . . . "WOW and Oh My God!" and he hadn't even seen the area where Vic had staked out as his private quarters, which were three more rooms and a porch still covered with plywood. And although Vic wasn't in, I opted not to invade his privacy. However, what Trey did see was more house than he had ever seen in his life. He was amazed and excited beyond words.

The tour and a little more explanation of the mansion's history eventually led us back to my bedroom, which was now *our* bedroom. Interestingly enough, I felt at ease. There was a strength that seemed to magically overtake any nervousness or any doubt about whether or not I was doing the right thing. It was as if I had garnered an inner pride, giving myself permission to move on with my life, even if the situation was considered precarious, to say the least. I stood there with Trey's arms wrapped around me like a bow on a present. In a way, I was a present . . . his. And he was mine.

The Introduction

After Trey and I took our showers, we said a prayer, seeking the support of the ancestors before entering the lion's den. We were headed towards the kitchen area when we saw Vic in the hallway. "Hey, so you got yourself a pretty boy," Vic said as he approached us with a huge smile and his hand out. "So, you're my wife's boyfriend," extending his hand to Trey's.

Trey looked him dead in the face and said, "That would be me; how's it going, man?"

I began stacking dishes, trying to let them have their moment.

"The name's Trey, pleased to meet you. You are obviously, Victor."

Vic stood there in his white apron over a white T-shirt and pressed slacks, along with a multicolored headscarf, bouncing like he was *on something*.

"Yep, but everybody calls me Uncle Vic. Hope you're ready to work. Me and my wife work real hard around here. But it looks like you might be able to handle it," grabbing Trey's upper arm where he buffed a tight muscle.

"Hey, you might as well meet the rest of the family," my estranged husband continued.

Vic hollered out for the boys who were in the back; he had obviously picked them up the night before or that morning. They were on summer break, which meant that they would be spending quite a bit of it with us.

After a strange and quite awkward introduction, my previous sentiments of strength and courage began to weaken as I met the eyes of my stepsons. Although they knew what was up, I still felt guilt-ridden and embarrassed by what was happening between their dad and me. Being polite, the three of them cordially met the new extended member of the family. Whew! Talk about weird.

Despite the awkwardness, the day went rather smoothly. Most of our customers thought nothing of Trey being there. He was another new employee, finding his way around. For those who knew the situation, Trey was met with warm affection, but also with an occasional lift of the brow. I, on the other hand, was simply grateful that things were going as well as they were.

It was close to 3 o'clock before any of us were able to take a break. The regular staff left after cleaning and setting up for dinner. It had been too busy to really get to know the new kid on the block; nevertheless, there were going to be plenty of other times to get more of the 411. Meanwhile, Vic was making an effort to get to know how Trey liked his first day. Now that we had time to sit for a while, Vic sat down with his rival and had a beer. Surprisingly, as I watched from a not-too-far distance, they appeared to be getting along well, and that Vic was being civil and accommodating. Everyone seemed to be getting along quite well... considering.

Observation

I was proud of me and Vic for being mature enough to live our lives separately while living under the same roof; for not allowing jealousy and ignorance to keep us from working together or being loving (somewhat) and civil towards each other. Yes, we were being mature and understanding that shit happens, and that it didn't have to be about finding fault or blaming. After all, it is what it is. Or is it?

It was less than a month later when my estranged husband let me know that he had been checking out whether or not my new lover could *fit the bill*. His observation wasn't too hopeful. "You know, I'm pretty good at readin' people," Vic said one night as we talked about our situation. "He's a pretty boy and all that, but he's lazy. That boy ain't done no real hard work; his hands are too soft. I mean, he's all right as long as you're givin' him somethin' to do, but he ain't gonna do somethin' cause it needs to be done."

As I listened to Vic's observation, I had to face the hard reality that, unfortunately, he was right. I could see it, even though Trey would do whatever I asked him to do, with a few breaks in between, I'd noticed. He definitely wasn't what I was accustomed to. Vic did work his ass off. Maybe it was gonna take a little time for Trey to get used to restaurant work. Maybe I expected too much. I remember my goddaughter, Jackie, telling me once that I was a slave driver. *"Hell, girl, I know this bitch is a former plantation, but damn, you work a person like he's a slave on this motherfucker."* Maybe she was right.

THIRTY-EIGHT

What a Little Honesty Can Do

Tension was a new wave of energy between me and Trey. It was happening, the honeymoon was coming to a halt, after only a couple of months. We still made love, hugged and kissed, now and then. We even talked about a future together and what that would mean regarding the business and all. We rationalized and did the what-ifs. We did all the right things to keep a relationship moving forward. Yet something was not quite honest . . . not quite authentic.

Something must have been brewing in the air, because I also noticed that my agreeable, estranged husband was beginning to snap at times, raising his voice (often unwarranted) when we tried to have a conversation. While I never expected us to be stress or trouble-free, I did think that the three of us were adapting to our unorthodox lifestyle quite well. I just didn't have a clue how it would pan out in the long run.

After some contemplation regarding the way I was treating Trey, I decided to have a talk with him, assuring him that all was cool and that I would try to give him some slack. I shared Vic's observation of him, which he took without any outburst of ego or male pride. I even noticed him making an effort to own up to a little more of his responsibilities to the business as "my man." For a while, it appeared that things were back on track. However, unbeknownst to me, Vic had decided to get on another track; one that would take us in two, totally different directions.

Since the summer was coming to an end, Trey drove to Chicago to visit with his kids and to spend a few days with them before they went back to school. Although absent, Trey called his two children a few times a week, in which some of those times, they also got an opportunity to speak with me. I also spoke with his wife a few times, which gave her a sense of trust regarding allowing her children to come and visit. We were much more civil towards each other than Vic's ex-wife, and she didn't seem to carry any residual feelings for her estranged husband. Truth be told, she sounded as if she were quite happy with the setup. Everyone was being upfront and honest.

Speaking of honesty, Vic and I got together to talk while Trey was away. Like I mentioned, he had been somewhat— different, almost like jealousy. At least, that's what it seems like to me.

It was a hot August day, and the house was empty with the exception of me and Vic. It actually felt good not having a bunch of people around, to have some real quiet time. I made the suggestion that we go out on the balcony and talk. At first, Vic was a little skeptical . . . said he didn't want to get into any arguments. I assured him that I only wanted to talk... to clear the air. Personally, I was still extremely angry about his lying about Daisy, and why he stopped treating me like his wife. And even though we had moved on with our lives, I suppose you could say, I still needed closure.

Although it was hot and sticky, a faint breeze gave some relief from the humidity while we sat on the balcony. Vic had brought us a glass of iced tea and a turkey sandwich. After eating in silence for a few minutes, I took a couple of deep breaths before speaking to make sure I didn't come off as hostile or angry. Since we both seemed to struggle with having a conversation, I decided that I would break the ice.

"Okay, Vic, first understand that I am NOT trying to start any shit. I just want us to be completely honest with each other . . . completely honest. There is no need for either of us to lie. We are separated and have decided to move on with our lives, and I'm suggesting that we come clean so that we both can *really* move on." I paused for a moment to see if Vic was on board.

"Yeah, you right. We do need to talk." He, too, took a deep sigh and leaned against the edge of the window. My back was pressed against the iron railing, facing him.

"You want a pillow for your back?" Vic asked, concerned for my comfort.

"That would be nice, Vic; I would appreciate that."

After retrieving a pillow, Vic helped to place it behind my back before sitting back down. We resumed our talk.

"Vic, you know that I have dreams and visions, right?" Vic nodded in the affirmative.

"It's hard for me to say this, Vic," I cautiously continued. "But I have had dreams about you and . . . your best friend."

I took another deep breath as Vic froze— as if he stopped breathing for a brief moment.

"I know about your relationship . . . I know why you are unable to love me as your wife."

My husband nervously moved around to adjust himself to face me. His eyes instantly turned red and swelled with tears. I had never seen my husband cry. He dropped his head as he began to speak.

"You know my father left when I was only twelve years old," he whispered. "There was no man around, and my mama always... well, she didn't know any better. She would always perm my hair; she made me suits. Hell, I was the only kid in elementary school that wore suits."

I could tell he was struggling with trying to tell me "why" he couldn't be the man that I needed him to be as a husband. His sentences were jumbled and incomplete. But I knew what he was trying to say. As much as it hurt . . . I knew.

"When I met you, Nailah . . .," my husband smiled as if thinking of the past as he looked at me briefly before continuing. ". . . you saved my life."

While I wasn't sure exactly what he meant about *saving his life*, I didn't say anything.

"You're right . . . and all I can say is that I'm truly sorry . . . and I mean that. I am so sorry."

I knew then, that all those horrible, frightening dreams were no figment of my imagination. In a strange way, I was glad that I was right about my feelings that my husband was... gay. There, I said it! At least now I knew that I wasn't crazy or that God wasn't playing tricks on me. We were both quiet for what seemed like an eternity. My heart sank deep into my stomach, for I ached for my husband. Every sad emotion I could possibly feel was felt at that moment. I couldn't say anything. I could only cry. Not profusely, but slowly, like a dripping faucet.

"You were right about Daisy, too," he managed to continue. "I got high one night and . . ." I watched him closely as each word that fell from his lips seemed to take a weight off his shoulders. ". . . I know it was wrong. And I've been sorry ever since. The last thing I wanted to do was hurt you."

At that point, I had to ask the question. "Why did you keep lying to me, Vic? You knew that I knew. My dreams don't lie to me, and you treated me as if I was crazy or stupid."

"I didn't know how to tell you. I truly didn't want to hurt you."

I silently thought about those words: *He didn't want to hurt me.* WOW! That was an understatement, if I ever heard one. I was way beyond hurt! *Damn! Why didn't God, the ancestors... somebody SHOW me this before I said, "I do!"* I cried in the privacy of my mind. It was only "after" we were married that I began to have the dreams about this. The dreams I could never speak about and was too afraid to admit what I was being shown. My beautiful husband with another man! What could I say?

Vic somberly continued his confession. "I am still a man, Nailah, and I do love you . . . not the way you want me to . . . but I do love you."

Even though I had heard those words before, they sounded different this time. I actually believed him. I grabbed my husband and held on as if my life depended on it. It was the first time that Vic actually *let me cry on his shoulders* (except when Mark died), and cry, I did! The tears came like a broken dam. I was devastated to the core! But what was really crazy, as Vic wrapped his arms around me, I realized that . . . I *still* loved him.

In that short time span, everything was finally out in the open. Our souls had been set free for the first time in five years. And I knew Vic had to be as happy as I was to get the truth out, once and for all. And although Vic's reasoning as to *who* he was (due to the absence of a father and how his mother treated him), I wondered if he was simply "born" that way— no fault of anyone's, and no need for shame or guilt. Either way, I was thankful that he was finally able to acknowledge the truth... not only to me, but to himself!

Neither one of us had much to say after his confession, and we never spoke of that day again. However, something else happened that threw me completely off guard. Vic's moment of truth was NOT the final straw that broke the proverbial camel's back, but rather *mine* . . . and my heart, again! Yes, he had something *brewing* in the air.

THIRTY-NINE

Something Brewing in the Air

Just when you think you know a little something... that you've gained control over your emotions and have love in your heart for *everyone* (because that's what *spiritual* people do, right?)...well, that's when the shit really hits the fan . . . flying everywhere.

I never spoke of the conversation between me and Vic to anyone. That was our secret. However, there were times when I wanted to tell everyone the whole sordid story, especially since some people were referring to me as a bitch, blaming me for our separation. But I kept my mouth shut. And, as of late, we lost a couple of old customers whom I thought were open-minded, such as my friend, Martha, the one who was so supportive in our purchasing the mansion and offered to loan me $25,000. Surprisingly, she was quite angry with me when I ran for governor, especially since I chose to run as an *Independent* with the Natural Law Party (now why she would get upset because of that... I have no clue). However, when she heard about Uncle Vic and me, she *completely* dropped me as a friend.

We also lost a couple more friends because we allowed gays as a part of The Java House extended family. These were people that I thought were true friends or at least die-hard customers who supported us because we served the community in so many ways. On top of that, the Christian radio stations blasted on the airwaves that I was a devil and bound for hell for condoning homosexuality, which was a little unnerving, to say the least. Bottom line, The Java House embraced ALL people, and I wasn't about to change that for anybody! Meanwhile, there were some . . .

Strange Happenings

I'm not sure what happened to Vic after our moment of truth and his confessed *love* for me, but he got weird. He started arguments for no reason. His ability to take an order got really crazy, having to repeat an order four or five times. While he did that in the past, and me thinking that it was because of his being out of practice for more than a year, only to find out that it was due to *crack*... seemed to have gotten worse. At times, his look was wild and crazy as if possessed by something or someone. To tell the truth, I was getting scared. I had also noticed that one of his prosthetic clients was coming around quite a bit. He was from Cuba and was acting quite differently with me since our separation. This really made me suspicious.

One poetry night, Vic was in rare form. He came out into the restaurant area and started talking really loud and crazy. He then got on the mic, and to everyone's surprise, he began to recite a poem: *"And then the Cocaine Came . . ."* Of course, he got everyone's attention, for we hadn't heard that particular poem. Plus, he did it in the form of Spoken Word . . . right off the top of his head. I can't speak for everyone else, but I was shocked that he would actually do a poem about *cocaine*, especially since I had found out the truth. He got a standing ovation!

As usual, it was extremely busy, and Trey was running around half crazy, but loving every bit of it. He had been unusually supportive since our talk and working hard to keep me happy. He was enjoying the art that was taking place and even complimented Uncle Vic on his poem. He, like everyone else, probably surmised that Vic was speaking from experience. Yes, that night was a shocker . . . and unfortunately, that was just the beginning. Vic was on a mission with a few other things brewing. Not only was Vic acting strange and sneaky, but his disposition also seemed to create a dark energy that lurked around the twenty-two rooms that I hadn't felt before— even when there were *Presences* that had me running out of the mansion on a couple of occasions. This was no friendly or playful Spirit, and I was beginning to feel . . . threatened. Yes, something was different.

A Little Help From a Friend

The summer heat had no mercy on the fact that our air-conditioner wasn't working upstairs. On this particular day, Trey was out, and Vic had been out all night. When I heard the knock on the door, I had just been praying for some guidance and clarity on the disturbing feelings that seemed to taunt me. That knock would prove to be an opening into finding some answers. It was Rita, a dear friend who had been another spiritual blessing in my life.

Seeing Rita again made me happy. She was a voluptuous Sistah who carried it well, along with great pride for her African ancestry. Her kinky twists sprouted from a warm, colorful Kente head-wrap, which highlighted her bright and cheerful smile. Her teeth sparkled with whiteness, emphasizing her rounded, mocha cheeks.

"Hey, Sistah Nailah," she beamed, giving me a genuine hug, which I truly needed at the time. "I've been picking up on your energy and thought I would drop by," she continued before releasing me from her passionate embrace. Rita had been a Java House family member since its inception, and always supportive. Amazingly, Spirit knew once again just what I needed. And it couldn't have come from a better person.

Before we got upstairs, my dear friend began to pick up some energy.

"What's going on with you and Uncle Vic? And I'm not talking about the breakup."

"Funny you should ask. I've been getting concerned," I began to explain. "I'm not sure how to explain it... but he's been looking and acting really weird, lately."

We had made our way upstairs and sat on the balcony off my bedroom, trying to catch some of the infrequent breezes.

"I ran into a close family member of Uncle Vic's the other day, and I didn't like the way she was talking. You know, she is really jealous of you. I don't trust her, and I think she's doing something." Rita paused briefly, as if to choose her words . . .

"I think she's been talking to someone who does Black Magic, and I believe Uncle Vic is involved, as well as one of our friends who's been hanging out with Uncle Vic and this family member. I would rather not mention names since I'm not positive. But I'm sure you know who they are."

Rita had lost the sparkle she came in with, and she was right. I had a really good idea as to who she was speaking of, and what she said was no surprise. She was saddened. She once looked to these people as good friends; the disappointment was apparent. However, Rita's love and friendship for me were even more apparent. And for that, I was truly grateful.

Our conversation gradually took on a less somber aura. We laughed and talked about the fun times and future possibilities for The Java House. She also took time to share her warm feelings for Trey. I had her blessings, and before my friend left, she made it quite clear that I should see our friend Shangodora (my Yoruba teacher) to get more clarity on what was surrounding me. Rita felt that her warnings were just enough to assure me of the severity and as a confirmation of my distraught feelings. And believe me, I took her suggestion very seriously.

The Brew

It took two days before I could get an appointment with Shangodora. It was good to see her again; it had been well over a year since our last conversation. An indication that I hadn't had the time or energy to finalize my training as a priestess. She looked bright and happy. Her life had its own challenges as a priestess, as well as raising six sons. However, she always took time to help others, and often with little or no compensation.

Shangodora's new home mirrored the reflections of Africa. Masks, artifacts, pictures, and other memorabilia from her many visits to the Motherland were the focal points of her decor. Her spacious, four-bedroom home was beautiful. No comparison to the crowded, three-bedroom public housing that she came from only a few months earlier. Her oldest son, a professional football player, had made the big times, and he made sure his mother benefited from his success. And God knows, she deserved it.

After sharing and catching up with what had been going on with our lives, Shangodora prayed and ritualized the space before consulting the ancestors. While the Cowrie Shells were used as a tool for divination, she never asked too many questions; she had that gift of tuning right in and picking up on what was surrounding the querent.

"So, you have learned of your husband's secret," she stated instead of asking. "He is ashamed . . ." She pondered for a few moments before continuing. "He thought things would change when he married you. He tried . . . he does love you the only way he knows how." Pausing again briefly, she continued to tell me that one of Vic's close family members was jealous and working with negative energy (Rita was right on it) to get me out of the building, and that their intention was to run the business with Vic. She also alerted me that there was a container of some sort in a room on top of a mantle.

"Don't touch this container," she warned me. With her eyes still closed, she shook her head. "Um, um, um, they really want you out of the way," she continued. "I see a very dark-skinned man around him who has worked with the dark side. Do you know who I mean?" She frowned as she inquired.

"Yes, I believe it's one of his clients. He's from Cuba, and he's been acting rather strangely here lately."

"Yes," she nodded in agreement. "That's him; he's no good. Watch him."

She took a deep breath before continuing. "There's also a woman who you think is your friend . . . she helps out a lot at the restaurant, and she has two daughters and wears glasses."

She shook her head in disbelief before continuing. "She and your husband are doing drugs together... and she's working to help get you out of the way. She hasn't been around lately, but she'll show herself at some point; she won't be able to be around you."

At that instant, I felt I knew who she was talking about but decided not to say anything. I continued to listen with a stiff upper lip and a feeling of defeat, that I had somehow failed to *see* what was right under my nose.

"Your husband is very weak right now, and this family member is using that weakness to do their dirty work. There are drugs and alcohol... it's getting worse... you have to watch him closely," she warned me before taking another deep breath. "There will be some dark times... but you will get through them." She got quiet for a few moments as I sat there in astonishment, unable to believe what I was hearing, and yet, it confirmed my suspicions, as well as Rita's.

"Keep praying," she continued in a soft-spoken voice, almost whispering. "Your ancestors are with you, and no harm will come to you. You will be guided and protected."

There was more, and by the time I left, I was dumbfounded. The only consolation was that I was protected and would be guided. And the way things were going, I was really in need of all the help I could get. For now, I needed to know who my enemies were . . . at least one of them.

Reflections of a Sweat

On the way home, I gave some more thought about the woman who was pretending to be my friend. The more I thought about it, the more I realized who it was. It made me think back to a Sweat Ceremony I attended not long after we opened at the mansion. My friend, Nasheed, often facilitated Sweats during the summer in remote locations in Northern Kentucky, which on several occasions, I attended.

On this particular Sweat, we were greeted by Nasheed and one of his sons, and two other young brothers from the college campus where

Nasheed was employed. The tepee-style tent was unusually large, which was a sign that several people had RSVP'd for this auspicious occasion. Right in front of the tent, various-sized rocks were piled high on an open, fiery pit. The intense heat spread out about five or six feet, making the heat of the day even hotter. My goddaughter, Jackie, and a couple of other people from the restaurant, along with this woman that Shangodora was telling me about, all went to participate. Anyway, we drove in two different cars, and *this woman* chose to ride with another driver. Although odd, I didn't give it much thought.

As with most spiritual rituals, it was necessary to be cleansed with Sage before entering the tent. Wearing as little as possible without being inappropriate, Jackie and I were among the first to enter with "me and my relations" (a statement said upon entering). However, the woman in question could NOT go into the tent (although she made the attempt) and made an excuse that she wasn't feeling well and thought she should go sit in the car. Jackie and I overheard the sister and looked at each other, with lips sealed.

Since I knew what to expect regarding the *heat* situation, I immediately went to the back of the tent. That way, if it got unbearable, I would cunningly lie on the ground and slightly raise the bottom of the tent— just enough to get a little air, and hope that no one would notice. But, as the ancestors would have it, Nasheed rearranged those of us who were veterans and put the novice ones in the back. I ended up sitting right in front of the pit. Jackie was directly across from me.

By the time all twelve of us were tightly fitted around the small pit of hot rocks, Nasheed sought out the Elder of the group to get permission to begin our Sweat. An obviously older man spoke up as the Elder and graciously gave permission to begin. And in that short span of time, it was already hot! Prayer and invocation were led by our leader while dippers of water were being passed through to raise the heat. The water hitting the rocks caused a cascade of hot rain, landing on my legs. The amazing thing was, by the time the water hit my sweaty skin, the drops were a cool reprieve from the torturous heat. Nasheed reminded us that if it got too hot, to quietly go outside until we were able to come back in... if we chose to come back, which was always an option. Seeing who could stand the heat the longest was by no means a goal.

In that session, several participants went into trances. Some prayed while others sang Negro spirituals. I, on the other hand, began to *channel* what appeared to be one of my Native American ancestors. With my closed eyes, the vision of a campfire appeared with dancers and drummers, and I began to sing what seemed to be a chant. I could hear myself sing this unfamiliar tune, but had no way of understanding what it meant, nor could I stop it. At this point, I was not conscious of any heat; I was pleasantly comfortable.

I'm not sure how long I was in that state, but the next thing I heard was Nasheed making the suggestion that we call upon our "animal totem." Not knowing what would show up, I took a few deep breaths and silently requested that my totem make itself known. Then what seemed to be in no time at all... a Black Panther was IN MY FACE! Was I scared? No! It almost looked as if it had a smile. Its huge, dark eyes were peaceful and serene-looking. After a few brief moments of leaving me in a state of wonderment, the huge feline slowly turned, exposing its long, lean body of muscles before taking off into a "slow motion" sprint. Then, magically, I noticed that my sacred animal guide was carrying two passengers; a white Serpent lay coiled in the center of its back, while a Dove perched peacefully on its back. It was like nothing I had ever seen–it was beautiful and surreal, leaving me with a feeling of deep tranquility and a sense of being divinely protected. I had not one... but 3 powerful totems ready to serve as guardians and as guides on my life's path.

I don't know how long our sick friend was in the car, but it was dark by the time we came out of the tent. We all moved around gathering our things with little conversation. The vast sky highlighted millions of stars and a colossal full moon, with no buildings to obstruct its beauty. The entire area was only landscaped with clusters of aged trees separated by wide open spaces. Enjoying its magnificence, I silently gave thanks to the Gods, Mother Earth, and our Ancestral Guides.

Jackie tapped on the window where our friend was slumped in the back seat and asked if she was okay. Half asleep, she yawned and nodded her head that she was fine. Neither one of us questioned her about her illness. We knew something else must have been going on. She appeared to be fine when we left, and she was laughing and talking with several people while we were preparing for the Sweat. When we all met at Nasheed's home, his wife and daughter had made vegetarian chili for us. After eating, Jackie and I got with Nasheed to get his take on "our girl" not being able to go in. He proceeded to tell us about a time when he and his son had a disagreeable session while doing a Sweat, which resulted in his being burned several times on the arm, which was uncommon for him. He surmised that his *spirit* was not in alignment with what he was doing, and getting burned was showing him he needed to 'check himself.'

"Her spirit was not right," he went on to explain. "And the ancestors would not allow her to go in." Jackie and I left it at that without trying to get more details about the "why." However, at that point, I knew that if the ancestors wouldn't allow our friend to go into the **sacred space** (after traveling over 30 miles), that told me that whatever was going on, she definitely warranted watching!

Anyway, back to that day after leaving Shangodora's house . . .

When I returned to the house, I immediately looked to see if Vic's van was around, it wasn't. I ran upstairs from the back entrance since he had the door that led to his part of the house blocked off from the inside. Lucky for me, the back door could only be locked from the inside. I was so eager to find the container that I didn't bother to look and see how my estranged husband was living on his side. I went straight to the room where the fireplace was, the room Shangodora had seen. There it was, just like she said.

I walked closer to get a look at the vase-like container that sat on the mantle. Swirled with silver and grey, it was pretty . . . not threatening at all. As I went to pick it up, to get a closer look,

Shangodora's warning resounded in my mind, *"Don't touch it!"* So, I leaned forward to look inside. Unlike the container, the dark, mud-like substance was horrible looking, and it looked to have blood mixed in it. I shivered as I backed away, sickened to my stomach.

Suddenly, a burst of tears poured like a broken sprout. I was angry... devastated and deeply hurt that my husband, although estranged, could hate me so much to take such drastic steps to hurt me. At that point, I didn't care about the excuses of drugs and alcohol or someone else's influence, or his Cuban friend or my so-called friend's support in this devious attempt to destroy me. I was married to this man . . . how could he?

I don't recall much once I returned to my side of our home, and I couldn't control the waterfall of pain and anguish. I must have been in shock when Trey shook me. I hadn't heard him call my name the three times he said he tried to get my attention. I was sitting on the edge of the bed, and I had no idea how long I had been there.

"What's wrong?" Trey asked, obviously frightened.

I knew my eyes were swollen; his face blurred as I gazed at him before laying my head on his shoulder, unable to speak. Trey's concern for me was so warm and genuine, yet I could not speak about what was so troubling. I eventually was able to tell him that I would be okay; that I had come to realize just how much Vic wanted to hurt me. Without any further explanation, I assured him that one day I would be able to share with him what had happened. We then lay down while Trey rocked me until I fell asleep.

FORTY

Open House

For the next few days, it took all I had not to blast Vic, letting him know that I knew what his plans were. However, planning for our upcoming Open House kept me extremely busy. Lining up the entertainment, setting up the yard and ordering food and cooking and getting the press to come through for what I considered, a historical event, was overriding any frustrations or fears.

The Harriet Tubman Cultural Center was being honored as a "Not-for-Profit" and had been awarded a few thousand dollars from the City's Alderman for our district. Grateful, isn't the word. By the grace of God, I had been stable enough to maintain our businesses by doing the necessary fund-raising and applying for grants to keep us financially afloat. Nevertheless, the politics were horrendous, and I found myself in the middle of a potential scandal. With the determination to be honest and run our business with integrity, I was able to unmask some unscrupulous behavior, which led to an audit and an investigation that eventually led to the resignation of an accountant and a closer look at our Alderman.

However, in the interim, before the shit hit the political fan, I was able to pay myself a stipend as the Center's director, which afforded me the opportunity to keep my promise to pay Vic's child support. No matter what our personal problems were, as Vic's wife, I was determined to keep my end of our agreement by making sure the boys got what they deserved. I also had the Center to pay the café rent, since they were two separate entities.

Keeping account of every penny, particularly for the Center, proved to be at times arduous, but it was mandatory for accurate records, allowing our public donors (if necessary) and board members to see where every penny was spent. I took pride in keeping good records, saving receipts, etc., it was what I considered business integrity. And having a Certified Public Accountant (CPA) was essential for maintaining those records in a format that satisfied the powers that be. My CPA, owned and operated by an African American female, was invaluable to me and the businesses.

The Open House went exceptionally well. All my troubles temporarily took a back seat as I was swept up in the energy of music, gaiety, and a sense of accomplishment. Saria performed along with several other newfound talents. Vic smoked turkeys, grilled Salmon and fresh corn. I made an array of salads, baked mac & cheese, and home-made desserts. And I blew up so many balloons that my mouth felt like cotton. But in the end, it was all worth it. We sold-out of all the dinners, and the café was able to benefit financially. It was everything we could have hoped for, as Vic and I smiled and carried on the pretense of being the ideal couple, while Trey gave us the space to play the game. However, the masquerade would soon come to a halt. . . big time!

FORTY-ONE

The Threat

One would think that after a great opening, Vic's attitude would have improved and be like old times. I had managed to suppress my knowledge of his concoction and refrained from letting him know that I knew about his partner-in-crime and his Cuban friend's intentions. I stored it all in a corner of my mind, trying to keep a lid on it; hoping that we could still work together as a team for the sake of our business, and not allow our personal differences to destroy everything we had worked so hard to achieve. After all, Vic and I had our *talk;* he confessed his love for me, albeit *unique*. Hey, maybe he had changed his mind about his intentions to hurt me. Well, at least that's what I was hoping for . . . even with Shangodora's warning. However, what I had *hoped* for was not in the cards . . . or in this case, Cowrie shells.

I can't recall exactly what happened this particular day in late July, but for whatever reason, Vic and I had gotten into an altercation. I remember being at the top of the stairs and I was complaining about how he had been treating me like shit. He was rude to me when I wanted to see the boys, although they, too, began to treat me... differently, which really hurt. I had loved those boys as if they were my own sons. I don't know how I thought our relationship would stay the same. The fact was, their father and I were separated—we both had relationships that fell short of what they had come accustomed to. For the past five years, there was security, frequent visits, and real family time— and now, all that had changed. And, of course, I was to blame.

Anyway, Vic and I were going back and forth with each other to the point that I blurted out something about what had come between us was not my fault; that his relationship with his best friend and getting Daisy pregnant were the real reasons we weren't together, not to mention the drugs. And while the details as to how our argument got started are somewhat vague, what I do remember, quite vividly, was how he looked! His eyes bulged with fire; his face tightened with anger, while his eyes roamed up and down me with a vengeance. I had seen him enraged before, but this was like a "he could kill me" kind of look.

"You the one that's gay— always with your girlfriends," Vic spat the words out like fire from a dragon. "Whoever heard of such? You think you're important. Ain't nobody gonna wanna come here after we're finished."

I listened in shock. I had never heard Vic talk like that. I stood there with no ability to offer a rebuttal.

"Just wait, you ain't seen nothin' yet. Me and Jim (Cuban friend) done already pissed all around this fuckin' building. Just wait, you'll see. We'll fix it where you won't have any more customers!"

I'm not sure what eventually came from my lips, but whatever it was must have added fuel to the fire, for his next words left me fearful for my life!

"Before I see you make it . . . **I'll serve you up on a silver platter, bitch!**" Before I could utter a word, he vanished from my sight. My legs weakened. I held on to the banister to support myself before I found the strength to sit down. My mouth must have fallen open, for I felt myself drooling while the salt of my tears curved to the corners of my mouth. Stunned ain't the word. Shocked, ain't the word. I was horrified!

The sound of Vic's van starting up brought a little ease to my pounding heart. I'm not sure how long I was glued to the step before I was able to stand up and walk. But even then, I depended on the wall to support my lifeless body as I made my way to the security of my bedroom — locking the door behind me. The pain was so deep, I could barely breathe. I sat on the edge of the bed and stared at the blank wall. I was comatose.

A Friend in Need

Vic had left, and there was no telling when he might return. Trey had gone to Chicago to visit his kids, and I was scared shitless. Fortunately, Trey called that night to let me know he would be home late the next day. I couldn't speak on what had happened, and I tried to be calm to keep from showing that I was near a nervous breakdown. I didn't want him worried, especially since he was with his kids. This was possibly his last visit before school started.

After talking with Trey, I decided to call my friend, William, whom I had met through the Department of Public Health. The cultural center served as a forum to educate the community on subjects such as STDs and the importance of "safe sex," as well as other health concerns that affected the community. Our open discussions had become quite popular, which started when we were over the bookstore. Conversations on relationships became a hot topic, encouraging honest and open dialogue that often ran into the wee hours of the night. Our *square* table discussions brought all types to the table to feast on food for the heart and mind, everyone from schoolteachers, social workers, PhDs, janitors, and other professionals of various backgrounds, set the tone for a broad range of interesting and dynamic philosophical ideas.

It's amazing what having an honest and authentic conversation will do for healing what ails us. To sit down with my sisters and brothers, having intelligent and passionate conversations was one of the highlights of our little business. We were truly a community. But now, more than ever, *I* needed some "healing".

I left a message for William, asking that he call me as soon as possible. Besides working for the health department, my friend had a sultry voice. He wooed us with ballads and jazz on several occasions for special events, which were usually fundraisers. But for now, I needed him to serve as a friend and a confidant.

It was after six when the phone rang. It was William. Once we were past the niceties, I got to the heart of my call and explained to him what had happened. William was somewhat familiar with the circumstances that brought Vic and me to our current situation. As a matter of fact, I learned later that he knew a little more than I thought. Being openly gay, William heard talk in the community about Vic. He had chosen not to say anything, knowing I would be extremely hurt. But, after learning what was happening, especially with the latest ordeal, he felt it warranted sharing what he knew. Of course, the news was not as painful as he anticipated, since I was aware.

We talked for about an hour before William suggested that Trey and I should come and stay at his house until I could get a restraining order against Vic. As scared as I was, just the thought of having to do that was extremely painful. Yet I knew it had to be done. Before hanging up, we decided that I would get in touch with him when Trey got back. As I put down the receiver, I felt the warmth of a tear run down my cheek. That's when I realized I was crying. The pain had returned, and my heart felt heavy with grief, shame, and even guilt. Was I responsible for Vic's rage and determination to destroy me?

I don't know when I fell asleep, but it was close to 9 o'clock the next morning when I looked over at the clock. I still had my clothes on, and the pain over my eyes was the first sign of a major headache. I managed to get up and stagger over to the open window. I walked out onto the balcony and met the sun with squinting eyes. Still early, its rays already reflected a mid-day heat wave, and my tired, worn body welcomed it with favor.

Vic's van was nowhere in sight. I was relieved. As I looked out over our near acre of land, I could not help but give thanks. The fragrance of Honeysuckle and fresh-cut grass danced in the slight breeze, and I was blessed to inhale its scent; a sweet gift of being alive. Gratitude can be a game-changer. And for that short time, as I stood and looked around, it gave me hope and reminded me why I was sent to this place that seemed to bring only hard work, sorrow, and lots of questions. My gratitude also included the fact that it was Monday, and

I was not on the clock; that I had been gifted with time to pull things together. There was a lot facing me, and until Trey came home, I would take the time to pray, meditate, and seek more guidance. Only God knew just how desperately I needed it. My mission bequeathed from the ancestors was turbulent at times, but I would soon learn that my Soul would have an even greater mission– one that would bring me to a place of greater submission and even greater humility.

Another Temporary Home

I spent most of the day meditating, praying and seeking guidance in the situation I had gotten myself into. By the time Trey got home, I was calm enough to explain to him what had happened the day before. I also let him know that I spoke with William and told him that it was suggested that we come to stay at his house for a while. And of course, after reiterating all the events (including the container situation) that had led up to this time, he agreed with William to take a restraining order out on Vic. I have to admit, just thinking about it was unnerving. I knew that it would have a major effect on my relationship with his boys (which was already precarious) and his family, as well as our customers. However, with Vic's state-of-mind these past few weeks, I couldn't take the chance with my life possibly being in danger, even though I had been told that no harm would come to me; that I was being protected. Nonetheless, after much contemplation, I realized that I had to take precautionary action.

Trey and I went to visit William later that evening to work out our plan. William's home was cozy, warm, and inviting. The decor was masculine but exuded a feminine touch. It was a townhouse with two bedrooms upstairs, in which one would become my and Trey's temporary home. It was a nice-sized room, and like the decor downstairs, it was warm and inviting. There was a small TV and a radio. Colorful drapes hung from the window. It also had a nice-sized closet and a small dresser drawer. William assured us he would make sure that we had enough room for our clothes, even though we felt our stay would be short. He encouraged us to make ourselves at home and to feel free to use anything, and that we were welcome to eat whatever was there, as well.

Headed back to the café, a deep sadness covered my heart. Although I was grateful to have such a great friend in William, I felt lost and unsure of myself. Trey and I spoke a little more about the situation; however, I wasn't able to find any joy or a sense of guiltless release. All I could think about was how it would affect the boys and what little family structure we had left. And the thought about what it would do to Vic was horrifying. The one thing that gave him purpose would be taken away. The Java House had become his claim to fame. He had become somebody. He was no longer a mere small-time drug dealer. No longer the black sheep of the family, and for once in a long time, he was considered a good father and family man. And I was about to tear down everything that we had built over the past five years. And to those who did not have a clue as to what was REALLY going on, I was about to become, "A Super Bitch!"

It was after nine by the time we got back, and I was relieved to see that Vic still hadn't come home. It gave us time to pack a few things and to make sure everything was set for lunch the next day. I figured I would call later that night to alert Vic that I would not be at work the next day. I would tell him that I needed to take some time off; that I was pretty shaken by our last conversation. But, as I should have expected, Vic was not happy about my decision.

"You know I was just talkin'," Vic said as if he had no idea that I took him seriously.

"No, Vic, I saw the look in your eyes and heard the tone in your voice," I reminded him. "I have never seen you like that before— ever."

"Well, I was probably just upset," he stuttered. "And I was a little high," he confessed.

I took a few more minutes to explain my fears and concerns and reminded him about what he said–that he and Jim pissed all around the building, making sure I would lose customers, lose business. He got quiet for a moment before mentioning his concern about needing help.

I assured him that while I was away, there were employees scheduled. Of course, he wasn't happy at all. He mumbled a few more sentiments about being upset and high, which to me was no excuse. Actually, I believed his threats even more so, because he was . . . high.

There I was again, feeling like a lost lamb without a Shepard. It wasn't easy for me to stay away from my business. I was one of those types that felt if I wasn't around to make sure things were done right, to expect chaos. Apparently, it was time for me to let go of control and trust that everyone would do what was needed. I really didn't have the strength, nor the desire to worry about the business. There were greater concerns, and time was of the essence.

FORTY-TWO

Restraining Order

Going to file a restraining order against my estranged husband, took more than I thought. Guilt laid heavy upon my heart. As I read the forms, tears swelled and landed on the fresh ink as I wrote out my complaint. I took a deep breath to help pull myself together. *How?* I thought to myself. *How did Vic and I get here?* Thoughts of how we used to be, surfaced briefly, which made me cry even more. This was definitely one of the most devastating things I ever had to do.

Maybe I was making things worse than they actually were. Maybe I was being too hard on the man that I once loved... maybe I still loved him. But, how? How could I possibly love someone who wasn't capable of loving me? Was I a glutton for punishment? The fact that there was the possibility of still loving him made me wonder if I even knew what love was. To say the least, I was confused.

With all the musing and self-questioning, Vic's words, **"I'll serve you up on a silver platter,"** took precedent over all the other thoughts. That statement haunted me. I had no choice but to protect myself, and maybe even possibly, Trey as well. With tears and all, I decided to finish the paperwork.

By the time I left the police station, it was rush-hour traffic. The last thing I wanted was more time to think. I was eager to get home, get a glass of wine, and a cigarette. I turned on the radio to help drown out my thoughts, but the music only served as a background to my mental torture. One thought led to another, with most of them beating myself up for everything that had happened over the past eight months. Now, I was beginning to doubt every decision I had ever made, even though they were for damn good reasons. But with everything that had been "brought to the light," maybe I should have been asking myself, why did it take so long?

Once I got to William's house, I told Trey I didn't want to talk about the situation, and he understood. Later that evening, when William got home, he asked if I went downtown. I told him yes. He could tell that I didn't want to get into any details. He assured me the right thing was done, and to not be hard on myself. I took a desperate sigh of relief and a huge gulp of wine.

It was the weekend, and I hadn't spoken with Vic since our initial conversation, when William announced that I had a phone call . . . it was Vic. When I took the receiver, my heart raced because I was afraid Vic had been approached by the Sheriff. But I managed to calm myself down with the fact that I had filed the papers only the day before.

"Hi, Vic. What is it?" I sucked in a quick breath of air, so my voice wouldn't quiver.

"Hey, you need to come on home. I really need your help, and you know it's poetry night; we're gonna be swamped."

"I'm sorry, Vic, but I can't... not yet. I'm sure everything will be okay. I have two waitresses on duty, and I'll call our cook to see if he wants some overtime."

My mind started its mental, nagging chatter again, and the guilty feelings began to resurface. I felt myself getting nervous. William overheard my conversation and beckoned for my attention. To my surprise, he offered to go work in my place and thought it would be a good idea for Trey to go as well. After forwarding the message to Vic, he agreed that it would help if they came and that it wouldn't be necessary to have the cook work overtime. I talked with Trey and asked if he felt okay with going without me. He was cool. They both changed clothes before heading out. I watched as they drove out of the driveway before shutting the door. Once again, I was alone with my thoughts and my guilt.

It was around 2:30 a.m. when I heard them come in. They were laughing and talking as I headed downstairs. I hadn't been able to sleep.

"Wow! It must have been a busy night," I inquired with a yawn.

Simultaneously, they both agreed that it was a pretty good night. William was all geeked up and smiling through what appeared to be pain, as he was slightly bent over.

"Hey, I made some good tips," he exclaimed. "It was busy as hell, and I thought I would drop dead."

"Oh, I'm sorry. Poor baby. Now you know what I have to go through." I shared with little pity.

"How in the hell do you do it . . . all the time?" He asked.

I laughed as he and Trey flopped down on the sofa.

"Man, now you see what I've been having to deal with," Trey managed to say, exhausted.

I sat down with them as they shared their take on the night. This was William's first time at a poetry night, and he was amazed at the quality of talent and how packed it was. Whatever tips he got, he said he definitely earned every dime. I asked how Vic dealt with everything. William said it wasn't too bad, and that most people were ordering coffee drinks, our famous Juice-Joint, and beer. Trey said he helped Vic with the salads and that he was pretty cool . . . he didn't talk about me, other than to ask how I was doing.

Before long, Trey had fallen asleep when we finally decided to call it a night. It was after 3:30 and I was ready to hit the sack. I woke Trey, said goodnight to William, and thanked him again for his support before we all headed upstairs. I was relieved that Vic hadn't given them grief about me not coming. I was even more relieved that, for the next two days, we were closed.

Monday rolled around before I could think straight. I knew that any day now, Vic would get a summons, and everything was going to change . . . drastically! I was beginning to question myself, again. But it was too late. Monday evening, I got a call from Vic, and it wasn't about me coming back to work. His voice was somber, yet with that Scorpion sting. I was being attacked with venom, and I couldn't say anything to my defense that hadn't already been said. Nonetheless, I attempted once again to explain that I had to protect myself; that I couldn't trust him. He was so angry! Yet I could hear the hurt in his voice . . . the pain from the thought of losing his purpose, losing the Java House. He assured me that I would be sorry and that it wasn't over. Yes, it was "V-Day," and I don't mean victory— but rather, Vengeance.

Meanwhile, at some point, Vic filed a counterclaim against me in response to the restraining order. I received a summons to appear in court.

Yarbrough VS Yarbrough

It was a typical, hot, late August morning. I wore all white that day, including a white head-wrap. I had prayed and sought guidance before going. White was a color that repels negativity and helps with spiritual purity. And when I saw Vic, I knew I needed all the help I could get.

He looked nice wearing a light suit jacket with dark trousers. He masqueraded his twists with a black hat. His eyes were wild and distant. He looked high, and I could only hope he wasn't crazy enough to come to court, hyped. But what was even more of a concern, was why he brought his son, Barren.

I had missed my stepson. In a not-so-distant past, we shared a great relationship. We shared long talks about girls, school, drinking and other teenage challenges. Born a Cancer, he was sensitive and unusually wise for his age. Since I had meditated, it allowed me to maintain a sense of poise and control over my mixed emotions.

"Why would you bring your son into our stuff, Vic?" I looked at him calmly and glanced at Barren.

"He's my witness," he uttered.

"Witness to what?" I asked, feeling a crease form between my brows.

"You'll see! You're the one that's gonna be in trouble! You'll see, I ain't goin' nowhere! If anybody gonna leave, it's gonna be you!"

Vic's word cut deep, like a rusted blade right in the pit of my stomach; however, this time, my meditation failed to come to my rescue. I felt sick.

I looked at Barren and apologized to him for bringing him into our mess. His chest rose with a heaviness and looked at me with watery eyes. He made no comment.

"Yarbrough versus Yarbrough," a male voice, shouted. My eyes, with a mind of their own, began to fill with tears. Although overwhelmed with anxiety, I was determined to show no fear. So, I fought back the tears that felt like a dam waiting to rush down my cheeks and walked through the door that read: Family Court. Straightening my back, I held my head high, knowing that the truth would prevail.

After the announcement of the Judge, we were told to have a seat. I sat on the left side of the female Judge, while Barren and Vic sat on the right. Vic laid a manila envelope he was carrying on the table in front of him. I laid my purse on the table before me, sat erect, and made direct eye contact with the woman who would serve as my judge and jury. After taking a few moments to review the papers before her, she looked at me and said, "Mrs. Yarbrough, first I would like to commend you on your run for governor. Your community should be quite proud of you."

Of course, I was shocked. However, I smiled and thanked her.

"Now, I understand that you filed a restraining order against your husband, Mr. Victor Yarbrough. Is that correct?"

"Yes, Your Honor," I responded.

"I've read your complaint," she continued, "so it's not necessary to explain the reasons, again."

She then looked at Vic, glanced down at her papers and looked back at him. "Now, Mr. Yarbrough I see that you have countered and wish to have a restraint against your wife . . . Is that correct?"

"Yes, Your Honor, you see . . ."

"Yes, or no, Mr. Yarbrough," she interrupted.

"Yes."

"And who is with you today?"

"My son. He's... my witness."

"And what is your name, young man?"

After Barren answered, the Judge turned to me and asked me a few questions. My answers were yes or no and straight to the point. She, in turn, asked Vic some questions, and he constantly wanted to explain his answers. When she asked Barren if he had anything to add, his response was hesitant and with an obvious struggle, as he looked back and forth at his dad.

"Young man," she interrupted. "That will be enough. It appears to me that you don't want to be here. Is that correct?"

Barren slightly hung his head before saying, "Yes ma'am."

"Okay. I see what's happening," she stated. "Thank you, young man, and I must tell you that it's a shame that you had to be a part of this. You seem like a nice young man, and I don't think you're the type that would lie unless you were told to." She then turned her attention to Vic and continued.

"Mr. Yarbrough, I want you to know that I don't believe that your wife has threatened you, and I don't believe that she pulled a knife on you, as you stated in your complaint. However, I do believe that Mrs. Yarbrough has every right to be concerned for her welfare. My judgment is for Mrs. Yarbrough."

I looked over at Vic and immediately became sad, or should I say . . . sadder. Although pleased with the Judge's decision, I was deeply hurt. I sat there brokenhearted as Your Honor continued.

"Mr. Yarbrough, you are hereby ordered by this court to stay no less than 100 yards from Mrs. Yarbrough and The Java House Café. You are to make no contact with her by telephone or any other form of communication. If you need anything from The Java House Café, which I understand is where you both live, should be gotten by a friend or family member. Do you understand, Mr. Yarbrough?"

Vic once again began explaining himself, but she cut him off and repeated her question.

"Yes, I understand," he sheepishly answered.

The Judge then turned to me and ordered me not to telephone Vic or make any contact with him. The Order was for three years. Before she stood to leave, she made one more announcement.

"Mrs. Yarbrough, I'm gonna have a guard walk you out to your car. And if you should ever have any reason for concern, call the police."

She then wished me good luck and thanked me again for what the café was doing in the community. I thanked her in return.

I suppose I should've felt happy . . . should have jumped for joy. On the contrary, I felt so much guilt. Even though my husband had blatantly lied about me, I wanted the Judge to know that The Java House was what it was, because of Vic's support. I wanted her to know how hard he had worked; what a great spirit he was. I wanted her to know how much I once loved him, and how painful it was to be in court. That I didn't want to hurt him, but the end had to come. I knew now that nothing would ever be the same.

I looked over at Vic and Barren. The tears were trying to surface again, but I fought them back. My heart cried instead. Vic made sure he didn't look at me as he swiftly moved toward the door. I looked at Barren and told him he was always welcome at the café, and that I was sorry things had to be this way. He gave me eye contact and said, "Yes, ma'am. I understand. See you around."

I could only hope that he did understand. It wasn't that far back when I told him about his father getting Daisy pregnant. I was in a rage that day. Vic's lies and making the boys think that everything was my fault, had taken me over the edge. And without thinking, I blurted it out. Barren looked at me as if he knew I was right; as if he knew about Vic and everything else that was haunting me . . . us, as a family. That day I could see it in his eyes . . . he knew something.

It took all of 15 minutes for our lives to be changed, merely by the thump of a gavel. I would never see or talk with my husband again, at least for three years. As I walked back to my car, escorted by a guard, the tears began to fall like a gentle rain.

"Are you okay, ma'am?" the guard asked sympathetically.

"I'm okay. Thanks for asking."

After I was safely in the car, and the guard bade me farewell, the tears finally gave way to the pressure that had built up. I'm not sure how long I sat there and cried, but by the time that I was able to pull myself together, my eyes were swollen; my throat was dry, and I felt like my stomach was being torn out through my navel. My God, what had I done?

By the time I got back to William's house, my head was pounding. The first thing I did was to pull off my head wrap, hoping it would take some pressure off. Trey was at the café, and I really needed to get there because it was close to lunch. I found a couple of aspirin in William's medicine cabinet. When I looked in the mirror, my reflection made me want to cry even more. I splashed some cold water on my face and put my mouth under the faucet to swallow my aspirin. The way I felt, it would take at least an hour to pull myself together; so, I called Trey to let him know that I would get there around 11:30. Of course, he wanted to know what happened, so I gave him the short version and told him I would share the rest later.

It was 11:50 by the time I reached the café. Trey took one look at me and gave me a hug. Fortunately, we only had three customers, so he told me to go ahead upstairs and that he would call me if it got busy. I gladly took his suggestion. And although I no longer had a headache, I felt lifeless and in no mood to be serving anyone. As I moseyed upstairs, using the wall as support, it suddenly felt strange to be at home. There was no doubt that things were going to be quite different, and I could only hope that life would get better. As my body slumped onto the bed, I looked over at my altar and mentally promised the ancestors fresh flowers, a new candle and something good to eat.

By the time I awakened, it was 4:30. I felt rested and a little more energized. I could hear the music downstairs and some laughter. So, I got up, took a quick shower, and put on some fresh clothes. My eyes looked much better, and I put on a little foundation and lipstick. I brushed my teeth and brushed my hair back into a ponytail. Having micro braids really helped. With a little oil and some brushing, it was all good.

When I got downstairs, Trey was talking with Alice and Jacque. They were two of our favorite poets. Alice loved hosting and Jacque had found a new talent. He was truly a Spoken Word artist.

"Hey, you guys, good seeing you," I said, walking toward them. We all hugged as they expressed being happy to see me, but sorry to hear the news about Vic. Since Trey had mentioned the restraining order, at that point, as my extended family, I felt they deserved an explanation. They truly cared for Vic, as most of our customers did.

By the time I finished telling them the situation that led to the restraining order, there was a deep sadness with us all. Jacque was the first one to express how sorry he was for both of us. However, he admitted that he understood why I did what I did and that he felt it was the right thing to do. Alice agreed. I explained to them that everything would be quite different and that I really needed their continued support.

The rest of the day was slow, but steady, and that night I did the cooking for dinner. It didn't take long to get back into the swing of things, even though I had been away for a couple of weeks. Normally, Vic cooked every night, and it dawned on me that it would be my responsibility from here on. It felt strange. And with everything that had happened, I didn't wanna think about the future. It was too much. I had to take one day at a time and pray that I kept it together and not give any more thought to Vic's threats. Especially the ones about making sure I lost customers. No customers . . . no business!

Keeping the Distance

The following week, I got a call from Vic's brother. Vic wanted to come over and get some of his things and to see me, one more time. I awkwardly explained to his brother the Judge's orders, and that I could not go against them. I told him that he or one of Vic's sons was more than welcome to pick up their father's things. I could tell by his tone that he was pissed off, and I tried to explain again my situation; however, he called me a bitch and hung up.

A few days later, Barren came by with his older brother to get Vic's things. They barely spoke as we headed to the back entrance to collect their father's belongings. There were no conversations while I hurriedly put some things together and stacked them in a corner near the door. With tears in my eyes, I looked at my stepsons and told them that I loved them and that I was sorry for everything. The oldest boy gave me a look that made me want to leave as quickly as I could. He obviously had no love for me or any understanding as to what had been going on. But what could I expect? As the old saying goes, "Blood is thicker than water."

When they finished packing, I said my solemn goodbyes as I watched them head down the back stairs. As I headed back through the house, I was drawn to the mysterious *vase* that was on the mantle. I knew I couldn't touch it but, I thought about how to get rid of it. As hot as it was, I suddenly felt a chill, and I could vaguely hear the ghostly whispers that Vic and I had encountered on several occasions. All I could think about was gettin' the hell out, as quickly as possible.

However, first the barricade of chairs and the stack of heavy boxes (which Vic put up to keep us from coming on his side of the house) had to be moved from against the door which led to the hallway.

I hurriedly removed the obstruction as the eerie feeling was growing almost to a point of panic. I had to get out of that room!

Finally, safe and secured on my side of the house, I went into the kitchen and sat at the table, pondering on what to do next, when I heard the boys leaving from the back. Looking out the window, I watched as Vic's van backed out of the gravel driveway. Although it felt uncomfortable being around them, the thought of not seeing them again was disheartening. I returned to my seat and thought about the phone call from Vic's brother, saying that Vic wanted to see me one last time. For a moment, I had actually contemplated the possibility, but quickly thought—*What if he wanted to kill me? What if he came around and actually took me and Trey's lives?* My mind was all over the place. Nevertheless, I quickly dismissed the gruesome thought and put the blame on the Judge. Meanwhile, I needed some advice on eliminating the threatening situation that still had me alarmed.

Shangodora wasn't surprised when I called and shared with her about our day in court; she knew it was bound to happen. I asked her about the container, and she asked if I had someone who would be willing to take it out. She said that Trey couldn't do it because we were too close. Then she strongly suggested that I find someone else who could make sure that the vase was put in a box and buried. My friend also reminded me that jealousy was still a motivating factor in some negative energy around me, and that an attempt to take The Java House was still being sought. However, she encouraged me to not let it stop me from doing what needed to be done; reiterating that no harm would come to me; to keep praying and meditating, and all would be well.

As she continued, she explained that much of what was happening was for my spiritual growth. That I would become stronger and more in touch with my *Higher Self*. She then paused for a few moments before continuing.

"There will be more sadness in the future, but it has to happen," she warned me. "You're strong, Oshun, and you will be okay," she assured me. "I will keep praying for you, and remember the ancestors are with you. If you need me, please know that I am here for you."

I placed the phone on the receiver and tried to think about what *else* could happen. I needed some normalcy in my life; it had been one thing after another. Taking a deep sigh, I decided not to give it any more thought. Whatever was going to happen, I would deal with it. I recalled my mantra and began to silently repeat, *"One day at a time, Nailah . . . one day at a time. Everything will be fine".*

FORTY-THREE

The Burial

The next day, remembering the container I needed to have buried, I called my friends, Betty and her husband, Ubie. They both were strong supporters of The Java House but were rarely able to come around because of their busy lives raising children, their own, in addition to two more after the death of Betty's sister. When I asked Ubie about removing the container, he let me know that it wasn't necessary to explain the details, but to just let him know when I wanted it done. Ubie was an extraordinary Congo player, whose talent was well-known in and around the city. As one of the drummers for our initial cleansing rituals, he was well aware of ceremonial rituals, even those that dispelled any unwanted or negative energy.

The following Sunday, my friends came over to support me in following the instructions regarding the vase. It was great to see them; it had been several months since they had been around. Although neither felt it necessary to explain anything, I made the decision to at least give them a synopsis of what had been happening. While they were sorry about Vic and our relationship, they understood why he had to leave.

In preparation for what we considered to be a ritual, my friend came with his Congo drum under his arm, wrapped in an African print, burlap cover. He then asked me to show him where the vase was. Before I took them upstairs, I went to the kitchen and got some rubber gloves to make sure none of the contents got on his hands. I then got a towel and a shoebox, as well as a piece of aluminum foil and a rubber band to cover the top and handed it to him. He stood in front of the mantle . . . bowed his head . . . and then proceeded to cover the container with the foil, securing it with the rubber band. He meticulously wrapped the vase with the towel as if it were an ancient, expensive relic before placing it in the box.

"I'm getting ready to take this outside; could you bring me a glass of fresh water and meet me outside?" he asked. His wife and I went into my private kitchen, where I found a crystal glass that was a wedding gift. I filled it with water, said a quick prayer, and blessed it with love. Before going outside, I went into my bedroom where Trey was still asleep. Since we were essentially performing a ritual, I wrapped my head in the traditional white. By the time we got outside, Ubie had begun digging the hole where he was set up with a chair and his drum. The tree that draped over the back fence into the alley was huge, with large branches and heavy foliage. We quietly stood near as he finished digging.

The early September air was still and unusually warm. Streaks of sunlight glistened across the box as it lay in the rectangular-shaped hole. Betty's premature, silver hair was highlighted by the sun. Her youthful and unblemished olive complexion radiated. She was so beautiful. I was truly blessed to have them in my life. Ubie proceeded with a chant as he perched on the edge of the chair with his drum between his knees. With eyes closed, his hands moved up and down-- beating out a message to the ancestors. At his command, I poured the water in increments upon the earth and silently prayed to myself, giving thanks to God and to the ancestors for my safekeeping, as well as others. I asked that I be forgiven of any transgressions toward anyone, knowingly or unknowingly, as well as forgiving my enemies.

As I was praying, I felt a strong breeze. I opened my eyes to witness the tree's branches swaying forcefully. I looked around and noticed that it was the only tree that was affected by the unexpected wind. I smiled. After our prayers, Ubie covered the box with the rich, red soil that the property was known for. The burial was complete.

Just after the ceremonial rite, I felt a sense of relief, while at the same time, feeling a strong tug in the pit of my stomach. I guess my facial expression showed my discomfort; and when asked what was wrong, I didn't quite know how to answer. Nevertheless, I assured my friends that I was fine; that it was probably just an emotional release—which was understandable, considering. We then hugged before moving toward the house.

By the time we got in the house, I began weeping, and I could find no explanation for the tears. Trey had been awakened by the drum and came down to offer his thanks and to say goodbye. After our hugs and well wishes, they reminded me of their availability if I should need Ubie's services again, and to not hesitate to call. That day, I had no idea I would soon be making that call . . . no idea that *it wasn't over.* And that the circumstances would be so bizarre, that even if you were there to bear witness . . . you would probably *still* question your sanity.

FORTY-FOUR

Moving On & Creating Art

During my spiritual studies, one of the hardest challenges for me to accept was the excruciating fact that I was the *creator of my reality;* that there was nothing or no one outside of Myself that I could blame for the picture I was not so eloquently painting on the canvas of my life. The whole idea that the madness that I had been dealing with was self-created... was mind-blowing! And with the prediction of more *sadness* in the future, it was mandatory that my daily prayer ritual (which was the only thing that had sustained me thus far) didn't suffer due to the extra workload, since Vic's departure. As a matter of fact, it was imperative that some serious changes take place, particularly since my life had become a virtual hell. And things had gotten way too hot to make it a permanent residence.

Since 1991, I had been studying *A Course in Miracles,* which I found a lot easier to do with a group. But after my marriage to Vic and my hectic schedule, studying with a group was no longer an option. Therefore, I decided to go back to my book *"The Science of Mind,"* authored by Ernest Holmes. Reading his words gave me a sense of not being alone, validating my thoughts and spiritual concepts about my relationship with and about God.

Now I pretty much understood the importance of my connection with the ancestors, along with having daily gratitude for my life and purpose. But "Getting an understanding" about **my** relationship with God—was becoming more confusing than I anticipated with all the *lessons* that I obviously had not mastered. But like my dear friend, Shangodora, reminded me, that no matter how difficult the challenges, it was for "my spiritual growth". And like it or not, my *spiritual growth* . . . be it good, bad or anything in-between . . . was not only inevitable, but was kicking my ass!

The first few weeks after Vic's *mandatory* departure were awkward, to say the least. Just about everyone wanted to know where he was, and I told those *inquiring minds* that Uncle Vic decided to leave; that our *unique* living arrangement was just a *little* too much. Not that my story would *hold water* (not for long), it was guaranteed that the *real reason* would be the talk of the town... in no time. Meanwhile...

Business for the next couple of months was off and on. There were some busy days as well as days that made me think that Vic's Mojo was working. Fortunately, we had several school tours scheduled for almost the entire month of October, which were one of my favorite activities for the cultural center, especially with the elementary schools. The young ones were *open* to receiving truth about the past and how they could be *better*. Their innocence made my job easy when I explained about slavery and how it hurt so many people—black and white.

Having students slip their small hands into the iron shackles, which I usually used as a visual, were pivotal moments in their ability to understand the meaning of being a slave. Even at their young ages, they knew that shackles were like being 'locked up'. I recall when a young white boy, around 6 or 7 asked me, "Am I gonna go to jail?"

With older students from Middle & High Schools, I talked more about slavery's brutal treatments–the castrations, and babies ripped from their mothers' arms. I took them into the cellar where many felt the cold presence of death . . . and would ask to leave. Some vomited, most cried. Whatever the emotion, all were touched in some way. And before they left, I would encourage them (particularly those of African descent) to research the *Willie Lynch Theory* and to think about how they were going to break the mental chains that were set up to imprison their minds for years to come. To think twice (or more) before using the word, Nigger. And that no matter what their race, they had a responsibility and an obligation to do things differently–IF they wanted a better world.

On slower days, I managed to keep myself busy with other creative outlets. With the support of one of my young customers, (of Caucasian persuasion) whose gift was drawing and painting—she brought my vision for a mural of *Billie Holiday* into a beautiful reality. However, in keeping with the theme of the plantation, my enthusiastic friend went beyond my request and added a landscape of cotton fields being worked by female slaves wearing huge bonnets to protect them from a sweltering sun. She also included a male's body hanging from a leafless tree in the background. The visual, being artistically beautiful and distressing at the same time, served as a constant reminder as to *why* I was there, as well as a source of empowerment to keep my '*Eye on the prize'*.

Playwright Seeks Forgiveness

With what was to be a grim outcome for The Java House, our doors continued to welcome newcomers. People of all persuasions from as far as Florida came to Spoken Word. Many foreign-exchange students from various countries came through, sharing their language and culture. Furthermore, there were those who brought us gifts, who came with good news and a strong desire to support the racial healing, and also to help rid themselves of generational guilt, which was exactly what John, a white guy, came to do.

John was new to the café, and like everyone, he was greeted with love and a warm welcome. Tall, slender, and very nice looking, he sported a conservative haircut, which was quite becoming. There was a gleam in his eyes, slightly tainted with a sadness that he tried to cover with a contagious smile. After our former introduction, he ordered a Mr. T Burger with our famous lemon iced tea... upon my recommendation. Once served, he gazed upon his hearty lunch. "This looks great!" he exclaimed. "Are these raisins in the salad?" It was great to see such enthusiasm, especially from a newcomer. We were proud of our unique style of sandwiches.

"Yes, we like adding a little sweetness. You do like raisins, right?" I asked, concerned. After all, raisins were automatic with our salads, even though we learned that one or two of our extended family members had a dislike for the dried grapes.

"Oh, yes!" He beamed. "I love raisins, just never seen them on a salad before . . . nice touch."

I left John to enjoy his Java House experience and continued with my work. When I checked to make sure all was well, and to refill his iced tea, he invited me to sit with him. I promised to join him after checking on a few more customers. Trey was in the back helping our cook, and I was working alone in the dining room. It had become necessary to cut back a little on hours with my waitresses, especially during the times we were slow.

John's energy was warm and infectious. I liked his spirit. "So, how did you hear about us?" I asked.

"I was talking with some friends of mine who do poetry, and they told me how cool this place was." His smile framed his beautiful, straight teeth. It was obvious they were well taken care of and that he didn't smoke. "I don't do poetry," he continued. "But I write a little bit. That's what I would like to talk to you about," he continued, leaning in a little closer while trying to keep his sleeve out of his plate.

"Here, let me take your plate. I don't think you're gonna get anymore off of it," pleased that he ate every bite... down to the last raisin.

"By the way, that was the best sandwich I have ever eaten . . . and I'm not just saying that. It was fabulous! And the raisins were perfect. I think I'm gonna put raisins on my salads from here on. Thanks!"

After blushing for several moments and expressing my gratitude for his kind words, I excused myself and took his plate. While up, I took the opportunity to bus a couple more tables and do refills. I had a feeling John had a proposition for us worth listening to.

"Thanks for waiting. Now you have my undivided attention," I said, sitting back down. John leaned in again with his hands under his chin. "You know," he began with his eyes unconsciously drifting off to the side, avoiding eye contact. "My . . . my great-grandfather was a slave owner," he managed to confess. I listened attentively with no outward emotion, except for a discerning smile.

"And I know that . . . the **real** reason I came here . . . is for my healing." He nervously adjusted his position as he continued sharing his generational guilt. "Ever since I was old enough to realize that my family had a past that I'm not proud of . . . I've had this drive, so to speak . . . that in some way I could try and correct it. I mean, not that I can change what my grandparents did . . . but I felt I had to do something. So, I wrote about it." John managed to regain his composure while his eyes sparked with compassion. I continued to listen without interjection.

By the time my new friend finished sharing, I had taken two more breaks to close out my remaining customers and drank two cappuccinos. During our conversation, John stated that he had written a play that dealt with a white family whose slaves were considered family. I shared a little more about the café and our not-for-profit sector of the business, the Harriet Tubman Cultural Center, as well as my mission regarding the trapped souls, which he found to be so intriguing that he suggested that **I write a book about it.**

Trey came through a couple of times before I introduced them. Of course, at first, when John saw him walking around, he thought that he might be Uncle Vic. But I told him that my husband and I were no longer together. He offered the normal response of 'being sorry' and shook Trey's hand. I then shared with Trey about John's play. He lit up like a lightbulb.

"Hey man, that sounds great. I'm an actor and I've been looking for an opportunity to put my skills to work." We both chuckled at Trey's enthusiasm. "Yeah, let's do it," he exploded with excitement, looking at me while pulling up a chair.

I told John I would love to take a look at his script and see what happens from there. After a little discussion about the possibility of doing the play as part of the cultural center, John asked if he could come back at a later date and bring the script. I agreed that it sounded like something that we might be interested in, but it would be necessary to read it first. Trey later excused himself to head out for a while to meet with a couple of his new friends.

Three hours had passed before John finally got up to leave. Meanwhile, he had ordered our delectable, sweet potato pie and a cup of coffee before making his departure. I walked him to the door, and we gave each other a hug; and as he stepped back . . . looking at me with watery eyes, John stood before me and began to apologize for his great-grandfather, again.

"I can never express the guilt and humiliation I feel for what my family did . . . and there are not enough apologies in the world . . . but I am so sorry!" John's sincerity was deeply felt. I knew that he was genuinely sorry, and at the same time, happy that he could begin his healing. "Thank you for being here," he continued, before hugging me again.

"My divine pleasure," I assured him. "My work in the community and the Mansion is a part of my soul's purpose, and I have a responsibility to my ancestors and my community." Once again, we embraced and agreed to get together soon.

The idea of producing a play dealing with slavery was definitely an opportunity to bring more attention to what we were doing. Plus, it would serve as an educational tool for teaching about the atrocities that slavery had on the people of African descent, as well as how its stench was still permeating the air, keeping us from the sweetness of true equality.

I watched as John drove from the parking lot and waved goodbye. I stood there for a minute just thinking about our talk. Yes, it was happening. Healing was taking place in more ways than I had imagined. And the idea of a performance brought a little spark of sunshine to what had been some dark times, generating some hope for the future of our business, as well as my state of mind. Whereas John needed a reprieve from his haunted past of enslavement by his great-grandfather, I was needing strength and a reason to keep going. At times, I felt as *trapped* as those souls who were depending on me for their ultimate freedom. And trying to fulfill that commitment was becoming more daunting every day. Not only did I sometimes feel as trapped as my ancestors, but my unorthodox spiritual beliefs often left me with no one to talk to. I was abhorred by local, Christian Churches and only tolerated by others, especially after the ordeal with Vic. I desperately needed someone to be in my "*Amen corner.*"

FORTY-FIVE

Saved by Agape

It had been several months since I had attended a local Unity Church. It brought back a nostalgic place in my spirit where I felt a part of something that resonated with my soul's yearnings. The female leadership of the church was an extra benefit, for I had grown accustomed to seeing a reflection of my gender during my spiritual development in California. And most recently, fellowshipping with my partner in *peace*, Virginia, who was also of "the cloth" (with a Degree in Divinity), had served as my educator and supporter in my becoming an ordained minister . . . primarily to officiate weddings. My spiritual beliefs and teachings did NOT necessarily vibe with the average, southern... pulpit. And I could only pray that my "walk and my talk" was a testament to what I claimed to believe.

It was a quiet Saturday afternoon, and I was busy polishing and cleaning the Cappuccino machine when my waitress came to tell me someone wanted to see me.

"Who is it?" I asked.

"I don't know. I haven't seen her before... some white woman," she replied.

I checked my headscarf and lipstick in the shiny chrome that reflected back approval for meeting a possible stranger.

"Okay, tell her I'll be right there." I tried to figure out who it could possibly be, but no one came to mind. When I walked into the dining room, I noticed two white females next to the window. One had her back to me, so I couldn't see her face. The other woman wasn't recognizable either. Since they were the only women in the room, it was obvious that one of them had to be the one asking to see me. I didn't recognize her at first as I started to introduce myself...

"Hi Nailah, you remember me? —Shelly," she asked, smiling before I could get my name out. "I'm the Spiritual Leader at Unity," she continued. "I met you a few months ago."

"Oh yeah, I'm sorry. So glad to see you. How have you been?"

"Wonderful! I told you I would come. This is my friend, Melissa."

I turned and greeted her friend and received an invitation to sit down. They had already ordered and were drinking their iced tea. We started talking like we were long-lost friends. When their food arrived (both had the vegetable lasagna), they complimented the presentation and were eager to dig in. I offered to leave and come back after they finished, but they insisted that I stay. After a few more salivating comments about their meal, they dug in while we continued what was becoming a delightful and spiritual conversation. One that I hadn't been privy to in many moons. They were speaking my language. I was high on The Most High! And before I knew it, I was being offered a gift that would literally get me through some of the most challenging times in my life.

"Nailah, it is such an honor to meet and talk with you," Shelly gleamed. "You sound just like a female, Michael Beckwith," she continued.

"Who?" I asked curiously.

"Michael Beckwith of Agape," she said as if I should have known who she was speaking of.

"I don't know who Michael Beckwith or Agape is," I responded, still baffled. Looking at me as if I instantly grew a third eye, she went on to try and explain to me who this person was ... with no real luck.

However, I told her I was grateful for what seemed to be a compliment.

Realizing the fact that I really had no clue, she continued. "Nailah, I'm gonna bring you some cassettes I have of Beckwith's messages from his services at Agape International Spiritual Center. He's African American, and you're gonna love him. You remind me so much of him."

As we all walked toward the door, Shelly was still raving about this minister and how he got started and how he married Rickie, the Music Director, and how good the music was. She went on for about ten more minutes before we finally hugged and said our goodbyes.

Shelly, standing around five feet, tipped on her toes to give me a hearty hug. Her petite stature carried the persona of someone tall and confident. Melissa, who was much taller, grabbed me with vigor. Her hugs were a lot like mine—warm and filled with passion. I looked forward to their return, especially Shelly's. I was quite eager to hear this person that I reminded her of. I had listened to more ministers than I could count. And with the exception of my friend Virginia, I had yet to hear a minister of African descent (especially a man) *teach* from a "spiritual" perspective. Yeah, I had to hear this man. This was going to be interesting.

Fourteen Cassettes of Truth

The following week, Shelly stayed true to her word. It was a late Saturday afternoon when she walked in with a shoebox under her arms. She was alone this time as she came in, glowing with excitement.

"Just like I promised," she exclaimed, handing me the heavy box.

Our sparse lunch crowd left me plenty of time to visit with my new friend, so we sat down, and I offered her a glass of iced tea. Although she had eaten lunch already, Shelly was determined to patronize the business and insisted on paying for her complimentary tea. She also bought dessert . . . a slice of sweet potato pie.

When I opened the box, I was surprised to see a mass of cassettes. I counted fourteen in all (which equals a 5, meaning Change), which were labeled: Agape International Spiritual Center. As I looked at the dates and subject titles, pulling them out one at a time, Shelly boasted about the messages and the Center in general, where she was fortunate to have visited in California during trips for conferences and visiting family.

"When I wasn't able to be there, I ordered cassettes from the Center directly," she delightfully shared in between bites of pie and sips from a freshly brewed cup of coffee. "These cassettes are all during the 90s'," she continued. "I love these services; they have been a big help in my own ministry. I was even blessed to attend one of his workshops last year. Nailah, you're going to love this man and his explosive sermons."

By the time my new friend left, we had talked for over an hour. I was geeked and couldn't wait to play a cassette. Trey had been working in the back and keeping things bused for me, so I asked him to cover for me while I took a break. I grabbed my shoebox full of treasures and headed upstairs. Fortunate for me, my old "Boombox" had a cassette player, which I kept in the office. I explained to Trey that I didn't want to be disturbed unless it was absolutely necessary. It was slow, so he had no problem with it, and besides, he could tell that I was excited, which was something rare.

I hurriedly ran upstairs to my office to listen to my first cassette. As I held the box in my hands and mused over Shelly's enthusiasm, I found myself holding the box close to my heart and praying that somehow this Beckwith guy could help me get through the hell I had created. Now, more than ever, spiritual support was mandatory or risk losing my mind. I needed to hear others who believed as I did. I needed to be assured that I wasn't crazy.

As I liberated the boom-box from a corner near the high-backed chair, it was embarrassingly obvious that I hadn't dusted in some time. I wiped the top with my hands and transferred the dust to an inconspicuous place on my jeans before putting it on the desk and finding an outlet. Once I plugged it in, I damn near fell off the chair; it was LOUD! *"Damn,"* I thought to myself, *"I must have been jammin' the last time I had this on—Or high!"*

After a brief moment to compose myself, I switched the nob over to "tape," smiling to myself as I began to finger through the cassettes. This time I said a little prayer asking Spirit to guide me as I closed my eyes and energetically selected a tape. I placed it in the open slot . . . closed it . . . and hit play.

For the next hour or so, I jumped up and down, cried, and gave praise and thanks to God! My sanity had been confirmed, and my unorthodox beliefs, validated. Much like the teachings of "Ifa," Agape believed in the One God. That we were all created to live a life filled with goodness; that we were created in the Image and Likeness of the One Infinite Intelligence (God) and were here to have a life of joy, happiness, love, wealth and prosperity along with anything else which was good. Heaven was truly at hand—and I didn't have to die first to get to it!

By the time Trey came upstairs, it was late evening. By then, I was lying on the sofa with red, swollen eyes.

"Are you all right?" he asked, moving toward me with a concerned look.

I explained about the tape and how it affected me and assured him I was okay. As a matter of fact, I was more than okay. I was filled with hope and renewed energy.

The two of us sat and talked for a while and thankful it was an off night for poetry; we were hoping to close early. Trey had been working extra hard lately, and I was running out of steam. So much had been going on that we hardly had time to really sit down and talk.

We got our wish and closed around 8:30. Our last customer was a take-out order for a Mr. T and a Veggie Lasagna, which I prepared while Trey cleaned and mopped the floors. By 10:00, we were ready to call it a night, and after a hot bath together, we managed to muster up enough energy for some long, overdue intimacy, which usually was a recipe for some goooood sleep! However, I was so hyped and thrilled about the Agape tapes that I couldn't sleep. I lay next to Trey (who was snoring) with a smile on my face and Rickie's song on my lips.

"I release, and I let go, I let the Spirit run my life. And my heart is open wide, yes, I'm only here for God! No more struggles, no more strife, with my faith I see the light. I am free in the spirit. Yes, I'm only here for God!"

FORTY-SIX

The Message on the Wall

The bedside clock had inched its hands towards the noon hour by the time my wandering soul returned to the body. I looked over at Trey. He was still in some far-off place exploring other dimensions. His face was peaceful and child-like, looking as if he was enjoying wherever he was . . . and with no intentions in coming back to the present, anytime soon.

I stretched like a cat from a well-deserved rest before throwing my legs over the edge of the bed. Sitting there for a few moments, I gave thanks for the time off and the quietness of the house. Kenya, my Doberman, was lying on the floor next to me. She had made it a special point to stick close to me since Vic had left. She laid there as if to say in her "dog" language: *If you wanna get by, you'll have to step over me.* So, I did and headed for the kitchen to put on some coffee. Of course, my bodyguard wasn't too far off my heels.

After putting Kenya outside on her mile-long leash, I then headed for my altar to do my meditation. Only now, I had a great addition that I added to my time of reflection and contemplation. I had Agape and its powerful songs of praise and messages of Life-Giving food for my spirit. Once again, my soul rejoiced as I listened to Beckwith's words of Truth: ". . . It's not that we believe IN Jesus, we BELIEVE Jesus when he said, 'These things that I do, Ye shall do also, and greater things than these.'" By the time I got through the service, I was pumped and ready to stand up to Any problem! Little did I know that challenges would be lined up like soldiers, ready to take me on and test my faith. Talk about "Nailed to the cross."

It was after 2 o'clock by the time I heard Trey rise from his slumber. He was a late sleeper, pretty much like me in comparison to Vic. But I really couldn't say anything about Trey sleeping late. I pretty much ran the place like a "plantation." The only difference was, as the Master, I worked harder than anybody.

Yawning with a backstretch and an obvious boner, Trey stood in the doorway. "Got any plans for today?" he asked, as he descended the two steps leading into the kitchen. I sorta smirked at the rise in his pajamas but decided not to make a comment... just in case last night wasn't enough. I was so fueled with the Spirit, I knew trying to go into a "Barry White" moment was out of the question.

"Not really," I replied. "I may need to do some shopping, but I can do that tomorrow. I was thinking about working on some tunes, just to do something creative. I need a release." Trey had heard me sing and was quite supportive when I got an itch to be in a Billie Holiday state of mind. He loved my voice.

Before heading to the theatre to be creative, Trey and I decided to hang out for a while and go out to eat, since neither one of us wanted to cook. When we returned home, we thought it would be a good idea to call Saria to see if she wanted to come over and mess around in the theater with us. Since Vic had left, Saria felt more comfortable about coming over. However, it had been some time since we had visited, and it felt good to hang out with a true friend, again.

Saria looked so radiant, and seeing her brought back some great memories. We laughed, talked, and drank some wine. She did her ritual smoke, which I hadn't participated in since before my political endeavors. Trey got out his trumpet which he rarely played, and we all laughingly went upstairs to the theater.

The evening had turned to night, and with only a lamp for light, the room had a cabaret feel to it, only we didn't have an audience . . . except ourselves. I was sitting on a tall stool at the mic off in my own world making up melodies and scaling high and low vocal sounds with no particular structure. Trey was off in a corner tuning up his trumpet, while Saria started blending in her rich alto with what I was doing. Before we knew it, we had a groove going on that we thought was pretty tight. And the acoustics were awesome.

While we were clowning around, we heard some voices calling my name from outside. It was Jacque and one of his musician friends coming over to hang out, which was nothing unusual. We seemed to have an open house policy . . . even when we were closed. It didn't take long for our added guest to fall into the creative flow. Jacque tried out some new poetry, and his friend turned one of the tables into a Conga drum. I lit a white candle for the stage and burned some incense.

Time flies when you're having a "whatever comes to mind" type of party. We were definitely in a creative mode. We went from making up unconventional melodies and spoken word, to singing Motown favorites, mostly a-cappella, with the exception of occasional table raps and Trey's intermittent blows from his Angelic, Gabrielle horn. And I do mean "angelic," and here's why.

Trey had been playing his trumpet off and on for a few years. However, he could NEVER play the upper notes. He claimed it was too much strain on his face and neck. But to Trey's wide-eyed surprise, when he placed the trumpet to his lips and started blowing, he started hitting high notes without any effort. Needless to say, he was completely "blown" away — and so were the rest of us. What was even more surprising, was that he wasn't even trying to hit high notes—it just happened!

He was so shocked after the first time it happened that he figured it was a fluke–only a one-time thing. So, a little later, he tested his ability to reach higher ground once again—and he did it! But, as magical moments are known for, it never happened again after that. And speaking of magic, his hitting those high notes wasn't the only mystifying encounter that night.

After Jacque and his friend left, the three of us sat around and talked about what happened with Trey and his trumpet-blowing. I was still on the stool and found myself turning around toward the stage area. The light from the candle cast a dim glow on the walls surrounding the stage, along with a little moonlight peering through the window on the left. I could hear Saria and Trey talking, but I couldn't help but pay close attention to the far-right wall.

"Do you all see that?" I asked, still turned towards the stage. And before either of them could answer, I continued questioning,

"Are those hands . . . can you see it?"

"See what?" Trey responded with a clueless look on his face.

"On the right wall . . . there are hands with shackles. And look! I know that's a shadow of a hanged man," I stated as if he surely had to see what I was seeing.

"Yeah, I see it," Saria finally chimed in.

Slowly, the three of us got up and walked onto the stage. It was silent for a few moments before I turned to the center wall, and what I saw made my legs weak. I reached out to brace myself on Trey's shoulder—Saria was still enthralled with the first images. When I grabbed hold of Trey, he turned and asked what was wrong.

"Stand back," I instructed Trey. "Saria, you won't believe this.

Stand back and look at this." Saria, without question, took a few steps back.

"Do you see what I see?" I asked, once again. Stunned, we stood there staring at the shadow-like image. The shape was undeniable; I knew it quite well. It was a woman's "pregnant" belly. It wasn't an entire figure of a woman, but from her breast down to the end of her stomach. And what looked like two hands, suspended alongside her stomach as if pulling her stomach apart. Neither of us could speak! It was horrifying and unbelievable! Tears swelled, and a lump formed in my throat. I turned to look at Saria—she, too, had tears running down her dark cheeks.

"Old my God!" Trey finally exclaimed. "That can't be what I think it is!"

"Yes, it is," Saria and I said simultaneously, "a woman's baby is being ripped from her stomach." We each looked at each other before taking our seats, staring at the three images that faced us. No one said a word, at least not for about five minutes.

Being the first to break the silence, I asked my friends what they saw again—still unable to believe it. Neither one could repeat the horrors. Trey stated that he needed to leave because he was getting sick to his stomach. Saria sobbed as she cursed the ghosts of the plantation, damning them to hell for what had been done to us. Barely able to breathe, I stood and hugged the both of them and explained that we had a lot of work to do — a lot of healing had to be done. As we broke from our embrace, we all turned to take one last look at the images our ancestors were showing us—They were completely gone!

After walking Saria to her car, and with tears still in her eyes, she looked up at me and assured me that I was where I was supposed to be, and that the ancestors were pleased with the work that was being done. I bent down to give her another kiss and thanked her for her friendship and her support.

Going back into the house, Trey and I didn't speak. And we didn't mention what had happened anymore that night . . . or any other time. However, it was a night that I knew would be imprinted in my subconscious; a vivid reminder of my mission—one that I could not run from or give up on. And, most importantly, the realization that any work, pain, frustration or agony that I was going through, was NOTHING compared to what my ancestors had undertaken for me to be where and who I was today. Their debt for my freedom was far greater than mine would ever be.

FORTY-SEVEN

Gratitude & Family

Thanksgiving was always my favorite holiday, even though it did not come into existence without the savage deeds of greed and control. However, it was a time to celebrate with family and friends and to reflect on the year's blessings . . . despite its challenges. Having my sons and their families come down made this one even more special. It had been a year and two months since my grandson's death, and having family around in a festive mood, along with a traditional Thanksgiving feast, made the sadness bearable.

We, as a family, did a conference call with my daughter. We all cried, laughed, and reminisced about the good old days for almost an hour. Considering the circumstances, Jenia was coming along quite well, and deciding to go back to school was proving to be rewarding. Before hanging up, Jenia decided that she and the kids would come and visit for Christmas. She anticipated a small amount of money from Mark's accident and was working part-time. We were thrilled, to say the least. My heart felt a release knowing my daughter could laugh again, and that the children were doing well. They still claimed to see their brother from time to time, which gave them joy and a sense of still having him around.

Shortly after my family's departure from our celebration of giving thanks, I felt a sense of loneliness and a slight depression. The sound of tiny tots running through the mansion gave my home a sense of life... joy and happiness. Their shrieks of laughter rang throughout the halls while playing hide-and-go-seek. I began to think about how grandchildren are lifesavers and give answers to the whys of all the questions that come up when you're struggling with raising children. They make all your tribulations worthwhile. I was blessed to be a grandmother and honored to look back at my children and take note... that I did good.

We closed for the entire holiday weekend, which gave some reprieve from the hectic schedules Trey and I were both keeping, along with the preparation for Thanksgiving. With business being rather slow, I regrettably had to cut hours for my waitresses to help keep things afloat. They understood and often came through to help out just for tips, which were also a little lean since things had slowed down. And, of course, whenever it was unusually slow, I thought about Vic and his "curse." Even with constant prayers, meditation, and relentless pleas to the ancestors, there were times when fear took precedent over my faith, even if it were short-lived. I yearned for a break from the mundane, the fears and doubts about the future. I needed to release the pain and frustrations of everything. I needed to sing.

FORTY-EIGHT

A Ritual with Lady Day

That Friday (the day after Thanksgiving), Trey and I decided to set up the Karaoke machine, so I could work on my voice. While we were setting up, I got a telephone call from my new sister-friend, Wanda, whom I had met a few months earlier.

The night we had met, William was doing a fundraiser for the Tubman Center, when he invited me to sing. I had only rehearsed once and didn't feel comfortable performing in public. Even though I had sung in the past at various clubs and events, I never quite had the confidence I needed to be considered a "professional." However, with a little coercing from William and the band, I sang two of my favorite songs: *Lover Man* and *Good Morning Heartache*. Thankfully, I was well-received and encouraged to sing more often.

After the show, Wanda said she wanted to introduce me to her man-friend, who had a knack for music, and whom she felt would love to meet me and possibly introduce me to his friend, who was opening a recording studio. Although quite thrilled, I really didn't think much about it after that night. So, when I got her call, I was pleasantly surprised.

After a few moments of girly chit-chat, Wanda went on to tell me why she called.

"Look, I know you're closed . . . but my man, Chuck, is in town and I wanted to bring him over to talk to you about singing. I told him how I thought you reminded me of Billie Holiday . . . and Chuck loves him some Billie."

"Girl, Trey and I just set up the Karaoke machine so I could work on my voice." I shared. "It's fine with me if you wanna come over. Maybe, if your friend is interested, Trey can play a video that he recorded of me a few weeks ago. I did a few of Billie's songs."

Like Wanda's friend, I loved me some Billie Holiday. Our voices were different, but our style of delivery was like we were twins. I knew her stories of unrequited love and heartache deep in the core of my Being. She was my idol, and singing "our" songs made me feel good—– the kind of good that kept me hopeful for the kind of love we both knew existed. The kind of love I found myself *still* longing for. But, even more than yearning for *true* love, singing allowed me to pull up buried pain that often lay dormant, as I tried to stay strong and hopeful about life and all its upheavals.

"That would be perfect! What about around eight tonight?" Wanda asked.

"Sounds great. I look forward to meeting your friend and seeing you again. You know it's been a while."

"Girl, I know. I've been really busy, but we will catch up tonight. I'm excited. See you tonight."

We said our good-byes, and I told Trey that they were coming. He, too, was excited. He was quite proud of the video he recorded of me and was happy that he could show it off. So, we put away the Karaoke machine and set up the video camera instead. We then hung a twin-sized, white sheet on the back wall over the stage to serve as a screen.

Wanda and Chuck arrived shortly after eight. It was a delight to see Wanda again. As usual, she was wearing an Afrocentric outfit and a huge, colorful scarf around her head. Chuck, on the other hand, was more casual, dressed in jeans and a sweater. They looked good together as a couple. He was a nice-looking, brown-skinned brother with a fresh haircut, lined to the shape of his oval face. His personality was warm and contagious as we welcomed him.

After a quick tour of the mansion for Chuck, his overwhelming excitement reminded me of the good job we had done... restoring my enthusiasm. I then made fresh coffee and served some leftover cake from our Thanksgiving dinner, while Trey began talking about the video and the techniques he used to get the look and feel of the 30's and 40's. How he used a sepia-tone effect instead of black & white. We listened as he described the grainy texture and how he burned incense, filling the room with a cloud of misty smoke, while capturing a swirling ceiling fan that hung over the stage, which he called his Casablanca look. He even had me dress up in a long, white dress accessorized with elbow-length gloves and sparkling costume jewelry. And of course, my look was topped off with a silk Gardenia (Billie's signature flower) placed on the right side of my hair. I have to admit, it was pretty cool.

Although I had seen the film before, watching it with strangers, I could feel myself getting a little tense. . . concerned as to whether or not it sounded as good to Wanda and Chuck, as it did to me and Trey. But after the half-hour performance, I was praised with accolades beyond my expectations . . . as well as Trey. Chuck was genuinely impressed with both of us.

"Man, you did one hell-of-job, and I really like the effect you got . . . it was like watching an old movie." Trey blushed with gratitude as Wanda dittoed his sentiment and before Chuck continued.

"Nailah, I have a friend who just opened a studio in Iowa. I know it's late, but I'm gonna call him tonight to see if we can't go and do a demo this weekend. It won't cost you anything but time. Would you be interested?"

"Are you kidding me? Of course, I would love to go. Do you really think your friend would do it . . . especially at such late notice?" I asked, feeling pretty good about myself and my singing, while Trey damn near floated in mid-air. I think he was more excited than I was.

That night, around 11:00 pm, Chuck called with the news. He was able to set up a time for us to drive to Iowa early on Sunday morning and come back that night. I called Saria the next morning to see if she wanted to go; she was more than eager to tag along. I told her the plans and that I would call before picking her up. She was one of my biggest supporters when it came to my singing; she and Trey made me feel good about my voice. She also knew of my obsession with Miss Holiday as a kindred spirit and reminded me of the importance of getting Billie's "permission" before I went trampling off to do "her" songs.

Billie Shows Her Approval

The sun was shining when I went out to buy a white candle and fresh flowers. But the sharp, chilling wind reminded me that the harshness of winter was right on our heels. Trey had decided to stay in and take a nap, so I had some quiet time to reflect on our journey. I beamed on the inside while both the car and I warmed up a little before pulling off. The whole idea of it all sparked a lightheartedness in my spirit. I was about to do something for me . . . something for my creative spirit. And it felt good.

After gathering my items for my ritual, I smudged myself and the theatre. I found a mat and placed my items meticulously on the stage and prayed before lighting the candle. It was cold upstairs, but I took off my coat and removed my shoes. I was wearing a beautiful, multicolored nylon sweater with reds and oranges with a white background and jeans. And although this was not an ancestral ritual, I wrapped my head in a scarf. As I knelt and called forth the energy of Billie Holiday, I thanked her for all she gave us as a singer and as a person who endured extreme racism and human injustices, just for being Black. I thanked her for her soul's passion for her music and her dedication to giving all she had. So many drank from her bitter cup and tasted her pain with little or no mercy for her struggle. I adored her, as well as admiring her weaknesses, because she owned up to them with no shame. Nor did she seek pity or excuses for her choices, which ultimately caused her demise.

As I was talking with Billie, seeking permission to echo her songs, I watched the yellowish, orange flame flicker gently. I glanced at the white Carnations and briefly wished they were Gardenias before bowing my head to listen for her response. Suddenly, a raging flame ignited on my left shoulder. Why I didn't jump, scream or beat the hell out of my shoulder, I do not know. Instead, with a sense of calmness, I began *tapping* the flame until the fire turned to a smoldering smoke. That's when I distinctly heard Billie's voice resounding in my head, saying, *"By the way, I wear my Gardenia on the left."* (When I sang for the film, I wore her signature flower on the *right*.) Once again, the flame from the candle *gently* flickered as if nothing had happened. I then looked at my nylon sweater, only to find that every fiber was in place . . . with NO signs of ever being aflame. I guess you could say, I got her permission.

After my encounter with Billie, I called Saria to tell her what had happened. She wasn't surprised and said she was on her way over. I suppose it did warrant a more in-depth conversation. Showing my friend where I had set up my altar, she knelt and honored Billie's Spirit before we headed downstairs and landed in repose on the two bottom steps. We went into a deep conversation and contemplation about what had happened.

"You know you and Billie are connected, don't you?" Saria asked as her deep, dark eyes connected to mine, waiting for my response.

"I've always felt that way but wasn't really sure why," I hesitantly answered.

"Nailah, with the exception of the drugs," Saria began to explain. "You and Billie have lived very similar lives. You know her... you know her pain, especially when it comes to relationships".

"Yeah, I know. But a lot of women can identify with her pain . . . her unrequited love affairs." Again, I found myself unable to allow myself to have any *special* privileges. After all, who was I? Saria took my hands in hers and looked up at me. "Nailah, didn't you just have a spiritual encounter... a connection with Billie? I mean, she set your sweater on fire and didn't even leave any evidence of it. Now, how many people can say that?"

The truth was, we had no idea whether or not anyone else could say that or not. Or if anyone else had encountered her at all. But Saria's point was well taken, and I resolved to the possibility that what she believed was true, and what I felt in my heart was real; that we did have a connection. Or did I?

Although I had the honor of singing in California on numerous occasions at jazz clubs, the Navy Officers Club, and private functions, as well as singing in the church choir most of my life, I was still shy and lacked confidence in my ability as a vocalist. So, it didn't surprise me when, later that night, I began to feel the onset of a cold–self-sabotage, maybe? When I awakened early that morning with a cough and laryngitis, I thought for sure my solo performance would be canceled. Trey took my temperature, which was 102°. We were both dumbfounded. How could I have gotten sick so quickly? Less than twenty-four hours earlier, I was feeling great.

I sat up on the side of my bed and wondered what could be happening. It came to me that somehow, I didn't think that I deserved this rare opportunity. In some of my psychological studies, it has been hypothesized that many of us often sabotage any opportunities for accomplishments due to feelings of unworthiness. I mused as to whether or not I was a victim of this ideology. If, in fact, I was, I was going to do everything in my power to make it a lie. Whatever I had to do to get ready for this trip, and to sing 11 songs, I was going to do it.

By the time Chuck called, I had drunk three cups of herbal tea, sucked on Halls cough drops, and gargled with warm saltwater. Chuck immediately knew that I was sick and asked if I was still up to going. I assured him that I was up to it and that somehow, I would sing those songs. There was no way I was going to let this opportunity slip away. He was pleased to hear my commitment to going. After all, he had worked hard to get this appointment, and I certainly didn't want to disappoint him or myself.

Iowa Bound

On schedule, with the exception of Wanda (she had to work), we were on the road by 6:00 a.m., headed to Iowa. I sat in the back and laid across Trey's lap. I felt like shit and began to question my rationale for making the trip. We pulled over a few times for aspirin, a Ginger Ale, and more cough drops, and finally to get a pint of brandy and a fresh lemon.

After several hours of driving through various neighborhoods, I knew we were close when I saw black folks in packs and not just sprinkled here and there. Before long, Chuck pulled into a driveway behind a small truck and blew his horn. The freshly painted, small brick building appeared to have been a house at one time. A large empty lot on both sides gave it privacy, along with barred windows for extra security. I looked around, still blowing my nose and trying to suppress a cough, when a young man came to the front door.

"Hey there, my man... come on in," the young man hollered to Chuck. His smile was warm, and his eyes were lit with excitement. I could tell he was proud. Hell, he had his own studio.

During introductions, it was obvious he was definitely young and part of the Hip-Hop Culture. Thick dreadlocks fell from his turned-around cap with a large diamond-like stud in his left ear. Dressed in baggy pants and a black T-shirt, he looked like he was ready to get down with some sounds. And as sick as I was, so was I.

The tour of the brothers' studio was short but rewarding. I was delighted by his accomplishments as an up-and-coming studio engineer. The 32-track soundboard was massive with all the latest bells and whistles; you could tell he was excited. In his excitement, I reminded him that this was gonna be "old folks" music. He assured me he was cool with that, since he grew up in a house of jazz and blues.

He started bragging about listening to Sarah Vaughn, Nancy Wilson, etc. I was impressed.

Trey and Saria walked around admiring the recording room while the young man showed Chuck and me more of the Board. After explaining to the brother that I was singing with a Karaoke CD, he explained that he wouldn't be able to separate or adjust the musical instruments, but he could put my voice on a separate track. I pretended that I understood and asked that he just do his best, considering it was a "demo." In other words, it wasn't going to be *professional,* per se.

An hour or so had passed before I found myself standing in a room all alone with an extended microphone at my lips and headphones cushioned to my ears. After several sips of brandy and lemon juice, along with a cup of hot tea, I was feeling pre-tty good. Saria fired one up and assured me that one hit was not gonna get me high but help me to relax. Since I never smoked when I had something important to do, hesitantly, I took a tiny hit.

Still barely able to talk, I silently prayed to my angels and to Billie, asking them to give me the strength to sing. I took a deep breath, concentrated on my diaphragm, and listened for my first note. I was shocked! My voice was clear and smooth. With Saria and Trey watching me through the glass window, their thumbs-up motivated me to keep the momentum going, although there were moments when I felt weak, especially after singing the "cover" of one of my favorite southern belles, Lena Horn's *Stormy Weather.* By the time I got to *God Bless The Child,* my Cinderella moment of having a *voice* began to turn back into a frog. My fans encouraged me to do it over with a little more energy. And somehow, I found the strength to do it again.

It was dark by the time I sang 11 songs straight, and by the time I re-did *God Bless the Child,* I was tired, weary, and with virtually no voice. But, as I sat with my friends while the young brother played my tracks, I was quite amazed at how clear and strong my voice was. And even though the musical *mix* left a little to be desired, we were all thrilled with the final product–especially me, causing a smile to part my dry lips and my cotton-like mouth—I had no saliva. But I was cheesing.

It was after 5 a.m. by the time we pulled into the driveway. Trey had taken over the wheel while Chuck got a few zzzz. Saria sat in the back with me and offered her lap as a pillow. Her cushioned belly rose and fell gently while she quietly slept. I hated to wake her. Although I didn't get any sleep, I rested well, musing about what I had accomplished. Professional or not, I was pleased with the outcome of my demo and pleased with myself for following through and having the ability to borrow from the strength of my angels and Billie to get me through it. And I was especially glad it was Monday . . . another day off. Hallelujah!

Over the next few weeks, I shared my accomplishment with a few selected close friends— one of whom was a professional publicist and makeup artist who began to envision costumes and media coverage for my new career as a vocalist. Unfortunately, as life would have it, a budding career in the singing department was not in the plan. However, months later, I received a $1200 grant (which I applied for earlier) from a local women's foundation to further my aspirations as an artist. Now, that put a gigantic grin on my face!

FORTY-NINE

A Reunion

The winter months slowly but surely brazened their way into the familiar season of freezing temperatures. It was only December, and we were already experiencing temperatures in the low 20's. With Jenia and the kids coming for the holidays, I wanted to make sure there were enough blankets and heat. So, I bought a few more blankets and purchased a couple of electric heaters.

Business was extremely slow, which I assumed was due to the one time of year that the average person spent more money than any other time of the year. It was typical to an extent for it to be slow, but somehow, I kept thinking about Vic and his threat to ruin what we had worked for. The only thing that gave me any peace was the fact that my child and grandchildren were coming, whom I hadn't seen since Mark's death. And having them home for Christmas was my "gift . . . my joy to the world."

I was an hour early picking up the kids. I was so excited, I didn't want any possibility of being late in case of traffic, which was usually heavy around the airport, especially during the holidays. It took a while to find a parking place, which meant I had a way to walk. The still, icy air stuck to my exposed face, freezing my licked lips together. With my gloved hands in my pockets, they still managed to feel like frozen popsicles—and my feet felt like they were glued to my socks, making my boots feel tighter than they were. I was miserably happy.

When I saw Jenia come through the door, she was carrying the baby girl. The other three who were dressed in sweaters and furry, pullover hats were hanging onto Jenia's pant-leg. Once they spotted me, they broke from the security of their mother's leg and ran into my arms. I was beyond elated. After several minutes of crying, hugging, kissing and wiping snotty noses, along with a mandated pit-stop, we headed to the baggage claim.

"Grandma! What a big house you have," they all said in unison as we pulled up in front of the house.

"Dang, mom, you said it was big, but this is a mansion!" Jenia exclaimed accompanied by a huge grin. Mouths fell open as the kids filed out slowly, one by one. I grabbed hands and hurriedly moved them towards the huge, red door. With popped eyes and gasping sighs of awe, their small heads fell back upon their shoulders, taking in the 14-foot ceilings and giant doors.

Iniah, the eldest, was 8; Jonathan, who was right behind her, recently turned 6, and then there was Kamonnie, who was 4. And last, but not least, was the baby, Siarra, she had just turned 2 on the 5th of December, which of course, gave her the privilege of being carried most of the time.

As we all stood in the doorway, the children sited the Christmas tree in the next room. And although Jenia never allowed her children to believe in this particular season of a white-bearded man coming down a chimney, they jabbered about its beauty with all the lights and candy canes. I called Trey down to meet my family and to get the luggage from the car. Of course, Jenia was very much aware of him and had spoken with him on the phone a couple of times, so meeting him was putting a face to the name.

Trey took second place to the beautifully decorated tree but managed to meet and hug each one before they took off for other adventures. Even Siarra eagerly climbed down from her place of security to follow her oldest sister. They, as well as I, were as *"happy as a hog in slop"*. My babies were home, and the rest of my small tribe was due in a few days.

It was one o'clock in the morning before the cowboys, dancers and hide-n-go seekers fell dead to the world of enchantment and amazement. And I was beat to the bone. Nevertheless, my joy and happiness took precedent over my aching body as Jenia and I talked into the wee morning hours. Trey had fallen asleep along with the kids. They had run him ragged with their games and as their personal tour guide. He really enjoyed them. Two days later, he headed to Chicago to spend the holiday with his own kids.

They were some of the happiest days I had felt in a very long time; watching my family come in over the next few days made my heart leap with joy. All the anguish and disappointment seemed to melt away. As instructed, they brought sleeping bags, pillows, and extra blankets. By nightfall, my bed was filled with children and storytelling, and I was enjoying every moment.

The next night was poetry, and for the first time, Jenia got to see what it was like, which was our last one for the year. She had only heard about it through our conversations. She was completely amazed and overwhelmed with excitement over the talent, the music and the overall ambience of joy and creativity. My children, and especially my grandchildren, where astonished by the speed and flair that I showcased while being a waitress. They were very proud of me, being a business owner and all, and even more proud that I was able to keep my head held high and continue to move forward, in spite of the breakup between Vic and me. Of course, they all pitched in with serving, making salads, pouring drinks and most importantly, cleaning up.

We spent the next couple of days and nights after Christmas reminiscing; the stories had us all laughing until we hurt. We prayed, sang songs and ate as if the cupboards were overflowing. We were having the time of our lives — so much so that Jenia and the kids were thinking about moving to Kentucky. And the fact that Jenia and her husband weren't getting along made it seem almost certain to make the move happen.

FIFTY

Theatre in the Making

Remember John, the writer who had written a script? Well, he kept his word and returned to drop it off for consideration. As promised, I took a good look at his story in detail and thought it was an excellent idea, especially since that night with the wall images. To "educate" our community about the atrocities of slavery in a theatrical format seemed ideal. However, I knew it would take a lot of work, and we would have to solicit costumes and find actors to participate... for free. Actually, I found myself getting excited about being busy again. After my daughter and grandchildren left to return to California, about two weeks into the new year, I was stricken with a deep sadness and loneliness. I missed them deeply. This project was exactly what I needed!

John was ecstatic when I called him, saying I was ready to get started with the play. I had a lot of hard work ahead of me. Not only did I have to find actors and costumes, but I also had my responsibilities with the restaurant, as well as running the cultural center, which could not be put on hold. The play of course, would be a part of the cultural center's activities, so there was the possibility for donations to help with the cost.

John was thrilled about doing the play— and so was I. We committed to getting together again to sit down and organize everything, now that the holidays were over. And since we were tentatively looking at June, we had just under six months to pull it all together in time to commemorate "Juneteenth." (A celebration of the ending of slavery, which was first held in Austin, Texas on June 19, 1866)

Rewrites, Actors & Costumes

Business had been relatively slow, so it gave me a little more time to work with John in revising the script. He left the script with me because I told him I needed to consult with the ancestors to see what changes had to be made. He was unselfishly open to any of my suggestions and had no problem with me making changes. I explained to him that it was not necessarily me who would be making the changes, but instead, I was seeking direction as to what the ancestors wanted to tell "as their story."

Once getting the word out that we were looking for actors, it didn't take long for some of my customers to jump at the opportunity to perform. We made up fliers and put an ad in a local magazine that was geared towards the arts. It was free and a great resource for getting some professional people to take part in what was an integral (although horrific) part of America's history.

I contacted a couple of actors that I had worked with in the past, when I produced *A Raisin in the Sun* by Lorraine Hansberry while serving as director for the Family Life Center at a local, well-known church. I had previously performed in three productions: *Picnic* by Willian Inge and A *Night In Tunisia (Humana Fest)* by Actress Regina Taylor, and the musical *Tintypes* by Mary Kyte. So, you might say that I had a little experience in theater, although acting wasn't something that I pursued as a career. However, albeit on a small scale, my participation in theater would prove to be an asset for our upcoming play.

As a former slave state, Kentucky's history and its relationship towards the descendants of Africans were still marred by the inability to relate to us as equals. So many of our elders were still trapped in the "slave mentality," which carried a seed that germinated and rooted deeply in the minds of so many of my generation, and the sluggish uphill battle to promote pride, equality, and self-sufficiency was almost impossible. After all, Kentucky did **NOT sign the Emancipation Proclamation until 1976, 111 years later.** Talk about being determined to keep us enslaved.

Nevertheless, the story needed to be told, especially for the sake of our youth. And what little "freedom" we had, it was so whitewashed that the memory of our past had become saturated with the illusion that we "had made it." Anytime I had black folks telling me, "The white man ain't gonna let you…" I knew we were a far cry from being free, especially in the mind. And what better place than a *former plantation* to awaken our sleeping consciousness. So many of my people needed a desperate "wake-up call," and we were determined to give it to them.

I worked feverishly for the next couple of months rewriting the script and finding costumes. The ancestors had given me a few ideas on what changes to make, and John was open to them all. We were both satisfied with the final outcome, thus creating our first "Murder Mystery," *The House Warming.*

Putting it all Together

The fact that we had been in the papers, on television, and known for Spoken Word, getting donations was not an uphill struggle. A restaurant specializing in African cuisine donated appetizers, a local costume shop provided the *period* clothing, and getting professional actors was the icing on the cake. In speaking with prospective donors, it seemed as if folks had been waiting for an opportunity to support the African American community, and in particular, The Java House Café & The Harriet Tubman Cultural Center. Everything was falling into place.

With April springing forth, it was now time for rehearsals, which made my days even longer than usual. But I managed to muster up the strength. We were embarking on a period in history when my ancestors worked from sunup till sundown. At least I avoided the "whip" when I fell asleep or took time off to rejuvenate, reminding me once again that what I was doing was Nothing compared to what my ancestors had to experience.

I suppose, with any project, especially one so sensitive, I should have expected some challenges. One of my actors just couldn't deal with the subject matter, although she was aware of what it was about beforehand. However, I suppose when you have to be called nigger and pushed around and treated like shit, it was just too difficult to handle. So, quite naturally, I had to take on an additional role, as well as the role of director and producer. It was good that I had written some of the dialogue, which made it easier for me to remember lines. As they say in show business . . . "The show must go on." And that it did.

The House Warming

The hot, humid sun has no mercy on the guests of local plantation owners and their families as they arrive on a glorious Saturday afternoon. Approaching the gate with a huge, floral fan and a brightly colored parasol, two women are greeted at the entrance to the mansion by a young black butler. Chairs are lined on the front lawn on each side of a wide sidewalk as the butler directs them to their seats.

(Being that this is a play, Blacks and Caucasian guests are arriving, and in this case, a black woman arrives with a white coworker. As they walk through the gate . . .)

"Ma'am, you on this side," the butler bows to the white woman as he directs her to the right.

"And you, Ma'am," being *less formal as he* greets the colored woman. "You on this side," directing her to the left.

(Not realizing that the "separation" was a part of the performance, both women tried to explain to the young man that they were together. However, the young man was insistent as they continued to explain their position. Finally, the young man, somewhat frustrated and practically yelling . . .)

"White folks on this side and Colored folks on that side," he exclaimed while pointing in opposite directions. With his eyes wild with fear, he continues . . .

"Whites and Coloreds can't sit together!"

(At that point, still in character, I slowly walked over as I casually fanned myself and whispered in a southern drawl to our perplexed guests.)

"You are now a part of the reality of a Southern plantation."

(Still obviously confused, they hesitantly went to their "separate" sides.)

As the servants serve drinks and appetizers, colored children from nearby plantations, with tattered and worn clothes, scurry playfully on the freshly cut lawn with their new neighbors. Their cheerful laughter fills the air as they play with wooden sticks and half-deflated balls. Happy and *free* as the birds . . . suddenly . . . their laughter turns into screams of terror as they run in different directions when they hear gunshots while two, black male slaves yell while chasing a runaway slave, along with their white Master with a shotgun.

"Stop nigguh. I's is gonna shoot ya ifn't you don't stop. I's got em Masser . . . he ain't gets too fur. I catch em fo ya, Masser."

Just as the children are being taken into the house, and the runaway slave captured, a male guest takes center stage on the front porch.

However, with all the commotion, the guests are not aware of his presence until he speaks:

Gentlemen:

 My name is Willie Lynch. First, I shall thank you, the gentlemen of the colony of Kentucky for bringing me here to this festive occasion as we welcome back one of our own. It is my understanding that this young family has forgotten the ways of the South while living in Africa as missionaries. And based on what we all just witnessed with one of your runaway niggers, I feel this is a most appropriate time to help you, and especially our host, as how to solve some of the problems with your slaves.

I caught the whiff of a dead slave hanging from a tree a couple of miles back. You are losing valuable stock by hangings; you are having uprisings, slaves are running away, as we just witnessed. Your crops are sometimes left in the fields too long for maximum profit, you suffer occasional fires, your animals are killed. Gentlemen, you know what your problems are; I do not need to elaborate. I am not here to enumerate your problems; I am here to introduce you to a method of solving them. In my bag, I have a foolproof method for controlling your slaves. I guarantee every one of you that if installed it will control the slaves for at least three hundred years. However, due to time and the fact that this is a celebration of sort, I will outline just a couple of my methods for the "Making of a slave." These methods have worked on my modest plantation in the West Indies, and it will work throughout the SOUTH. And being that I feel it is the most beneficial in making a good nigger slave, here's what you do.

For example, take the case of the wild stud horse, a female horse and an already infant horse and compare the breaking process with two nigger males in their natural state, and a pregnant nigger woman with her infant offspring. Take the stud horse, break him for limited containment. Completely break the female horse until she becomes very gentle whereas you or anybody can ride her in comfort. Breed the mare and the stud until you have the desired offspring. Then you can turn the stud to freedom until you need him again. Train the female horse whereby she will eat out of your hand, and she will in turn train the infant horse to eat out of your hand also. When it comes to break the uncivilized nigger male, use the same process, but vary in degree and step up the pressure so as to do a complete reversal of the mind. Take the meanest and *most restless nigger, strip him of his clothes in front of the remaining male niggers, the female, the nigger infant . . . tar and feather him, tie each leg to a different horse in opposite directions, set him afire, and beat both horses to pull him apart in front of the remaining niggers. The next step is to take a bullwhip and beat the remaining nigger male to the point of death in front of the female and the infant. Don't kill him, but put the fear of God in him, for he can be useful for future breeding.*

Don't forget you must pitch the old black VS. the young black males, and the young black male against the old black male. You must use the dark-skinned slaves VS. the light skin slaves. You must use the female VS the male, and the male VS, the female. You must always have your servants and Overseers distrust all niggers, but it is necessary that your slaves trust and depend on us. Gentlemen, these are just a couple of keys to control your slaves. Never miss an opportunity. My plan is guaranteed, and the good thing about this plan is that if used intensely for one year, the slave will remain perpetually distrustful.

Then, suddenly, out of nowhere, a female servant runs up to Lynch, raging with anger. "You's will burn in hell!" The servant screams while violently shaking her fingers. "May da good Lawd strike you down, and mays yo soul never have no peace!"

Fear for her servant, the hostess runs up and lovingly takes the woman's hand and leads her into the house. Still fuming with anger, the woman continues her ranting until she is out of hearing range.

"You see, my friends," Lynch continues before stepping down. "You must control the nigger female first... break her down by making her totally dependent on you as I proposed, and this type of thing will never happen. I hope that the owner of that nigger woman does what he knows is necessary, making sure that that type of disrespect is no longer tolerated." Lynch then takes a wine glass from one of the *servants who's standing nearby . . . raises his glass and makes a toast . . . "To all my fellow plantation owners — here's to 'The making of a slave!'"*

Note: The original speech of "The making of a slave" was penned by Willie Lynch in 1712 and espoused throughout the South. I took only parts of this speech (along with added text for the benefit of the play), however, the "methods" he recommended are verbatim. The original speech is a total of over four-pages . . . explaining in gruesome detail as to the recipe for making a "good nigger slave." This is history that many of us (particularly African Americans) are NOT aware of.

Once Lynch steps down from his soapbox, the bewildered guests are ushered into the mansion where the plot thickens . . . and where Lynch meets his demise as the *murdered victim!*

The Effect

After two hours of intrigue and harsh realities of slavery and plantation life, our audience was left stunned and in deep thought. The production was awesome! The comments were beyond my expectations, especially from our younger audience. I recall one young man who was the son of one of our lead actors who came to me after the performance. As a theatre student and an avid theatergoer, he said:

"Miss Nailah, this is by far the best play I have ever seen. And thank you for teaching me about slavery and what it was like. I will never forget this story, and I'm glad my dad was a part of it."

Needless to say, the young man's statement validated just how important and impactful our "Murder Mystery" was—which by the way, received rave reviews in the local newspaper's Arts section. And after seeing the production, the sponsors who had been happy to participate beforehand, assured us that we would have their continued support in any of the Center's future productions.

Putting on a production of that size took a lot of energy and hard work, but everyone did a great job, and I was extremely proud of their professionalism and dedication. Since the production was well attended, we were fortunate to make a few hundred dollars in profit after a few expenses. Everyone worked in the spirit of love for our ancestors, but also for hope and equality in our current affairs as Blacks in America. And most importantly, I hoped that the memory of our ancestors who endured the pain and suffering of Lynch's' theory be etched upon our hearts and minds, as a reminder that we can NEVER let the sickened words of Willie Lynch and people like him, continue to set the precedent as to how we live . . . love . . . worship (our God), or die in this country.

FIFTY-ONE

Bitter Sweet

Business was getting scarce, and the profit we made from the play definitely came on time. The cooling system wasn't doing any good upstairs, but the utility bills looked as though the entire 22 rooms were "chilled" almost to the point of freezing. I wasn't used to $1300-$1500 a month, and it was a struggle to pay it, to say the least. Between that and the mortgage and the cost of food and sales and payroll taxes, I was getting a little panicky. I was still tired from the production; however, there was no rest for the weary. I had to find more ways to make money, or I would not be able to keep up with the expenses.

As much as I hated to, I knew we needed to start charging an entrance fee for poetry. Five dollars was the decided amount, but only three dollars if you were participating, but I still hated doing it. We had never charged before. Surprisingly, after making the announcement one Saturday night, everyone was in agreement. Ready, willing and supportive . . . no one ever complained.

I missed Vic and I felt sorry for him. Hard to believe, I know. But, in spite of his seeming hatred and defiance towards me, I prayed that he would find peace and happiness.

My Child Comes Home

Jenia and the children kept their promise to come back and live, and they came just in time to celebrate "Independence Day." Seeing them gave me a ray of hope and lifted my spirits, even though there was a slight fear of how I was going to be able to take care of an additional five people. However, they were my babies, and I knew we would make it... somehow.

The celebration was filled with music, dance, poetry, and fireworks. Folks from nearby cities came to help us celebrate our contribution to America and Her glory. We understood that it was the backs of blacks that built Her, and in many ways, we continue to sustain Her. As leaders in the sports arena, music and entertainment industry, and inventors of thousands of amenities and products that are used every day, we truly have reason to celebrate. There would be no America if it were not for US!

Having my daughter and my grandchildren to fill the empty spaces in my heart was more than I anticipated. Trey, of course, took care of my physical needs, but my heart still longed for laughter and a sense of worth. My grandbabies made me feel wanted . . . their love was pure with no conditions or expectations. It was free and unselfish; wrapped with long hugs and lingering kisses on each of my cheeks, along with reciprocated tickles that exploded with back-aching laughter. They gave me pure joy.

On the days that my daughter fell down from her tower of strength, we became each other's foundation for renewal and newfound strength. Mark's death still weighed heavy on her soul, as it did mine, so I knew I had to call upon the souls of ancient times to hold me up so that I could hold her up. We took one day at a time, with some days crying for hours, while other times we laughed until we cried.

Spoken word must have given my grandbabies ideas about entertaining. There were times when they took to the stage upstairs to dance and sing. My one and only grandson, Johnathan loved to dance, and at the tender age of eight years old, he swirled his sister, Kamonnie around as if he was Frankie Manning and she was Norma Miller (both Lindy Hop Legends). They were unbelievable!

The eldest, Iniah, twirled around like a rag doll, kicking her long, thin legs up in the air like a ballerina, while her long, thick hair bounced from side to side. And the youngest, Siarra, only two, flit around like a butterfly trying to imitate her siblings. Their reward for their performances was always met with roaring applause and, oftentimes, a crisp dollar bill, which made their eyes light up, making the experiences even more joyful.

With all the joy and laughter around me, there were still times I felt I would fall apart and lose complete control. I must have worn my ancestors out . . . they, too, had been taken through the ringer. I called on them every day trying to hold it together while the bills were piling higher, and less and less money was coming in. The irritation towards Trey resurfaced, and I found myself comparing him to how Vic and I worked. And even when he was doing what he could around the mansion, I often made him feel as if he wasn't doing enough, even when there wasn't anything to do. I was scared!

Trey Gets a Job

I have no idea why I was so disappointed that Trey wasn't doing more. However, being that business had slowed down considerably, and there wasn't a lot to do, I guess I expected him to *man-up* and take the initiative to look for an *outside* job. But maybe the problem wasn't Trey . . . but rather ME! After all, I knew who he was when I met him. He worked a part-time job, had two kids and a wife with high aspirations to be an actor. Anyway, I finally told him he had to find a job to help out. So, I took him to a couple of places to put in applications, including FED-EX, where he eventually got a few hours a week. The problem was, I had to drive him to work because his car had broken down.

Trey's hours at FED-EX were crazy, to say the least. Midnight till four in the morning was maddening. There were a few times I slept in the parking lot for those four hours, just to save gas. The only good thing was that it hadn't gotten really cold yet, so a blanket usually kept me comfortable. However, that didn't last more than a month. Not only did he complain about the work, but I also complained more about the *added* work that I had to do. Things were getting pretty crazy, and I hadn't been able to make the mortgage payment for at least three or four months. I was sending partial payments when I could, but even that became a problem by December, and I was barely able to pay the utilities and buy food. Not only for our few customers, but for five additional mouths in my family, as well. Yep, it looked like my dear husband's final words had come to fruition. Just like the song by Nina Simone, *"I put a spell on you,"* Vic's hex was working its mojo on my life and the business. And I would soon find out; it was only the beginning.

FIFTY-TWO

Ghost and Homework

It didn't take long for the Spirits in the mansion to reveal themselves to my family. One day, Jenia saw a young boy and girl peering at her from under the kitchen table in our private quarters, dressed in what she thought to be from the 1800s. She said they curiously watched her as they began to whisper to each other, before quickly vanishing.

Kamonnie, also a seer, and who had seen her brother Mark on several occasions in the past, ran to me one day, telling me about a white man she saw.

"Grandma, where did that white man go that I saw on the steps?" she asked in a high-pitched voice. Since we were closed that day, I immediately felt that she was talking about David, the rapist, the one seeking forgiveness for raping several women and for the attempted rape of Bessie (the one who "showed" me her story in the cellar).

"What did he look like?" I inquired nonchalantly.

"He was white, Grandma, and he was wearing a black hat and a white shirt, and he had a big mustache". Her voice was excitable as she shared all the details, as only a five-year-old can. "He was standing right there," pointing at the top of the stairs. "Then he went in the room, and I went to see where he went…and he was gone, Grandma. I couldn't find him."

I explained to her that his name was David and that if she saw him again, to let me know. She seemed to be satisfied with just a name and ran off to play. I knew it was David. Other than the time I saw him in the vision with Bessie, he showed up again not too long after we started the renovations.

It was late at night, I recall. I had used the van to get some things from our current home to bring to the mansion. When I pulled into the back, I noticed the lights were on upstairs. I figured Vic was still working, as we were trying to get our soon-to-be living quarters in good enough shape for us to stay while we were renovating. Right after I turned off the ignition, I noticed a man with a white shirt and dark trousers going down into the cellar. I had turned the van lights off, so the only light was coming from the upstairs windows. Of course, I knew it had to be my husband. I jumped from the van and called out his name.

"Vic..."

However, there was no response. So quite naturally, while still calling his name, I rushed over to the top of the steps leading into the cellar. The door was closed.

"That's weird," I thought to myself while heading down the steps to open the door. When I peeped in, it was pitch black and quite obvious that there was NO ONE there. Being just a *little* frightened, I quickly ran inside the house and went upstairs. When I saw Vic in the hallway, I intuitively knew that the man I saw was David. And like the other wandering souls, day after day, he relived a virtual hell.

Getting back to Kamonnie and her "seeing" abilities, I recall another incident. One day, she had been playing with her siblings and some neighborhood kids in the laundry room at the rear of the house.

"Grandma," she screamed, running into the kitchen where I was cleaning. "What's the matter, baby? You look scared . . . is anything wrong?" I nervously asked. Panting and out of breath, her eyes were as large as light bulbs as she described what she saw. "I saw a real big man in the back, and he was real black, grandma and he had on some big blue jeans, and his hair wasn't combed either."

"Did his blue jeans come up high on his chest?" I asked, demonstrating on my own chest. "... with two straps that held them up with shiny buckles like the ones on your coat?"

"He didn't have no coat on, Grandma, but he had shiny things right here," pointing to her upper chest on both sides. I smiled and explained that he was wearing a different kind of buckle and that his big jeans were called overalls. "Okay, Grandma... is he a good man? cause he looked mean," she asked, scrunching her face into a frown. I assured my granddaughter that he was a good man, and that his name was Joe, and that if she saw him again, to let me know. She agreed and eagerly ran back to what was more important... playing.

I, too, had seen Joe's apparition a couple of times and was given his background during a meditation. Although obviously a grown man, Joe had the mind of a child, and he loved playing with kids. That's probably why he was around. One thing about children is that it doesn't take them any time to make new friends, and in this case, a young white boy and his sister, whom I had never seen until my grandchildren came to live with me. I eventually met their mother one day when I heard her calling them home. I made it a point to introduce myself and assured her that her children were in good hands when they came over to play. During our relaxed conversation, she expressed her delight in our being in the neighborhood, that she had read all about us and thought we were helping to change the "attitudes" of many of her white neighbors. And although she never came as a sit-down customer, she occasionally ordered a Mr. T to go. **Teaching . . . again**

The summer flew by like a jet plane, and although the weather was cooling off, I still found myself in a *hot* situation. There was less and less money and more and more responsibility. While most kids went back to public schools, my daughter and I decided that homeschooling was probably the best for my grandchildren, at least until I could find a more suitable situation. From what I knew of the public-school system, I didn't want them to be subjected to its poor quality of education.

Fulfilling the role of an educator took more time than I was able to swing. So, I found myself teaching between our lunch hour and dinner, as well as some late evenings. Meanwhile, Jenia had registered for college to work on her bachelor's degree in social work at a local

Jesuit College. She helped when she could, but because of her studies, those occasions were quite rare. I needed help, and getting it was looking rather bleak.

By the time October rolled around with its unique winds and falling leaves, my friend, Virginia, also a retired school teacher, offered to teach the kids three days a week at her home. This gave me a little more time to try and maintain the two businesses that were draining the bank accounts dry. However, her support provided very little hope in finding a cure to my dilemma. And, unfortunately, since my allegations of the City's "possible" misappropriations of funds, the year before, I was "blacklisted" for any more funding. (Remember, I unmasked some unscrupulous behavior right after our open house, leading to an audit and an investigation) Of course, they offered a more eloquent excuse for non-support . . . "We have overspent our quota."

Just after a couple of months, Virginia could no longer serve as the children's teacher. Johnathan's behavior had become a little more challenging than she could handle, especially with a sick husband. So, I ended up homeschooling, once again. Understandably, my grandchildren were still dealing with Mark's death. On occasions, there were bad dreams, crying spells, and questions that my daughter and I fought back tears to try to answer. And the story of "Your brother has gone to heaven" was losing its power and becoming less palatable. And for Johnathan, it seemed to be harder on him; he had lost his *only* brother— and heaven or not, he was having an extremely hard time. And with everything else that was going on with overdue bills and the lack of business, so was I.

FIFTY-THREE

More Chilling Encounters

There's an adage that states, "When it rains, it pours," and believe me, I was in a storm with lightning flashing and thunder roaring. And to top it off, a most bizarre thing happened that made my life even more tenuous.

It was cold, and Jenia was on her way to school. I had gotten up with her to start my day. But when we headed out to leave, we both noticed that it was colder than usual at the bottom of the stairs. I started looking around to see what was causing the chill, only to look into the Henrietta Marie dining room to find a brick on the floor. Bewildered, I wondered where it had come from; that's when I felt a gust of cold air coming from a broken window. Before I could speak, my daughter and I looked at each other with a blank stare.

"Damn, somebody threw a brick through the window," I thought out loud while searching the rock's cold surface to see if there was any note of a threat. There was none, and yet, I could tell it was intentional.

"Mom, who in the hell would do some shit like that? That's a fuckin' shame . . . oh, sorry, Mom, but that don't make no damn sense," my daughter expressed with anger.

I solemnly agreed, still pondering over who did it, and why. I gave a sigh of despair and told her to go ahead to school, and that I would call my friend, Al, to come and fix it. Obviously still angry, I could tell my daughter was attempting to be calm as she gave me a hug for encouragement before leaving; promising me that everything would be all right. A part of me felt that it was Vic's doings, but again, I wasn't sure. So, I took a deep breath, found a towel to cover the giant hole and called my friend. Before the day was over, the window was good as new. However, the situation was beginning to cause concern and fear for my daughter. She was going through enough. And having to deal with my insurmountable problems, as well, was affecting her coping abilities.

All in the Toilet

My daughter's morale improved somewhat after meeting a young man by the name of Jerry. He brought a new, young group of rappers to perform at the Tubman Center. They were outstanding! Their lyrics rocked with a positive and revolutionary flair; they educated young minds while keeping the funk relevant to their taste. They ended up being one of the several successes of our efforts to support the arts in our community and went on to record their first CD, honoring The Java House Café & Harriet Tubman Cultural Center as a major part of their success, along with a picture of the mansion on the CD's back cover. I was extremely honored and truly impressed with their professionalism and dedication to raising consciousness. At least some good was coming from our efforts.

Over the next few weeks, there were more bizarre happenings that made me uneasy. At the time, besides listening to Agape every other day, I often read the "Daily Word," which was spiritual prayers and affirmations that usually gave me a sense of hope. I had a few books in my bathroom above the commode, and on this particular day, Jenia and her friend, Jerry, ran out into the kitchen. Both breathing heavily, and Jenia, with a smirk on her face... suspiciously cheerful...

"Mom, I told you about those books," she boasted. I turned and looked at my daughter, trying to figure out what she was talking about.

"What books? What are you talking about?" I asked, somewhat confused.

"Those fake Christian books you had on the back of the toilet," she spouted. "They just flew off the back into the toilet. I told you!"

"They did, Miss Nailah," Jerry interjected. "They flew out of the basket, right into the toilet, and there was no wind or anything. It was weird."

"See, the ancestors were trying to tell us something; that they don't care nothing about the white man's religion," Jenia ranted. "They used their religion to enslave them and took them from what they truly believed in . . . and their culture." I could tell my child was serious. Jerry had been teaching her about the Holy Tablets of ancient Egypt.

"Somebody just dumped those books in the toilet, and it was probably that woman I saw in the bathroom one day," she continued. "I had to use the toilet really bad, but as soon as I walked inside the door, I saw a heavy-set black woman standing by the sink... and I knew it wasn't you!" Wide-eyed and almost out of breath, she continued. "Now, even though I've seen some strange shit, she still scared the hell out of me, and I almost peed on myself trying to get out."

Not that it was funny, but Jerry and I couldn't help but chuckle.

"How come you never said anything, honey? That sounds like the woman I saw when we had our cleansing ritual." I responded.

"Mom, there has been so much going on, I hadn't thought about it until now. Plus, you probably wouldn't have seen it as any big deal anyway. I just wanted you to know that the ancestors ain't into that religious stuff."

My daughter knew the Bible inside out and could quote Scripture better than most ministers. So, for her to kinda "kick religion to the curb," in a way that basically questioned her own religious beliefs, I knew the Holy Tablets had to be pretty powerful. I didn't know exactly what it was, but its origin was "African," and it was broadening her thinking; encouraging her to seek more knowledge about her ancestors, and that was good enough for me.

FIFTY-FOUR

Saving My Sanity

Things had gotten pretty bad financially, and with deep regret, I had to lay off my cook. However, a few months later, with homeschooling and all the other responsibilities, it became evident that I couldn't keep up with everything. So, I started asking around and eventually was asked if I would be willing to give a young man an opportunity to get his life back on track. Since he was the brother of a dear friend, and he really needed a job, I overlooked the fact that he had recently gotten out of prison. After talking with him, I offered him a deal that neither one of us could pass up. He would work part-time, cash minimum wage, and free meals.

After teaching him the ropes and showing him our way of doing things, he seemed to be a good match. I still cooked in the evenings and weekends, while the new cook gave me time to do homeschooling with the grandkids. The extra time also gave me more time to "think"! Jenia, when she wasn't in class, worked the cash register for the few customers that sprinkled in.

While I abhorred winter's brutal nature, it had a way of slowing one down; allowing for Inner reflection and Self-evaluation . . . which I found myself doing on a daily basis, to some extent, if no more then to keep my sanity. My mind threw so many questions at me about my intentions, that I hardly had time to reflect on any one situation. Situations such as: Was I sabotaging me and Trey's relationship by finding faults . . . finding reasons to make him a problem? Had I given

Vic a real chance to make things right? Did I truly believe that I deserved success, in spite of all the hard work? These questions laid heavily on my mind. I needed a break!

During the wintry days of freezing temperatures, it was great that there wasn't much snow, which was good for me because I had talked with Jackie (remember, my cursing goddaughter?) about coming to Buffalo, New York, to visit. Just like she had planned, she moved to Buffalo a few months after she graduated –landing a job close to her new apartment. We had talked a couple of times once she moved, bringing her up to date about Vic's leaving and Trey's moving in. After telling her about Jenia and the kids coming to live with me, and the fact that Trey and I were having problems, and that business was virtually non-existent, she strongly encouraged me to take a break and come to visit.

Neither Trey nor Jenia took my decision to go away for a long weekend very well. With the kids and homework, my daughter immediately felt burdened with more responsibility, while Trey felt it was too much work without me. I looked at him and told him he had no clue what "too much work" was. And the fact that he was getting on my last nerve these days, anyway, gave me just the edge I needed to tell him off. Words like lazy, childish, and a few other not-so-kind, descriptive antics of my disappointment flew out of my mouth. He got my point loud and clear and came to the conclusion that a break would do me some good. Plus, get me off his back.

With poetry night coming up, I had to delay my trip for another week. I knew my daughter would be stressed about being alone, so I called one of my friends who had offered to help if I needed her. Fortunately, she had recently gotten a new job with the weekends off. And although she would only be working for tips, she didn't mind.

And it was only for a weekend. Trey could help in the kitchen while Jenia and my friend handled the floor. Everything was set so I could take-off with a clear conscience. However, before I left, I had one more issue to deal with.

It was Thursday night after we closed for dinner when one of my poets came by to work on a new piece for Spoken Word. Since we were closed, I told him he could work on his piece while we were cleaning. About a half-hour or so of running through his new lyrics, he came to the steps where I was sitting in the foyer to talk. As he approached me, I could tell he was excited.

"Mama Java, how did you like my new poem?" he asked, beaming.

"As usual, baby, it was great!" I assured him. "And I really liked the added flair of the jazz beats . . . did you make the CD yourself?"

"Thanks, Mama Java. I had a couple of my boys to lay down a track for me. I still need to work on the timing, but it should be tight by Saturday. Thanks for letting me work on it."

"Not a problem, sweetie, glad to help. It really sounds good. I know it will be a hit."

"Look, I wanted to talk to you about something else as well," he continued, a little more serious. "You know my lady-friend, right?"

"Sure, if you're talking about the one I've seen you with for the past couple of months . . . or is this somebody new?"

"Naw, it's the same one," he chuckled. "That's what I wanted to talk to you about. You know she and I have been seeing each other for a couple of months now, and we decided to get married . . ."

"You what?" I asked, shocked.

"I know, it's rather soon, but we talked about it and we think we'll be good for each other. What I want to ask you — is will you marry us?"

"Look, sweetheart, thanks for asking me, but I can't do that." I began to explain while his smile turned upside down. "I know, without a doubt, that it would never work," I continued. "For one, you've only known each other for a very short time, and . . ."

"I know, Mama Java, but we're sure it will work," he interjected. I know you're probably looking at the fact that she was once a prostitute . . . and that she has four kids . . . "

"No, I'm not judging her," I continued. "And having kids is not the issue either. What IS the issue, is that every time you guys come around, I get a strong sense that something is not right. Now, don't get me wrong, your girl seems very nice . . . I like her. I can't explain it . . . but I know if you guys got married, your relationship would be very turbulent. There would be fighting . . . and I mean serious, physical violence!"

My friend tried very hard to convince me that I was wrong, but everything **within** me told me that I was right. As much as I cared for him and his lady-friend, I knew in my heart that I could not be a part of "joining" these two together. I knew it would be disastrous. And at the same time, I knew he was determined to go through with it. So right before he left, I made the suggestion that they go to the Justice of Peace. And, that he would give some serious thought to what I felt.

After he left, I sat on the steps pondering, not quite understanding how or why I felt so strongly about their relationship. Nevertheless, I knew the words I spoke would prove to be true; I could *feel* it! But for now, I had a trip to plan.

A New York State of Mind, Buffalo... That Is

Jackie stood behind me in her small bathroom with her hands on her hips and an attitude of frustration drenched in love; demanding me to tell myself that I was beautiful. "Come on now, bitch. Say you are beautiful. We ain't going nowhere until you say it!" Now don't get all hung-up on her calling me, *bitch*. Remember, this way of communicating is Jackie's own unique signature, especially when she's trying to make a point about something serious. And saying that *I was beautiful,* was a serious matter.

Damn, saying those words were harder than I could have ever imagined. Every time I glanced up from the sink, I could only see how the last twelve months had wreaked havoc on my face . . . my spirit . . . at least from my perspective. However, Jackie saw something quite different as she continued her psychological profile.

"Look, damnit, you are one of the most beautiful women I know — inside and out. You need to get a grip and realize that no matter what you have been through, you are a beautiful woman! Now say it. I AM BEAUTIFUL!"

The forced words came slowly as the tears began to stream down my sullen face. "I am . . . I am . . . " I threw my hands up in the air and turned to Jackie. "I just don't feel it". Jackie, standing all of 5'2, reached up to put her arms around me. Her extra-large breasts pressed up against my heaving chest, as I cried profusely. She held me tightly, not saying a word. But after a few seconds of sisterly love, she continued with her demands.

"Look, Nailah. I ain't gonna stand here all night. We got places to go and things to do," she strongly encouraged me as her voice shifted to a lower gear. "Now, look in the mirror and tell yourself that you are beautiful, . . . before I smack the shit out of you."

My red, swollen eyes didn't help, as I managed to take a good, long look at myself. For a moment, I felt silly for being so hard on myself and found a smile surfacing. My lipstick had worn off, while the black mascara made its artistic debut along my nose and cheekbone. I laughed while a surge of love and warmth came over me rather suddenly. I straightened my spine and pulled back my shoulders before the words found their way to my lips.

"Nailah, you are beautiful." The words came softly at first, however, with a little more persuasion from my drill sergeant, I was instructed to say it again . . . louder. "Nailah, YOU ARE BEAUTIFUL!" I screamed. Tears overtaken by laughter, continued to flow as I bribed myself to believe what I was saying. "With everything you have been through, you are still a beautiful woman," I continued, turning to my beautiful Sistah, who was more like a daughter. I hugged her, until she hollered for air.

"Can a Sistah breathe, now? Damn, it's a good thing it didn't take your ass that long to decide to bring your ass up here. Hell, after talking to you, I thought I was gonna have to come to Kentucky and kill a few nigguhs." Jackie then took a few moments to look around to remind me of her situation and to fire up a joint.

"Now look," she continued taking a long hit and passing it. "I told you that a bitch ain't got no furniture yet, so we'll have to sleep in sleeping bags." Smoke filled the empty space as we both coughed. "I called my friend, Jeremy, after finding out you were coming, and he brought over his sleeping bag and some blankets. You'll meet him tomorrow night after we go get our nails and stuff done." Looking up at me and smiling, we hugged again after taking another hit and giving me another look-over. "You do need to do something to that head," she announced. But instead of weeping in anguish, I laughed in agreement.

Jackie's work schedule turned out to be perfect for my last-minute escape from prison. She had the entire weekend off. I stopped to let the warm sun shine on my newly made-up face while I gave thanks for a beautiful day and the joy of being around a true friend. Jackie had been like a daughter; reminding me of the one I lost at the age of two. They were both Cancers and fiery. While I believe my daughter would have been tall and slender, Jackie was stout with thick hips and legs. She was beautiful, and her copper skin glistened in the sun's rays, as she walked out of the house. The weather was colder than Kentucky, but there was no snow; and with the sun shining, the weather was perfect for a February, Friday morning.

"Come on, Mommy," (which she called me at times) "We gotta get some breakfast and then go see about getting our nails done. You look nice; I see you put on some makeup."

"Yeah, I thought I better, since we're going out in public. I didn't wanna embarrass you."

"Look now, we ain't startin' that shit, again."

"I know, just kidding," I admitted. "I can't believe I'm actually in Buffalo, New York and not working my ass off at the restaurant. And girl, I ain't gotta cook either. Thank you, God!"

"You got that shit, right," Jackie agreed. "Thank you, Jesus. Look, fire up this joint while I run back in the house. I forgot my sunglasses."

During breakfast, we laughed until my back hurt. It felt so good to be away from the business and all the bullshit. Being with Jackie was a period of rejuvenation; she was so loving and consoling. Her gift as a "seer" always gave me hope and clarity on any concerns that I may have had during stressful times. As she often reminded me, I was always there for her when she needed someone — having the same gift, however, not as refined. And during her college days of being broke, she could always depend on The Java House to keep her fed and offer a quiet place to study.

"Look, girl. What do you think about getting our hair dyed? I'm ready for a new color," Jackie asked, exuded with excitement.

"Sounds good," I agreed. "What color you thinking about? I need something different — really different."

"I don't know. Maybe a reddish copper . . . something that will look good with a natural hairstyle. I took my braids out, and I don't wanna do a perm." Jackie pondered for a moment before she blurted out what color I should have. "Girl, you should go blonde!"

"Blonde! Are you kidding me? Girl, I haven't gone blonde . . . like, forever. I ain't 30 years old anymore; I'll be 53 in a few months. What the hell would I look like going blonde at 53 years old?"

"Sexy, bitch. Fifty-three and sexy!"

The Mall was crammed with shoppers, even though Christmas had been over for almost two months. I guess many stores were having post-Christmas, New Year's and Black History sales all intertwined together.

After a few temptations to fall into the trap of spending money on something we didn't need, we finally saw a salon that had pictures of "women of color" taped on a large display window, which was a good sign they were capable of dealing with "black" hair. The smell of perm and dyes permeated the air as we were greeted by a cute, blonde stylist.

"What can we do for you ladies today?" Of course, Jackie spoke up before I could respond.

"We both want to get a color. We have some ideas, but not really sure."

"Well, we have a couple of books with color swatches that may help," she explained, eyeing us both and stepping closer to get a better look at our hair. "Are you looking for a permanent color or a rinse?"

"Permanent," we said simultaneously.

The young lady then gave us a couple of books and offered us a seat. "After you find something you like, let me know, and I'll be happy to assist you." She smiled broadly before returning to her client, who was wearing huge rollers, to put her under a dryer. The two other customers who were already under the dryer, both nodded before gazing back into their magazines. Jackie and I were the only ones of *color* as we patiently looked through the swatches to make our determination.

By the time we got ready to leave, three hours had passed, and the other women that were there earlier were at the register being checked out. At first glance in the mirror, my mouth dropped when I saw my reflection. "Oh my God, girl! I am a true blonde. Oh, my God, I'm almost platinum!"

The young stylist looked on — pleased with her work. "You look great, blonde. I hope you like it. I also trimmed your ends and gave you a nice shape in the back. It really does become you." I surely needed a cut, since I had no luck with taking out my microbraid hairstyle. It was so bad that Jenia had to cut them out, losing all my length, which I was so proud of.

"Well, I must admit it's gonna take some getting used to," I acknowledged while fluffing out a couple of curls, trying to get used to my new look, while Jackie raved.

"Girl, I told you it would look good. When you take your ass back home, everybody is gonna love it. It's you. Go on, sexy momma. Now tell me what you think of my color." I had been so preoccupied with my own hair that I hadn't noticed Jackie's before now. It was awesome!

"Jackie, it's gorgeous! Copper with highlights . . . It looks hot. Are you gonna let it stay natural?" I asked, beaming with delight. Jackie ran her fingers through the kinky-curly style, admiring herself in the mirror. "Yeah, I'm gonna leave it this way. She trimmed it a little and took off the split ends. I like it . . . I like it a lot."

Before getting out of our chairs, the two women at the register dittoed our sentiments, while one of them really looked surprised with the outcome. "You look very nice as a blonde; a lot different from when you came in," one of the ladies announced. "You both look very nice. Enjoy your new look, ladies," the other woman said as they were leaving out the door. We thanked them for their compliments as they were leaving and took one last look at our new hair-dos before checking out.

Stepping Out

We looked too hot and sexy to stay cooped up in the apartment, so later that evening, we decided to go to a local bar that Jackie frequented. We both had changed into something more suitable for the nightlife and freshened our makeup. It had been far too long since I felt cute, let alone sexy. But that night I felt sexy and flirtatious.

It was around six o'clock, and the temperature had dropped once the sun went down. We wore just enough to keep us warm without taking away our swagger. Being cute was more important than being warm, and wearing a hat, even though warranted, was not happening.

My ears were freezing . . . but I was cute.

The club sat on a corner street not too far from the apartment. When we walked in, a small bar was situated in the middle of the quaint space about thirty feet from the door. To the right, along the front wall, were two tables with an old model jukebox in the middle. An opening led to another room with a pool table, lit by an overhead, multicolored, oblong fixture. It was quiet, but it was still early. There was only one guy at the bar... he seemed to be engrossed in a... hockey game?

"Hey, beautiful," the bartender beamed as he greeted Jackie. She was definitely someone you didn't easily forget.

"Hi sweetie," Jackie called everybody sweetie, baby, love, mostly because she was terrible at remembering names. But you would never know because she treated you like you were a longtime friend. "Where's everybody? Kinda quiet," she said, while we propped ourselves on padded barstools.

"Hey, it's still early. They'll be coming in soon." His smile was wide and genuine. His chocolate complexion and large eyes pulled you into his space, making you feel comfortable and welcome. "I haven't seen you for a minute, where you been?" He continued. "And who's your friend?" Jackie and I both began taking off our coats while getting situated on the narrow stools.

"This is my real, good friend, sister, mama . . ."

"Nailah," I interrupted and held out my cold hand.

"Yeah, she just drove in from Kentucky for the weekend."

"Clarence . . . pleased to meet you." His handshake was warm and firm as he made sure to make eye contact. "Now I understand, good friend and sister, but mama . . . I don't think so," he questioned, stepping back, giving us both his attention. "What can I get you ladies to drink?"

Jackie ordered a beer. But for me, drinking anything cold was out of the question. "You got fresh coffee?"

"Sure do . . . cream and sugar?"

"How about some Bailey's Irish Cream?"

"You got it."

With the warmth of the coffee and the calming effect of the Bailey's, I finally began to relax as the realization of being in Buffalo sank in more deeply. My tan, silk blouse, (which peeped with cleavage), set off my jeans and boots, giving me a casual but sexy look. Jackie, being well-endowed, wore a white sweater with jeans and platforms, while our new hairstyles glistened with a light coat of coconut oil. We were cute!

It didn't take long before the locals began to make their way in. There wasn't a name that Clarence didn't know; everyone was like an extended family living in the same neighborhood. Most brothers came in as loners, while a couple came in with southern style Sistahs carrying a month of groceries in their trunks (big butts), runway makeup, and big hair wigs.

The pool room was finally coming to life, and there were only a couple more hours for the "happy hour" half-priced drinks. The Brothers and Sistahs were getting their drink on before the clock struck 9 . . . and so were we. Running a tab, we ordered another drink, along with some fish and fries, as we shook our hips to the funky sounds coming from the box. I don't know about Jackie, but I was feeling good... real good.

Flirting

The two of them stood out like a flower in six inches of snow. One was around 5'9, built, pleasingly brown, and easy on the eyes. The other one, a little taller and a little lighter, was boyishly cute with dimples. They looked to be around late thirties or early forties. Whatever age, for me, it was robbing the cradle . . . and I was tempted to do a little stealing.

"What-up, baby-girl? Long time, no see." With a gleam in his eyes, Mr. pleasingly brown leaned down to shower a kiss on Jackie's cheek.

"Hey, baby," Jackie delightfully responded. "Bitch been working like a Hebrew slave. What you been up to... and who's your friend?"

"Oh, this is my man, Les. Man, this is the sister I was telling you I met at the poetry jam a few months ago. This is Jackie."

"Nice to meet you."

"Likewise, yeah, Ron told me about you."

"And this is my friend, Nailah," Jackie continued, letting them know that I was an out-of-towner. "I had to rescue her ass from Kentucky. She came in this morning."

"Hi, the name's Ron." Reaching across Jackie, we shook hands.

"Some handshake. Did she say . . . Nailah?"

"Yes, pleased to meet you."

"Nailah, this is my friend, Les." He repositioned himself to avoid having to reach over Jackie's legs. Holding my hand, his smile was infectious as he repeated my name.

"Nailah . . . that's a beautiful name for a beautiful woman. Very pleased to meet you."

I struggled to keep from blushing. I didn't want the brother to think I wasn't used to compliments (although it had been ages).

"Thanks. It's a pleasure meeting you, too."

"And what's this about having to . . . rescue you?" Les asked, smiling.

Ron and Jackie were in their own world, talking about the poetry slam and her job as a mental health therapist, while leaving us to get better acquainted.

"Well, I'm one of those people who doesn't have sense enough to take a break. I manage a restaurant and culture center." It felt strange looking into the eyes of a man who wasn't a customer. Someone that I wasn't asking if he wanted cheese on his Mr. T.

"A restaurant <u>and</u> a cultural center? Sounds like a 24/7 job," he asked, leaning against the bar and getting close enough to make me feel . . . should I say, like a . . . woman? It felt good, although somewhat awkward.

We both continued some small talk, until he saw that my glass coffee cup was nearing empty. "Can I get you another drink?" he asked, while deep dimples creased his jaw.

"Thanks, but I've had my quota for the night," I graciously declined. After another hour or so, along with a few dance steps to help offset the effects of my buzz, we decided to hang out in a more private setting, which meant us following the young men back to their house.

The ride was only about ten minutes or so before we drove into a long driveway, leading to a shotgun house tucked between two homes in a quaint neighborhood. The porch light was on, dimly lighting the weather-beaten, wooden frame. Upon entering, we were met with the sound of jazz coming from a back room. The small living room was cramped with leather furniture and glass tables. As we meandered through the dimly lit rooms, I found it amazingly clean and orderly for two bachelors.

Soon after sinking onto a back-wall sofa in another room, I got a whiff of a familiar scent. Les called for pizza delivery, while Ron got us some snacks and bottled water. I took a short hit from the supersized joint and leaned back, wondering what else the night would bring. The vegetarian pizza tastefully satisfied my munchies. Everything was easy and spontaneous. I was really enjoying myself. The conversations, the attention, and the fact that I didn't have to get up a few hours later to work, was beyond *icing on the cake*.

Jackie and Ron had gone to another room, leaving Les and me alone. Feeling completely safe and sure of what I was and wasn't gonna do with this delightful, young man, I relaxed even more. That's when I saw that Les was rubbing the back of his neck, which the *healer* in me wanted to come to his aid.

"Neck bothering you?" I asked.

"Yeah, and it's causing my head to hurt as well."

"If you would like, I can probably get rid of it for you." (I always sought permission before "touching" someone — something I learned as a student of Reiki, a "laying on of hands," energy and healing art form.)

"Sure, of course," he stated, looking rather skeptical. "I would appreciate that very much, especially if it works. Go for it. Should I lay down or what?" he inquired.

"Get a towel so you can stretch out on the floor."

I began to rub my hands together as I said a little prayer to myself, calling on my Higher Self to do the actual healing. By the time Les returned with a towel, my hands were hot with tinkling energy flowing from my wrist down through to my fingertips; I was ready, and so was Les.

"First, take off your shirt . . . if that's okay."

"Not a problem," pulling his shirt over his head.

"Now, take a deep breath through your nose and exhale slowly through your mouth," I instructed. "Do that three times . . . and relax your shoulders . . . let it all go."

Les lay there breathing with intent, while his lightly, hairy back rose with each deep inhalation, causing his muscles to expand and retract. As I kneeled by his side, I raised my hands about four inches above his back. I could feel the heat as I moved my hands in circular and up and down motions before I began the massage. He immediately responded with gratitude as I dug deep into each muscle from the base of his spine to the nape of his neck—up through to the crown of his scalp.

I manipulated his tired, tight muscles for about a half-hour before they finally gave release to the tensed muscles in his head.

"Wow! That felt great," he exclaimed with gratitude while he slowly sat up and gently moved his head to both sides. "Hey, my headache's gone; I can't believe it . . . it's really gone." He moved around with a little more vigor this time— assured that it was no illusion. "You are good," he said, with a few more pleasantries before offering to ease my tension.

As Les moved his long hands up and down my back (with my clothes on), I fought to keep my moans and groans under wraps to avoid any possibility of anything suggestive, if you know what I mean. And since Trey and I had been having problems, our sex life had petered out for the past couple of months, and I was feeling a little vulnerable. Les had no idea how his touch was making me feel, and I did all I could to make sure it didn't turn into something more . . . intimate. However, after a few more minutes of being sensuously relaxed, we both drifted into a rather unexpected, titillating situation.

The sun was peeping over the horizon by the time Jackie came into the room to announce that it was time to go. I had blissfully fallen asleep. Les lay quietly beside me, while his breathing became a light snore — I smiled, before gently shaking him.

"Good morning, Les, it's early morning and we are about to leave," directing my words a few inches away, knowing my breath had to be reeking with garlic and onions.

"What time is it?" he whispered, rousing himself to a sitting position.

"Almost 6 o'clock," I whispered back, putting my shoes on and looking around for my coat. "I had a wonderful time. Thank you so much for everything."

"Believe me, the pleasure was all mine," he assured me, scrambling to a standing position to help us with our coats. "Can I make you girls some coffee before you leave?"

"Naw," we both said. "We're straight, but thanks for asking. We'll get some on our way," Jackie sleepily continued. "And please tell Ron I'll holler at him later, and thanks for everything." Les gave us both a hug and a kiss on the jaw as we prepared ourselves to greet Mr. Weather.

There was a thin mist in the air. It was cold and damp as the dew glistened on the sidewalks and roads. We stopped to get coffee about two blocks away from the guy's house. With neither one of us being morning people, the radio was the only thing that broke the sound barrier. Finally, after several sips from the steaming cups of caffeine.

"How was it? Did you have a good time?" Jackie finally asked.

"I had a great time — and before you ask—no, we didn't have sex."

Jackie took her eyes off the road for a second to make sure she was looking at me when she asked . . . "You *do* know it would've been okay if you did?" she said, looking at me with one raised eyebrow. "Well, did you at least kiss?"

"Girl, that Negro could kiss . . . but they weren't the kind of kisses that made me feel like he was trying to *get some* . . . they were sweet and tender," I explained, reminiscing. "You see, I gave him a massage to get rid of his headache . . . and it worked. He was shocked! Then he gave me one. I didn't have a headache, but I sure needed to release. My muscles were tight! Anyway, we ended up kissing, right?"

Jackie slowed down her speed and changed to the right lane as if she really wanted to hear all the details.

"You know how some guys kiss... like really aggressively, with roaming hands all over your body and heavy breathing with hopes of scoring?"

Jackie nodded her head and said, "Um-um, I know what ya mean."

"Well, Les was different," I continued. "His touch, his kiss... was like he was saying . . . 'thank you.' You know what I mean?"

"Yeah, I think so." Jackie kinda whispered as if trying to imagine what that would be like.

"The brother was really cool . . . no pressure at all," I continued.

"Besides, I'm through with babies; it's bad enough dealing with Trey's young ass."

"I hear you. Well, we didn't do anything either, but smoke another jay and talk," Jackie began to explain. "As horny as my ass was, I decided not to pounce on him. But you know, since I've known Ron, he has never approached me like that. You think they might be gay?"

"Naw, just because a brother ain't trying to get in your pants, don't make him gay. But, then again, you never know these days. Uh, I should know!"

Getting the Needle

By the time we got back to the apartment, we were starving. We made some breakfast, talked some more about the night, and then took a nap. We had an agenda for later that day to get our nails done and buy me some new glasses to match my new hair color. Jeremy, Jackie's friend and coworker, was also taking us out that night to a local Reggae club.

The sun sprouted through trees stripped of their green foliage, while patches of brown grass lay matted to the cold earth. It was afternoon before we started on our journey to find the perfect eyewear. Being that it was Saturday, I knew that wherever I found them, it had to be one of those "glasses in an hour" places since I was leaving on Monday morning.

After we finished getting our mani/pedi, we wandered through the Mall looking for a place for my glasses. And as the universe would have it, we didn't have to go far. After my examination, I was guaranteed to have my glasses in about an hour.

It took several pairs of various styles and colors before I found something that Jackie and I both agreed on. Trading in my large, roundish frame to a sleeker and rectangular shape, was not an easy task, and it took a little time for me to get accustomed to the reflection I saw looking back at me. She was definitely not the same person who drove into Buffalo, two days earlier. I strutted out not only with a fresh, new look— but with a new attitude. Yes, I understood my girl, Patty Labelle, when she sang her song: *I Got a New Attitude*. My attitude was so new that I blurted . . .

"Girl, I wanna get a tattoo. I've never had one. Think there's a place here in the Mall?"

"Damn! Are you serious?"

"Yep, I sure am. I've been thinking about getting one for some time . . . but never found the time to look into it."

"What kind? Cause you know once you get one, there ain't no taking that shit off."

"Something Japanese or Chinese that says: I Am. You know, for I Am that I Am."

"Okay, that's cool. There's got to be one around close. Maybe we can ask somebody. All right now, mama, you are really going all out. I ain't mad at ya."

After a couple of inquiries, we were told of one not far from the Mall.

Books and magazines lined a long shelf on the back wall. The eerie sound of vibrating needles filled the air from several stations, which at first was a little frightening. However, no one was moaning and groaning or screaming out in pain, so I decided to move forward. I was about to get my first tattoo. After a polite greeting by a young, blonde female with several tattoos along her bare arms, I explained to her what I was looking for, and she handed me two sheets of Asian symbols.

"Is there a symbol for I Am?" I asked the young artist when she came over to see if I had found anything.

"No, not really; the language is strange. There's no letter or symbol for Am. It's complicated to explain. Will the "I" work by itself for you?"

"Actually, the 'I' by itself is fine. I'll know that it stands for I AM, and that's all that matters."

As I got in the chair, I decided to meditate to take my mind off what was happening. Taking deep breaths slowed my heart rate, and I could feel a sense of calm overcoming my anxiety. "Just where would you like your tattoo?" Her voice was soothing and compassionate as she assured me that she would be gentle and that I would love my tattoo. I placed my hand right above my left breast, next to a tiny mole.

The tiny pricks into my skin were, at first, a little discomforting. But I think it was the grinding sound that was actually more intimidating. I forced a smile and put my hands on my stomach –feeling it as it gently moved up and down. I could feel myself drifting.

"Well, that's it," she announced, handing me a small mirror. "It's gonna be a little red for a while," she explained, wiping off the excess blood. "But it's beautiful. Great choice: I hope you like it."

"I love it!" I exclaimed, admiring the reflection in the mirror. "You were so gentle. I barely felt it. Thank you so much." I called for Jackie to come see my latest whim. She, too, thought it was beautiful and the perfect choice. 俺

After a few recommendations on keeping it clean and safe from germs, I buttoned my blouse and gave her a hug, along with a gracious tip. I was excited! Here I was, blonde—new glasses–and a tattoo. Who would have ever thunk!

A Reggae Good Time

Jeremy came by around 9 o'clock. We had taken a nap after our long day and were well-rested. My new, off-white blouse was a hit with a new pair of jeans and 4-inch heels. For the first time in ages, I truly felt sexy, and my confidence had soared up a notch or two. I even looked and felt better than the night before, and I was ready to par-tay.

Jeremy was tall and slender with medium dark hair and bluish, green eyes. He was very handsome, and dressed in a dark sweater, jeans and boots with a wool scarf hanging loosely around his neck. He and Jackie had been working together for the past few months and really hit it off. He was a cool... "white" Brother.

After introductions and a hefty hug, we all left with great expectations to have a reggae good time.

We could hear the Jamaican rhythms before we got to the door. I was already doing my little reggae moves before we got in the door good. It was packed, and the six-piece, live band was jamming. As we danced our way to the bar at the back of the room, the sounds got more intense. Dreadlocks swung from side to side to the heavy rhythms of guitars and Congas painted in the traditional Jamaican colors of red, yellow, and green. Hot bodies gyrated to the funky groove as the drummer beat out deep, rich tones from his fabric-covered drums. Sweat poured down their dark, glistening faces, landing on opened shirts exposing ripped six packs. What a site! I was enjoying the "eye candy."

I maneuvered through the crowded dance floor, heading to the bar as I checked out the band members. Most of them were young, but the lead singer was from the old school with mixed-gray locks hanging down to his waist. His lips kissed the mic as he spit out lyrics of freedom and culture. I was getting warm as I stopped to groove with a couple for a hot second. They smiled as I took off my coat before landing a seat at the crowded bar. I hadn't noticed that Jeremy and Jackie had found seats on the other side of the room when Jackie came up to me.

"Hey girl, we found a table over in the back, unless you want to stay at the bar." Jackie loudly whispered.

"Cool. Yeah, I'm coming. I hadn't realized that you guys found a seat. The band is hot, and they have some real cutie pies. Does your friend dance?" I asked, ready to get my groove on. Not that I needed a partner, I was known to dance solo on many occasions.

"Yeah, he probably does, but I haven't danced with him before. He looks like he might have a little soul, though. Girl, the band is hot, and did you see grandpops— the older guy? Jeremy said he's been around for a long time. That's why he brought us here; he thought we might really like the group. I've heard about the band, but it's my first time hearing them."

I danced my way over to the other side. Jeremy had found a table up on another level, which looked over the dance floor. I pranced up each step eager to get the night going before I finally sat down.

"Look like you ready to party," he said, smiling. "What you want to drink?" he continued.

I pondered his question for a few moments, trying to think what I could sip on for a little buzz—just to loosen up a little. "I'll have a *Grand Marnier, please* . . . with a water back. Thanks." I knew I had to have the water to ward off any potential headache, which I often ended up with when I indulged in alcohol. It was probably my subconscious way of not overdoing it, since both my parents had established a comfortable, long-lasting relationship with liquid spirits. Jackie ordered a *Red Stripe* (Jamaican Beer) and Jeremy ordered a *Jack and Coke*.

By the time the drinks came, Jeremy and I had the opportunity to know each other a little better. He had been a Social Worker for the past 7 years and had started working at the hospital, where he met Jackie only a few months earlier. He talked about how he felt he *knew* her; that she was easy to be around and great to work with. They often went out to people's homes for evaluations, once they were released from the hospital. Most of their patients were former drug users or suicidal. They worked so well together, that they were often asked if they were married.

It didn't take but a couple of sips before I began to feel the effects of the warm, orange liqueur. Before swallowing, I rolled it around in my mouth with my tongue as it gently burned the back of my throat. It was strong and tantalizing—opening up my sinuses as an extra delight. Back in the day, it was my favorite drink when I had singing gigs. And my customers kept them lined up on my table.

It wasn't long before I strutted out to the dance floor with a young brother who saw me dancing in my seat. By now, the music was sounding *really* good, and my drink was doing what it was supposed to do. I felt light and . . . free. We must have danced through at least three straight songs before the young man said he couldn't go any further.

Jeremy and Jackie had come on the floor by the time my partner pooped out, so I kept it moving with them for a couple more tunes. By the time we left the dance floor, the cutie pies in the band had gotten to know me as one of their biggest fans. I was being my gregarious self—

getting everybody into a "call and response" mood with the band. Pops had even started pointing me out and dedicating songs to me before the night was over. I was having a Reggae good time . . . ball!

A Shocker

It was after 3 o'clock by the time we fell into the doorway. Jeremy expressed how much fun he had and that he was really happy to meet one of Jackie's best friends. We were safely locked in when we heard him pulling away from the driveway. I was so high . . . not on booze, but on the remnants of Jamaican bliss. I hadn't danced that much since the night I met Vic. And even though from time to time we went out for a night of relief— the three of us— yes, Greg as well, it was never the same as that night at the Paradise.

We hadn't taken our coats off before Jackie began talking about the great time we had . . . especially me. "Girl, I haven't seen you have that much fun since I've known you."

"Yeah, girl, I had a ball. And the old man, Pops, I thought he was gonna propose before the night was over. He was all over me."

"Hell, yeah, he was. Can you blame him?"

"What you talking about? I was just having fun."

"Girl, before me and Jeremy came down, he was looking at you dance and talking about what a good time you were having. Then he looked at me and said . . . 'Jackie, she's not wearing a bra! I can see right through her blouse.' "I looked, and sure enough, your ass had no bra on. No wonder Pops was on your ass."

Stunned, I pulled off my coat. My blouse was still damp from sweating. I looked down, and sure enough, my nipples were standing at attention like soldiers. I could barely talk. "Oh, my God! How in the hell did I forget to put on a bra?"

"Bitch, I didn't even notice until Jeremy pointed it out. Couldn't you tell your shit was bouncing up and down? Now there was a time you didn't have any titties, but your ass got some now. I can't believe you couldn't tell; you didn't smoke that much! Girl, Jeremy was in shock, and that's why we came down to dance to make sure he was seeing right."

Now, as you read this, you're probably thinking the same thing. How in the hell did I not know I wasn't wearing a bra? Well, it goes to show you how messed up I was in the head . . . things had been a little weird . . . what can I say?

After a few more laughs from embarrassment, I took one last look at my slightly risqué attire before washing my face. And since I was void of intoxication, I decided to do a little communicating with the ancestors and Spirit Guides before retiring. We both had been so focused on my "finding" myself that I hadn't taken the time to stop and connect, which is something I obviously should have done before I left the apartment.

Jackie was more than willing to join me. She was very much aware of my initiation into the Yoruba Spiritual Principals, as she, too, had connected with a particular Orisha. I was Oshun and she was Jemoya, the Orisha of lakes and seas and the patron of women and of motherhood. She may not have been a mother, biologically, but she was definitely a mother to many children, particularly those in the "system." It was 4 o'clock in the morning before we made our last petition, as sleep finally won out.

A bright sun bled through the drawn curtains as I rolled over to check the time on my phone. It was 1 o'clock. I lay there for a few minutes musing over the fact that I wasn't rushing around buying groceries and cleaning. As I began my cat stretches, I couldn't help but notice that my body didn't feel like I had been beaten with a broomstick, even though my makeshift bed was no different than the last two nights. Maybe it was because I danced as if my life depended on it, or because the alcohol numbed any feelings of pain and distress. Whatever the case, I was happy to be alive and actually feeling good – for a change.

Three days had come and gone much quicker than I would have liked. I was having such a great time, so much freedom and relaxation.

However, it would all come to an abrupt end in less than twenty-four hours when I headed back home. But for now, I was determined to keep my joy and enthusiasm before returning to my dreaded and confused life.

Jackie and I decided to stay in the rest of the day to rehash some earlier conversations about our lives over the past couple of years. We both had gone through some major transitions —some good, and some that made us wonder what the hell life was all about. During our sacred time of bitching, we managed to giggle between tears over our stupidity and choices before bursting into fanatical laughter after a few hits from our morning ritual. No matter how much suffering and anguish we had put ourselves through, with a little help from Mother Nature, we could laugh while vowing never to fall in love again.

FIFTY-FIVE

Back on the Plantation

I had left the blissful habitat of serenity and freedom in the wee morning hour at around 4 A.M. on Monday morning. I still wonder what the ride to Buffalo was like — truth is — I don't remember. Strangely enough, it was during a telephone conversation with Jackie, during the writing of this book, when I realized that I had absolutely no recollection of driving to OR from New York. I must have really been in a major funk. How can you forget that you drove nearly eleven hours, each way? Well, to this day, I don't remember!

What I do remember, is my beautiful grandchildren meeting me at the door, screaming, "Grandma, you back. Grandma, yo hair look pretty, its yellow!" They made it all worth coming back, and although it was hard trying to homeschool along with everything else, they gave me joy and made me laugh when I wanted to cry. It was great to see their smiling faces as they peered around, looking for a bag of surprises. I had gotten them all a small, inexpensive gift, which you would have thought cost hundreds of dollars. Children really teach you how to appreciate the little things in life.

Trey and Jenia really liked my new look. I knew that if my daughter said it looked good, I could rely on it being true. Jenia would always tell me what was "really" on her mind, and believe me, if it didn't look nice, she would have been the first to tell me, in no uncertain terms.

It didn't take long to fall back into the routine of being a cook, waitress, shopper . . . back to the old self of all work and no play. The sense of loneliness began to slip back into its groove after a few days, as well. Things hadn't changed between me and Trey; I was still frustrated with our relationship.

My sexiness slowly began a metamorphosis back to a life as Cinderella, with my glass slipper lost somewhere between Buffalo and home. And my tattoo, that no one else saw besides Trey and Jenia, was now for my eyes only. No more see-through or low-cut blouses and four-inch heels. I was back to T-shirts, jeans and tennis shoes. And after two more weeks of arguing and complaining, I was man less as well. Trey finally got tired of my finding fault with everything he "didn't" do. He left in a huff back to Chicago. But, then again, what did I expect? The Java House wasn't his dream.

Hating to say, I Told You So

Trey left a few nights before Spoken Word, but with a little help from my family, I was able to get through it without feeling overwhelmed. Although our numbers had fallen considerably, that night, it was a nice crowd, and I was very grateful, especially since it created a little revenue.

Before the night was over, I noticed that one of my female customers was wearing a cast on her arm. I hadn't noticed her earlier, probably because I was busy running back and forth to the kitchen, since I was cooking. However, once I had time to slow down a little, I realized that the woman was the girlfriend of my poet friend, the one who asked me if I would officiate their marriage before I took off to New York, the one I turned down. So quite naturally, I went over to speak and to find out what had happened.

"Hey sweetie, how's it going?" I asked, sitting down next to her.

"Hi Miss Nailah, not too good," raising her casted arm slightly upward.

"Do you mind if I ask what happened?" I hesitantly inquired, nodding at her arm.

Just before she started to explain, she gazed up at me with tears in her eyes; that's when I noticed that makeup was camouflaging a black eye. I sat back and took a deep sigh, knowing what had happened.

"I started it, Miss Nailah . . . I hit him first. It was a couple of days after we got married . . ."

"Wait a minute," I interrupted. "You did get married?"

"We went to the courthouse almost two weeks ago."

"I haven't seen him since I got back," I stated. "I've been out of town. Are you guys still together?" I asked curiously.

"We decided to get an annulment, but he's here tonight in the other room. We're both sorry to disappoint you. He told me what you said."

Fortunately, my daughter had an order for me, and I had to get back to work, which left me no time to continue our conversation. I was too angry to really get into details, anyway. So, I just took another deep sigh, gave her a hug and encouraged her to stay positive and to take care of herself and her children.

By the end of the evening, just as I was heading upstairs, I heard my name being called. It was him.

"Mama Java . . ."

I turned and looked at him with obvious disappointment.

"I don't know how you knew, but you were right . . . But Mama Java, I didn't start it . . ."

"I don't care who started it," I quickly interjected. "You are a man and could have walked away. I told you what was going to happen, but you wouldn't listen."

"I know, and I hope you will forgive me. Can I still come to The Java House?"

"Look, I still love you, and you are always welcomed at The Java House. However, I am extremely disappointed, and I have lost respect for you."

After dropping his head for a brief moment, he then looked up at me with obvious shame and asked again if I would forgive him. I assured him that I was not the one he needed to be asking forgiveness from. I then turned away and headed upstairs. I had my own guilt to deal with.

A Little Reprieve From Guilt

Thank God for friends and credit cards. Jackie had gifted me with my new hairdo and my mani-pedi, as well as helping with gas; the rest was put on my credit card. I was pretty good about not using my credit card unless it was absolutely necessary, and getting new glasses and a tattoo, was necessary . . . at least for my morale and self-esteem. However, now that I was back on the plantation, guilt flourished in wiping out my rationale to sustain my sanity and self-esteem. The reality was, I couldn't afford the trip without suffering the consequences. However, as the Universe would have it…

The phone rang right in the middle of lunch. I scurried around a few minutes serving a couple of lunches before answering. "Good afternoon, The Java House Café, how may I help you?" It was a woman's voice on the other end. She introduced herself as Trina and began to explain that she had heard about us through a friend that attends our Spoken Word.

"Yes, well how can I help you?" I asked, needing to get back to my few customers.

"I am looking for a place to rent to host an event for the company I work for." She explained. "I was told about your café, so I thought I would give you a call to see if you might be interested."

I kindly rushed her into making an appointment to come and talk with me in detail about the event. However, before we ended our conversation, she assured me there was a nice sizable budget to work with. We scheduled an appointment for that weekend. Meanwhile, she offered to mail me some literature about the product and some information about the proposed event. I thanked her for her interest in The Java House and assured her I was looking forward to meeting and talking with her.

I damn near skipped back to the dining room, wearing a huge smile and a gleam of hope. I had no idea what kind of money she was talking about, but I knew that whatever amount, it was more than we had. As I stood in the doorway of the dining room, I heard my two younger grandbabies in the Vault playing as if they hadn't a care in the world.

Their giggles were contagious as I peeped in. They were skimming through the worn pages of children's books; amazed at the images that resembled themselves. They ran over to me to share the bright colored images.

"Look grandma, the little girl has a dog like Kenya," Kamonnie excitingly shared, half smiling, and Siarra in agreement. A big red dog was licking the little girl in the face as she attempted to push the dog aside.

"Can you read what it says, Kamonnie?" Of course, I had to test my homeschooling skills. Not to my surprise, at five years old, she was able to read most of the words, one at a time while Siarra looked on trying to echo her sister. They had no problem entertaining themselves, and they had plenty of books, games and homework to keep them busy.

The older two were busy bussing tables when I went back into the dining room and heard a familiar voice.

"Hey Nailah, looks like you have some new employees, and they're doing a great job." The voice was that of a dear friend who had loaned me his shoulder to cry on, on a couple of occasions. After my friend handed them both a crisp, dollar bill, I thought I was going to have to peel the grin off their little faces. The fact that I was under tremendous pressure, gave way to the happiness and joy of that moment, and the fact that we could be making a little cash in the very near future.

The Meeting

Trina called that Sunday to let me know she was running behind schedule and would be about an hour late. I appreciated her call and informed her it would be fine. I hadn't said anything to the cook or Jenia, yet. I wanted to be really clear on what the proposal was, first.

She was stunningly attractive with long hair; coffee with cream complexion, slender, tall and nicely built . . . and professional. After our formal introduction, we sat in the library to talk about her plans. She worked for a name-brand liquor distributor, and they were promoting their latest "mix." They would offer giveaways of various prizes, including a case of the "latest thrill." They were to provide virtually everything: DJ, appetizers, greeter staff, clean-up crew, and security. Plus, there were going to be vendors as well. One of them was a customer of mine (a jeweler) who suggested the referral. So far, Trina's proposal was sounding great.

"Why don't I show you around so that you can get a feel for the space and see if it works for you?" I suggested.

"Sounds great. This is a very beautiful room," she said, looking around admiringly.

"Thank you. This is the Fredrick Douglas Library," I stated, thus beginning the tour.

We walked and talked for forty-five minutes to an hour, and by the end we were completely relaxed with each other, however, still handling business. Trina appeared to be enthralled with the place and thought it was perfect for her event. It had the right ambience, plenty of space, rich in history and the right price. After she heard our rules and regulations, such as No Smoking or Drugs of any kind—No

Vulgar Language— No Inappropriate Conduct—No Fighting, plus a few other No's, we then agreed to the amount of $4,000.00. And all I had to do was keep my eyes on things.

Two weeks later, I received the 50% deposit to move forward. Talk about right on time! I was able to pay the overdue utility bill and my sales taxes, which was a small amount. Nevertheless, it was a blessing to have *some* sales, period. We had agreed that the balance would be invoiced to be paid in full, 10 days after the event.

After getting the deposit check, realizing Trina was serious about leasing our space, I told Jenia and the cook about the upcoming event in the middle of March. I assured Jenia they would not be in our living space, and it wasn't necessary to take the kids somewhere else. I asked my cook to come and hang out with us just to make sure there wasn't any shit popping off that we two women couldn't handle. Our own personal security, if you will. He agreed and said he would ask his brother-in-law to come as well.

Meanwhile, my stress levels were a little lower; however, still stressed. I had gotten a couple of letters from the bank threatening the worst— foreclosure. While the bank had been understanding and trying to work with me, I finally resigned to signing papers that would allow the bank to take back the deed in lieu of foreclosure. Although at the time I really didn't know what that meant, I was so distraught and confused that any chance to keep a roof over our heads and the business going a little longer gave me hope.

As busy as I was, getting ready for the event, I still took the time to honor my ancestors, and listen to Agape and meditate when I could. It was a means to keep my sanity. After listening to Agape, if only for a few days, I felt uplifted and energized to keep going. But, as life continued its ebb and flow, it was guaranteed that something would happen to drain all my energy.

The Event

It was unseasonably warm that second Saturday in March. Trina's crew started arriving around six o'clock to set up. I showed the four of them around as they raved about the building, talking among themselves about how great things were going to be. They had a small truck loaded with a portable bar, bean bags, candles, tablecloths, and

DJ equipment, along with several boxes of "product." I left them to their work and told them I'd be upstairs if they needed anything.

Meanwhile, I was upstairs fixing the kids dinner. Jenia and Jerry were out and promised to be back by eight o'clock. The festivities were to start at 9 till 2 a.m. When Jenia returned, I had the kids ready for bed, but they were too excited to sleep, so I allowed them to watch TV until the Sandman took over.

By the time I dressed, it was a little after 9. I looked out the window to check the parking lot and noticed there were not many cars. My stomach fluttered just a little; fearful that it wouldn't be a good turnout. I wanted it to be a great night for everyone. I said a quick prayer for a successful night and went back to finish getting ready.

After putting on my makeup and fingering through my new haircut, which was much shorter, I took a long look in the mirror and recalled my time with Jackie. "You're beautiful, Nailah," I said out loud. "You are a beautiful woman, and don't ever forget it."

Before I went back downstairs, I called Jacque to see if he wouldn't mind coming by. Although Bobby, the cook, was sticking around for extra safety, I thought another male and familiar face would make me feel more at ease. There was Bobby, his brother-in-law, who promised to come later, Jerry and now Jacque. I was covered, just in case.

By ten o'clock, Jacque was calling my name from the top of the stairs. I met him in the hallway going towards the theatre. "Damn, Mamma Java, you look good!"

Smiling, I did a quick sashay and gave him a hug. "Thanks, Jacque. It feels good to get cute for a change." From the top of the stairs, I could see that as usual, we black folks never like to be the first ones to show up at a party. We have to make an entrance, and it appeared that every guest had that idea.

Before long, my quick prayer was being realized. It had gotten pretty crowded, and the music was jumping. I felt a sense of freedom and excitement . . . and cute! Every room, with the exception of our living space and the room where the vendors were, was dimly lit with red light bulbs, which was their color scheme. The DJ was set up in the theatre with a cabaret theme, with tables draped in red tablecloths and glass candles. The music was a mix of Techno and Urban... definitely for a younger set.

By eleven o'clock, there were well over a hundred people, and the average age was probably between 25 and 35. Jacque, being the average age, took off to scope things out and to keep his eye on things. Being that Trina had her own fan base, none of the guests were Java House people. They mostly came from nearby suburbs around the Cincinnati area. My jewelry friend, who referred us, introduced me to a fellow jewelry designer who had a booth in the vendor section. He was from Chicago and a Hebrew Israelite, which I had never heard of. I must say, he was a different kind of man, looking like he just stepped off the pages of the "Old Testament."

Before I had a chance to get into a conversation with him, and as I was admiring his exquisite jewelry, he immediately... with a softness, began reprimanding me for wearing a mini dress. He said I was showing too much skin and that I needed to change clothes. Of course, I thought my shit looked good and wondered who in the hell did he think he was to tell me how to dress. But of course, I didn't express that.

For some strange reason, after listening to him speak more about what it was like being a Hebrew Israelite, and how the women were considered Queens, I found myself surprisingly intrigued, but not quite sure . . . why. Of course, being acknowledged as a Queen wasn't anything new, particularly in the African culture. But for whatever reason, the next thing I knew, I was going upstairs, rummaging through my closet until I found a "long" off-white dress. I didn't know it at the time, but that was my introduction to an entirely new community. One in which I would find myself in the midst of, and all its "Old Testament" ways of life.

After Jenia got the kids to sleep, she and Jerry joined the festivities. Bobby was having a ball, trying out the new craze and checking out all the honeys. Everything was straight and going quite well. The only incident that I knew of, was when Bobby found a dude trying to "fire one up" in the men's room. He politely led him outside with no problem and then asked one of the Security guys to have the DJ make an announcement to reiterate the rules, making sure it didn't happen again. Other than that, everyone was nice, respectful, and having an awesome time. And so was I . . . long dress and all.

The couple of times I saw Trina, she was doing her thing, making sure the promo videos were constantly playing, and surveys were filled out to see what the word was on her new product. It was good, and it only took a few sips for me to feel the effects. I had danced, met new friends, and passed out flyers about our Spoken Word, and by the time two o'clock chimed in, I was feeling really good. However, my professional persona was never compromised. I gave Trina the final invoice and thanked her for the business.

The next morning, I noticed that Bobby had taken about four/five bottles of the product that Trina left me. I called him on it when he came to work on Tuesday, and he said he thought I wouldn't mind. Like I told him, he was probably right; however, *asking* would have left no doubt. I later found out that there were a few other things he took without asking, like food. Well, needless to say, his stay was cut short.

FIFTY-SIX

Terrorized

I'm not sure how long it was after the event that I had the dream, but I remember waking up crying and shaking. Prophetic dreams were common for me, and usually gave me a heads-up on upcoming events, which allowed me to be prepared for any sudden changes. However, this particular dream was quite disturbing, and NOTHING could have prepared me for what was to come.

It was our wedding day, and Vic and I were kneeling down before the minister. His brother was standing on the other side of him. As the observer, I was watching the two of us saying our vows, when suddenly I noticed that Vic was disappearing right before my eyes. Too shocked to say anything, I watched in horror as his entire body faded away before me.

I jumped straight up! I was sweating, sobbing, and terrified! It immediately came to me what it meant when a person "fades away" in my dreams. I shuddered with fear and anxiety, shaking my head. "No! No! It can't be," I cried out loud. "Oh my God! Vic is going to die!"

I cried until my head hurt, and I felt paralyzed; unable to speak or move. Since I was at the very back of the house, no one could hear my outpour of tears. My stomach knotted. My throat tightened. I felt my eyes swelling shut. I was sick!

Only God knows how long I cried before I finally began to talk to myself. Told myself I was tripping; that I was wrong, and just because I'd seen people fade in the past before their death, didn't mean that it was happening this time. There was a chance I was wrong . . . right?

I eventually made it to the bathroom to put some cold water on my face. I looked in the mirror. Damn, I looked terrible! I staggered over to the commode and relieved myself, and once again, I started crying and shaking all over again. By the time I got back to the bedroom, I had convinced myself that I was wrong. That there was no way Vic was about to die. Hell, he had never been sick a day in his life. The dream must have meant something else. Maybe a warning of some type. Maybe he was leaving town, going someplace else to make a new start. I decided to call Jackie.

"Hey Mommy, what's wrong? And don't try and tell me ain't shit wrong, I can hear it in your voice."

"You're right. I had a dream about Vic," I continued, telling her of my nightmare. After telling her the dream, I told her about people fading in my dreams as an indication that they were about to make their transition. "Jackie, is Vic getting ready to die soon?" I solemnly asked, holding my breath while listening to the silence, before she sighed and took a deep breath.

"I get a yes. But it could be that I'm picking up your energy."

Again, there was silence. Finally, after clearing my throat, I made the statement that I believed it meant something else. That sometimes dying meant a new beginning. That maybe it meant he was leaving town. She agreed that it could have meant any or all of what I had just said. Or, she said, "It could be that Vic is about to make his transition. You know, he hadn't been happy since he left. He hasn't gotten over you and being at the café ."

As much as I trusted my goddaughter's gift, I refused to accept what she was saying. At that point, I decided that my dream meant something else entirely and that we were mistaken. I don't know what came over me, but before I hung up with her, I was determined that everything was fine and that it had simply been a nightmare. Of course, Jackie thought I was in denial, and to prepare myself anyway. I shunned her off and told her I would be fine. She assured me that everything was gonna be okay, that she was there for me if I needed to talk.

"*Okay, Nailah, get it together*," I began to talk to myself; trying to assure myself that all was well and to keep praying, knowing that everything would be all right. So, I took a shower, put on some makeup and got dressed. There were things to do, and since I no longer had a cook, I had to take on that responsibility as well. Believe me, I had enough problems during my *awakened* state that had me scared and worried. So d*reaming* that Vic was dying, had to be just that . . . a dream.

I forced myself to think about more positive things, such as, it was the end of March, and I could expect to get the $2000.00 balance from Trina any day. However, it was already spent, and things had gotten worse if that was possible. There were fewer and fewer customers, and I was becoming terrified of the inevitable.

"Hi Trina, how are things going. Yes, I'm happy to hear that everyone enjoyed themselves. Yes, I had a very nice time." I hadn't anticipated Trina's phone call, let alone anticipated that she would call to say that my payment was delayed and that it would take two more weeks. But that's exactly what happened. She apologized profusely and assured me that I would get it. What could I say? There was no point in telling her how badly I needed the money; that I was facing foreclosure; that I had bills to pay, and that I felt like I was losing my mind.

Getting a Break

Spring Break, what a relief. It was so good to have Jenia home to help out. She needed the break and so did I. Getting rid of Bobby didn't help my situation, so I called him and told him that I could use his help. He promised to keep his sticky fingers to himself and that I could depend on him to be honest. He thanked me for giving him another chance. What he didn't know, was that I did it for my sanity. And at that point, there wasn't a lot of food to steal, anyway.

Strangely, there hadn't been much paranormal activity as of late. I suppose the Spirits thought I had enough going on without adding to the drama. Actually, I missed seeing them or hearing from them through visions or during my meditations, which, by the way, were waning. I kept my altar going, and I listened to Agape almost every day. But sitting down to still my mind was becoming more of a problem than not. It became a time when I really gave attention to all my problems, whether I wanted to or not. The thoughts of losing my business, Vic's threats, and juggling all that I had to do ran rampant.

April Fool's Day came and went. Fortunately, I was bypassed from getting fooled. I did call my mom and stepdad to wish them a happy anniversary, which had become a joke for them. Mom used to say that getting married on April Fool's Day made them the biggest fools of all. At least it was easy for me to remember. Speaking of my mom, she and my Aunt Lillian were becoming quite concerned about me and all that was happening. They knew times were hard, and there was nothing they could do to help.

Mom told me one day that she wished I had stayed with Vic; that he was a good person and a hard worker. Yes, she was correct. Vic was a good person and a hard worker; however, he "could not" love me as a wife, had issues with drugs, and was doing "Black Magic" to ruin me. And let's not forget the baby. Now, what part of that my mom didn't understand threw me for a loop.

Even with all of that, there was a time I thought about the possibility that my husband and I could still be partners . . . not married, but able to run the business together. I was willing to help with the baby, overlook the fact that he loved another man, and hoped that if we worked together, the evil intent would cease. However, the drug use was an entirely different story and a guarantee for a Not-so-happy ending. That thought lasted all of 30 seconds!

FIFTY-SEVEN

OMG, Not Again

It was April 7, 2002. I believe it was a Sunday morning because I was still in bed, when I heard a knock at the back door. As I looked over at the clock, it was a little after 9:00 a.m. I thought to myself, *"Who could it be this early in the morning?"* I got up and put on my robe as I moved towards the back porch. "Who is it?"

"It's Candy," she almost whispered. Now I was really wondering what was going on. Why on earth would Vic's sister be coming to see me at 9 o'clock on a Sunday morning? I opened the door and invited her in. Standing at the foot of my bed, I asked how she was doing, and without answering me, she looked at me rather solemnly.

"Vic is dead," she calmly said with hardly any emotion.

My legs immediately gave out from under me. She grabbed me to keep me from falling, and I began to tremble all over. It felt like someone had kicked me in my stomach, and all the breath escaped from my mouth, leaving me unable to breathe. Candy helped me to my bed and grabbed a glass of water that was on my bedside table. I could not even take a sip. "Is there anyone here with you?"

"Yes, my daughter is upfront," I barely managed to say, trying to breathe with some steadiness. Then, after a brief silence, I looked at my sister-in-law as she affectionately held my hand. "What happened? How did he die?"

"He had a massive heart attack. He was with some white girl. It happened around 2 o'clock this morning. That's all we know for now."

Strangely enough, Candy was pretty calm. I suppose from the time they got the call until the time she came to me, she had cried most of her tears already. And, oddly enough, she gave me a warm and comforting hug before getting up from the bed. We had practically been enemies, especially since I felt that she was the one who coerced Vic to do Black Magic, to try and ruin me, so that she and my husband could take over the business.

"Thanks for coming over, Candy. I sincerely appreciate you taking the time to come and tell me."

"Well, mom told me to come over. You may want to get your daughter so that you won't be alone," she continued. "I'm sure someone will be getting in touch with you".

After she left, I sat on the bed comatose for no telling how long. And as I sat there, it came back to my remembrance—that just a couple days earlier, I found a bookmark in my mailbox. On the bookmark was scribed some sort of eulogy. It was written like a poem, asking the reader *not to mourn their loss; to stay strong and to remember the good times.* When I saw it, I intuitively knew who it was from, maybe because of my dream, which I refused to believe. But somehow, I knew my husband was saying goodbye. And, like my dream, I wouldn't allow myself to believe what was happening.

With all the pre-warning signs, I still couldn't allow myself to accept the truth. And as I sat there, reliving every emotion I felt from the dream, I didn't think I could make it. I immediately felt responsible; somehow, his death was my fault. *"Oh my God, what about his sons*? I thought. I knew they had to be completely devastated. My mind began to race with thoughts, thinking that they might somehow blame me. *"Would their father be dead, if I hadn't put him out?"*

The next few days were hazy and disconnected. I was so grateful that my daughter was with me; I'm not sure if I would have made it without her support. There were outbursts of crying spells, without any forewarning. The pain I felt was so deep that it was difficult to believe we had been separated for over a year. Mysteriously, it was as if we were never estranged and that I had lost my best friend and the love of my life. What was wrong with me? After all the hell he had put me through . . . I couldn't understand my grief. Yet I was totally devastated.

I remember times when Vic and I would have discussions about his dying. "Look, don't be cryin' for me," he would say. "I want you to have a big party and celebrate my life." He would talk as if we were discussing what we were having for the lunch special. "And I'm goin' out this world, just like I came into it . . . naked," he assured me.

Of course, it was never a subject I wanted to talk about. We were both still very young (especially him, being I was nine years older), with a long life ahead of us. When we would argue about him being unfaithful, and I would threaten divorce, he had that same type of attitude. "I will never divorce you," he would proclaim. "You might divorce me, but I'll never divorce you. I'm in this until I die." And since we were still married, for once, he actually told the truth.

Being legally married, Mother Yarbrough made it a point to make sure I was a part of the funeral arrangements, albeit to the disdain of her children and his former wife. To say that it was strange and awkward to be with my estranged in-laws and family is an understatement. They never missed an opportunity to show me how they felt about me; how much they blamed me for Vic's unhappiness. But what hurt the most was how my stepsons treated me, as if I were poison. That was almost as painful as Vic's death.

Up until the "Wake," I was pretty much in a daze. And before I knew it, I was at the funeral home viewing my husband's body. He had shaved his head, which is something he would do when there was going to be a major change in his life, like when we got married. I stood there looking at the grayish tone of his skin, still unable to accept that he was gone. His brother must have picked out his dark suit, for if it were up to Vic, he would have been laid out in a bright colored jacket with a matching tie. I placed my warm hand on top of his, kissed him on his forehead, and said goodbye. I had cried so much that at that point, there were no more tears.

After I said my goodbyes to my husband, I turned to look at Greg, who was sitting with his lady friend... the same one he knocked around. I walked over to him and looked him straight in his eyes and said, "I'm really sorry for 'our' loss; I know you loved him, too." He glanced at me before saying, "Yeah, he was my best friend," then dropping his head, which was my signal to leave. I acknowledged his friend and moved on.

While moving around and speaking to people, I was approached by several of our customers offering their condolences; some of whom were true friends, while others pretended to care and couldn't wait to talk about me once I turned my back. Believe me, their energy was so obvious, I just wanted to say, *"Cut the crap, you don't give a damn about me or Vic."* But of course, I never voiced my feelings. It truly wasn't worth my time.

Vic's Final Hours

By the time I got to the door, I noticed a young white woman standing around some people. I didn't recognize her as one of our customers, but she was staring at me as if she recognized me. That's when she grabbed my arm. "Aren't you Vic's wife?" she asked with some trepidation.

"Yes, I am." Her hand was slightly shaking as she shook mine and began to explain to me who she was as we started moving away from the small group of people she was standing with. Not knowing why or what she wanted to talk with me about, I barely paid any attention until she said...

"I tried to save him . . . I really did," she whispered. And of course, she had my full attention. "You see, we were doing some blow... coke, and uh... I don't know what came over him, but he started stripping off all his clothes," she stuttered.

I stood there numbed as I listened to the last minutes of Vic's life.

"He really did love you, you know. He talked about you all the time, you know . . . how you gave him reason to live and stuff like that," she went on to explain. Her speech was rapid, and her eyes widened as she relived that night. "He jumped up on the table and started talking out of his head . . . hell, I was fucked . . . sorry, messed up myself. I had never seen him like that before. Then, all of a sudden, he fell out on the table. I called his name, but he never answered."

I stood there, still shocked at what I was hearing, and yet wondering why my husband was with this stringy-haired, white girl. He didn't even "like" white women.

I wondered why I had such a negative thought about the woman being "white." Would it have been better if it were a Sistah? Did it really matter? Here, Vic was dead, and I was angry because he was with a white woman. Was I being "prejudice"?

Still rambling, she continued her story. "Well, that just fucked... sorry . . . blew my high! I listened for a heartbeat, and I didn't hear anything . . . then I started doing CPR, and nothing happened. I called 911 and told them that I thought my friend had a heart attack."

I could see how terrified she was, so I reached out and gave her a hug. I held her trembling body close to mine; letting her know that it was okay. I thanked her for sharing with me and trying to save Vic's life and expressed my sincere apologies for the fact that she had to be a witness to such a horrible tragedy. We made our final eye contact, before I turned to leave.

Just about everyone had left during our conversation. Just a few of my in-laws and my stepsons were still there. I turned to say goodbye and got a "cool" response, except for Mother Yarbrough. She walked over and gave me a hug and told me to hang in there. She reminded me of the order of things for the next day; that I was to meet at her house to be picked up in the family car for the funeral. I loved Mother Yarbrough; we hit it off the first time we met, and she knew her son better than anyone. She told me, regardless of what had happened between me and her son, she loved me and that she knew I loved Vic, and to stay strong. Just those few words meant the world to me.

The sun had fought its way through an overcast day as I walked to my car. Still pondering the conversation, I tried to visualize that last night of Vic's life while asking my inquiring mind . . . *Did he plan all of this?* After all, he had shaved his head; he stripped naked, and his last words were about me. Besides, he had told me on a few occasions, during some of our emotional conversations, that he would rather die than to give me up and The Java House. I thought again about the bookmark and what it said. Suddenly, all the racing thoughts made me feel even more guilty. Or maybe this was Vic's way of "sticking it to me" as one last hooray? The thought was unbearable.

The Funeral

The next morning, I made it a point to dress in bright colors, Vic would have wanted that. I didn't have to wear black for anyone to see that I was in mourning. The hollowness in my eyes showed it; my unsteady walk showed it. And although it wasn't visible, my heart screamed it loud and clear that I was in deep, deep pain for a man I didn't know whether to love or hate.

My immediate family met at Mother Yarbrough's to follow the family car. Mom had picked me up so I wouldn't have to drive. I sat quietly in the front room waiting for the family car. Vic's ex was there and wanted to ride in the same car with me and his sons. Mother Yarbrough explained to her that she couldn't; that she was no longer Vic's immediate family. To say she was pissed, is an understatement.

The church was packed. Vic was well known, if not necessarily loved by many people. His former employer and those he worked with were there and offered their condolences. My father-in-law and his wife had flown in the night before. I could tell that their love and concern for me was genuine. I was happy to see them and thanked them for coming. My daughter decided to stay home with the kids, although she wanted to support me. I assured her, I would be fine. My mom, stepdad, aunt Lillian and my sister and brother were there to help hold me up . . . in more ways than one.

The minister made no attempt to paint Victor Yarbrough as a fine, upstanding citizen. No, he spoke on Vic's weaknesses, i.e., his jail time, his drug dealing, his infidelity, and a few others. However, he also spoke of his generosity; that big warm smile that touched everyone. He spoke about his hard work ethics and how much he loved being a part of The Java House. He spoke of his love for his sons and how he worked hard to be a good father. Of course, there were bouts of laughter and a few Amens. In spite of Vic's imperfections, he was a good man.

All was going quite well, considering. But then Vic's oldest son got up to say a few words. For the most part, he was talking about his dad's good qualities, his love for The Java House, etc. And then, he had the audacity to say, "And my dad told me. . ." clearing his throat, "that he loved my mother and that he always had . . ."

You could hear a pin drop. Just about everyone in that church knew how much Vic detested his Ex! My mouth dropped. My bewildered heart sank into the pit of my stomach, and the tears ran down my face, uncontrollably. My mother, who was sitting behind me, put her hand on my shoulder and whispered, "Everyone in here knows that's a lie, baby. That child's mother put him up to that. You hold your head up . . . you hear me? Don't buy into that." I straightened my slumped posture and wiped my eyes with a tissue. And to think, that was not all I could expect from the Ex.

As we were leaving the church, there were many that came to me to offer support; letting me know that if I needed anything, to call. Although Vic and I had been separated, the last five years were evident to just about everyone who knew us . . . knew how much I loved him. We worked extremely well together, as it was often mentioned; and in spite of our problems, we kept things pretty amicable. There were never any public outbursts or blatant disrespect in front of others. And there were only a couple of people that I told about Vic's relationship with Greg, and that was mainly for support in keeping my sanity.

Just as we were getting into the family funeral car, Vic's Ex, rudely tried to get in. Vic's mom saw the situation and stopped her.

"You can't ride with them, Lisa. I told you this car is for Vic's wife and his sons." She then directed her to a car that was more appropriate. As Mother Yarbrough left to get in the car behind me, Lisa ran and jumped into the front seat with the driver. I couldn't believe it! The driver tried to tell her she couldn't be up front, but she refused to leave. All four of Vic's sons looked and didn't say a word. Of course, I just sat there shaking my head. It was really sad. She was determined that she was going to be the "important" one in this bizarre situation. Granted, I gave her credit for being the boys' mother, but bottom line, I was STILL Vic's wife. And it obviously made her quite sick.

It was silent pretty much the whole time as we drove to the gravesite. Vic's oldest son, the one he had as a teenager, made it a point to sit next to me. We talked a little . . . nothing serious, just casual conversation. I was pleased that he befriended me during this complex time. But, then again, he had always been on my side, begrudging some of the poor decisions his dad had made. Especially, having another baby . . . that really pissed him off.

As I got out the car, I noticed the procession looked to be at least a mile long. Lisa had jumped out and grabbed a seat in front near the coffin. I just smiled inwardly and sat across on the opposite side, where I was directed. She looked pitiful, and I actually began to feel sorry for her. She always resented me and the fact that Vic and I had accomplished so much together; that I had a good relationship with her sons, even though now, she had obviously given them instructions to "tune me out." Hell, I understood their dilemma, she was their mother, after all. Nonetheless, it still hurt, painfully.

I was so grateful that funeral homes had stopped lowering the coffin in the ground while people were still there. I think I would have fainted if I had to look at the finality of that process. It was already bad enough. I felt so alone and ostracized. I tried to fight back the tears, but they flooded as if the protective dam that I thought I had in place, had broken. And, to make it worse, my so-called friend, Martha, the one who liked me until I had the "audacity" to run for Governor, and the one who offered me $25,000 to help start my business, walked up to me and said, "How could you? Vic was a good man, and you destroyed him."

"Was she crazy?" I thought to myself. Nevertheless, I stood there to hear her out.

"Vic told me all about how you kicked him out and had a Judge to keep him away from The Java House."

I couldn't believe this woman. I wanted so badly to scream out– DID HE TELL YOU THAT HE THREATENED TO KILL ME OR THAT HE WAS FUCKING ANOTHER MAN? DID HE TELL YOU THAT? DID HE TELL YOU HOW HE AND HIS SISTER AND HIS FRIEND PROMISED TO PUT A CURSE ON ME AND THE JAVA HOUSE? DID HE? But being somewhat dignified, I held my tongue, gave her a shit-eaten grin and walked away. Whatever beloved feelings I still held in my heart for my late husband, she vehemently managed to remind me—it was all in vain. All I wanted to do was go home and pray that it was all a nightmare.

God knows, the last thing I wanted was to go to the repast (a dinner after the funeral). The idea of having to grin and pretend in people's phony faces made me sick to my stomach. And eating was the last thing on my mind. I had to replay my mom's last words to me to muster up the energy to keep going. "You hold your head up . . ." So, I took a d-e-e-p breath, lifted my head and walked in. It helped that my mother was right beside me.

I did have something to drink, and even that was a little difficult to swallow. A large lump had formed in my throat, probably because I was holding back the words that wanted to spew from my mouth. It was a damn shame; I couldn't even bury Vic in peace without a bunch of drama!

At some point, I went outside to get some air. The weather was still relatively cool, but the brisk air felt good on my face. I had to redo my makeup a couple of times during the course of the day. It was one thing for them to see me saddened, but an entirely different thing to see me look bad. I carried it off . . . the sadness, being distraught, the anger, and still managed to look better than most people expected.

Standing on a wooden porch, Barren smiled at me and gave me a quick hug. I told him I loved him and how sorry I was about everything. Barren was the one that I believed knew his dad better than any of his brothers. He knew how I had treated his father for the five years we were a family, and there was no way he could have any "real" animosity toward me. He knew it, and I knew it.

The youngest son, on a couple of occasions that day, would raise his eyes up to look at me and give me a quick wave. And what really surprised me, was when the oldest, the most distant one, the one that got up and said that his father still loved his mother—came up to me and gave me a hug and said, "I'm sorry, Miss Nailah, but she's, my mother." I wanted to break down and cry, but once again I held back the tears. I assured him that I loved him and that I understood.

Vic's brother and best man at our wedding looked at me and expressed that he felt like I could have given Vic another chance; that it wasn't necessary to put him out. I was at a point that I had no rebuttal, nor did I feel it necessary. I simply stated that I did what I had to do and walked away. On the other hand, his wife gave me a warm hug and a most sincere apology for everything I was going through. She, of all people, knew very well what I had gone through with her brother-in-law. When Vic and I were still together, and we had our "girl talks," I learned that her husband had been cheating on her for years, but she opted to stay because of their young son.

Continuing to flow through the crowd of people who came to honor my late husband, finally came to an end. I was tired and ready to go back home and crawl into my bed and hopefully get some much-needed sleep. Although the business had been closed since Vic's death, I was inundated with telephone calls and well-wishes after an article in the newspaper headlined: "Victor Yarbrough of The Java House Café Dies!" Even long after the funeral, I continued to get letters and cards, which made me feel better. It was good to know that there were people who, regardless of our separation, knew we were an unusual couple who worked hard together in creating one of the most talked about Spoken Word venues in the state ... and surrounding states, even as far as Florida.

FIFTY-EIGHT

A Spiritual Quest

It was April 22, our would-be seventh wedding anniversary, when I finally received the check for $2000.00. Since Vic had left his insurance policy to his sons, which I totally understood, getting the check was a blessing. However, money was still a problem, and time had run out for any saving grace.

Later that evening, I got a call from my new friend, the one I met at the big event the month before, the one who looked like Moses and told me to put on a long dress. We had spoken a few times after the event about the Black Hebrew Israelites and their celebration of the Shavuot Harvest Festival that was taking place in Israel, in May. My new friend, Mocksherril. had become a listening ear for my problems, basically a confidant. And he was quite adamant about the fact that he thought I needed to go.

The idea of going to Israel sounded great. God knew I needed a serious break, but I wasn't sure it would work out. I began to pray and meditate on the possibility. In the meantime, I needed to check on getting a passport while my friend researched a round-trip ticket, which he assured me he could get at a great price. He also alerted me that I had to have a written invitation from the Abba, Ben-Ammi Israel, to enter Dimona. Without that, I wasn't going anywhere— at least not Israel.

After overcoming the guilt of not attempting to catch up on the mortgage, which was at least seven or eight months behind, and in which the $2000.00 wouldn't put a dent in, I realized it wouldn't make any difference. At least the utilities were paid up, and I was able to stock up for the restaurant.

Once I told Mocksherril to move forward on getting the ticket, I was able to get my passport in less than two weeks. I was scheduled to leave on the 18th of May, which meant the festivities were already into the second day. I would return the first week in June, right after my birthday.

While I was greatly excited, my daughter was panicking a little. Our home was being threatened, as well as the business. Plus, she had to send Kamonnie and Siarra back to their father, who had filed kidnapping charges against her. With everything she had been through, she was too weak to fight it. Fortunately, I was able to convince my child that everything would be all right; that she needn't worry.

I was scheduled to be interviewed by a local magazine regarding The Java House, a few days before my departure, to let the public know that we were in financial trouble, in hopes of stirring up some business by the time I returned. During the interview, I stated, "I will have to be dragged away from The Java House before I let it go." That statement would prove to be the force behind what was to come in the not-too-distant future. The article was scheduled to run in the June issue.

I started looking around in second-hand stores for long dresses. My mother loved that idea, and she was more than happy that I was getting away, especially to the Holy Lands. I also started my vegan diet, which was the diet of the Black Hebrew Israelites. That transition, I found very easy since I only ate chicken, turkey, and fish.

While my mom and family members were very supportive of my going to Israel, there were some concerns for my safety. Israel was not the safest place to be traveling to at the time. But I was not afraid, even though I was going by myself. Besides, there were hundreds of people flying from the States to celebrate the Shavuot Harvest Festival, the Jewish holiday celebrating the Torah. And in this case, Black Israelites were celebrating their heritage as the true descendants of the exiled ancient Hebrews.

Headed to the Holy Land

The plane was to its capacity with Jews, especially Black Hebrews. The fourteen-hour flight gave me plenty of time to think, although that was the last thing I wanted to do. I was tired of thinking! Nevertheless, for most of the journey I mused about everything that had happened since my dreams about meeting Vic, the mansion, and the very strong probability of losing what we had worked so hard for. Vic was gone, and the only thing left was The Java House Café & The Harriet Tubman Culture Center with all its faded glory.

Landing in Tel Aviv was nothing like any airport I had ever seen. I've seen security, but nothing like this. There were soldiers and guards everywhere with holstered guns hanging from waistlines and rifles strapped across their backs. I anxiously looked around for someone holding up a sign with my name on it…but, to no avail. I sat around for a while, expecting someone, but didn't know who. That's when a Brother came up to me and asked me if I was going to Dimona, (a small southern town in the Negev desert). I immediately said, yes. I explained that someone was to pick me up, but I wasn't sure who it was. "Listen," he said. "You better get on the van with us; that's where we're headed. Vans come periodically, but there's no need for you to keep waiting." I followed the man, dressed in African garb to the parking lot where a van was waiting.

While in the van, there was small talk and discussion about the event. Most of the passengers had been coming to this auspicious occasion for several years. After reaching our destination, we were greeted by some young brothers who bowed before us with the salutation, Shalom. After assisting me from the van, they took my suitcases and took us to a waiting area. I was already impressed!

Although my time in Dimona was one I shall never forget, I won't take up a lot of writing space to tell you all the details. However, from polygamy, self-sufficiency, African culture, their own schools… to the most awesome, delectable vegan food I had ever eaten, I was smitten by all the talent, female camaraderie, and the entire communal way of living. And even while both male and female soldiers walked around with rifles strapped to their backs along the streets (besides the airport), I found Israel to be an amazing country. However, I was about to discover something even more amazing. A tour to remember . . . or *remembered*.

Deja Vu?

The sun was smoldering hot, as its rays beamed through the window pane of the tour bus. Looking out at the glorious countryside, it blew my mind that people were dressed like it was winter, covered from head to toe, literally. I was told that being covered, actually kept them cooler. As we slowly moved up the winding hill, a feeling came over me, that to this day, I can't explain.

Just as we came to the top of the hill, I could see Jerusalem coming into focus. As I sat there, with my eyes wide open, I began to have a movie-like vision play out in my mind's eye. *I saw myself in a small boat with two other women, rolling down a river.* I blinked a couple of times to make sure I wasn't hallucinating. (Well, in a way, I guess I was. But it was so real). The closer we got to Jerusalem, I had this overwhelming feeling that I had lived there before. Somehow, I knew this land. Then, out of nowhere, I started crying . . . profusely. And the energy I was feeling, deep in my soul, was that I was home!

Alarming the rest of the tourists, the driver, peering through his review mirror, called back to see if I was okay. I attempted to explain to him what was happening, and surprisingly, he understood. "You know," he started saying. "You're not the only one who has had this experience. You are remembering a life here. Let the tears flow, Sister; you are at home. This is your original land."

I did just that. I let the tears flow. All the tears that I had been holding back since Vic's death, poured like a waterfall. I wailed for almost a half-hour, non-stop. I felt like I was home, after many lifetimes of being away.

Finally arriving in Jerusalem, and although we were doing the tourist thing, I really felt a connection as we walked around what felt like familiar surroundings; I even rode a camel and visited the "Wailing Wall." At one time, while strolling through what seemed like a tunnel, lined with tiny stores and apartments, some children ran out of a small apartment onto the cobblestone street. Their beautiful dark faces lit up with smiles as they ran towards me and started talking in a language I didn't understand; grabbing my hands and trying to pull me into their modest home, which I could see through a wide-open door.

Hearing the children, finally, an adult male came out to see what the commotion was about. He then invited us in for tea. Can you believe that? Complete strangers! And the children acted as if they knew me. Since our guide spoke Hebrew, and the older gentleman spoke a little English, we were able to have a casual conversation. They thanked us for our visit and said we were always welcome, whenever we came back.

On our way back to Dimona, we stopped at a small village and visited some of the native women who were cooking flatbread on an open fire in a huge, bowl-shaped pan. I suppose it was part of the tour since we were invited in and were offered the opportunity to learn how to make the bread.

The women were squatted around the hot flames with wrapped skirts pulled between their legs. Since I could squat (back then), I joyfully joined them. Everyone was taking turns to see if they could flip and stir the dough onto the hot surface. People complained that it was too hot and were unable to stand the heat.

Of course, when it was my turn, I picked up the hot dough, swirled it around on the hot surface, and then flipped it over. The women, as well as my fellow tourists, were thrilled and wondered how I did it. So, I told them my secret—that I worked in a restaurant and cooked on a hot grill all the time. They laughed.

Hell Getting Out of the Holy Lands

During my three-week stay in Israel, I had the time of my life. From sailing the Red Sea, to floating like a feather on the Dead Sea (we called it the "Live" Sea due to its healing properties), to jogging every morning, climbing steep mountains, to talking more trash than the law allowed when it came to multiple wives— my trip was amazing! And to top it off, the Abba (spiritual leader) bestowed upon me the Hebrew name, *Eemijah*, meaning: "Woman of God." It was an experience that I would never forget, but the time had come for me to leave my Oasis and head back home. However, getting "out" of the Holy Lands would prove to be . . . hell!

The time frame from when I arrived to boarding the plane was at least 2 hours, so I knew I had plenty of time. The lines were long, as most of us traveling from the States were headed back. However, I thought it would be less crowded, since I stayed three weeks as opposed to the two that most folks stayed.

By the time I got to the counter, the agent looked at my name and said, "To the side, please." Now mind you, this is the line to check my ticket and check in my bags. Like I said earlier, security was tight! As instructed, I moved to the side where I was met by a female officer strapped with a pistol. Of course, I immediately thought, *"Oh shit, what's going on here?"*

"I need you to follow me, please," she ordered. Although nice, her tone let me know she meant business. Like a puppy dog, I followed her to a nearby room, in which an agent followed me with my luggage. Two other women agents, already in the room, took my luggage and began searching it. Piece-by-piece was taken out and shaken out as if they were going to hang them on a clothesline, with the exception of my *dainties*.

Meanwhile, while my bags were being searched, so was I. And yes, I had to strip down to my panties and bra. I was devastated! In the meantime, time was quickly ticking away, and I had a flight to make. So, I very kindly and softly reminded the lady who had me spreading my legs that I must get to my flight. She took a look at my ticket, which was in her pocket, and realized that I only had a few minutes to get to the plane.

"Okay," she said, agreeing that time was of the essence. "Sorry, I will give you a pass to get through security, that way you won't have to wait in line or be checked again."

"No, shit," I thought in the privacy of my mind.

"We will take your luggage and check it in for you," she continued. "You must hurry and get dressed." She quickly gave me my ticket, along with a pass and my purse, then pointed in the direction for me to bypass security. It was a damn good thing I wasn't trying to smuggle anything; cause girlfriend would have been carted off to the nearest jail. That is, if I wasn't shot first.

Finally, over the trauma, and once we took off, I was settled down enough to muse about the wonderful time I had with my Hebrew Sisters and Brothers, and how different their culture was compared to ours. Although many Black Israelites had several communities in the states, I could only imagine how hard it was to get Sisters to go along with their husbands having multiple wives, and whether or not it was something "I" could deal with. One thing for sure, polygamy meant a man would never be accused of "cheating." But my real curiosity was . . . could a man deal with **his** wife having another husband . . . or two? Makes you go . . . um!

FIFTY-NINE

Back to My World

My only brother, Mark, who (like most of my family) never came around much, picked me up from the airport. He couldn't believe it was me. I was three shades darker, and I loved it. I was so brown that I would need to buy much darker makeup. However, in Israel, makeup was taboo, which was cool with me. I remember a few days after I had been there, one of the Brothers who met me the day I arrived, looked at me and said, "Sister, you look so much better. Just in the few days you've been here, you've got a glow. Not that you looked bad, I could just tell that you were stressed. Being here is good for you." I knew the Brother was right. Hell, I was more than stressed. I was wrecked!

It was so late when we arrived that I was too tired to talk about my trip. I did let my brother know I had a great time. He, too, said I looked great and that he had never seen me that black.

"Damn, Sis. You are as black as me and Lonnie (my only sister). Can't nobody call you high-yellow no more; now you look like us." We laughed.

I went in through the back, since I didn't want to wake Jenia and the kids. Kenya heard me and met me at the door. It was good to see her; she jumped on me and started licking on me. Damn, I hated that. I loved her and all, but I hate for a dog to lick on me, especially my face. Yuck!

"That's a big-ass dog, Sis; you sure she won't bite?"

"I'm sure, little Bro. She's all bark . . . unless you try and grab me or something like that. Then, she will bite your ass."

Mark hurriedly put my luggage in my room. We talked for a couple more minutes and he promised to stop by soon, which, by the way, I knew was just talk. But it was okay. At least he came to our wedding and the funeral. Besides, he was no different than the rest of the family. Everybody was busy living their lives . . . trying to survive. Hanging out at The Java House wasn't a priority. I gave my brother a hug and walked him to the door, while Kenya stood guard.

My bed looked so good. I had a marvelous time, but I was sure glad to get home to my bed. And as tired as I was, I knew there was no way I could get into the bed without taking a shower. I grabbed a nightie from the drawer, took a short, hot shower, and brushed my teeth. I then pulled back the covers and flopped onto the bed; that's when I heard Kenya on the porch making a weird, low, like howling and whining sound, which was unlike her. I yelled for her to stop, but she continued. It then dawned on me that she was probably seeing Vic. She soon came in and tucked her head under my chest.

"Did you see your daddy, Kenya. I know he's out there," I told her in a baby voice, rubbing her head. She laid down beside the bed, guarding me the rest of the night.

(Now, I know you're probably wondering how I figured that Kenya was seeing Vic. Well, let's just say . . . I had a *feeling*).

The next morning, I woke up early. I must have still been on Israel time, because I wasn't really tired since I managed to get some sleep on the plane. I had made sure that I arrived home on Sunday, so that I would have two days off ... not that it was going to be busy. I stayed in my room for a while to meditate and give thanks. I also put in an Agape tape. I sure missed hearing Rev. Michael and his wife's music.

It had been a minute since I had some time to myself, with the funeral and all ... then preparing for my trip, which in a way, was more like a spiritual quest. I was rejuvenated, inspired, and motivated to keep pushing forward, no matter what the future held.

Jenia was sure glad to see me; although it had been slow, she said things were not the same without me. But she and Bobby and the kids made out okay, and the fact that she was on summer break from school meant there was less stress. Jerry made her life a little easier to bear by supporting her with the kids, as well as being a shoulder to cry on during her bouts of depression, and for having to let her two younger kids return to California. Needless to say, he was an Earth Angel; and not knowing what the future held with a place to live, my daughter and I were on shaky ground!

Bobby, on the other hand, had some good news. He found a full-time job working for a factory. I was happy for him and thanked him for all his help. He had been a blessing, even though he had taken advantage of my kindness, by stealing. But all was forgiven, and it never happened again.

SIXTY

Two Events Save the Day

Things continued to get worse, at The Java House, and I was beginning to lose hope. There were so few customers, that I knew the time had come for me to accept the fact that I was "going out of business." Even with the anticipation of doom being the final outcome, I needed to make some money, and at that point, even a "little" money would help tremendously. As I sat in the office, trying to come up with possibilities—albeit, far-fetched, the phone rang.

"I hope this is enough time," the voice inquired. "But it would be great if you could accommodate... say around at least fifteen of us for lunch next week. We already have your menu, so we could pre-order, if that would help."

It was the Black Dental Association of Kentucky; they were having an annual meeting and decided to do lunch at a restaurant, and it was agreed that The Java House would be ideal, having the room for privacy, and a great meal.

I took a pre-order, so I would have everything I needed, and since Jenia and the kids were spending a lot of time at Jerry's apartment, I knew I would be by myself. However, I didn't want Jenia to feel like she had to work. She deserved a break.

I had everything laid out when the dentists arrived. I set them up in the Henrietta Marie Dining Room for more comfort, and so that they could have their discussions without distractions. I also was blessed to have a few customers on the other side. The challenge was, I was alone.

For those who ordered the Veggie Lasagna, it was pretty simple; but for those who ordered the Salmon or sandwiches from the grill, I had to cook to order, and I made sure I didn't have to keep refilling drinks by putting pitchers of lemon iced tea and water on the table for self-serving.

By the time I served those fifteen, and at least four other customers on the other side, I had moved non-stop for over an hour. Back and forth I went, serving both sides. At the end of the luncheon, everyone complimented me on the great service and how well everything was prepared. One customer, who had the Salmon, said to me, "Tell the chef the Salmon was excellent." I grinned and said, "Thank you, I am the chef." That's when they found out that I was alone. Amazed and completely baffled, they wondered how on earth I handled everything so efficiently. And then, while cashing out, and realizing I had customers on the other side, they really shook their heads. Needless to say, they all tipped generously.

Contributing our little windfall of luck to the local magazine that did the article on us, later that week, I also got a call from my dear friend, William who worked for the Department of Public Health. They wanted the Cultural Center to host an AIDS Awareness event in August. He assured me that once he got the paperwork confirmed, he would mail a deposit. And they also approved The Java House as the caterer.

This news not only gave me a little hope for our financial future, but also a reprieve from the guilt of spending money on myself. And to top it off, the special guest speaker was the renowned author, E. Lynn Harris, an openly gay man who wrote several books about men on the DL (downlow) and the signs women needed to look for. Talk about happy! The Department of Health agreed to do all the publicity, as well as provide vendors. There would be T-shirts and other promotional-type items along with pamphlets and educational tools regarding this important cause. On this one, I was going to need HELP!

With the AIDS upcoming event only a week away, and with virtually no help, I had to rely on the support of a couple of my male customers to move some large tables and do some heavy lifting. I may have been looking better since my return, but my back was still reminding me that it wasn't getting any better. There was a lot to do, and Jenia and the kids were a big help with decorations and extra cleaning. The deposit check helped tremendously, enabling me to buy all the food we needed to feed up to a hundred people.

We had a large gay community, so I knew the event would be well-attended. Although it was mostly geared towards this community, the heterosexual community, especially the women, showed a lot of enthusiasm about the event. And the fact that E. Lynn Harris was coming, didn't hurt. It didn't matter that he was gay, he was one fine man!

The event was fabulous, absolutely fantastic. E. Lynn Harris gave an excellent talk on his personal life and spoke very candidly about being a man. "Look," he said. "I am a man, who happens to love another man. Just because I love a man, doesn't make me any less than one." Silence fell upon that room so tough, you could hear a cotton-ball drop. It made me think of my Uncle Vernon, who was such a man, I would have NEVER known he was gay, if he didn't tell me.

And the booths! One Sister was selling an array of "sex toys," and they were flying off the table (I had my eye on the portable vibrator). There were all types of information, including Harris' books, that brought an educational component that I was amazed at. And let's not forget about the spread I made for the buffet-style luncheon. I must say, I outdid myself.

There was a fresh fruit section, alongside huge salads with all The Java House's special ingredients. I baked chicken over steamed rice, Veggie Lasagna, and hot rolls and garlic bread. The dessert table was filled with miniature fruit tarts, sweet potato pies, carrot cake and cookies. And to drink, was our special lemon iced tea. One guy, who had never had our iced tea, said it was better than an orgasm. Hello!

After the event, Mr. Harris was so impressed with The Java House that he asked if there was some place we could talk in private. I took him to my office, upstairs. He asked questions about the business and as to whether or not we had a 501-C 3 status. I told him, we did, under the Harriet Tubman Cultural Center. I shared a little with him about our history and our purpose. When he expressed his admiration for all that we were doing, he offered to make a contribution to our cause once he returned and talked with his board members. I felt overwhelmed and blessed that he would even consider supporting us. Things were beginning to look up— so, I thought. But something else was brewing in which I had no forewarning . . . this was going to be something that would take me completely by surprise.

SIXTY-ONE

The Invasion of the Flies

Damn, it was hot as hell upstairs, and it wasn't even 8:00, and that's A.M. There was a tiny breeze coming through my bedroom window, but it offered no reprieve from the August heat. When I went to wash my face, hoping to cool off a little, even the *cold* water was warm. And it made no sense to turn on the air conditioning, since it didn't work anyhow. So, I went into the kitchen to open the windows, hoping to get some airflow. And what I saw made me stop dead in my tracks.

"Oh, my God1" Is all I could say. All the bottom windowpanes of three windows were completely covered with tiny, **black flies**! For a moment, I couldn't move. I stood there wondering how the sun could shine so beautifully on the top panes and have such a horrific sight on the bottom ones. "What the hell?" were my next words. I really couldn't come up with anything that didn't warrant some three and four-letter words to describe what I was seeing. I was shocked! To say the least!

Of all the crazy shit I had seen thus far, this was by FAR the wildest and scariest thing I had seen. I moved cautiously toward the window to the far right, hoping not to disturb them and have them flying all over the place. There I was, right up on the window . . . and not a one moved. And what was even more bizarre, they were ALL the same size. Now go figure!

Since my daughter's bedroom was to my right, I tapped ever so gently to wake her up and to make sure I wasn't having another nightmare. "Jenia," I whispered. "Jenia, wake up; you've got to come and see this." Of course, that early in the morning, she grunted that she was sleepy. "Can't it wait, mama? I'm tired." This time, I opened the door and walked up to the bed.

"Baby, you will not believe this; you have got to get up! Please."

When Jenia walked into the kitchen, she didn't immediately notice the windows. She was still half asleep. "Jenia, look," as I pointed to the window closest to her. At that point, she almost fell on the kitchen table.

"What the fuck? Damn, mama, I'm sorry, but what the hell is going on?" My daughter may have *once* been a devout Christian, but she cursed like a bona fide sinner. She didn't always talk that way. But, when you go through the kinda hell like she had been through, cursing becomes a huge part of your vocabulary. Call it "Anger Management."

As we both walked around, looking at each other, dumbfounded and struggling to understand what was happening, we were completely awestruck as to the massive amount of flies. We knew it was nowhere near normal. Yes, you get flies in the summertime, but hundreds, at one time . . . this was something beyond summer and all its little nuisances. This was something **evil,** and we both knew it.

Armed with a rolled-up newspaper and magazine, we both got ready to go to battle. I went first, since Jenia was a little skeptical about getting too close. And what was so very strange, was that when I went to splatter the little demons all over the window pane, with a single blow, not a one attempted to fly away to safety. Now, that was creepy.

BAM! I blasted at least ten or so at one time. They fell onto the windowsill, and some hit the floor. Now, check this out. THEY CAME BACK TO LIFE AND CRAWLED BACK ONTO THE WINDOW! That's when I knew I was going to need more than a rolled-up newspaper.

"Did you see that, Jenia?" I nervously asked. Shaking her head and backing up at the same time, Jenia was ready to book!

Of course, I tried to rationalize it by saying I probably didn't really hit hard enough—that I just knocked them off without killing them.

"Mom, this is some crazy, devilish shit going on here. I watched how hard you hit them. Have you checked the other rooms?" Jenia and I locked arms and started tiptoeing through other parts of the house. I had already been through the kids' room, which I had to pass through to get to the hallway. Fortunately, the kids were not there. My oldest son had picked them up a week earlier to spend the summer vacation with his two daughters. Based on what was happening, it looked as though a spiritual warfare was imminent, and having children in a war zone, was not good.

We walked through Jenia's bedroom to my office—all was clear. Then we crossed over to the theatre—that's when we saw that the first window was completely "shaded" with the same type of flies. Not bothering to do anything, we headed downstairs . . . still holding hands and walking softly, as if the flies could hear us coming. At the bottom of the stairs, to the left, we peeped in the Henrietta room—all clear. Then we creeped over to the Fredrick Douglas library—NOT clear. However, like upstairs in the theatre, only the first window was infested.

"My God," I thought. *"What were we going to do?"*

Jenia and I went back upstairs to my bedroom to try and figure out a plan. First, we started praying, which my daughter ended up praying in "tongues." Then we started making a list of some items that we might be able to use for artillery: Sage, Anointing Oil, Holy Water, insect spray, and the Bible.

"Mom, where are we gonna get some Holy Water and Anointing Oil?"

"I don't know of any place to buy any. Maybe we can get some purified water and bless it, along with some Olive oil."

Agreeing to improvise, we both dressed and headed out to purchase our weapons. On our way, we tried to think of every conceivable possibility as to how or why we were being terrorized by an invasion of flies. Was Vic still working his mojo from the grave? Well, even if he were, I knew the ancestors had my back, and that NO harm would come to me or my family.

First, we tried spraying the winged pests with the insect spray–they didn't even move. Shit, it may have made them stronger. Next, we started sprinkling Holy Water and Anointing Oil and decreeing them to be gone in the name of Jesus. I thought for sure, the way my daughter was praying and speaking in tongues, that surely Jesus was the answer–NOTHING! Both of us looked at each other completely bewildered, as I broke out our last solution—the Sage. Surely, we could smoke them out.

I took a really large piece of Indian Sage and lit it. Once it had a nice blaze, I blew it out. The smoke was thick and darn near black as I started fanning the windows, just knowing they couldn't take the smoke. But the only ones that couldn't take it—were us! We both ran outside, coughing.

Frustrated, we called it quits for about an hour to think about some more strategies. Coming up with absolutely nothing, I finally decided to call Mocksherril. Surely, he would know what to do. After all, he was my last hope.

"In the name of Yeshua," he proclaimed. "Command them to be gone in the name of Yeshua, that's Hebrew for Jesus. You are dealing with ancient, dark spirits." He was quite adamant and was certain that it would work. "And after they are gone, cleanse the rooms with the Sage," he continued. "Then make sure you use a sweet fragrance afterwards, like Frankincense & Myrrh."

Well, we had tried everything else under the sun; it certainly couldn't hurt. So, we prayed—got the remaining blessed water and oil and went back to the battlefield. However, since it was getting late in the day, and with so many windows, I decided to call my friends, Ubie and Betty, to help.

"You're not going to believe me," I started the conversation.

"Believe what? Is this Nailah?" Betty asked.

"Yes, girl, and I have a request. I need you and your husband to come around here ASAP. There's no point in trying to tell you anything over the phone. You wouldn't believe me."

"Okay, but it may take a while. I have to wait until my brother gets back to stay with the kids. Then, we'll be right over—probably about an hour or less."

"All right and tell Ubie to bring his drum. We're gonna need to summon the ancestors for this one."

Jenia was pleased to know there would be reinforcements; there was no telling what might pop off. We headed for the kitchen armed with holy water and oil, along with our rolled-up newspaper and magazine. Commanding in the name of "Yeshua" to be gone, we doused the enemy with water and oil while whacking them with all our might. Masses fell to the floor as if ambushed. The ancient name, Yeshua—worked!

We had just won the battle in the kitchen when my friends yelled from the backyard. I yelled back that I would meet them downstairs, out front. By the time I headed out the front door, they were just coming around to the front.

"What's going on? You sounded as if it's serious." Betty said, hugging me tightly, followed by her husband.

"Girl, you are not gonna believe what I have to show you. Ubie, I see you got your drum." He held it up in agreement and said he was ready when I was. Then, just as I turned to go toward the door, I looked over at the window above the porch–the one that peered into the Henrietta Marie room.

"Oh my God," I damn near screamed. "That's what I'm talking about," pointing at the window. "The flies! You see all those flies?" They both stopped, looked, and got completely silent— then, Ubie finally whispered, "What the hell is going on?"

Betty still hadn't spoken, as she stepped closer—stepping up on the porch. I immediately called Jenia from upstairs. We had looked earlier that day at the inside of that window, and it was . . . clear. And unlike the other windows, this time, the thick patch of flies was on the "outside" of the window.

I waited for Jenia to come down before I gave my friends the short version of what had happened and what we found to be the solution. Jenia confirmed every word, and alluding to the fact that black magic had been cast upon the mansion.

"Somebody don't want us here," she said with conviction. "This is some evil shit going on here. You should have seen the upstairs windows in the kitchen before mom, and I finally got rid of them— and we still have three more windows to do."

"They don't even fly away when I get up close," Betty said, finally able to speak. "Usually, flies take off when you get close . . . they didn't move . . . and they're all the same size . . . and they're all this dull, looking black . . . with green on the wings."

Ubie took his drum from its African cloth and started tapping out a call to the ancestors while we held hands and prayed. After our prayer, I went back upstairs to get the blessed water, however, it was pretty much gone, so I made up some more and got the Olive oil and grabbed my newspaper and the magazine. I could hear the rhythmic sound of the drum—and I began to feel a sense of hope and victory.

While Ubie kept the "call" going, Betty joined me and Jenia as we doused water and oil upon what we had surmised as demonic. We continued to call the name of Yeshua as groups of flies fell to the concrete surface. We then moved into the library and were able to witness the same effect as we continued the powerful ritual. The window in the theater was our last station for battle, and like the others, it was no contest. The victory was ours.

I cannot begin to tell you how many hundreds, if not thousands of flies laid dead on the floors of the affected areas. Jenia went to get a broom to begin the clean-up; however, I knew this was a job for the "vacuum cleaner." They needed to be "sucked up" and then "burned." So, we dug a hole in the back, put the bloated bag inside, and soaked it with kerosene before I dropped the blazing flame into the hole. We then stepped back and watched as a giant billow of black smoke spread into the open space . . . slowly dissipating into the vastness . . . leaving no trace.

At that very moment, as I watched the smoke disappear, I KNEW in my spirit that not only had the battle been won, but my MISSION had been fulfilled. The "spell had been broken," and the Lost Souls, trapped in their own virtual hell, were finally free! Their Souls could move on. However, with everything that had happened over the past five years, from dreams to reality, and everything in between, I didn't know whether to feel relieved or sad that it was all over. I wondered what was going to happen next, as I questioned in my mind as to whether or not "I" could move on.

Continuing Mocksherril's orders, we cleansed each room with Sage to purify the space. We then each took a stick of Frankincense & Myrrh (used since the days of Yeshua) to freshen every room with its citric and piney aromatic scents. It was done! Thank you, Yeshua!

SIXTY-TWO

The End of a Mission

Just when I thought I could exhale, two days later, coming back from the store, I noticed from the car that there was a sign on the back door. I figured maybe someone came to see me and left a note. Jenia was over at Jerry's, and the kids were still visiting their cousins. By the time I reached the top step, it became quite apparent that it wasn't a note from a friend.

EVICTION NOTICE! I struggled to hold onto the bags I was carrying, as I continued to read what felt like a death warrant. I had 15 days to vacate the property. I lay one of the bags down and took the stapled sign from the door. My hands were shaking. Picking up the bag, I used my foot to push open the door. With "notice" and all, I went into the kitchen and put the bags on the table. I sat down and gazed at the paper as if I could magically change the wording. But those big red letters didn't budge; they sat there on that page staring back at me.

For months, I had refused to heed the bank's warnings. I couldn't or wouldn't accept the inevitable. It was just too painful! All the backbreaking work; all the sacrifices—the blood, sweat, and tears. Was it all for NOTHING? I screamed inside my head until I thought it would explode. My stomach knotted up like the time I got the phone call about my grandson's death. But, in this case, not one tear surfaced to release some of the excruciating pain. I wanted a cigarette, and yet grateful there were none to be had. So, I got a glass of wine– and just sat.

I don't know how long I was glued to the chair before dragging myself to the bed. I was a little woozy and had to use the wall as support to keep from falling. I was drunk— not from the fermented grapes, but from the "grapes of wrath". Where was I going? What would happen to my child and grandchildren? I felt like everything was in vain; that none of what I thought the ancestors were asking of me held one ounce of truth. All my faith; all my praying and meditating and paying homage and rituals and studying and burning candles and giving and giving and giving . . . I felt like the biggest hypocrite that ever lived!

Tears finally began to flow like a broken dam—trailing down the mounds of my cheeks to my trembling lips. "Why! Why?" I mumbled over and over to anyone who could hear me. That's when I heard the voice . . . *"My darling daughter . . ."* the voice whispered in my mind. My breathing paused–my heart pounded like a heavy hammer landing upon a huge boulder. I listened.

"Will you let it go? Will you allow Me to take you on a journey far beyond this small sacrifice?" the voice continued.

"You call this small!" I yelled out loud.

"Yes, I do. Compared to what is in store for you, this has merely been a test. YOU called this into your life. YOU agreed to answer the call from your ancestors, in which they are well pleased—You have set them free."

I had no choice but to continue to listen, for deep down in my soul, I knew it was true. I had called this entire, freaky, bizarre situation into my life for my own spiritual development—To Seek and to Find that Divine Essence that Agape spoke about. That the teachings of *Ifa* blessed me with. Nevertheless, while my soul knew, my flesh was still at war . . . it continued to try and make a deal. "But I have given all that I've got to this business. Can't you make it work? Can't you have someone donate some money or let me win the lottery?" I begged.

"No one promised you that THIS would be where you would find your success . . . although successful it has been in many ways. It brought creativity to a famished land, love where there was hate,

forgiveness towards those that were misguided, and it taught you that perceived failure is only a doorway to your Divine purpose." The Voice continued speaking things that I still wasn't ready to hear. Yet I knew it was the Truth.

"Have I not always been here for you—even with your free will? Trust Me, daughter—there are things unseen—But, if you continue to have faith, I will show you your True Calling, your Soul's Purpose. One that no man can take away or keep from you. So, I ask you again. Will you let it go?"

The "Voice" I heard, resonated as my very own. And yet, I had no control over the soundless words that poured out with love and compassion for my life. I knew there was no way I could continue down this road. It was literally killing me. This time, I needed to fully "let go" and let that which was "within—that Voice" take me through the next phase of my life. And to **know** . . . that no matter where I was headed—it was for my good. So, I wiped my eyes, blew my nose, and laid flat on my back and softly professed, **"Yes, I will let it go."** Ahh, the sweetness of submission—It certainly gives one peace.

You know what's really strange? I had actually started collecting boxes and packing–three days before I got the Notice. Goes to show that my God consciousness was already preparing me for what was coming, even when I was too stubborn to believe it would happen. Or maybe it was my way of self-preservation. There were times I felt my sanity was at stake, and I didn't know how to give up–at least that's what I felt I would be doing if I didn't try everything in my power to hold on to what we had worked s-o-o hard for. But I understood now–that this purpose–The Call, had been heeded, and the mission was successful.

The Divine Eviction

What on earth could be "divine" about an eviction? Well, I'm gonna tell you.

It was the morning of September 3, (my mother's birthday) 2002. It was a bright, sunny day and I had gotten up early, took my shower, washed my hair and put on my robe. Jenia was getting ready for her class, and the kids were due home the next day. I had been packing, realizing I was past the due date to be gone. But I hadn't found a place and was hoping I had a little more time. And even more important—I had No Money! Anyway, I heard a loud knock at the front door and Jenia yelled that she would get it.

The next thing I heard was my daughter running upstairs, crying. "Mama, mama, there are about seven Sheriffs at the door."

"Okay, Jenia, it's gonna be okay. I'll take care of it," I tried to assure her. Amazingly, I wasn't upset, angry, sad or any of those emotions one would have under such circumstances. I wrapped a towel around my wet hair and proceeded to the stairway with Kenya and Jenia close behind.

"Are you Mrs. Yarbrough?" a Sheriff asked, standing with his feet far apart.

"Yes, I am," answering from the top of the stairs.

"Ma'am, we have a warrant for your eviction from this property. Could you get dressed, please, and come down?"

"Sure, come on in. Can I get any of you some coffee?"

"No thanks, and we need you to hurry."

I quickly found some jeans and a T-shirt and hurried, per instruction, back to the front. At least four of them had come inside, standing with legs slightly spread and strapped with guns. There were at least three or four more standing guard around the front steps. I could also see several young men who looked like "movers" outside. Kenya began to bark and started to follow me as I descended the stairs, while Jenia sat on a step, terrified. Then one of the Sheriffs that had come inside, goes for his gun and threatens to shoot my dog.

"There's no need for that, Sheriff. She won't bite," I politely explained.

Jenia, who was now about to lose it—was really crying. "Jenia, take Kenya in the back and shut the door and you go to class. I'll handle this. Don't worry, everything is fine. I'll make sure that your and the kids' clothes are packed. Go to Jerry's after class, and I'll call you this evening."

"Mama, they ain't gotta treat you like this. Mom, he threatened to shoot Kenya!"

"Jenia, I've got this. Please leave and go to class . . . please."

When I got to the bottom of the stairs, I stood face-to-face with the leader, as he handed me the official warrant. I then took a brief look and signed the paper. Stern and very official, the Sheriff showed me that he was accompanied by several young men who were there to remove my items from the property. He then introduced me to their coordinator. I smiled, shook hands and told him I would show them around when they were ready. The Sheriff then asked if I would show him around before they got started. He wanted to make sure that none of the business items were taken.

We walked upstairs together, and as we were standing in the doorway of the theatre, the tall, slender, dark-haired man looked at me and said, "Miss Yarbrough, I'm really sorry we have to do this. I have followed you in the papers for a while, and I must say, you have done a fine job for this community. Now, you may not believe this, but my wife and I voted for you when you ran for governor."

I thanked him for his kind words and told him they meant a lot to me, especially under the circumstances. We both chuckled, and he shook my hand. "I truly wish you the best, Miss Yarbrough. I really mean that." We both headed back downstairs. I then realized that he really didn't need to see everything; he only wanted the chance to speak with me in private. Radioing his men, the Sheriff told them they could leave; that everything was under control.

Once back outside, the coordinator asked if I would show him around. His face was kind and gentle-looking, not like someone who was ready to put all your shit out on the street. As we walked through,

I pointed out my personal items. He then took out a card from his wallet and said, "Here's a number for a guy that can help you to move. He's African American and lives in the neighborhood. Give him a call. I believe he will help you." I thanked him and told him I would call. Meanwhile, when the young men came upstairs to get instructions, the gentleman gathered them together and said, "I want you all to pack everything as if she were being moved professionally. Place her items in the yard, not the parking lot. Be careful and don't break anything. Got that?"

Looking surprised, with half smiles, they said in unison, "Yes, sir; we got it."

I had already packed most of my personal dishes and kitchen items, as well as some artifacts and books. Periodically, the guys would inquire as to what was what. It took a few hours to box and carry out what didn't belong to the restaurant. I also took the man's advice about calling Mr. Jones about the possibility of helping me to move.

"Hello, is this Mr. Jones?" I explained to him that I was given his card.

"Yes, how can I help you?" His voice was deep and strong.

"My name is Nailah, and as we speak, I am being evicted," I explained quite cheerfully and informed him that I was the owner of The Java House Café.

"Yes, I've heard of your place; I've heard some good things. It's that mansion over near the river. Yeah, I know where it is."

"Well, I'm gonna need some help moving all my stuff to the storage."

"How much stuff do you have?"

"Quite a bit, I'm afraid. However, I'm only taking my personal things; the restaurant stuff stays here. Now, I must warn you, before you agree to help, I only have $60.00 to my name."

"Hey, anyone who can sound this cheerful being evicted, I've got to help them. I'll be around shortly."

I called my mom to wish her a happy birthday, then told her what was happening. She was actually happy. "Baby, I hope you understand when I say, thank you, God. I've been so concerned for you. You've been killing yourself trying to keep that place open.

Baby, it's just too much. Everything is gonna be all right."

I explained that I would need money for storage and wondered if she could help. She put my stepdad on the phone, whom I had never asked for anything. He said they would be over in about an hour.

As their boss instructed, the young movers had everything well organized. Boxes were stacked, and furniture was placed meticulously on the front lawn. It looked like a furnished apartment, complete with a stove and refrigerator, while the fresh, cut grass served as a lush green carpet. I offered all the guys' beers to take with them before they left. Their boss said it was okay. They thanked me and wished me well. One guy told me that he had never met anyone as nice as me who was being evicted. I didn't doubt it.

Before their boss left, he pulled me to the side and explained to me that once they took everything out, it was his responsibility to lock everything up and board the doors. "But, Miss Yarbrough," he started to explain. "I'm gonna leave that back door open in case there is something you left. I know you won't take anything that you shouldn't. I wish you the best, and I'll come back and board that back door tomorrow."

I gave him a hug, and he reciprocated. Just as he was leaving, I noticed someone pulling into the parking lot. It was my banker. Not Mr. Roland (the one who gave me the loan), but an Associate. I had only seen him a couple of times; however, he was a major factor in facilitating the "move." Anyway, as he walked towards me, he paused and looked around before extending his hand to me.

"Mrs. Yarbrough, I am deeply sorry about all this," he said while holding my hand. "I truly wish that things could have been different. But the bank had no choice." His light blue eyes began to fill with tears; however, he was able to successfully keep them at bay.

"I understand," I stated, allowing him to continue to hold my hand. "I truly understand, and I am grateful for the banks' leniency. But business is business, and I take none of this personally. Please let Mr. Roland know that I appreciate everything that he has done, and that I am sorry for how things worked out."

"I will, and believe me, he's just as sorry as I am . . . heck, the entire bank is. The Java House has been a very positive influence in this community, and you should be very proud. You gonna be, okay?"

"Oh, yes, I'll be fine, "I assured him. "And thanks for your kind words, I appreciate that. We tried our best . . . but . . . life happens." After a gentle squeeze, he finally released my hand. He then smiled, gave me a hug, and wished me luck before returning to his car.

My Moving Angels

It must have been one of the biggest moving vans they made, as it pulled up in the driveway. It certainly was big enough for my stuff, with probably room to spare. I leisurely walked toward the van while Mr. Jones stepped out of the cab. He was a big guy with chocolate skin and broad shoulders. He looked like he could pick up a sofa by himself. But he had another guy with him, not quite as big as him, but big enough.

"Now, you can change your mind if you want to. I know this is a lot of stuff." I said, smiling, and shook his hand.

"Naw, I ain't gonna do that," he said, looking around. "I'm here to help, just like I said."

Ubie and Betty were loading their car when the van pulled up. I had called them earlier to see if they wanted anything. As a matter of fact, I gave away quite a few things that day, including Kenya. That really hurt. But there was no way I could keep her. I actually kissed my dog and let her lick my face. I was gonna miss her. At least I was assured she would be taken care of. The guy that took her raised Dobermans and said that Kenya would be in good company.

After my moving angel and his friend finished loading the van, I gladly gave him my last $60.00 and a couple of beers. He didn't drink, but his friend was happy to take them both.

"I know what you've done is worth far more than what I have, and I can't thank you enough for your kindness. You will be blessed for your good deed."

"I am blessed," he kindly stated. "That's why I knew I had to help you. God has been good to me." We hugged, and he wished me the best and encouraged me to keep my positive attitude.

Mom and my stepdad arrived just in time to lead them to the storage place. Thank goodness, it wasn't that far. After giving both of them a hug, and mom reminding me that everything was going to be fine, I told my stepdad that he could write the check out to the company for $145.00 – a 3-month special. He also assured me he would make the monthly payments, after the 3 months, if necessary, until I got on my feet. I watched as they maneuvered their way out the driveway.

Now, that's why I call it "Divine." That was nobody but God!

Final Good-Byes

Dusk took over the sun's rays, and the cool breeze had replaced the humidity of that early September day. My auntie and her new husband came by with their truck and took the things that were being stored at her and my mom's house. She looked sad, but I assured her that I was fine. She, too, worried about me, my health, my state of mind.

"Well, niece, do you have plans as to what's next?" Her voice was soft and concerned. I sighed in relief from the day's hard work before telling her my plans.

"Well, I'm gonna stay at mom's for the next two nights, then I'm headed for Chicago, where I've been invited to live with the Ambassador and his wives. You know, the Black Hebrews I met while in Israel. I'm gonna work at their restaurant. I tell you auntie . . . if it weren't for their invitation, I'm not sure where I would go. I know I couldn't stay here in Louisville. It would be way too painful."

"I understand. Where's Jenia?" she asked, looking around.

"Jenia called earlier today, and I told her not to bother about coming back over here; that I would drop her luggage off at Jerry's. It had been devastating enough, and seeing me sitting out on the porch with half my life in the front yard, would have been too much. By the way, Jerry invited her and the kids to live with him".

"That's good. I knew they had gotten pretty tight," my auntie expressed, smiling. "I like him. He seems like a nice young man."

"I do too. He's a good person, and I'm sure they'll do fine. And the kids love him."

"How much longer are you gonna be here? You know it's getting dark."

"Not much longer, I have to check and make sure I have everything before I leave. Plus, I just want to take it all in, one more time."

"I understand," she said.

"You know, today the bank guy . . ."

"You mean the Brother that gave you the loan . . . wasn't his name, Roland?"

"Yeah, but it wasn't him. This was a white guy. He works with Roland."

I shared my story with her about what happened when he came over, and she didn't seem to be surprised.

"Niece, everyone knows what you did for this community. And the way you and Vic renovated this place . . . no one would have done what you all did . . . not on that little money. You have more faith than anybody I know, and you worked your tail off. You were a gift to this community, and believe me, they are gonna miss you! That I know for sure. You gave it your best shot, and now God has something else for you to do. Bigger and better."

"Thanks, Auntie. You have always had faith in me, and I love you for that. And you're right, I'm gonna be just fine."

"Look, Rob is ready to go. You sure you're gonna be okay?"

"I'm sure. I'll talk with you before I leave. And thanks for everything."

The light from the porch spread out almost to the parking lot. Between that and the moon, I could see the entire front yard. Now, only a small patch of items stood solo, with a sign that read: Free stuff. I made sure the yard was nice and neat and that no trash was lying around. I looked, for the last time, at the pink Dogwood that hovered over the fence. I stepped up on the long porch that served as a huge windowsill for the formal dining room and then took one last saunter around "my dream."

"Did I serve you well, my dear ancestors?" I cried out. "I heard you when you called, and I came. And I came with ALL my relations, for it was the only way I could come. And while I thought it was all about YOU calling me to free 'your' Souls—I have miraculously 'awakened' to the reality that **I** also called you—to free Mine! Thank you! I am truly blessed and humbly honored to have been your servant!"

I couldn't go back inside, even though the door was open. I reminded myself, again, that I "Answered the call". It was finally over. It was time to move on. No matter what had been left, it was no longer needed. And as I made my way back to the front, I stood before the mansion and smiled. And as I lifted my gaze towards the heavens, I then turned around and walked to my car. I was tempted to turn and look back as I drove from the parking lot—but, the *Voice* said, *"There's no looking back. There's only what's ahead of you. Go forward, my child. **I AM** with you, always!"* I then remembered that I had been listening to an Agape tape the last time I was in the car. I pushed it in, and just as the Universe would have it, my favorite song resounded throughout the car as I began to sing along *". . . I release, and I let go; I let the Spirit run my life, and my heart is open wide; yes, I'm only here for God!"*

The End

ABOUT THE AUTHOR

Nailah Jumoke (Yarbrough), a native of Louisville, Kentucky, was the founder, proprietor, and visionary of *The Java House Café* and the *Harriet Tubman Cultural Center*. Recognized as a forum for **racial and social healing** through the art of the Spoken Word and various other community art forms, The Java House and Tubman Center hosted distinguished visitors and performers that included Bahamian Diet Guru and Comedian Dick Gregory, Comedian June Boykins, aka "Just June," and Author/Poet Jessica Care Moore. During its five years of operation, The Java House emerged as *the* gathering place for local and regional artists.

Listed as **"One of the Most Notable African Americans in the state of Kentucky,"** in 1999, at the age of 50, Jumoke-Yarbrough was the first African American to run for governor in the state of Kentucky. In 2000, Jumoke received the Louisville Historical League's Preservation Award for the Renovation of the Irvin House in Portland,

Kentucky, which became the home of the Harriet Tubman Cultural Center and the new home for The Java House Café.

She was also acknowledged in an edition of "Who's Who" in Business. Jumoke was known as a poet, community activist, Kentucky/Indiana Girl Scouts volunteer, and a youth advocate. She also counseled and mentored "at-risk" youth in the public-school system.

Jumoke, who has been a seer of ghosts since childhood, is a staunch believer in *life after death, psychic forces, ancestral reverence,* and the importance of *dreams… all of which* ultimately led her to the penning of ***Abebi, "We called for her and she came to us."*** *It is based on a* true story that spans a five-year period of Jumoke's life in which she performed African rituals while enduring tremendous sacrifices to "heed the call" in helping to *free* the trapped souls in a real-life, former plantation.

www.ingramcontent.com/pod-product-compliance
Lightning Source LLC
Chambersburg PA
CBHW071144070526
44584CB00019B/2658